THE HARPER ERA IN CANADIAN FOREIGN POLICY

THE HARPER ERA IN CANADIAN FOREIGN POLICY

PARLIAMENT, POLITICS, AND CANADA'S GLOBAL POSTURE

Edited by Adam Chapnick
and Christopher J. Kukucha

UBCPress · Vancouver · Toronto

© UBC Press 2016

All rights reserved. No part of this publication may be reproduced, stored in a retrieval system, or transmitted, in any form or by any means, without prior written permission of the publisher, or, in Canada, in the case of photocopying or other reprographic copying, a licence from Access Copyright, www.accesscopyright.ca.

25 24 23 22 21 20 19 18 17 16   5 4 3 2 1

Printed in Canada on FSC-certified ancient-forest-free paper
(100% post-consumer recycled) that is processed chlorine- and acid-free.

Library and Archives Canada Cataloguing in Publication

The Harper era in Canadian foreign policy: Parliament, politics, and Canada's global posture / edited by Adam Chapnick and Christopher J. Kukucha

Includes bibliographical references and index.
Issued in print and electronic formats.
ISBN 978-0-7748-3319-6 (hardback). – ISBN 978-0-7748-3320-2 (paperback).
ISBN 978-0-7748-3321-9 (pdf). – ISBN 978-0-7748-3322-6 (epub).
ISBN 978-0-7748-3323-3 (mobi)

   1. Harper, Stephen, 1959-. 2. Conservative Party of Canada. 3. Canada – Politics and government – 2006-2015. 4. Canada – Foreign relations – 21st century. I. Kukucha, Christopher John, author, editor. II. Chapnick, Adam, author, editor

FC640.H34 2016	971.07'3	C2016-902901-8
		C2016-902902-6

Canada

UBC Press gratefully acknowledges the financial support for our publishing program of the Government of Canada (through the Canada Book Fund), the Canada Council for the Arts, and the British Columbia Arts Council.

This book has been published with the help of a grant from the Canadian Federation for the Humanities and Social Sciences, through the Awards to Scholarly Publications Program, using funds provided by the Social Sciences and Humanities Research Council of Canada.

UBC Press
The University of British Columbia
2029 West Mall
Vancouver, BC V6T 1Z2
www.ubcpress.ca

To our colleagues at the Canadian Forces College and the University of Lethbridge

Contents

Acknowledgments / ix

Introduction: Conservative Foreign Policy in the Harper Era / 3
ADAM CHAPNICK AND CHRISTOPHER J. KUKUCHA

Part 1 Setting the Context

1 Debating the Proper Role of Parliament in the Making and Conduct of Canada's International Policies / 25
DENIS STAIRS

2 Foreign Policy and Minority Government: The Cases of Lester Pearson and Pierre Trudeau / 41
JOHN ENGLISH

3 The Constitutional Politics of Parliament's Role in International Policy / 56
PHILIPPE LAGASSÉ

Part 2 Key Issues

4 Did Minority Government Matter? Thinking Counterfactually about the Canadian Mission in Afghanistan / 73
JEAN-CHRISTOPHE BOUCHER AND KIM RICHARD NOSSAL

5 The Evolution of the Harper Government's Defence Policy: Minority versus Majority or Surplus versus Deficit? / 89
DAVID PERRY

6 Stephen Harper's Israel Policy / 105
   ADAM CHAPNICK

7 Explaining Canada's Foreign Environmental Policies during the Harper Era / 121
   MICHAEL W. MANULAK

8 Canada and the United States in the Harper Years: Still "Special," but Not Especially Important / 135
   GREG ANDERSON

9 The Harper Government's Approach to Energy: Shooting Itself in the Foot / 151
   MONICA GATTINGER

10 Canadian Aid Policy during the Harper Years / 167
   STEPHEN BROWN

11 The Shaping of a Conservative Human Rights Policy in the Harper Era / 181
   DAVID PETRASEK AND REBECCA TIESSEN

12 Canada's Incremental Foreign Trade Policy / 195
   CHRISTOPHER J. KUKUCHA

13 Diaspora and Canadian Foreign Policy: The World in Canada? / 210
   DAVID CARMENT AND JOSEPH LANDRY

Part 3 Additional Perspectives

14 Minority Report: Covering Canadian Foreign Policy in a Minority and Majority Government / 231
   LEE BERTHIAUME

15 Foreign Policy and the Senate: Microscope and Telescope in Turbulent Times / 244
   HUGH SEGAL

16 Concluding Thoughts: The Prime Minister of the Few / 258
   NORMAN HILLMER

Contributors / 269

Index / 271

Acknowledgments

This book represents our shared fascination with Canada's foreign policy during the Conservative governments of Stephen Harper. When we started our work, we understood that previous Liberal priorities would have been altered but were struck by the shift in tone and focus of this new era in Canada's foreign relations. As a historian and a political scientist, respectively, we had slightly different perspectives on the reasons for this transformation; as we searched for a framework for our analysis, however, we were continually drawn back to one central question: did a change from minority to majority status in Parliament have an impact on Canada's foreign policy during the Harper era? The answer to that question was somewhat surprising to both of us. We encourage readers to form their own opinions as they consider the thought-provoking chapters from our contributors.

Not surprisingly, given the scope of this project, there are numerous people to acknowledge. First and foremost we want to thank our authors. Our intent from the outset was to select emerging and established scholars who would represent the wide range of diversity in our fields. This is never an easy process but we were surprised by the willingness of most to accept our invitation and by their ongoing enthusiasm in the face of numerous requests, often on short timelines, of their volume editors. We are grateful for the generosity and insight of our colleagues.

Individual contributors also noted specific acknowledgments. Several chapters, for example, benefited from comments on earlier drafts, including Jean-Christophe Boucher and Kim Richard Nossal (Frank Harvey and Justin Massie), David Perry (Gene Lang), Michael Manulak (Norman Hillmer and Tom Keating), Adam Chapnick (students in the 2014-15 National Security Programme), and Monica Gattinger (Maya Jegen and others providing input during her presentation at the 2015 annual conference of the Canadian Political Science Association). Research assistants receiving thanks include Shannon Smith (Adam Chapnick), Pavle Levkovic (Adam Chapnick and Christopher Kukucha), and Sirisha Valupadas (Greg Anderson). Stephen Brown and David Carment also noted the hospitality and funding of the Käte Hamburger Kolleg/Centre for Global Cooperation Research at the University of Duisburg-Essen (Germany), where both were Senior Fellows. Boucher, Nossal, Brown, Carment, Chapnick, and Philippe Lagassé further recognized the financial support of the Social Sciences and Humanities Research Council. Finally, on a personal note, Denis Stairs expressed his immense gratitude to his wife, political scientist Jennifer Smith, for her comments and suggestions during the writing of his chapter. He further notes that none could wish for more encouraging, helpful, and authoritative support and that any deficiencies that remain are there in spite of her, not because of her. Striking a similar chord, Lee Berthiaume thanked Melanie and Kai for their love, patience, and support.

We have both published with UBC Press in the past and once again this was a very positive experience. Everyone involved was supportive and professional throughout the project. As always, our editor, Emily Andrew deserves special recognition for her input, praise, and mentorship. Similarly, Holly Keller's production team is unsurpassed in its speed, efficiency, and general good nature. Laraine Coates facilitated the co-publication of our promotional blog with the excellent team at University Affairs, including, in particular, Tara Siebarth and Ashleigh Van Houten. Kerry Kilmartin was her usual and helpful self in shaping our marketing plan. The copy-editing for this book was done professionally and without complaint by Joanne Richardson, and Megan Sproule-Jones, who produced the index, was, as always, a pleasure to work with. We are also extremely grateful for financial assistance provided by the Canadian Forces College, the Collaboratory on Energy Research and Policy, and Philippe Lagassé.

Finally, this collection would not be possible without the love and support of important people in our lives. Chris thanks his family for their ongoing inspiration and patience, as well as the many colleagues he has worked with over the years. This collaboration with Adam, however, will always be a highlight. Adam would not have undertaken this project without Chris's partnership, and would not have completed it without the endless patience of Erica, Alana, and Avery, as well as the support of the Chapnick and Berman families.

THE HARPER ERA IN
CANADIAN FOREIGN POLICY

Introduction

Conservative Foreign Policy in the Harper Era

ADAM CHAPNICK AND CHRISTOPHER J. KUKUCHA

Barely three months after he was sworn in as Canada's twenty-second prime minister, on 17 May 2006, Stephen Harper introduced a motion in the House of Commons that could have ultimately ended his political career. The issue was Canada's commitment to Afghanistan, and at stake was the slender minority Conservative government's credibility as a defender of the Canadian national interest.[1] At the time, the opposition Liberals, led by an acting leader with only limited control over his caucus, were divided on extending the mission. The New Democrats and Bloc Québécois wanted to bring the troops home. The Conservatives had only won 124 out of 308 seats in the January 2006 Canadian federal election, and with 294 members present in the House of Commons for a late night emergency debate that lasted for over six hours, they needed 148 votes to extend the mission for two years. Losing the vote would have embarrassed the prime minister; undermined his, and Canada's, credibility as a Western ally; and put into question the competence of the government as a whole. When the votes were tallied, 149 members of Parliament (including thirty Liberals) had supported the motion, and the first potential crisis of the Harper era was narrowly averted.

The close call seemed to indicate that the Conservatives' minority standing in the House of Commons would be critical to how Prime Minister Harper approached world affairs. Indeed, it was one of the only plausible indicators of how the Harper era in Canadian foreign policy was set to play out. The Conservative campaign platform, *Stand Up for Canada*, had hardly acknowledged the country's role abroad, and the prime minister himself had limited international experience. Since Prime Minister Harper led a new political party and a minority government, looking back to the Brian Mulroney *Progressive* Conservative era could hardly have been instructive, and the previous minority (and still Progressive) Conservative regimes – of Joe Clark in 1979 and John Diefenbaker in 1957 and 1962 – governed in decidedly different times.

By the end of the year, and in the aftermath of the Afghanistan debate, two comprehensive academic publications had attempted to make sense of the worldly outlook of what Conservative ministers referred to as "Canada's new government."[2] Editors Andrew F. Cooper and Dane Rowlands named the 2006 volume of the annual *Canada Among Nations* series *Minorities and Priorities*, and they included in it three essays that speculate on the broad contours of the Harper government's foreign policy future. Each chapter contemplates the potential impact of the government's minority standing in the House of Commons on how the Conservatives would conceive of, develop, and implement Canadian positions on the world stage. Senator Hugh Segal, who reflects in the present volume on his experience as a foreign policy practitioner in the Upper House during the Harper era, argues that, so long as the Conservatives held a mere plurality of seats in the House of Commons, they had to "put forward sensible proposals that [could] withstand the scrutiny and gain the acceptance of parliamentarians from more than one political party." The government's indeterminate term in office, subject to end at virtually any moment through a vote of non-confidence by the opposition parties, would likely act as a constraint. "Concessions will be required," he notes, "to balance Conservative goals and objectives with the parliamentary prerequisite of consensus."[3] In contrast, the political scientist John Kirton was impressed by the boldness of the new prime minister's actions on Afghanistan, discussed in more detail in this volume by Jean-Christophe Boucher and Kim Richard Nossal, and by how he secured a resolution to a long-standing softwood lumber dispute with the United States, mentioned here by Greg Anderson. Kirton also concludes, however, that the government's minority standing would "hamper its ability to create favourable conditions at home for genuine global leadership abroad."[4] Finally, Adam Chapnick analyzes the situation facing the Conservatives from a historical perspective. He advocates "a modest, disciplined – and indeed – conservative approach to world affairs" as the best way for a new, minority government to navigate the challenges of Canadian international policy.[5]

A fourth view of the future is provided by a past and future political adviser to Stephen Harper, Roy Rempel. In *Dreamland: How Canada's Pretend Foreign Policy Has Undermined Sovereignty*, Rempel offers a scathing critique of contemporary Canadian foreign policy as it had been practised by the Liberal governments of Jean Chrétien and Paul Martin. He notes that, in at least one instance, rather than promoting and preserving Canada's national interests, the latter's minority government had been "driven by a desire for domestic political gain." Canadian international policy, Rempel laments, had "become disconnected from the reality of the country's international position and from real national needs." Values had come to serve as the basis of popular and political conceptions of Canada's national interests. "But values such as democracy, human rights, and the rule of law (all central to government policy statements) are continuously engaged everywhere," he notes. "They offer few bases on which to make choices."[6]

Rempel advocates a divorce between international policy and domestic politics, a reinvigoration of the Canada-US relationship through a return "to the tradition of 'quiet diplomacy' that served Canada well in the 1950s and into the 1960s," and a reinvestment in the "capabilities" that Ottawa was able to bring to the foreign policy table.[7] Whether he believes that such changes are possible in the minority context is unclear, but Rempel's commitment to a foreign policy grounded in the national interest appears to be absolute.

Nearly ten years, two minorities, and one majority Conservative electoral victory later, some – albeit not all[8] – analysts have come to refer to the Harper government's approach to international policy as a "Big Break," or even as a "diplomatic counter-revolution" – one in which the longest-serving Canadian foreign minister of the era took explicit, if not also ironic, pride in "promoting Canadian values."[9] None of them, however, emphasizes the political stability provided to the government by its majority electoral victory of 2011 as the primary driver of that change.[10] As teachers of Canadian foreign policy who believe that Parliament's voice in international affairs has been regularly discounted by analysts of Canada's global posture, we were surprised by this incongruence. In light of the Harper government's defeat in the October 2015 election, we therefore set out to test it more comprehensively. It follows that *The Harper Era in Canadian Foreign Policy*, which presents the first comprehensive review of the international policy of the Harper era, is also prompted by a specific question: Did the shift from minority to majority government have a significant impact on the way that the Conservatives conceived of, developed, and implemented international policy on Canada's behalf? The answer, our contributors suggest, is sometimes –

but not nearly as often as that initial Afghanistan experience might have suggested nor as often as it had during previous minority government eras.

As Denis Stairs notes, measuring the impact of any individual Canadian government in world affairs is difficult even at the best of times.[11] When one seeks to analyze international policy as it happens (or immediately afterwards), without access to confidential government memoranda that will only later be made available to historians, the task is that much more complicated.[12] Moreover, there are times when even the most insightful analysts will struggle to isolate a single variable in the policy process. Consider, for example, the then Department of Foreign Affairs, Trade and Development's aggressive embrace of Twitter in 2014. Under the leadership of Foreign Affairs Minister John Baird, the department opened over 290 new social media accounts.[13] How the Harper government's majority standing in the House of Commons did or did not affect this decision is difficult to discern. At the most basic of levels, the Conservatives embraced digital diplomacy during the majority era, having ignored it completely as a minority government. But correlation does not necessarily imply causation. Note that they also embraced it under one particular minister, suggesting that the personality and power of the individual in charge of the file – perhaps regardless of the government's standing in the House – could have played a role. (Indeed, a number of the contributors to *The Harper Era* indicate that Minister Baird was pivotal to the 2011–15 period.) The embrace of the digital world also took place not long after the University of Ottawa political scientist Roland Paris published a widely read and scathing report on Canada's diplomatic backwardness in June 2013. And his essay did not even mention the minority/majority issue.[14] So Canada's about-face could have represented a response to public pressure or an indirect acknowledgment that Paris was right. There cannot be, at this point, a definitive explanation.

Consider also two widely documented and exceedingly rare instances of Conservative non-partisanship in discussions of international affairs in the House of Commons: (1) the appointment of an independent panel to examine the future of Canada in Afghanistan (the Manley Commission) in 2007 and (2) Prime Minister Harper's September 2014 call on members of Parliament to "put aside partisanship" and work collectively to support the international campaign against Islamic State militants.[15] If, as Senator Segal suggested in 2006, minorities force governments to reach across the aisle, then it makes sense to view the Manley Commission as a minority government outcome. But what about the 2014 threat of the Islamic State? The Conservatives held a clear majority at that time. Could both actions simply reflect the view of a government that believed that there were times and places for non-partisanship, regardless of any party's standing in the House of Commons?

These are not easy questions, but they are important ones considering the history of Canadian politics in the twentieth and twenty-first centuries (not to mention the pledge of Prime Minister Justin Trudeau's Liberal Party to introduce some measure of electoral reform in the post-2015 period). Canada's federal elections have resulted in minority governments nine times since John Diefenbaker ended twenty-two years of uninterrupted Liberal rule in 1957. Three of those governments were Progressive Conservative, two more were Conservative, and four were Liberal. No government lasted fewer than nine months (Joe Clark, 1979), and none survived longer than two years and eight months (Lester Pearson, 1965–68). While Diefenbaker's successful transition from minority to majority seems to have had little to do with international affairs, most analysts suggest that his government's reversion to minority standing in 1962 had a significant impact on how Ottawa dealt with plans to acquire nuclear weapons. The nuclear issue, along with the prime minister's outspoken opposition to Britain's entry into the European Common Market, is also thought to have contributed directly to the Liberal Party's election victory in 1963.[16] John English, the official biographer of both Lester B. Pearson and Pierre Elliott Trudeau, demonstrates in Chapter 2 (this volume) that the minority government context played a significant role in how both Pearson (1963–65 and 1965–68) and Trudeau (1972–74) made strategic decisions in international affairs. Joe Clark's minority tenure was perhaps too brief, and his government too inexperienced, for serious analysis of the impact of his party's standing in the House of Commons on his approach to foreign policy, but, as Stephen Brown suggests in Chapter 10 (this volume), it appears that the minority standing of Paul Martin's Liberal government (2004–06) played a role in its conduct on the world stage.

In spite of the significant impact of minority standing on international policy throughout Canada's history, there is a surprisingly limited amount of scholarship available to help us understand it. Philippe Lagassé's examination of Parliament's constitutional role in Canadian international affairs in Chapter 3 (this volume) is not the first such analysis, but it is the most comprehensive summary since James Eayrs's classic *The Art of the Possible: Government and Foreign Policy in Canada*, published in 1961. In it, Eayrs points out how the Liberal prime minister William Lyon Mackenzie King's condemnation of the secretive Allied diplomacy of the First World War helped him find common cause with the opposition Progressive Party and stabilize his minority government in the early 1920s.[17] In contrast, articles published by Denis Stairs and Kim Richard Nossal in the 1970s emphasize the limitations facing Canadian international practitioners, suggesting implicitly that party standing in the House of Commons would rarely ever be a primary foreign policy concern.[18] Four decades later, Professors Stairs and Nossal find similar dynamics at play, and not at play, in their contributions to *The Harper Era*.

As John English implies towards the end of his chapter, the challenge of understanding the minority Harper government is made greater by the possibility that Liberal and Conservative parties might manage their respective positions in the House of Commons in a minority context differently. With such thinking in mind, in 1980, George Perlin published the seminal guide to understanding (Progressive) Conservative behaviour in federal politics. He called his book *The Tory Syndrome*, and in it he tries to explain why the Progressive Conservative Party of Canada had found it so difficult to overcome what was, from the first victory of Sir Wilfrid Laurier in 1896 on, nearly a century of Liberal hegemony at the federal level. When John Diefenbaker formed his first (minority) government in 1957, his party had only been in power for five of the last thirty-six years. When his second minority fell in 1963, the Liberals ruled again, virtually uninterrupted, until 1984.

Perlin's "tory syndrome" refers specifically to "characteristics acquired by minority parties which tend to re-enforce their weakness."[19] Politicians in the pursuit of power, Perlin hypothesizes, "will generally be more favourably disposed to accommodation and compromise and more willing to conform to party discipline."[20] Such individuals typically avoid the opposition, leaving the latter rife with more principled, activist, and ideologically rigid Canadians. These traits, it is worth noting, lend themselves quite easily to values-based rhetoric, if not policy, on the world stage. More generally, minority party members tend to adopt what Perlin calls an "opposition mentality," characterized by "an attacking, destructive style,"[21] one that would play out both internally and, in the particular case of Canada's Progressive Conservatives, also against Canadian intellectuals (who, they believed, were inclined to favour the Liberal Party). Inevitably, even when such parties did gain power, either as majorities or minorities, they would quickly implode, leaving the so-called natural governing party to take over. How could one break the spell? Perlin concludes: "The party's ability to … survive in office long enough to change its competitive position would appear to require exceptionally adroit leadership and some considerable luck."[22]

Some of the themes touched on by Perlin – an activist government driven by an ideological view of world affairs, an opposition mentality – were evident in the thinking of Brian Mulroney's Progressive Conservatives when they took power in 1984. In their analysis of the international policy of the Mulroney era, Nelson Michaud and Kim Richard Nossal note that the Tories' initial "approach to foreign policy was indeed marked by simplicity." The government had embraced a "Manichean perspective" on the Cold War.[23] Moreover, as Mulroney's former secretary of state for external affairs Barbara McDougall reflects in the preface to the Michaud-Nossal book, her government was particularly proud of its "activism," as well as "the leadership role [it] played in the promotion of democracy and pluralism."[24] Perlin's themes, this time including the disdain for intellectuals and non-governmental organizations, also resonate with a number of the contributing authors to this volume. Many also point to Stephen Harper's leadership skills as the reason that his party was able to break yet another Liberal monopoly in 2006 and increase its standing in the House in the following two elections.

During the Harper era, a small group of scholars examined – some directly, others tangentially – the role of the Conservative Party's standing in the House of Commons on the government's international policy decisions. In *Two Cheers for Minority Government*, Peter Russell argues, as we imply here, that the Harper government's willingness to involve Parliament in discussions of the mission in Afghanistan during its first mandate was indeed shaped by its lack of a majority. Similarly, Prime Minister Harper's decision to assign John Baird, one of his strongest Cabinet members, to the environmental portfolio in 2007 at a time when the party was being criticized aggressively for its attitude towards the Kyoto Protocol in the House of Commons, a topic covered here by Michael Manulak, also appeared to Russell to reflect the impact of minority government on international policy.[25] In their 2011 textbook, *International Policy and Politics in Canada*, Kim Richard Nossal, Stéphane Roussel, and Stéphane Paquin identify a relationship between the seemingly constant rotation of Canadian foreign ministers between 2002 and 2009 (seven in total) and minority governments.[26] "The main consequence of a minority government," however, they conclude, is its "short life expectancy."[27] Even if a government were to attempt to effect strategic change, the constant reorganization of the political executive would act as a significant constraint. Political scientists Duane Bratt and Christopher Kukucha later echo and expand on this. They, too, recognize that – as Philippe Lagassé makes clear in this volume – regardless of its strength in the House of Commons, the governing party controls "the apparatus of government" responsible for international affairs.[28] Nonetheless, they also note the more frequent rotation of foreign ministers during the minority era and highlight – as does Lee Berthiaume in Chapter 14 (this volume) – the increased involvement of Parliament in foreign policy debates and the more active behaviour of parliamentary committees responsible for international affairs when governments lack the control that comes with a legislative majority.

The few preliminary assessments of the Harper era that benefited from having observed the Conservative government in both minority and (early) majority contexts did not provide definitive answers to our question. John Ibbitson differentiates between a period of "incoherence in foreign affairs," from 2006 through to early 2011, to one of "coherence and competence" during the early majority years.[29] He attributes much of that competence to "the security of a majority government," but his essay also leaves open the possibility, echoed by David Carment, Joseph Landry, and others in this volume, that the earlier incoherence could have been as much a reflection of a new government trying to find its way as it was of a minority regime.[30] In a memoir that is, admittedly, significantly less focused on international relations, a former policy adviser in the Prime Minister's Office (PMO), Bruce Carson, suggests – not unlike Stephen Brown does in his contribution to this book – that the Conservative government's minority standing had a significant impact on policy development and implementation in the 2006–08 period but that, once the party won its second minority mandate, "the Conservatives decided to govern as if they had a majority," and they continued to do so when that majority was confirmed.[31] By contrast, in his analysis of the Harper government's unwillingness to involve the broader Canadian public in international policy deliberations, Gerald Schmitz finds no difference at all between the minority and majority years.[32] *The Harper Era*, which benefits from having been completed after Justin Trudeau led a revitalized Liberal Party to a majority election victory in October 2015, offers a more nuanced view. Some of our contributors, like Jean-Christophe Boucher and Kim Richard Nossal, find that Parliament's role in shaping foreign policy in Afghanistan during the Harper era was limited to non-existent. Others, like David Petrasek and Rebecca Tiessen, correlate an intensification of what had been a more tentative Conservative human rights policy between 2006 and 2011 with the Harper team's majority victory. Still more, like Adam Chapnick, find the shift from minority to majority critical to some elements of the government's policy but largely irrelevant to others. Taken altogether, this book suggests that Parliament's role in shaping foreign policy in the Harper era was likely more limited than it had been during previous minority governments but that, as Norman Hillmer suggests in his conclusion, its role still cannot be entirely ignored.

The Structure of Our Analysis

The Harper Era takes as its inspiration the 2001 overview of the previous "Conservative era in Canadian foreign policy," which lasted from 1984 to 1993. In their book, editors Nelson Michaud and Kim Richard Nossal ask a collection of Canadian international policy scholars whether the shift from the Liberal governments of Pierre Trudeau and Lester Pearson to the Progressive Conservative government of Brian Mulroney represented a significant "departure" from Canada's diplomatic traditions.[33] Were the Progressive Conservatives, in the words of Denis Stairs, who penned an introductory chapter that framed the case studies that followed, "architects or engineers"?[34]

Like *Diplomatic Departures*, *The Harper Era* begins with an introductory section designed to establish the context for the analysis that follows. We, too, ask Denis Stairs to begin, this time by providing readers with a normative perspective on our central question: *Should* the government's standing in the House of Commons affect its conception, development, and implementation of international policy? In Chapter 1, Stairs argues that, even though Parliament lacks the constitutional authority to be actively engaged in world affairs, the House of Commons should nonetheless play an important role in the public education of Canadian citizens in matters of global importance. He advocates the foreign policy review process as a worthwhile if not necessary method of advancing popular and professional thinking, regardless of whether the government conducting the review has captured a clear majority of the seats in the House of Commons. In Chapter 2, John English offers a detailed analysis of the political and policy machinations of the minority Pearson and Trudeau governments. English was asked to assess whether the Liberal governments' minority standing *did* affect international policy, and his answer is a clear "yes." In Chapter 3, Philippe Lagassé then analyzes the same issue from a constitutional perspective: based on Canadian laws and constitutional precedents, *can* a government's minority standing affect its international policy? He concludes that, legally, the number of seats that a government holds in the House of Commons should make no difference. The executive is responsible for Canadian international policy decisions; nonetheless, politics always affects policy, and minority parliaments are inevitably political.

Lagassé's conclusion, focused as it is on the political side of policy making, is an excellent introduction to some of the main themes of the case studies that follow. Those cases are hardly comprehensive[35] – indeed, we doubt it's possible to cover every international policy decision of the Harper era in a single text – but we hope that they are sufficiently diverse to be indicative of the most significant issues facing the Conservatives, and Canadians more generally, between 2006 and 2015. The first case is Afghanistan, largely because it represented Prime Minister Harper's first major international policy decision in 2006. In Chapter 4, Jean-Christophe Boucher and Kim Richard Nossal use counterfactual analysis to assess whether Canada's role in Afghanistan would have been significantly different had the Liberals, under Paul Martin, won a majority government in 2004 or if there had been a Harper majority in 2008. In both instances, they find that the Conservatives' standing in the House of Commons had virtually no impact on Canada's Afghanistan policy. In fact, the issue of Afghanistan was largely absent from the 2004, 2006, and 2008 elections and had no observable influence on the electoral process. The authors also conclude that Martin and Harper majority governments would have made similar decisions regarding the deployment of a battle group in Kandahar for one year in 2005, the extension of that mission for another two years in 2006, a further deployment until 2011, and the decision to participate in NATO's training mission until 2014.

In Chapter 5, David Perry reaches a similar conclusion in his broader discussion of defence policy. Certainly, he notes, the Conservatives' pledge to increase defence spending was a cornerstone of their 2006 election campaign platform. Moreover, as prime minister, Stephen Harper trumpeted his government's exceptional commitment to defending Canada through a narrative that made reference to policy in the Arctic, Afghanistan, Libya, and the Middle East. Nevertheless, in reality, much of the 2006–15 period saw the Harper government cut the defence budget and delay or cancel procurement projects. In most cases, the cost-saving measures were tied to fiscal pressures within the federal budget, bureaucratic resistance to increased military expenditures, the 2008 global economic crisis and its aftermath, and the government's own decision to prioritize the domestic economic benefits of procurement purchases. In sum, to Perry, the minority/majority question was not irrelevant to Conservative defence policy, but it was largely secondary to these other considerations.

From the day he took office, Stephen Harper also made relations with Israel a significant international policy priority. As Adam Chapnick makes clear in Chapter 6, Harper had felt a strong personal connection to Israel since long before he was first elected to public office. Prioritizing Israel was therefore all but inevitable, regardless of the Conservatives' strength in the House. A few months after he returned from his first international trip to Afghanistan, in the aftermath of the July 2006 evacuation of thirteen thousand Canadians from Lebanon – in the midst of a conflict between Israel and Hezbollah – the prime minister informed his caucus that Canada would always "take a stand" against the destruction of Israel. Nonetheless, Chapnick also finds that the Conservatives' majority victory in 2011 enabled Cabinet ministers to travel more freely than they had done during the minority years and, thereby, contributed to the acceleration of Canada-Israel bilateral ties during that time.

It was also in the first year of its initial minority that the Conservatives staked out a clear position on environmental policy by refusing to participate in the Kyoto Protocol's second commitment period. In Chapter 7, Michael Manulak argues that popular explanations for Canada's position – namely, the personal and ideological views of the prime minister and the importance of the energy sector to the Canadian economy – were in fact secondary considerations in Ottawa's decision-making process; rather, the Harper government consistently attempted to align its greenhouse gas policies with those of the United States and to ensure that any Canadian multilateral commitments also included all of the world's most significant carbon emitters. To Manulak, then, the question of minority versus majority government was largely irrelevant to Canadian environmental policy.

In Chapter 8, Greg Anderson focuses on Canada-US relations, another early challenge for the first Harper minority. During their first year in office, the Conservatives concluded the 2006 Canada-US Softwood Lumber Agreement, an achievement that had been sought unsuccessfully by the Martin Liberals. The government also renewed the North American Aerospace Defense Command (NORAD) agreement in perpetuity and even added maritime security to its list of responsibilities. Other issues that appeared prominently between 2006 and 2008 include unsuccessful Canadian efforts to secure US support for an extension of the Keystone XL pipeline and the publication of the *Canada First Defence Strategy*, with its emphasis on continental security, coastal defence, and northern sovereignty. Like Manulak, Anderson posits that the Conservative government's approach to North American economic and security challenges was driven largely by international considerations. Once more, then, the minority/majority question appears to have been inconsequential.

In Chapter 9, Monica Gattinger focuses on energy, one of many defining issues of Canada-US relations in the Harper era. Gattinger is critical of the Harper government's failure to follow through on its commitment to transform Canada into an "energy superpower." She notes a long list of political disappointments, if not failures, during both the minority and majority years, including repeated delays in the negotiations to extend the Keystone XL pipeline; an inability to create a tidewater project for international exports; and struggles to contain fierce foreign and domestic opposition to a variety of energy-related projects. To Gattinger, these problems were the outcome of the government's "non-consultative, unilateral, and at times even combative" approach to dealing with Canada's provincial governments, environmental non-governmental organizations, Indigenous communities, and even opposition from within the general public. This confrontational attitude was adopted with remarkable consistency between 2006 and 2015, suggests Gattinger, leading her to conclude that the government's standing in the House of Commons was unimportant to Canadian energy policy.

Subsequent chapters focus on foreign policy issues that only gradually emerged as Conservative priorities. In Chapter 10, Stephen Brown notes that the new government's preliminary thinking on official development assistance was not revealed until 2007 at the G8 Heligendamm Conference, when Prime Minister Harper pledged to place greater emphasis on aid to the Americas. The *Official Development Assistance Accountability Act*, legislation that was supported more strongly by the opposition than it was by the government, followed in 2008. Not surprisingly, then, Brown characterizes this early period (2006–08) as marked by Conservative inertia. A more proactive phase followed (2009–11), and the majority era represented a final "intensification" of existing policies. Brown ties neither the heightened activity of the second minority period nor the stronger emphasis on development as an element of the Conservatives' post-2011 international agenda to the government's standing in the House of Commons; rather, development policy evolved to reflect the gradual decline of security considerations in thinking about Canadian aid, most notably in Afghanistan, and their replacement by a new emphasis on commercialization and the private sector.

In Chapter 11, David Petrasek and Rebecca Tiessen acknowledge early Conservative announcements of Canada's intent to pursue a "principled" foreign policy, but they argue that human rights priorities were not clear until 2009–10 when the Harper government introduced its signature maternal, newborn, and child health (MNCH) initiative. Petrasek and Tiessen are fairly critical of the program and how it was promoted. They suggest that both Prime Minister Harper and his first post-majority foreign minister, John Baird, were overly influenced by neoconservative social policy goals and too focused on capturing the political support of specific domestic constituencies, most notably those holding "traditional" attitudes towards women and young girls. Conservative human rights policy was also profoundly partisan and selective: the government condemned the human rights abuses of some regimes but deliberately ignored obvious problems and violations in others. Unlike Brown and others, Petrasek and Tiessen are more willing to speculate on the importance of the shift from minority to majority in 2011. Like Brown, they sense an intensification of Conservative policy, but they suspect that the new intensity was produced at least in part as a result of the political freedom granted to the government by the more stable parliamentary environment.

While the Conservatives pursued an aggressive international trade agenda as early as 2007 when they opened free trade negotiations with Colombia and Peru, Christopher Kukucha argues in Chapter 12 that a coherent trade policy that went beyond the standard neoconservative mantra extolling the virtues of reducing barriers to trade and investment did not emerge until 2009 with the release of the government's first major trade policy white paper: *Seizing Global Advantage*. The report called for greater engagement in global value chains, more secure access to international markets, and support for increased foreign direct investment. Negotiations to establish the Canada-European Union Comprehensive Economic and Trade Agreement (CETA) also officially opened that year. With its 2011 majority, the Harper government announced a new focus on "economic diplomacy," and the Conservatives released a more comprehensive *Global Markets Action Plan* in 2013. Ultimately, however, Kukucha argues that Canadian foreign trade policy is not tied to the standing of any governing party in the House of Commons; rather, it evolves incrementally.

In Chapter 13, our final case study, David Carment and Joseph Landry examine the relevance of diaspora politics to Canadian foreign policy. The authors condemn the Harper government for the favouritism that it demonstrated towards specific ethnic groups and for its politicized approach to diaspora-driven initiatives. Its actions, they declare, often risked compromising Canada's international standing in the crass pursuit of domestic political support. The political success of this approach ultimately helped secure a Conservative majority, but Carment and Landry suggest that the government's policies post-2011 did not change and therefore appear to have had little to do with the Conservative Party's standing in the House of Commons; rather, diaspora agendas were pursued consistently from the first minority era on, further eroding the vitality of civil society in Canada by giving Canadians the incentive to organize and vote along ethnic lines.

We complement the case studies with personal observations from Ottawa foreign policy journalist Lee Berthiaume, Senator Hugh Segal, and the acclaimed historian of Canadian international policy Norman Hillmer. In Chapter 14, in his reflections on the Conservatives' relationship with the media, Berthiaume concludes that, although the Conservatives' relationship with the media became increasingly worse over the Harper decade, it is difficult to judge whether the shift from minority to majority government was the catalyst. International policy is rarely critical to electoral outcomes in Canada, and it is therefore less likely that the standing of any party in the House of Commons will affect media relations. The Conservatives also adopted an exceptionally restrictive media strategy throughout, making it difficult to provide in-depth reporting. In Chapter 15, Segal's analysis focuses on the Senate's institutional role and, especially, on its committees. He emphasizes the professionalism and experience of Senate appointees and their ability to prioritize the substance of international policy ahead of the partisan stances of their House of Commons colleagues. Segal did not personally experience any difference in Senate processes after the Conservatives' 2011 election victory. Hillmer concludes, in Chapter 16, by focusing on Stephen Harper himself. Perhaps, he suggests, it was the force of Harper's personality – and indeed the certainty of his beliefs – that appears to have caused his party's standing in the House of Commons to mean so much less than it did to previous minority regimes.

Lessons to Be Learned: Reflections on the Harper Era

We end this introduction with four observations about the 2006–15 period that influenced, however indirectly, our editorial process. First, minority governments are inevitably shaped by the unpredictable and unstable environment in which they operate. John English describes the time-honoured

Liberal tradition of "tilting to the left" during minority government eras to secure the support of the NDP. When we started this project, we therefore expected the Harper government to behave similarly. Unlike the Pearson, Trudeau, and Martin Liberals, all of whom regularly courted the support of the NDP to maintain the confidence of the House of Commons, the Conservatives took a different approach. As Adam Chapnick's chapter on Israel and David Carment and Joseph Landry's contribution on diaspora politics indicate, the Harper regime targeted specific domestic constituencies, often at the individual riding level – and not always successfully, as Monica Gattinger demonstrates in her analysis of Canada's failure to fully access the global energy market. We were also surprised by the Conservatives' curious antipathy towards Quebec, at least on international policy issues – most notably climate change.

Second, we anticipated that Conservative international policy would be characterized by a consistency and decisiveness that would differentiate the Harper government from its immediate predecessor. Between 2003 and 2005, the Paul Martin Liberals were regularly condemned for their failure – real or perceived – to make definitive global commitments. Our authors add nuance to this hypothesis. Stephen Harper certainly prioritized the Canada-US relationship when he took office, for example. But he soon allowed that bilateral relationship to deteriorate. Select examples that span the minority and majority eras include Canada's explicit and outspoken opposition to US-led negotiations with Iran; comments that Ottawa would not "take no for an answer" on negotiations to extend the Keystone XL pipeline; and an unwillingness to provide political cover for President Obama's climate change efforts. As Greg Anderson suggests in his chapter, however, much of this policy was mere rhetoric that masked a relationship driven by much more than just executive posturing. David Petrasek and Rebecca Tiessen also observe the selective and often inconsistent application of the Harper government's "principled" human rights policy, especially as it related to China and maternal health, in similar terms. In all of these cases, although the Conservatives attempted to construct a "firm" and "principled" international policy narrative, the reality did not always match the rhetoric, irrespective of the party's standing in the House of Commons.

Next we assumed that Conservative international policy, particularly in the early years, would be dedicated in part to eradicating any memory of the previous Liberal eras. Consider, for example, the approach to Israel, the withdrawal from the Liberals' environmental commitments, and even efforts to eliminate government use of so-called Liberal language such as "gender equality" and "human security." In some cases, this policy of "erasure" does indeed appear to have been tied to broader political efforts at the domestic level or to attempts to build a uniquely Conservative narrative,[36] as David Perry notes with reference to defence policy, where the alleged abandonment of the Canadian Armed Forces (CAF) by the Liberals was decried regularly, even though Paul Martin proposed a $12 billion increase to the defence budget in 2005. At other times, however, the Conservatives seemed willing to subtly maintain, or even extend, existing Liberal policy initiatives until they had developed fresh ideas. As Stephen Brown points out, for over two years the Harper government hardly altered the official development assistance policies that it inherited from the Liberals. The government's relationship with non-governmental organizations also (d)evolved over time.

Finally, we wondered how regularly the Conservatives would draw lessons from Canada's history of minority regimes. Lester Pearson, for example, was a weak parliamentarian, and he did not fully understand the procedural powers of the institution. As prime minister, Stephen Harper was clearly the opposite. He leveraged his mastery of Westminster politics on matters of international policy repeatedly, perhaps most notably through his handling of the parliamentary committee on Afghan detainees. Party discipline was also weak under Pearson, who took a hands-off approach to most policy areas. Again, Harper was profoundly different, especially in his management of caucus dissent and media relations.

Like Prime Minister Harper, Pierre Trudeau came into office with few firm ideas related to foreign policy (except, perhaps, that it was too tightly controlled by the diplomats). While the 2006 Conservatives might have agreed on this latter point, they appear to have viewed the lack of strategic-level clarity as a mistake. In fact, there is evidence, as noted throughout this volume, that Prime Minister Harper was guided by clear social and economic neoconservative principles in many of his international policy decisions. Those decisions were not simply ideologically driven; they were also constructed to gain domestic electoral support and, as some have suggested, to advance a gendered narrative aimed at specific constituencies. Again, these trends did not appear to have been distinctly tied to the Conservatives' minority or majority standing.

In sum, the chapters that follow confound the thinking of the 2006 prognosticators as well as our own. And that, we think, is a good thing.

Introduction

Notes

1. We recognize that we should indicate that the results of the 2006 election produced a minority *Parliament*. The Conservatives, under the leadership of Stephen Harper, technically formed a *government* by virtue of having won a plurality of seats in the House of Commons and having convinced the governor general that they could carry the confidence of the legislature. To make this book more accessible, however, we use the much more common, if imprecise, term "minority government" throughout.
2. See, for example, Peter MacKay, 20 March 2007, in Canada, Standing Committee on Foreign Affairs and International Development, http://www.parl.gc.ca/House Publications/Publication.aspx?DocId=2778508&Language=E&Mode=1&Parl=39&Ses=1.
3. Hugh Segal, "Compassion, realism, engagement and focus: A Conservative foreign policy thematic," in Andrew F. Cooper and Dane Rowlands, eds., *Canada Among Nations, 2006: Minorities and Priorities* (Montreal and Kingston: McGill-Queen's University Press, 2006), 30, 27.
4. John Kirton, "Harper's 'made in Canada' global leadership," in Cooper and Rowlands, *Canada Among Nations, 2006*, 55. See also John Kirton, *Canadian Foreign Policy in a Changing World* (Toronto: Thomson Nelson, 2007), 232.
5. Adam Chapnick, "Caught in-between traditions: A minority Conservative government and Canadian foreign policy," in Cooper and Rowlands, *Canada Among Nations, 2006*, 67.
6. Roy Rempel, *Dreamland: How Canada's Pretend Foreign Policy Has Undermined Sovereignty* (Montreal and Kingston: McGill-Queen's University Press, 2006), 2, 4.
7. Ibid., 164, 15.
8. See, for example, Greg Anderson and Christopher Kukucha's chapters in this volume.
9. John Ibbitson, "The big break: The Conservative transformation of Canada's foreign policy," *CIGI Papers* 2 (April 2014); Adam Chapnick, "A diplomatic counter-revolution: Conservative foreign policy, 2006-2011," *International Journal* 67, 1 (2011–12): 137–54; John Baird, "Canadian diplomacy for the 21st century," address by Minister Baird at Foreign Affairs, Trade and Development Canada headquarters, 27 March 2014, http://www.international.gc.ca/media/aff/speeches-discours/2014/03/27a.aspx?lang=eng. See also Gerd Schönwälder, "Principles and prejudice: Foreign policy under the Harper government," *CIPS Policy Brief* 24 (June 2014), http://cips.uottawa.ca/publications/principles-and-prejudice-foreign-policy-under-the-harper-government/; and Roland Paris, "Are Canadians still liberal internationalists? Foreign policy and public opinion in the Harper era," *International Journal* 69, 3 (2014): 274–307. For other overviews, see the essays by Kim Richard Nossal, Justin Massie and Stéphane Roussel, Jean-Christophe Boucher, and Paul Gecelovsky in Heather A. Smith and Claire Turenne Sjolander, eds., *Canada in the World: Internationalism in Canadian Foreign Policy* (Don Mills, ON: Oxford University Press, 2013).
10. As we argue later in this chapter, Ibbitson comes closest to making such an argument, but his conclusions suggest that the experience gained by the Harper government between 2006 and 2011, rather than the increase in Conservative representation in the House of Commons, drove the "big break." See Ibbitson, "Big break."

11 Denis Stairs, "Architects or engineers? The Conservatives and foreign policy," in Nelson Michaud and Kim Richard Nossal, eds., *Diplomatic Departures: The Conservative Era in Canadian Foreign Policy, 1984–93* (Vancouver: UBC Press, 2001), 25–42.
12 On the Harper government's efforts to limit public access to information about how the government conducts international policy, see David Morin and Stéphane Roussel, "Autopsie de la politique étrangère de Stephen Harper: Un examen préliminaire," *Canadian Foreign Policy Journal* 20, 1 (2014): 1–8; and Gerald J. Schmitz, "The Harper government and the de-democratization of Canadian foreign policy," *Canadian Foreign Policy Journal* 20, 2 (2014): 225.
13 John Baird, "Modern diplomacy in the digital age," Speech, 26 November 2014, http://news.gc.ca/web/article-en.do?nid=909059. Even critics conceded that Canada made significant progress under Baird. See, for example, Roland Paris, "Has Canada finally discovered digital diplomacy?" *CIPSBlog*, 7 February 2014, http://www.cips-cepi.ca/2014/02/07/has-canada-finally-discovered-digital-diplomacy/. See also Eduardo del Buey, "Canada's effective Twiplomacy," *Embassy*, 13 May 2015, 18.
14 Roland Paris, *The Digital Diplomacy Revolution: Why Is Canada Lagging Behind?* (Calgary: Canadian Defence and Foreign Affairs Institute, June 2013).
15 Stephen Harper, quoted in Steven Chase and Daniel Leblanc, "Canada's military intervention in Iraq is 'noble,' Harper says," *Globe and Mail*, 30 September 2014, http://www.theglobeandmail.com/news/politics/top-general-briefs-harpers-cabinet-on-islamic-state-in-iraq/article20856118/. See also Mike Blanchfield, "Baird's 'one voice' in Iraq with Liberals and NSP a notable non-partisan change in tone of the Tories," *National Post*, 6 September 2014, http://news.nationalpost.com/2014/09/06/bairds-one-voice-in-iraq-with-liberals-and-ndp-a-notable-non-partisan-change-in-tone-for-the-tories/.
16 Robert Bothwell, *Alliance and Illusion: Canada and the World, 1945-1984* (Vancouver: UBC Press, 2007), 146–47, 170–75.
17 James Eayrs, *The Art of the Possible: Government and Foreign Policy in Canada* (Toronto: University of Toronto Press, 1961), 105.
18 Denis Stairs, "Publics and policy-makers: The domestic environment of Canada's foreign policy community," *International Journal* 26, 1 (1970–71): 221–48; Denis Stairs, "Public opinion and external affairs: Reflections on the domestication of Canadian foreign policy," *International Journal* 33, 1 (1977–78): 128–49; Kim Richard Nossal, "Allison through the (Ottawa) looking glass: Bureaucratic politics and foreign policy in a parliamentary system," *Canadian Public Administration* 22, 4 (1979): 610–26.
19 George C. Perlin, *The Tory Syndrome: Leadership Politics in the Progressive Conservative Party* (Montreal and Kingston: McGill-Queen's University Press, 1980), 198.
20 Ibid., 195.
21 Ibid., 199. For a more sympathetic view, see Hugh Segal, *The Right Balance: Canada's Conservative Tradition* (Vancouver: Douglas and McIntyre, 2011).
22 Perlin, *Tory Syndrome*, 201.
23 Nelson Michaud and Kim Richard Nossal, "The Conservative era in Canadian for-

eign policy, 1984-1993," in Michaud and Nossal, *Diplomatic Departures*, 6, 10.

24 Barbara McDougall, "Foreword," in Michaud and Nossal, *Diplomatic Departures*, 11.

25 Peter H. Russell, *Two Cheers for Minority Government: The Evolution of Canadian Parliamentary Democracy* (Toronto: Emond Montgomery, 2008), 50, 52. See also Brian Bow and David Black, "Does politics stop at the water's edge in Canada? Party and partisanship in Canadian foreign policy," *International Journal* 64, 1 (2009): 7–27.

26 Kim Richard Nossal, Stéphane Roussel, and Stéphane Paquin, *International Policy and Politics in Canada* (Toronto: Pearson Canada, 2011), 209. To further their point, the longest serving foreign minister of the Harper era, John Baird, served in his position exclusively during the majority years. See Chris Plesach, "Baird credited with giving Tories their foreign policy," *Embassy*, 4 February 2015, 4, 5.

27 Nossal et al., *International Policy and Politics in Canada*, 279. See also Russell, *Two Cheers for Minority Government*, 61.

28 Duane Bratt and Christopher J. Kukucha, eds., *Canadian Foreign Policy: Classic Debates and New Ideas*, 2nd ed. (Don Mills, ON: Oxford University Press, 2011), 235. On this point more broadly, see Peter Aucoin, Herman Bakvis, and Mark D. Jarvis, "Constraining executive power in the era of new political governance," in James Bickerton and B. Guy Peters, eds., *Governing: Essays in Honour of Donald J. Savoie* (Montreal and Kingston: McGill-Queen's University Press, 2013), 36.

29 Ibbitson, "Big break," 9, 13.

30 Ibid., 13. It is worth noting that the only published evidence we have of the Conservatives conducting a comprehensive foreign policy review seems to be found in the majority era. See Greg Weston, "Secret document details new Canadian foreign policy," cbc.ca, 19 November 2012, http://www.cbc.ca/m/touch/news/story/1.1152385.

31 Bruce Carson, *14 Days: Making the Conservative Movement in Canada* (Montreal and Kingston: McGill-Queen's University Press, 2014), 247.

32 Schmitz, "Harper government," 224–28.

33 Michaud and Nossal, *Diplomatic Departures*.

34 Stairs, "Architects or engineers?" See also Michaud and Nossal, "Conservative era in Canadian foreign policy," 3–24.

35 We deliberately limited each author to approximately fifty-five hundred words to make the cases more accessible.

36 Rebecca Tiessen and Krystel Carrier, "'The erasure of 'gender' in Canadian foreign policy under the Harper Conservatives: The significance of the discursive shift from 'gender equality' to 'equality between women and men,'" *Canadian Foreign Policy Journal* 21, 2 (2015): 95–111.

PART 1

SETTING THE CONTEXT

1
Debating the Proper Role of Parliament in the Making and Conduct of Canada's International Policies

DENIS STAIRS

To the question "How should Parliament affect the way international policy is conceived, developed, and implemented in Canada?" there are two kinds of answers. The first is simple, clear, and straightforward. The second is complicated, discursive, ambiguous, and subject to disagreements that are hard to settle. The arguments involved are frequently rooted in conflicting political interests as well as in differing views of how foreign policy decisions that are both efficacious and morally preferable can be most reliably made and pursued, and by whom. Whether the governing party has minority or majority support in the House of Commons can certainly influence the substance of the positions taken by those engaged in the debate, but the underlying question of what Parliament's *proper* role should be arises independently of the political composition of any particular Parliament.

It is easy to dispose of the first answer right away. The second answer, however, requires more discursive exploration and is the subject of most of what follows. My purpose is more to clear away the underbrush than to assert that any specific path is the best to take.

The simple, clear, and straightforward answer to the question before us is that, in pursuing a role in the making and conduct of foreign policy, Parliament has only one central obligation: to accept the parameters imposed on its freedom of action by the fundamental principles of responsible government upon which Canada's political institutions are founded and, hence, to operate within them. The limits are constitutionally defined (by convention as well as by written disquisition). Ultimately, they are determined by the courts. In practice, they are limited most often by what the ruling political authorities, whatever their party affiliation may be, are prepared to allow. The fundamental reality is that, by convention and written constitution alike, the conduct of Canada's international affairs is primarily an executive, not a legislative, function. This is "the law." The Canadian system of responsible government is "executive-dominant," and in the international policy field this dominance is especially evident.

That being said, and precisely *because* the system is executive-dominant, the government itself can determine how tightly the limits of the parliamentary role can be drawn. It can decide, for example, whether it will seek parliamentary support for overseas military operations or not. But, in the end, the political executive is *compelled* to go to Parliament only when it wants to do something abroad that requires it to spend money – and only then when the money it spends cannot be interpreted as falling within the budgetary approvals and latitude that it has already obtained. If, in conducting its international policies, the government appears to have exceeded its constitutional authority (e.g., by intruding without constitutionally defensible cause into an area of provincial jurisdiction or perhaps by treating, say, prisoners-of-war in ways that violate provisions of the Charter of Rights and Freedoms), it can sometimes be checked by the courts, assuming an aggrieved party decides to challenge it there and wins its case. For the rest, the constraints upon its freedom of manoeuvre are more political than legal and, hence, are essentially subjects of political prudence.

This general portrait is painted in much more detail and with great clarity by Philippe Lagassé (Chapter 3, this volume). The fundamental purpose in the present context is merely to remind us that Parliament's core normative obligation is simply to abide by the principles and practices of responsible government as constitutionally understood.

But of course this observation quickly takes us to murkier ground. If there is room in the system for Parliament to play an activist role, subject always to executive design or permission, then to what such role or roles should the executive agree? What measure of parliamentary involvement, in other words, is truly in the general public interest (as opposed to the narrowly partisan political interest of those currently in charge)? Alternatively, what kinds, or what degrees, of parliamentary involvement can reasonably be adjudged inappropriate because potentially damaging to the general public good? Put more directly, what forms of parliamentary participation should a truly conscientious and public service-oriented executive branch leadership encourage? And what forms should it eschew?

This is ultimately a normative question, not a purely empirical one, and like most normative questions in politics it resists a simple answer. Tedious though the caveats and stage-setting premises beloved by academics may be, therefore, two or three are very much in order before the core issue here can be identified, much less reasonably addressed.

The first of them derives from an obvious but often neglected reality. Canada does not have *a* foreign policy or *an* international policy. The question "What is Canada's foreign policy?" has no intelligible meaning in the absence of an identified context. It is true, of course, that governments sometimes issue white papers or other declaratory instruments that attempt to describe the evolution of pertinent conditions in the international environment and then identify the general principles and premises that they claim will underlie the responses they make to them. But these, as a rule, amount at most to statements of general orientation – broad frameworks that the political leadership of the day hopes will win the approval of pertinent attentive publics without at the same time hamstringing its own capacity to react in suitably flexible fashion to the kaleidoscopic particulars of the various problems with international dimensions that happen to come down the pike. Such documents thus have more to do with the rhetorical "discourse" of foreign affairs and with the "narratives" the government thinks are best suited to legitimizing its behaviour over time than with outlining concrete responses to specific challenges.

In reality, therefore, Canada has not one, but many foreign (or international) policies. There are different policies for different issues. Sometimes the issues are interrelated, and in some degree the responses to them may be coordinated by the interested players in the policy-making machine. More often, perhaps, they are not. It has become a commonplace to observe that almost every government department or agency has "foreign" policies of its own. In some degree this has always been true, but it has become much more so in an increasingly interactive age. Communications and other technologies, the extraordinary ease and pace of travel, the inexorable migrations of peoples, the international distribution of specialized patterns of economic production, and the long list of other engines and attributes of what we somewhat carelessly call "globalization" have seen to that. One of the results, as political scientists and others have been observing now for four or five decades, is that the line between the domestic and the foreign is becoming increasingly blurred. Regulate here, and the consequences are felt not only here but elsewhere.

However, the foreign policies that have to be constructed in response to these intrusive realities do not all raise the issue of parliamentary involvement in the same way or with equal intensity. Many – probably most – of them are not very different in substance from the sorts of policies that in previous eras were simply regarded as part and parcel of "internal affairs." They may attract the attentions of pressure groups. Certainly they can be subjects of political life and the rhetorical displays associated with it. That they have international (or transnational) dimensions can also make them both politically and administratively much more complex, introducing other interests – and the players who represent them – into the game. But there is a sense in which such matters are still not politically "special." They are the usual stuff of a pluralistic politics.

On the other hand, the generic term "foreign policy," when loosely used, has often been intended to refer to policies that *are* regarded in some sense as special – as different in kind, that is, from the sorts of policies traditionally associated with more or less routine internal affairs. Why? Because the foreign policies that trigger the special case argument are primarily concerned with matters directly related to the maintenance of international peace and security in general, and the promotion of national security in particular.

The distinction between policies that are primarily about security and policies that are primarily about other things is obviously not hard and fast. Nonetheless, it helps us to identify the core of the normative issue that bears on the proper role of Parliament in the making and conduct of foreign policy. This is because the politico-security issue area is where the subject has been most hotly debated, historically as well as in our own time. Parliament often addresses other sorts of foreign policy issues. Most of the items on Hugh Segal's list of the foreign policy topics explored in recent years by pertinent committees of the Senate demonstrate the point (see Chapter 15, this volume). But these pursuits are usually not regarded as exceptional. Like most of the very similar parliamentary inquiries that are applied to essentially domestic matters, they are "ordinary."

To illustrate, in June 2015, there were flurries of reports in the press on negotiations between Canadian and American transportation officials on enhancing and standardizing the specifications for new railway tank cars and establishing deadlines for replacing the cars still in service on North American railways with the newer and safer models. This was certainly an "international" matter of considerable importance on environmental, economic, and safety grounds alike, but few would argue that the subject warranted a normative debate over the role that the Canadian Parliament ought to have been playing in the formation and conduct of the Canadian position. It was simply another case of parliamentary business being conducted as usual. Even though the matter came prominently to the fore in Canada largely as the result of a horrendously tragic July 2013 accident leading to the loss of forty-seven lives and massive property damage in Lac Mégantic, Quebec, it did not resonate as would have a proposal, for example, that would have had the effect of putting Canadian military personnel in harm's way.

A second preliminary observation may also warrant attention. A central theme of *The Harper Era* focuses on the question of whether a government's general pattern of behaviour in international fields is affected by the degree to which it commands control of the House of Commons – that is, whether it is in a minority or a majority position. But when the purely normative question is raised of how and to what extent Parliament *ought* to be involved in the making and conduct of international policy, it is not clear, in principle at least, that its status in this respect is really relevant. It might be argued that a government in a minority position has a greater normative obligation than does one in a majority position to take the views of parliamentarians from other parties more sensitively into account since the mandate enjoyed by its own party is less firm and therefore weaker as a source of legitimacy for decisive action. In the abstract, however, if the executive has an obligation in certain foreign policy contexts to let Parliament enter more fully into the process by which the pertinent international policies are formed and implemented, then it presumably has that obligation irrespective of the number of like-minded members who are bound by party loyalty to support it. Minority status may strengthen the influence of the prudential considerations of practical politics by concentrating the minds of the political leadership on keeping the constituency votes it already has and seeking to attract more of them in the next election. But this is a practical power-seeking calculation, not a normative one.

Before we turn more directly to the Canadian case with reference specifically to the normative question before us, a third preparatory undertaking is also required. We need to address the question of the actual and potential roles played by Parliament in the governance process more generally. What, in generic terms, are its proper functions? These, after all, are the activities that we might expect to see in evidence, in whole or in part, were it to be actively engaged in the foreign policy-making and implementation process.

The most obvious parliamentary function, of course, is to pass legislation. Ultimately, Parliament approves the laws by which we are all bound and authorizes the government to raise and spend public funds in accordance with budgets that the executive proposes and of which a majority of those parliamentarians who are present and voting approve. In these capacities, Parliament really *is* a policy decision maker, even if in most situations what it decides to do will be determined by a government that expects the members of its own party to give its proposals their automatic support. If the political leadership happens to be in a minority position, of course, it will also need to entice support from a sufficient number of the members of other parties to allow its most important measures, including its money bills, to pass and, hence, to permit the government itself to remain in office.

But parliamentarians also perform a number of other, somewhat different, functions. Among them are the following:

- to play the role of "watchdog" and thereby hold the government publicly to account for its governmental and administrative performance;
- to seek, as watchdog, to educate its own members on the complexities of the various issues that are on the policy agenda, using parliamentary committees and the like for this purpose;
- by much the same process, and through discussion and debate, to educate the media and attentive members of the public at large;
- to act as a conduit for bringing constituency opinions, wants, and needs to the attention of those in the executive branch who really run the policy machine (although it is a characteristic of executive-dominant systems that this is usually – albeit not always – more efficiently done by organized interest groups focusing directly on executive agencies); and
- to lend legitimacy to the policy-making process and its outputs, so that decisions are generally accepted (or at least tolerated) by the public at large, even if many citizens disagree with them in principle or find their consequences personally inconvenient or otherwise painful.

In the context of foreign and international affairs, the performance of these functions by the Parliament of Canada in practice has varied enormously, depending partly on the attitudes and procedural preferences of the political leadership – and most notably those of the prime minister. The most extreme case of non-involvement prior to the government of Stephen Harper developed during the years between the two world wars – a time, it is fair to say, when Parliament's role in foreign policy was negligible. On the surface, it might not have appeared this way. With a very few exceptions (as in the case of trade policy), most foreign policy issues of the day were concerned with the high politics of international peace and security, and the leading politician of the time, Mackenzie King (the Liberal prime minister for most of the period), used to proclaim with respect to them: "Parliament will decide." In practice, however, this assertion was largely intended for the consumption and bemusement of the British, who were expected to take from it an understanding that Ottawa's hands were tied by parliamentary opinion and, hence, that the prime minister could not automatically come to their military aid if they got into trouble in the awkward outreaches of their empire or in the endlessly tumultuous interstate politics of Europe. A related concern was the danger that, as a result of the European-dominated politics of the new League of Nations (an organization of which the United States was not a member), Canada might be pressed by other international players to engage in collective security operations in parts of the world in which it had no direct interest.

But the reality was that the prime minister rarely asked Parliament for its opinion and assiduously avoided having foreign policy discussed in the House of Commons. Doing otherwise, he thought, would carry too much risk of inflaming divisions within the country – particularly, but not solely, between the French-speaking and English-speaking populations, a sensibility that originated with the political fallout from the conscription crisis of the First World War and continued through the Second World War.

After 1945, the new generation of political leaders proved to be somewhat more receptive to the idea that foreign policy issues should at least be *discussed* in the House, if only for purposes of public education. But for more than twenty years the debates that resulted were modest in scope and desultory (it must be said) in content. A standing committee on external affairs was established in 1945, but its work was confined mainly to examining the estimates for the external affairs department and to talking to public officials about them. The focus was thus on administration, not policy.

Very exceptional circumstances aside,[1] for evidence of Canadian practice at the other end of the spectrum of parliamentary engagement, it is really necessary to move ahead to the end of the 1960s and the years that followed (particularly, but not solely, when the Liberals were in power). The process was initially triggered by a combination of the recognition, on the one hand, that foreign policy was increasingly concerned with domestic issues that directly affected the daily lives and, hence, the personal agendas of ordinary citizens and, on the other, by the first Trudeau government's commitment to the precepts of what was then called "participatory democracy." The latter in particular resulted in an expansion in the number and operations of parliamentary committees that were charged with examining international policy topics; in a growth of consultations with attentive publics and interest groups of one kind or another (some conducted through House and Senate committees, and others directly with the executive branch through the pertinent public service bureaucracies); and in a multiplication of parliamentary reports, government white papers, and other declaratory accounts of government policies, broadly conceived.

This intensifying evolution of parliamentary and related activity in the international field continued under the Progressive Conservative governments of Brian Mulroney (1984–93), but its peak can probably be identified best with the Liberal government of Jean Chrétien in the mid-1990s. For illustrative purposes, some brief reminders of what it entailed are therefore warranted.[2]

The Liberals came to power in 1993, committed to what they called the "democratization of foreign policy." "We need," they said, "a foreign policy decided in a more democratic, open way. There must be consent of Canadians on important initiatives: – there must be a clear role for Parliament in making decisions. There must be more involvement by our [nongovernmental organizations] NGOs [and] business interest groups in defining our role in the globe."[3]

To launch the process, they held the National Forum on Canada's International Relations in Ottawa on 21–22 March 1994. Part of its purpose was to set the stage for two parliamentary reviews, one on defence policy and the other on foreign policy. The forum was organized by the policy staff in the Department of Foreign Affairs and International Trade (as it was then called); however, on strict orders from the minister, the department did *not* attempt to control the outcome. The gathering was asked to canvass the entire waterfront with the help of six working groups. Those in attendance included 130 "participants" (representing a wide variety of interests and walks of life, all regions of the country, etc.) and 120 "observers," including eight Cabinet ministers, four parliamentary secretaries, and all of the members of the Special Joint Committee Reviewing Foreign Policy and the Special Joint Committee Reviewing Defence Policy (called "joint" committees because composed in each case of members drawn from both the Commons and the Senate). Those among the "observers" from the various bureaucracies included five members of the parliamentary professional staff, fifteen members drawn from ministerial staffs, thirty-six senior officials from seven federal government agencies, and twelve representatives of the provinces. There were also seven rapporteurs.

This was a massive exercise in public consultation, and it stimulated sometimes astounding efforts in response. Domestic constituencies devoted substantial energy and resources to making the most of the opportunity that the process was providing. For example, a Toronto-based organization calling itself the "Canada 21 Council" spent approximately $500,000 in hiring researchers, developing a position, and disseminating the result. Its report as a physical document cost $15,000 to design and another $30,000 to print. Similarly, the Canadian Council for International Co-operation, an umbrella organization with a membership composed of some 125 non-governmental organizations (NGOs), had a meeting in Ottawa of seventy people over a four-day period simply to plot strategic guidelines for its members to follow in developing their submissions to the parliamentary committees. The Conference of Defence Associations and other military support groups had comparably elaborate strategies for orchestrating their inputs.

Here was consultative democracy through parliamentary (and related) channels on a substantial scale, with foreign and defence policy as its primary focus. On the defence side, the process may have facilitated the making of some difficult force structure decisions. It may have helped, that is, to legitimize the making of some hard choices. On the foreign policy side, however, the impact of the exercise was less clear, perhaps because its scope was too broad.

The process *did*, however, serve to educate parliamentarians; it *did* give all Canadians who really wished to be heard a chance to be so; and it *did* produce documents that, if carefully read, could impart a Canadian foreign policy education to anyone with the will to learn.

Nor were the opening policy reviews the end of the enterprise. The government's commitment to consultations continued for several years. Some of these, too, were pursued under the auspices of parliamentary committees but in an atmosphere in which consultation was becoming an expected norm; others were triggered by ministers through their own departments. This norm was particularly evident when Lloyd Axworthy was the foreign minister (1996–2000) and regularly consulted with NGOs and others who shared his general orientation, partly with a view to exploring ideas for new policy initiatives and partly (it would appear) as a way of demonstrating to Cabinet colleagues with more conservative dispositions that his ideas had strong public support. In effect, a display of parliamentary consultations with interested publics not only influenced parliamentary inputs into the policy process but created (for a time, at least) a consultative culture that led more directly to inputs aimed at the executive branch itself. This was far from the long ago practice of Mackenzie King, and it was clearly antithetical to the culture subsequently engendered by the Prime Minister's Office under Stephen Harper, renowned for its emphasis on the Centre's controlling both the rhetoric and the substance of policy.

This brings us, at last, to the core normative issue before us here: *Should* Parliament be substantially involved in the making of international policy, particularly in the politico-security issue area? Or should it be kept in the background so that the executive branch can both make and pursue its foreign policy agenda with a minimum of parliamentary involvement?

In the early phases of the emergent English-speaking liberal democratic world, the subject was rarely discussed, but the generally accepted premise was that international politics – then dominated by politico-security issues, often coupled with empire building, geopolitical manoeuvring, and the closely related pursuit of economic aggrandizement – were matters, on the whole, for elites within executive leaderships to manage with a minimum of intrusion from legislators or their publics. In the American context, the flavour of the argument is perhaps most clearly expressed in the founding debates by John Jay in "Federalist Paper Number 64," addressed "To the People of the State of New York." Jay has no objection to the provision in the proposed constitution to the effect that the president would have the power to make treaties "*by and with the advice and consent of the senate ...* PROVIDED TWO THIRDS OF THE SENATORS PRESENT CONCUR" (emphases in original). But that was because senators would be appointed, not elected, by state governments, a process that he thought would ensure that only suitably experienced and qualified individuals would be chosen. Such senators, with the president, would "best understand our national interests, whether considered in relation to the several states or to foreign nations." They would also be "best able to promote those interests" and would have "reputations for integrity" of a kind that "inspires and merits confidence." Those who wished instead to commit such matters "to a popular assembly, composed of members constantly coming and going in quick succession," Jay argues, "seem not to recollect that such a body must necessarily be inadequate to the attainment of those great objects, which require to be steadily contemplated in all their relations and circumstances, and which can only be approached and achieved by measures, which not only talents, but also exact information and often much time are necessary to concert and execute."[4]

In the British parliamentary tradition, similar arguments are mounted by John Stuart Mill in his 1861 treatise on representative government, although in his case they are intended to discourage the participation of parliamentarians in executive policy making. As he bluntly puts it:

> Instead of the function of governing, for which it is radically unfit, the proper office of a representative assembly is to watch and control the government: to throw the light of publicity on its acts; to compel a full exposition and justification of all of them which any one considers questionable; to censure them if found condemnable, and, if the men who compose the government abuse their trust, or fulfil it in a manner which conflicts with the deliberate sense of the nation, to expel them from office, and either expressly or virtually appoint their successors. This is surely ample power, and security enough for the liberty of the nation.[5]

Even in the mainstream liberal (and gradually democratizing) world, these sorts of opinions in relation to foreign policy were not significantly challenged until the First World War, following the revelation of the "secret treaties" concluded most notably by the British and French and aimed primarily at ensuring that they would each get chunks of the Middle East under their control once the hostilities were over. The exposure brought the underlying motives of the pertinent foreign policy elites under suspicion and produced a reformist response in the guise, most famously, of the first of the "14 points" articulated by President Woodrow Wilson in January 1918 as a basis for establishing a peaceful world order at the end of the war. There were to be "open covenants of peace, openly arrived at, after which there [would] be no private international understandings of any kind but diplomacy [would] proceed always frankly and in the public view."[6]

It proved to be a hopeless aspiration, not least because it made compromises at the negotiating tables of the Paris Peace Conference impossible. Concessions, immediately reported by the media, aroused righteous howls of protest from the negotiators' constituents at home, where it was commonly held that no quarter should be given in defending narrowly self-serving conceptions of the national interest. Doors to negotiating rooms were closed. Those on the scene who had taken the president's guidelines to heart became disillusioned, among them the erudite American journalist Walter Lippmann and the then junior British diplomat Harold Nicolson, who, at the end of the proceedings, reported in his diary (with regard to the experience) that he went "to bed, sick of life."[7]

As a general rule, the return to traditional practice that resulted came to be preferred by professional foreign policy practitioners in Canada and usually also by their political masters. Lester Pearson's view, broadly put, was that Parliament, and hence the public, should be informed of the government's objectives and purposes abroad and that it should certainly be advised of the substance of any agreements that were ultimately concluded. But it would not be in the general interest for it to be briefed in detail on the course of diplomatic negotiations.[8] There might be occasional exceptions, but in general – and even in the case of relatively amicable discussions with the United States on relatively routine matters – "quiet diplomacy" has been preferred. Representatives of interest groups, other levels of government, and even opposition members of Parliament have occasionally been given observer status in multilateral gatherings, particularly in the exploratory phases of developing responses to new issues (notably those relating to the environment). In most such instances, however, the outsiders involved have been excluded from the negotiating table (as at the World Trade Organization's ministerial conference in Seattle in 1999).

Just as there were criticisms from those suspicious of the quiet diplomacy approach some four and a half decades ago, so there are now occasional expressions of the view that Parliament and interested publics alike should have a greater role to play in deliberations bearing on international policy issues. Given the Harper government's reputation for maintaining centralized control of the policy process and insisting that both its parliamentary supporters and the public service stick to PMO-approved scripts, the pressure was not very optimistically advanced, although the pertinent parliamentary committees held hearings and delivered reports on a variety of foreign and security policy subjects.[9] In general, as Hugh Segal notes in Chapter 15 (this volume), those of the Senate were less driven by partisan majority influences than were those of the Commons, where party interests, electoral preoccupations, and PMO-driven marching orders held more sway. It is reasonable to assume that these exercises were useful sources of education for the committee members concerned, but (attentive special interests aside) the lack of media attention to the proceedings limited their educational impact on the citizenry at large.

There is a sense in some quarters that these limitations do not matter very much, the assumption being that Parliament itself does not matter very much. Abuses of the institution by the political leadership, when paired with the not unrelated impulse on all sides to practise a mindlessly partisan approach to parliamentary discussion and debate, reinforces the impression. With this self-indulgent spectacle before them day after day after day, citizens lose such faith as they may once have had that they have something to learn from what politicians say about complex issues – international politico-security issues not least among them. A larger proportion than ever before now have the benefit of postsecondary education. They also have access to the communications wonders of the internet and direct exposure to the myriad political utterances (and opportunities for taking part in policy advocacies, many on a transnational basis) that it delivers. Who, therefore, needs parliamentary help to reach sound policy preferences?

But this rhetorical question reflects an erroneous conclusion. The development of sound understandings of complex policy issues requires careful analysis informed not just by easily obtained factoids or exposure to 140-character expressions of raw, bottom-line judgments, often instantly formed. Seriously pursued, it requires lengthy experience, extensive study, and a nuanced understanding not only of political realities but also of the pros and cons – the competing arrays of probable consequences – that would likely be triggered, respectively, by the various practicable options at hand. In international matters, certainly, this process is rarely an easy enterprise. Uncertainties are inevitable. Plausible propositions abound: "If we free the people of country X from the tyranny of a dictatorship, they will quickly coalesce in their support for liberal democracy and implement its requirements in generous and accommodating spirit, and with practical sophistication." "If we free the people of country Y from the predations of their poverty, we will at once dissipate their anger and pacify their behaviour." The mobilization of such ideas from a well-intentioned and well-advised focus on "root causes" is in many respects an admirable phenomenon. But in the past two and a half decades such careless assumptions have encouraged – or at least rationalized – an impressive amount of killing. They have done so because they are grossly oversimplified, are often devoid of nuanced understandings of what is really going on in the targeted societies, are ignorant of the disruptive effects of even benignly intended fast-moving change (especially when externally driven), and so on. Interestingly, policy premises of this sort have enjoyed widespread currency, even among experts, in spite of the enormous supply of evidence from modern history that they should be regarded with scepticism – evidence that can be drawn, for example, from the frequent failure of imperial powers to succeed in persuading their colonies to govern themselves in the way they themselves have done or from the failure of so many development assistance programs (whatever their design) to accomplish the social and political objectives their sophisticated architects had in mind.

These comments are themselves contentious and open to argument. But there is enough truth in them to demonstrate that the educational functions identified long ago by John Stuart Mill as central to the parliamentary task and available only through careful, continuous, and well-researched debate, far from being outmoded, are now more necessary than ever. Some issues may be much as they have always been. But most are far more complex and are rendered more intricate still by conjunctions of multiple interacting circumstances that would never have disturbed those who made foreign policy in the age of classical statecraft. A modern executive branch of government thus has an obligation to promote considered parliamentary discussion and analysis, just as it has a need, if it is responsible, not to dismiss, but to encourage and consult, the professionals in its public service. Simple judgments about who are the good and who are the bad are not, in themselves, a foundation for efficacious, much less enlightened, policy.

It follows that the main vehicle for considered parliamentary involvement in the Canadian foreign policy process is the parliamentary committee. The activities such committees trigger do not imply that they will *make* policy, although they may sometimes be found among the myriad forces that have *affected* policy. Either way, they are essential to the effective performance of Parliament's watchdog, educational, and legitimation functions.

In an ideal world, the committees would be facilitated in these roles by considerably enhanced staff support, including research capabilities; sufficient financial resources to allow them to travel both at home (for consultative and legitimation purposes) and abroad (for exposure to the briefings and points of view of policy professionals and others in foreign jurisdictions); practices designed to ensure as much continuity of committee membership as possible so that expertise can accumulate over time; terms of reference that ask clear, concrete questions that focus on substantive policy issues; constructive and mutually supportive working relationships with the pertinent ministers and their senior staffs; access to sophisticated communications expertise; and internal operational cultures that encourage committee members to contain their partisan habits in the interest of open inquiry (at least until the report-writing stage, when dissenting reports can be accommodated as required).

All this sounds straightforward enough. But of course it is not. In the real world, some of these assets are hard for committees to acquire, and they have to make do with less. The party system is adversarial; nonpartisanship (especially in the Commons) is not natural to it. And ministers and prime ministers alike never find it easy to open up their policy domains to free-wheeling discussion that could call their own policy preferences into question (unless they have a clear political interest in doing so).

A less ambitious, but nonetheless significant, approach to fulfilling the parliamentary responsibility might be to augment the current operations of the pertinent committees with more elaborate international and security policy reviews after the pattern of the 1994–95 reviews whenever a new government takes office (as well as on such other occasions as political leaderships might think useful and appropriate). These enterprises can be expensive, and officials often complain that they are time-consuming and unhelpful from the vantage point of those who deal with the immediate and practical issues that clutter their desks from day to day.

But the parliamentary functions discussed above are important ones – and not only because educating our parliamentarians (who, in the Canadian House of Commons, turn over at an unusually rapid rate) on the complexities of international policy is essential to both the role they play in Ottawa and their credibility with the attentive citizenry at large. In addition, widely publicized exercises of this sort help to educate attentive publics, provide materials that can be used in university (and even high school) classrooms in which world affairs matters are addressed, inform discussion groups of various kinds all across the country, and so on. While governments may fear that such processes might lead to their being bombarded with pressures to do things that they may regard as impracticable, undesirable, or in conflict with their own political preferences, they will also gain both credit and legitimacy from demonstrating that they are willing to take serious account of the ideas of well-informed constituents. They may even find some of what they hear useful because it draws their attention to options they have not considered or, at the very least, gives them a feel for what foreign policy opinion leaders outside of official Ottawa are thinking and why.

In sum, the process as a whole, if repeated at reasonably regular intervals, could do a great deal to promote Canadian understanding of the complex world in which we live, while at the same time enhancing the capacity of Parliament to play a constructive role in line with its traditional constitutional functions in the international field. And, once again, this is a role that it can usefully play whether the governing party itself has a majority in the House of Commons or not. All that being so, public education is precisely what Parliament *should* do, and the policy review format is an admirable vehicle for this purpose.

Notes

1 The editors' introduction to this volume, for example, alludes to how parliamentary debate ran hot and heavy in 1962–63 when Prime Minister John Diefenbaker and his colleagues were struggling to deal with uproars over both the Canadian response to the Cuban missile crisis and the pros and cons of proposals to acquire nuclear warheads for Canadian weapons systems. Diefenbaker's minority government may have lost the 1963 election at least partly as a result, although that loss probably had less to do with the issues themselves than with the contribution they made to the impression that the prime minister was indecisive and vacillating.
2 The following details have been drawn from Denis Stairs, "The public politics of the Canadian defence and foreign policy reviews," *Canadian Foreign Policy* 3, 1 (1995): 91–116.
3 Ibid., 91.
4 Alexander Hamilton, James Madison, and John Jay, *The Federalist* (Franklin Center, Pennsylvania: Franklin Library, 1977), 463–65.
5 John Stuart Mill, *Utilitarianism, Liberty and Representative Government* (London: J.M. Dent and Sons, 1910), 239.
6 Woodrow Wilson, "President Woodrow Wilson's Fourteen Points," 8 January 1918, http://avalon.law.yale.edu/20th_century/wilson14.asp.
7 Harold Nicolson, *Peacemaking 1919* (London: Methuen, 1967), 571.
8 Pearson's views, heavily influenced by the Cold War context, are explored in his *Democracy in World Politics* (Toronto: R.J. Reginald Saunders, 1955). The most pertinent passages are on pp. 40–81. See also his *Diplomacy in the Nuclear Age* (Toronto: R.J. Reginald Saunders, 1959).
9 For a brief media assessment by an attentive, perceptive, and experienced observer, see Colin Robertson, "Circus act detracts from the real work of MPs," *Globe and Mail*, 26 May 2015, http://www.theglobeandmail.com/news/world/world-insider/circus-act-detracts-from-the-real-work-of-mps/article24608629/.

2

Foreign Policy and Minority Government
The Cases of Lester Pearson and Pierre Trudeau

JOHN ENGLISH

Lester Pearson loathed minority government. In the Conservative minority government of 1957–58, he proved politically incompetent in his leadership of the opposition in the House of Commons. As the prime minister during minority governments between 1963 and 1968, he called an unnecessary election in 1965, criticized and irritated American leaders, crowded the legislative agenda with bills too hastily prepared, and, in frustration, announced his retirement after only four years and eight months in power in December 1967. Pearson had received his political education during the governments of Louis St. Laurent in the 1950s, when large Liberal majorities gave him unusual freedom to shape Canadian foreign policy in the early Cold War. Freed from the constraints of the House of Commons, he spent months travelling to foreign capitals or rallying votes at the United Nations, where he became the closest North American friend of Dag Hammarskjöld.[1] The 1960s brought far more difficult times – times that were made much worse for Pearson by his inability to win a parliamentary majority.

Pearson believed that minority government placed shackles upon his governments' freedom. Many scholars, however, disagree with his interpretation and point to the remarkable legislative record of Pearson's governments, which included Medicare, the Canadian flag, the Canada Pension Plan, immigration reform, and federal bilingualism.[2] Nonetheless, Tom Kent, whose fecund mind and quick pen gave shape to so many of those initiatives, later described how difficult the minority Parliament was for

Pearson, whose oratorical skills were limited compared with the sharp wit and prosecutorial histrionics of John Diefenbaker. In the Commons, Kent writes: "Mr. Diefenbaker seemed to interact with Mr. Pearson in a way that produced what I think is the conventional reaction of the rabbit to the snake."[3] Pearson's pride in his domestic accomplishments is also apparent in his memoirs, but he is obviously dissatisfied with the foreign policy legacy of his governments, where Parliament was much less frequently the stage for action.

It seemed to start well. Promising an end to the anti-American excesses of John Diefenbaker, Pearson moved quickly and successfully to establish a strong relationship with President John Kennedy and, after Kennedy's death, with Lyndon Johnson. To establish a firmer base for the relationship, Canada and the United States appointed the former Canadian ambassador to the United States, Arnold Heeney, and the former American ambassador to Canada, Livingston Merchant, to study how future Canadian-American relations could avoid the angry public exchanges that had marked the last year of John Diefenbaker's leadership.[4] By 1965, when their report was ready, its tone and major recommendation – that Canadian and American political leaders should resolve their issues through confidential private negotiations and avoid public disagreement – had become controversial and, for Pearson, unworkable.

Yet Pearson yearned for the approach urged by Heeney and Merchant, who urged that, "wherever possible, divergent views between two governments should be expressed and if possible resolved in private, through diplomatic channels."[5] In the 1950s, as secretary of state for external affairs, Pearson had depended upon close personal ties with Western and, especially, American officials to achieve significant agreements and, in his own case, international recognition, including the Nobel Prize for Peace. But the 1960s were different: a combination of more complex political circumstances and an altered international context caused Pearson to abandon "quiet diplomacy," which, in the contentious 1960s, became a derisory term for Pearson's critics.

How much was minority government responsible for the foreign policy decisions he took while prime minister? First, Pearson's own recollections attribute many, if not the majority, of his problems to the plague of minority parliaments. There is a whine about minorities that extends throughout his memoir covering this period.[6] Nevertheless, one must acknowledge that Pearson was a poor parliamentarian whose lack of knowledge of the rules caused many of his problems and that these same problems would in all likelihood have occurred in majority circumstances. Certainly that was the opinion of Paul Martin and Jack Pickersgill, the finest Liberal parliamentarians of the period.[7] Similarly, many of his domestic accomplishments were in all likelihood the product of minority status. Social programs were popular in Western democracies in the mid-1960s, when poverty was suddenly "discovered" and budgetary surpluses permitted governments to introduce generous social programs. Robert Winters, a conservative presence in the Pearson governments, allegedly told a friend who asked why Canada had an abundance of new social programs in the 1970s: "Elections!"[8] With the support for the socialist New Democratic Party rising, the Liberals moved to the left to keep power in Ottawa and popularity in the nation.

Second, Pearson famously tended to leave his many talented and few incompetent ministers to operate their ministries free of his personal interference. The many memoirs of the period reveal that Pearson's own hand touched the tiller rarely in navigating Ottawa's bureaucratic and political waters. Scholars such as Penny Bryden verify the accuracy of Tom Kent's memoir, in which the former Pearson aide argues that he and select ministers and officials built Canada's extensive social programs in the 1960s with only minimal participation by the prime minister himself. More recently, Lorna Marsden discovered, to her surprise, that Pearson took little interest in the historic Royal Commission on the Status of Women, which he appointed and which many point to as a historic part of his legacy. Indeed, Marsden finds that he appears to have disagreed with many of its conclusions.[9]

Third, Pearson's distance from some of the most notable areas of government action was not the case in two areas: Quebec and foreign policy. With regard to the former, he was continuously active as he dealt with what, in 1965, the preliminary report of the Royal Commission on Bilingualism and Biculturalism called the "greatest crisis" in Canadian history. With little background on Quebec politics and almost no French, Pearson frantically sought policies and people who could respond to the "challenge" of Quebec. With regard to foreign policy, Pearson brought greater knowledge and skill than any other prime minister in Canadian history, but his knowledge of Quebec's history, its politics, and its people was weak. Moreover, as the Royal Commission on Bilingualism and Biculturalism pointed out in an extensive 1969 study, Pearson had done little as a diplomat or foreign minister to make the Department of External Affairs representative or even congenial to francophone Canadians.[10] One gets the sense that Pearson as prime minister was desperate to make up for lost time, but it would be difficult to attribute his approach to Quebec to minority government status. The leaders of the major opposition parties, John Diefenbaker and Tommy Douglas, were unilingual Western Canadians and, in the case of Douglas, there was an embarrassed willingness to accommodate Quebec's demands, undoubtedly to his political detriment. In examining the principal actions taken by Pearson to meet the "crises," which range from the move to bilingualism to the adoption of the new flag, one finds no explicit concern about minority government except for the normal parliamentary fussing that accompanies controversial legislation.[11]

If the New Democrats usually assured support for the Pearson government's major domestic initiatives, their votes became increasingly uncertain in the case of foreign policy. The Cold War consensus crumbled in the 1960s, and the NDP moved steadily towards neutralism. New Democrats became increasingly opposed to Canada's participation in the North Atlantic Treaty Organization (NATO) and the North American Aerospace Defense Command (NORAD), and the expansion of the Vietnam War was the principal catalyst for their growing opposition. For Pearson, this trend presented serious political problems, not least because in 1963 the Liberals had strongly supported the American alliance against John Diefenbaker's bitter attacks on the Kennedy administration's interference in Canadian affairs, when it urged the government to accept nuclear weapons for Canada's Bomarc and Honest John missiles. When Pearson announced that he believed that Canada must honour its commitment to take nuclear weapons, the NDP stood with John Diefenbaker in opposition to the "imperialists" in Washington and their Liberal Canadian lackeys. The conservatives Donald Creighton and George Grant and socialists Tommy Douglas and David Lewis joined to denounce American imperialism and its Canadian apostle, Lester Pearson.[12]

Pearson's appointment of Paul Martin as secretary of state for external affairs and Marcel Cadieux as the department's undersecretary meant that the principal architects of Canadian foreign policy in the 1960s were strong supporters of Canada's most significant alliances and, especially with Cadieux, the American intervention in Southeast Asia. Ministerial and bureaucratic advice was therefore consistently at odds with the policies of the NDP. In 1965, Pearson attempted to strengthen his domestic support in Quebec by recruiting Pierre Trudeau and Gérard Pelletier, prominent anti-nuclear activists and opponents of the Vietnam War, and Jean Marchand, a labour leader with similar sympathies. Simultaneously, the *Toronto Star*, Canada's largest newspaper, began to express increasingly nationalist and even anti-American sentiments on its editorial page. This tone troubled Pearson greatly because the *Star* was deeply linked with Walter Gordon, a nationalist,

Pearson's finance minister, and also his major political organizer in the winter of 1965, when the Vietnam War became a burning issue in American and Canadian politics.[13]

The shock of the assassination of John Kennedy bound Canada and the United States closely together, and, in the aftermath of this tragic event, President Lyndon Johnson told the Canadian ambassador to the United States that Pearson was the leader he "felt closest to."[14] The year 1964 was a good one for Canadian-American relations, with Pearson agreeing to allow Canadian diplomat Blair Seaborn to act as an intermediary with the North Vietnamese, and the Americans agreeing to a managed trade agreement in automobiles that was enormously beneficial to Canada. Pearson and Johnson met in Texas in January 1965 to sign that historic agreement, but they did not discuss Vietnam in detail, which was probably unfortunate. A year earlier, in the warm haze of post-assassination bonhomie, Pearson had told Johnson that "any drastic escalation [of the war] would give great problems both in Canada and internationally." It would be, Pearson added, "one thing to attack a bridge or an oil tank, but quite another to shower bombs on a village full of women and children."[15] At that time the prospect seemed remote, and Johnson did not disagree.

But bombs began to fall on North Vietnam in March 1965 as Operation Rolling Thunder commenced, and Pearson was troubled. On the one hand, Canada's most celebrated diplomat correctly perceived that Johnson was obsessed with the war and that he failed to recognize the impact of the expanded war upon the Western alliance. On the other hand, he knew that the NDP, Quebec public figures like Trudeau and Pelletier, and the nationalist Liberals clustered around Walter Gordon would strongly attack the American president and his aggressive policies. It was not difficult to imagine leftist votes drifting from the Liberals to the New Democrats, whose popular leader Tommy Douglas was increasingly strident in his criticism of the war. Similarly, hopes to reinvigorate the Liberal Party in Quebec could be undermined by Canadian support for the expanded war. Trudeau, for example, halted his drift towards the federal Liberals in 1962 when Pearson accepted nuclear weapons for Canada in January 1963. In *Cité Libre*, which he and Pelletier had founded, Trudeau denounced the Liberal leader as a hypocrite and as too willing to play games with the "hipsters" of Camelot. Both voted NDP.[16]

As Johnson's war expanded, Pearson's fears grew. He knew there was little hope of a quick victory in Vietnam and was attentive to the critics in the press, in the NDP, on Liberal backbenches, and in Quebec. He decided to grasp the opportunity to speak on Vietnam when he accepted an invitation to Temple University in Pennsylvania to receive a "World Peace Award" in April 1965. Prior to his arrival in Philadelphia, Johnson congratulated him, noting his "wisdom and courage." Shortly after receiving the award, Pearson told the university audience that the United States should consider a bombing pause in Vietnam. It was a carefully worded suggestion, but it outraged the president who immediately summoned the Canadian prime minister to his Camp David retreat, where he bitterly told him that he had come to the United States and "pissed on my rug." As Charles Ritchie explained: "Pearson had joined the ranks of the domestic opponents of his Vietnam policy [Senator Wayne] Morse, [Walter] Lippmann, ADA [Americans for Democratic Action], the ignorant Liberals, the 'know nothing' do gooders, etc."[17] It was not only Johnson's opponents that he pleased. At the Cabinet meeting upon his return, finance minister Walter Gordon "expressed warm agreement with the speech" and suggested that most Canadians shared his view.[18] Most who would vote NDP certainly did.

The Canadian ambassador to the United States, Charles Ritchie, did not share these supportive views, nor did external affairs undersecretary Marcel Cadieux, and the secretary of state for external affairs, Paul Martin, threatened to resign. On 10 February, Pearson had addressed the Canadian Club of Ottawa: "Our official doubts about certain US foreign policies should be expressed in private, through the channels of diplomacy, rather than publicly by speeches to Canadian Clubs ... Pulling the eagle's tail feathers is an easy, but a dangerous, way to get a certain temporary popularity."[19] Two months later Pearson strongly pulled these feathers and did indeed obtain a "certain temporary popularity." Trudeau, Pelletier, and Marchand agreed to come to Ottawa, the nationalists joined Gordon in applauding Pearson's boldness, and the Liberals rose in the polls. With Gordon's return as campaign manager, an election was called for 8 November 1965. But the majority the polls predicted was not to be, as the Liberals fell three seats short.[20]

The governing party also unexpectedly fell in the popular vote (1.34 percent), as did John Diefenbaker's Progressive Conservatives. Nevertheless, the advice of Gordon and campaign strategist Keith Davey to lean towards the left was justified by the 4.67 percent rise in support for the New Democrats, whose leader, Tommy Douglas, railed constantly against American involvement in Vietnam. While Pearson could never captivate a crowd as the eloquent Douglas regularly did in the Commons and beyond, Temple University offered the Liberal prime minister a unique pulpit that assured that his message was heard not only in the White House but also in the editorial office of the *Toronto Star*, university common rooms, and the coffee houses where young Canadians debated politics. Many years later, Paul Martin privately conceded that Pearson did what a political leader had to do. Upon reflection, he realized that the threat to the Liberals came from the left and that Pearson had used a foreign platform to win Liberal votes in Canada. The Temple speech and the recruitment of Trudeau, Pelletier, and Marchand ("NDP material," André Laurendeau wrote in his diary) pushed back the NDP surge even if it did not secure a total victory.[21]

Had Pearson won the expected majority in 1963 he would almost certainly have chosen different words for his Temple speech, even though he was much troubled by Johnson's Asian recklessness. Ironically, the disappointing electoral result also meant that Pearson wooed his ferocious 1963 foreign policy critics, Trudeau and Pelletier, when he sought to escape the shackles of minority government in 1965. Their appeal to the left enhanced their political value in the very different international environment of 1965. The peculiar needs of Pearson's minority government made possible the astonishing political ascent of Pierre Trudeau, who was a harsh critic of Lester Pearson, the Department of External Affairs, and Canadian international policy more generally. Trudeau had left the PCO because of Pearson's leadership in committing Canada to participation in the Korean War. He wrote to diplomat Jules Léger at the time: "I've just heard Pearson's speech on Korea in the House. Not a single original thought. A little current history, a lot of propaganda."[22] He later told other friends that Pearson was misleading Canadians by demonizing the Soviet Union. Pearson, he wrote, lacked the "courage" to acquaint "the public with facts which might tend to open an avenue of comprehension and sympathy" towards the Soviets. In his writings of the period, he championed the notion of a "third force" between the West and Soviet Communism, a concept thoroughly inimical to mainstream liberalism in Canada and the United States, but one that Trudeau promoted in his writings and deeds (such as a visit to Communist China in 1960, another to Cuba in 1964, and frequent participation in anti-nuclear demonstrations).[23] But in 1968 the domestic crisis caused by Quebec nationalism and separatism trumped earlier animosities, and Trudeau, with Pearson's strong support, became prime minister in that fateful year.

Pearson was an idealist with serious doubts about the faith. Trudeau was a realist but felt bad about it. Trudeau's stance created the unpredictability that marked his foreign policy, and the most sustained study of Trudeau's foreign policy is appropriately entitled *Pirouette*.[24] There were several turns, and in his final year in office Trudeau trotted about foreign capitals pushing nuclear disarmament in a most unrealistic fashion. It is therefore difficult to evaluate with precision just how much minority government affected Trudeau's international policies between 20 October 1972, when he barely escaped a defeat that would have almost certainly ended his political life, and 8 July 1974, when he won a solid majority government. The major debates about Trudeau's foreign policy and his attempt to break with Pearsonian internationalism, with its links to NATO and to UN multilateralism, took place shortly after he came to office and were largely settled by the time his government faced the electorate in the fall of 1972.

As early as his leadership campaign in spring 1968, Trudeau tried to break the Pearsonian mould by encouraging a debate among Canadians and within his government about what Canada's international policy should be. His *Foreign Policy for Canadians* document, with its cover of hundreds of "ordinary" citizens supposedly pondering what Canada should do in the world, set an anti-elitist, democratic tone that initially seemed to capture the Canadian anti-establishment mood of the late 1960s, when John Lennon and Yoko Ono wrote "Give Peace a Chance" in their bed-in at Montreal's Queen Elizabeth Hotel and revolutionary rhetoric abounded on university campuses. Trudeau made it clear that he thought peace had not been given a full chance during the Cold War. Canada, he said, to Pearson's great irritation, had no foreign policy in the past, only a defence policy. He hinted strongly that he favoured withdrawal from NATO, of which Pearson had been a leading founder and president of the assembly. In a foreign policy statement issued to set out the principles of the debate on foreign policy, Canada's peacekeeping role was summed up as being simply a "helpful fixer," sending off soldiers to deal with quarrelsome countries. While Canadians tried to fix the world, their own country became divided and now faced the possibility of disintegration. Canadians, Trudeau seemed to suggest, should heal themselves first and focus on their own self-interest. Pearson vowed to "have it out" with his successor but never did, satisfying himself with a memorandum he sent to friends in which he criticized a foreign policy that promoted Canada's "national interest" in such a narrow way. "Surely," he wrote, "a far better foreign policy is that which is based on a national interest which expresses itself in co-operation with others; in the building of international institutions and the development of international policies and agreements, leading to a world order which promotes freedom, well-being and security for all."[25]

Trudeau's foreign policy initiatives ran into roadblocks within the Cabinet, and the result was a diminished but far more bilingual Department of

External Affairs whose ranks were thinned in numbers and talent, a reduced Canadian presence in Europe, a smaller armed forces, and recognition of Communist China – but also continued membership in NATO and NORAD, and a foreign policy that was fundamentally the same. A disillusioned *Toronto Star* soon turned towards the NDP to fulfill its nationalist dreams. In his memoirs, Trudeau ignores the foreign policy review entirely and includes less than a page on international activities in his first government. It is probably an accurate reflection of his interests at the time.[26]

After the 1972 election, Trudeau faced a situation whose problems had some similarities to those Pearson encountered in 1963. His survival depended upon the support of the New Democratic Party, which had thirty-one seats compared with 107 for the Progressive Conservatives and 109 for the Liberals. It was a dangerous political terrain, and there was little doubt that Trudeau, like Pearson before him, had to move his party to the left. It was a turn easily negotiated for the erstwhile socialist, and by 4 January 1973, the *Toronto Star* was enthusiastically welcoming the transformation. Now, it declared, Trudeau "deserves a chance." NDP Leader David Lewis and the *Star* emphasized domestic policies in their support but they also called for a "nationalist" turn that would affect Canada's relations with the United States and President Richard Nixon. The first vote following the Speech from the Throne in 1973 was an NDP condemnation of the American bombing of Hanoi, which the Liberals decided to support. Trudeau sent a letter to Nixon explaining the domestic political situation that required the Liberal support of the motion, but this did not mollify the temperamental American president, who refused to send a letter of condolence to Trudeau on the death of his beloved mother in January 1973.[27]

Nixon's ire grew as Trudeau responded even more to the economic nationalists. He brought vocal economic nationalist Herb Gray into the Cabinet and finally agreed to allow his new minister of industry, trade, and commerce, Alastair Gillespie, to draw up guidelines for foreign investment in Canada.[28] He told Gillespie, "You know I'm not a nationalist and this is a form of nationalism, which I find suspect"; however, political realism carried the day. As Gillespie later wrote: "Trudeau did come to recognize the political and economic significance of the issue in vote-rich Ontario and, at the insistence of the NDP and many members of our own caucus, his minority government created the Foreign Investment Review Act."[29] The Cabinet minutes reveal the tensions between nationalists (such as Gray, Gillespie, and Donald Macdonald) and those who feared the impact of nationalist policies (such as Finance Minister John Turner and Foreign Minister Mitchell Sharp). The threat of a political hanging concentrated the Cabinet's attention upon what could be done to maintain NDP support while not alienating traditional centrist voters.[29]

After the creation of the Foreign Investment Review Agency came a torrent of nationalist actions inspired by the sudden increase in the price of petroleum products caused by the Arab-Israeli war of October 1973. Although the principal Canadian outcome was a nasty quarrel between Alberta and the federal government over economic rents, there was a huge spillover upon Canadian-American relations. Spurred on by an NDP resolution, the Trudeau government established a national energy company (Petro-Canada), an action that was anathema to Wall Street and the White House. Moreover, the government, with strong NDP approval, used an export tax to maintain two prices for oil, which in January 1973 was $9.60 a barrel for Americans and only $3.80 for Canadians. Although the government resisted NDP calls for a national heritage fund that would preserve the fossil fuel riches for future generations, as Norwegian Social Democrats successfully managed to do, the policies attracted critical comment in Washington and oil interests on both sides of the border. The Cabinet debates and those within the bureaucracy reveal a left-right split, with Simon Reisman, the deputy minister of finance and later a major negotiator of free trade with the United States, profoundly upset with Trudeau's tilt to the left. He left government service shortly after John Turner resigned from the Cabinet and joined the newly created Fraser Institute as an open critic of Liberal policies during the minority government.[30]

The minority government coincided with Richard Nixon's Watergate crisis, and the American response was affected by the enormous diversion created by the move towards impeachment in Washington. As Ivan Head and Trudeau himself point out, the minority government period did have many examples of Canadian-American cooperation, but, they admit, energy was an exception. In those times, however, no item was more important.[31] The interventionist approach of the Trudeau government aroused powerful opposition not only in Calgary's Petroleum Club but also in Congress and Wall Street. Although Trudeau was intellectually committed to redistribution policies, the strong whiff of nationalism associated with the policies of 1972–74 bothered him as much as it lured the NDP. In the election campaign of 1974, NDP leader David Lewis argued correctly that his party had "made a difference" between 1972 and 1974. But Trudeau and his Liberal team convinced Canadians that, although the NDP may have written the popular script, the Liberals were the better actors.

Does minority government matter for Canadian foreign policy? The Pearson and Trudeau governments suggest that it does, although both cases are different from the minority governments of Stephen Harper between 2006 and 2011. The principal difference is Pearson's and Trudeau's concern that their parties faced a threat from the left, specifically an increasingly popular New Democratic Party. Both Pearson and Trudeau believed that Liberal votes could move easily to the New Democrats, especially in urban centres and with younger voters. Indeed, Trudeau himself was proof of the tendency. Although there are areas in English Canada where NDP voters have been attracted by the populist appeal of Harper Conservatism, Harper did not target the NDP in his campaigns; rather, he concentrated on drawing centre-right Liberals and a few specific groups. The Jewish community, for example, apparently responded to Harper's pro-Israel policies and made what *Globe and Mail* reporter Craig Offman terms a "historic exodus" from the Liberal Party.[32] In a broader sense, Pearson and Trudeau made their political decisions in the so-called *trente années glorieuses* of the West, when strong and redistributive economic growth made possible a remarkable broadening of the state and expansion of social spending. The economic turmoil and lower growth of the twenty-first century made austerity, retrenchment, and the shrinking of the state a politically more effective appeal. There are differences, but some generalizations can be made.

Liberal governments in minority situations from William Lyon Mackenzie King, who successfully wooed the Western Canadian Progressives in the 1920s, through Pearson and Trudeau looked to the left either to maintain power in minority parliaments or to capture votes in the following election. More recently, Stéphane Dion and Jean Chrétien both pursued a coalition with the New Democrats when Stephen Harper stumbled on domestic issues after the 2008 election, this time unsuccessfully. In the cases of Pearson and Trudeau, foreign policy was significantly central in the appeal to the left, more obviously in the case of Pearson.

Lester Pearson was a career diplomat with deep respect for the Canadian foreign service. He famously favoured "quiet diplomacy" as a central tenet in Canada's critical relationship with the United States. While Pearson's 1965 speech was cautiously phrased, he was well aware of its potential impact.[33] But Pearson saw beyond the polls and thought of young Canadians (who, like American youth, were increasingly opposed to the Vietnam War) and of Quebec (where prominent voices in public affairs, such as Gérard Pelletier and Pierre Trudeau, were vocal critics of American foreign policy). Would he have given the speech if he had won a majority in 1963? Almost certainly not.

In his first government, Trudeau had stepped back from disengagement from the Western alliance and had successfully resisted harsh trade measures against Canada promoted by American treasury secretary John Connally. He met personally with Nixon, and they were "able quietly and without rancor to resolve the impasse to the complete satisfaction of each" in December 1971.[34] But he knew that Nixon was not his friend and would put American and Republican interests first. Would the Liberals have supported the NDP motion condemning the bombing of Hanoi so close to Nixon's inauguration after his decisive triumph over the anti-war Democrat George McGovern if Trudeau had won a majority in 1972? Almost certainly not. Would Trudeau have cloaked Canada's energy and foreign policies in nationalist rhetoric were it not for its appeal to the NDP, the left, and the critical *Toronto Star*? In conversations with his principal economic adviser, Albert Breton, he stressed political exigencies.[35] Political needs were the highest trump in 1973. While the Nixon administration disagreed with Canada's energy and investment policies, the Canadian rhetoric infuriated them. For Trudeau, Watergate was a fortuitous and fortunate diversion.

In Leopold Von Ranke's classic distinctions between *Primat der Aussenpolitik*, according to which a state's interests are preserved by shared values and an elite understanding of the state's relationship with other nations, and *Primat der Innenpolitik*, according to which domestic interests shape a state's interaction with others, minority governments tilt strongly towards the latter. For Trudeau, *Aussenpolitik* had held sway too long, and attention to *Innenpolitik* was overdue, even if some the nationalist flavour was distasteful. But even Canada's greatest internationalist could not avoid its unique power when his political legions were too weak to prevail. However uncomfortable, he took his political stand. For foreign policy, minority governments matter.

Notes

1 Brian Urquhart, *Hammarskjöld* (New York: Harper Colophon, [1972] 1984), 36. Urquhart confirmed his comment on Pearson's close friendship in a personal conversation.
2 L. Ian MacDonald, "The best prime minister of the last fifty years: Pearson by a landslide," *Policy Options* (June-July 2003), 8–12.
3 Interview with Tom Kent in Peter Stursberg, *Lester Pearson and the Dream of Unity* (Toronto: Doubleday Canada, 1978), 222.
4 The report was finally released in 1965. Heeney's account of the reaction is described in A.D.P. Heeney, *The Things That Are Caesar's: Memoirs of a Canadian Public*

Servant (Toronto: University of Toronto Press, 1972), 196. See also John English, *The Worldly Years: The Life of Lester Pearson*, vol. 2, *1949-1972* (Toronto: Random House, 1993), 369-70.
5 A.D.P. Heeney and Livingston Merchant, *Canada and the United States: Principles for Partnership* (Ottawa: Queen's Printer, 1965), 48.
6 L.B. Pearson, *Mike: The Memoirs of the Right Honourable Lester B. Pearson*, vol. 3, *1957-1968* (Toronto: University of Toronto Press, 1975).
7 Pickersgill, for example, told Peter Stursberg: "I once said that here was a man who played professional hockey and professional baseball, and maybe football too for all I know, and I am quite sure that when he played those games he learned the rules, and yet I said, here he is in the biggest game of all and I do wish he would learn the rules. So often in Parliament the invocation of the rules and the use of the rules in the right kind of way would have saved us endless grief." Stursberg, *Dream of Unity*, 221-22.
8 Conversation with J.W. Pickersgill who reported Winters's analysis.
9 Penny Bryden, *Planners and Politics: Liberal Politics and Social Policy 1957-1968* (Kingston and Montreal: McGill-Queen's University Press, 1997); Lorna Marsden, "Lester Pearson and the Royal Commission on the Status of Women," paper presented at conference entitled "The Pearson Government: 50 years on," Trinity College, Toronto, 9 April 2013.
10 See Gilles Lalande, *The Department of External Affairs and Bilingualism*. Special Study for the Royal Commission on Bilingualism and Biculturalism, vol. 3 (Ottawa: Information Canada, 1969).
11 Most of the initiatives on the domestic front were set out in the Kingston policy conference of 1960. See English, *Worldly Years*, 218-21.
12 Grant's celebrated *Lament for a Nation* appeared in 1965 and excoriated Pearson's diplomacy. Grant later claimed that, for Pearson, "the existence of the Canadian nation was not a priority." See George Grant, *Technology and Empire: Perspectives on North America* (Toronto: House of Anansi, 1969), 68-69.
13 On Gordon's influence on the *Star*, see Stephen Azzi, *Walter Gordon and the Rise of Canadian Nationalism* (Montreal and Kingston: McGill-Queen's University Press, 1999).
14 Charles Ritchie's comment is found in his *Storm Signals: More Undiplomatic Diaries, 1962-1971* (Toronto: Macmillan, 1983).
15 McGeorge Bundy, "Memorandum for the record of a conversation between President Johnson and Prime Minister Pearson, May 28, 1964," in *Foreign Relations of the United States, 1964-1968*, vol. 1, *Vietnam 1964* (Washington, DC: Government Printing Office, 1992), 394-96.
16 See English, *Worldly Years*, 251. Marchand also refused to run as a Liberal because of Pearson's stand on nuclear weapons.
17 See Ritchie, *Storm Signals*, 81-83 as well as his "The day the president of the United States struck fear and trembling in the heart of our PM," *Maclean's*, July 1974, 35-40.
18 See Cabinet minutes, 5 April 1965, RG 2, Privy Council Office Papers, vol. 6271, Library and Archives Canada (LAC), Ottawa.

19 "Extract from an address by the Right Honourable Lester B. Pearson, Prime Minister of Canada, to the Canadian Club of Ottawa, February 10, 1965," *Statements and Speeches*, 65/3 (Ottawa: Information Division: Department of External Affairs, 1966).

20 See Joseph Wearing, *The L-Shaped Party: The Liberal Part of Canada, 1958-1980* (Toronto: McGraw-Hill Ryerson, 1981), 168–73.

21 *The Diary of André Laurendeau* (Toronto: Lorimer, 1991), 152–54. Mr. Martin made this comment to me after he read a draft of *Worldly Years* in which I dealt with the Temple speech and the 1965 election. He asked that I not quote his remarks, which he made in 1991.

22 Trudeau to Jules Léger, 31 August 1950, MG 26, O2, Pierre Elliott Trudeau Papers, vol. 10, file 11, LAC.

23 The letters were written to Gordon Robertson and Douglas LePan, and Trudeau's attitudes while in the department are described in John English, *Citizen of the World: The Life of Pierre Elliott Trudeau*, vol. 1, *1919-1968* (Toronto: Alfred Knopf, 2006), chap. 5.

24 J.L. Granatstein and Robert Bothwell, *Pirouette: Pierre Trudeau and Canadian Foreign Policy* (Toronto: University of Toronto Press, 1990).

25 Pearson also gave his son Geoffrey, a foreign service officer, the Trudeau foreign policy document with his angry responses in the margins. For a fuller account, see English, *Worldly Years*, 384–85.

26 Pierre Elliott Trudeau, *Memoirs* (Toronto: McClelland and Stewart, 1993), 156. Trudeau and Ivan Head did write a book on foreign policy in the Trudeau years that is more expansive, but it is mainly Head's work and reflects his preoccupations. See Ivan Head and Pierre Trudeau, *The Canadian Way: Shaping Canada's Foreign Policy, 1968-1984* (Toronto: McClelland and Stewart, 1995).

27 Helmut Sonnenfeldt to Henry Kissinger, 17 January 1973, Richard Milhous Nixon Papers, National Security Council files, box 750, file "Canada, Trudeau," National Archives of the United States, Nixon Presidential Library and Museum, Yorba Linda, California.

28 Alastair Gillespie with Irene Sage, *Made in Canada: A Businessman's Adventures in Politics* (Toronto: Robin Brass Studio, 2009), 144.

29 A draft chapter of a thesis on the period being written by Beatrice Orchard divides the Cabinet into groups around economic issues and indicates how deep the divides were between the camps. Her work has been helpful for this section.

30 See Michael Walker, ed., *Which Way Ahead? Canada after Wage and Price Control* (Vancouver: Fraser Institute, 1977). The other authors in the volume, mainly economists identified with Milton Friedman's monetarist approach, are similarly critical.

31 Head and Trudeau, *Canadian Way*, 188–90.

32 Craig Offman, "Jewish community finds a friend in Stephen Harper," *Globe and Mail*, 30 November 2012, http://cached.newslookup.com/cached.php?ref_id=123&siteid=2115&id=3883398&t=1385798400. Offman indicates that Ipsos Reid reported that 52 percent of Canadian Jews voted Conservative in 2011.

33 Ritchie published an account of the incident as early as 1974 and offended many of Pearson's colleagues by doing so. See his "The day the president of the United States struck fear and trembling into the heart of our PM," *Maclean's*, January 1974, 35–40.

34 Head and Trudeau, *Canadian Way,* 188.
35 Breton warned Trudeau after reading a first draft of the nationalist December 1972 speech from the throne that he found it "so much at variance with what I believe are your own views" that it should be changed. Trudeau agreed to some moderation of language and some other details. See Breton to Trudeau, 21 December 1972, Breton Papers, privately held.

3
The Constitutional Politics of Parliament's Role in International Policy

PHILIPPE LAGASSÉ

In Canada, international policy is a responsibility of the executive. The legal authority to craft international policy belongs with ministers of the federal Crown, Her Majesty in right of Canada, not Parliament. Ministers must hold the confidence of the House of Commons to exercise executive authority over international policy, and federal and provincial legislation is often required to implement treaties that have been signed by the government. Yet, strictly speaking, Parliament has no formal control of international policy. By statute, common law, and the Constitution, international policy is conducted by ministers or by senior civil servants and military officers acting under ministerial authority. Equally important, the executive's responsibility for international policy is unaffected by a minority Parliament. Whether the governing party holds a majority or minority of the seats in the Commons, the executive's authority remains the same.

In practice, Parliament can play a larger role in international policy than the executive's legal dominance suggests. Parliamentarians routinely debate matters of international policy; the legislature shapes the executive's administration of diplomacy and defence through statute; and parliamentary committees conduct hearings on a variety of topics related to global affairs, broadly defined. With these efforts Parliament can hope to exert influence over Canada's international policies. Opposition parties, in particular, can critique the government's decisions, and during minority parliaments they are better placed to influence the government by threatening to implement non-confidence votes. That said, governments can also use Parliament for their own ends. Indeed, more often than not, when Parliament is asked to play a part in international policy, it is because involving the legislature serves the political interests of the executive. This, too, holds as much for periods of minority parliaments as it does for majority parliaments.

Parliament's degree of involvement in international policy, therefore, largely reflects political considerations rather than legal ones, and this is true during both majority and minority parliaments. Under a minority, the executive's political incentives to involve Parliament may be greater, but this is not always the case. Similarly, while opposition parties have more opportunities to pressure the executive on international policy during minority parliaments, their willingness to do so depends on the political benefits and risks involved. Although they can be a factor, minority parliaments are neither a necessary nor a sufficient condition for explaining the degree of Parliament's contribution to international policy. The search for political gains, or an effort to avoid political losses, offers a better explanation for increased parliamentary involvement.

International Policy, the Executive, and Parliament

Canada's Constitution operates within a Westminster system of responsible government. Ministers are solely responsible for the exercise of executive authority, provided that the governing ministry headed by the prime minister maintains the confidence of the legislature. While leading constitutional scholars argue that there is no separation of powers under this system,[1] they are incorrect.[2] While the legislature and executive are connected by the constitutional convention that ministers are (in the main) drawn from Parliament, the authority Cabinet exercises does not reside with Parliament; rather, that authority belongs with the Crown as the executive power, as per section 9 of the *Constitution Act, 1867*.[3] Formally speaking, ministers do not exercise these powers by virtue of being parliamentarians; they do so as servants of the Crown. Indeed, while ministers are almost always sitting parliamentarians, being a member of Parliament (MP) and a minister of the Crown are distinct positions with distinct legal capacities. Ministers do not need to be parliamentarians when they are appointed, and they retain their appointments and authorities when Parliament is dissolved. Ministerial powers remain in place regardless of the parliamentary cycle, including when Parliament is dissolved.

When they craft international policy, ministers rely on two sources of executive power: statute and prerogative. Statutory authority is vested in members of the executive by acts of Parliament. Elements of the authority that ministers possess over their departments are usually outlined in statute, as are the respective powers of senior civil servants and military officers, both of whom serve the Crown (like their ministers). Although Parliament is the source of statute, these laws do not grant Parliament executive authority; instead, they allow Parliament to give the executive certain authorities or to shape the powers that the Crown possesses independently of Parliament. Of the powers that the executive possesses independently of Parliament, Crown prerogatives are the most important.[4] As historic authorities of the monarch that have not been supplanted by statute, these prerogatives provide the executive with discretionary powers over key matters of state.[5]

A variety of statutes define the executive's powers over international affairs, including the *Department of Foreign Affairs, Trade and Development Act* and the *National Defence Act*.[6] Crown prerogatives provide the executive with a number of discretionary authorities that touch on international affairs, such as the power to conduct diplomacy, negotiate and ratify treaties, appoint ambassadors, issue and revoke passports, command and deploy the armed forces, and conduct certain intelligence and counter-intelligence efforts.[7] The full breadth of the executive's power cannot be understood without reference to these prerogatives. Indeed, statute and prerogative should be seen to provide the executive with parallel sources of authority in the area of foreign affairs, as the Supreme Court of Canada (SCC) suggested in *Canada (Prime Minister) v. Khadr, 2010 SCC 3 [2010] 1 S.C.R 44*.[8]

In *Khadr* and other judgments, the SCC has made it clear that international affairs should be conducted by the executive. As part of the *Khadr* ruling, the SCC noted that, while the courts can review uses of the foreign affairs prerogative, it is necessary for the judiciary to recognize that "the executive branch of the government is responsible for decisions under this power, and that the executive is better placed to make such decisions." "The government," the justices unanimously ruled, "must have flexibility in deciding how its duties under the power are to be discharged," and they state unambiguously that "the conduct of foreign affairs lies with the executive branch of government."[9] When read in light of previous SCC findings about the separation of powers – such as: "Our democratic government consists of several branches ... It is fundamental to the working of government as a whole that all the parts play their proper role. It is equally fundamental that no one of them oversteps its boundaries, that each show proper deference for the legitimate sphere of activity of the other,"[10] and "each of the branches of the state is vouchsafed a measure of autonomy from the others"[11] – the Court's declarations that foreign affairs are a responsibility of the executive reinforces the fact that, legally and constitutionally, international policy is set by ministers, not the legislature or the judiciary. Although the legislature can use statute to impose limits on how international policy is administered and treaties are implemented, and the courts must ensure that the executive's actions are constitutional, authority for Canada's international affairs does not belong with Parliament or the courts.

The executive's responsibility for international policy does not mean that Parliament has no say. Parliament has four functions that grant it influence. The first, the legislative, has already been mentioned but merits more attention. Because many elements of treaties, such as trade accords, require statutes to take effect in Canadian law, Parliament can veto these international agreements by refusing to pass implementing legislation. Under a minority parliament, this power can give opposition parties the ability to block a treaty. However, since the timing of legislation is at the executive's discretion, governments can always wait for opportune moments to secure the passage of enabling laws. Moreover, as the Conservative government of Prime Minister Stephen Harper has demonstrated, implementing legislation can be introduced as part of omnibus budget bills, which significantly raises the stakes of defeating it.

Parliamentarians also can attempt to use legislation to constrain the government's policy options. Provided that they do not involve the expenditure of money, which requires a royal recommendation (which is controlled by ministers), private members' bills can seek to force policy choices on the government by law. Although statutes are ill-suited to imposing policy direction, and therefore must be carefully drafted to have the desired effect, they remain a means of narrowing the executive's manoeuvrability. Moreover, private members' bills that aim to constrain the executive stand a greater chance of passing under a minority parliament. Yet, given the lottery system that determines which private members' bills will have priority and the limited policy scope that a statute not involving expenditures can have, legislation is not an especially effective means of constraining international policy, even under a minority parliament. Indeed, the clearest example of such an effort during the Harper minority era, an act meant to force the government to implement the Kyoto Protocol, had no policy impact and did not prevent the executive from withdrawing Canada's signature from the treaty because it failed to affect the foreign affairs prerogative.[12]

Parliament's second avenue for influencing international policy is the confidence function. A primary role of the House of Commons is to express confidence in a ministry. This is usually done through budget bills. Under a minority parliament, opposition parties can use confidence votes to exact concessions from the executive, including on questions of international policy. Yet, when they engage in such brinksmanship, the opposition risks defeating the government, at which point another party will be asked to govern or, as is more often the case, an election will be held. Consequently, opposition parties are cautious when pursuing this option (unless they are confident that the governor general will ask them to form the government or that they can carry more seats than the governing party during the election). Indeed, although opposition parties can withdraw their confidence at several points during a minority parliament, such a decisive action offers no guarantees of success. Of note, the motion that defeated the minority government of Prime Minister Harper in March 2011 dealt in part with the disclosure of financial details surrounding the acquisition of F-35 fighter aircraft. In the election that followed, the Conservatives won a majority of the seats in the House of Commons.

To increase the chances that they will form the next government, opposition parties leverage Parliament's accountability function. By questioning ministers on their decisions and policies, the performance of their departments and the armed forces, and the legislation they have introduced, opposition parties render government accountable to Parliament.[13] In so doing, they also hope to embarrass and shame ministers or at least give the impression that the government is incompetent. While the opposition's primary motivation in holding ministers to account is to impose political costs on the government, better policies and performances can be a second-order effect. Specifically, being held to account can compel governments to change bad policies, improve the performance of their departments, and amend poorly conceived bills. When the accountability function has produced this result, Parliament has had policy influence. The Harper government's decision to reset its controversial fighter aircraft acquisition process in 2012 after two years of criticism by the opposition and officers of Parliament, specifically the Office of the Auditor General and the Parliamentary Budget Officer, provides a good example. The accountability function, it should be noted, is not technically affected by whether there is a minority or majority parliament. Its success depends on the willingness of the opposition to engage in sustained criticism and on the government's willingness to change a policy or remedy a performance problem.

Parliament's investigative function offers a fourth way to influence policy. Through their work on relevant parliamentary committees, MPs can study questions of importance and publish reports that offer policy recommendations to government. Whether under a parliamentary majority or minority, however, the executive is free to disregard the committees' recommendations. Nor do committee reports have binding force. Although opposition parties have more opportunities to recommend alternative policies when they outnumber government party members on committees, a committee's influence remains contingent on the executive's sense of the politics of the situation or its willingness to heed advice. In November 2007, for example, the House of Commons Standing Committee on International Trade began to study environmental and human rights concerns surrounding the negotiation of a free trade agreement between Canada and Colombia. The committee intended that its report inform the minority Conservative government's negotiation with Colombia. However, the executive concluded its negotiations with Colombia before the committee's report was released, much to the opposition members' dismay. In addition, the government chose not to respond to the report of the committee, despite an explicit request to do so.[14]

Of the four functions, holding the government to account arguably gives Parliament the greatest influence. Not all treaties require implementing legislation, passing legislation takes time, and private members' bills are constrained by the requirement of royal recommendation and a system that limits which MPs have the opportunity to introduce a bill. Threatening the government with a non-confidence vote can push the executive to alter its policies, but it requires that the opposition parties coordinate and accept the risks associated with an election. Committee reports, meanwhile, are only as effective as the government's openness to their ideas. The accountability function, on the other hand, can be used relentlessly to critique government policy and raise doubts about the competence of ministers. If the government alters its policies or performance as a result, Parliament can claim to have influenced the formulation of a better policy. If the government refuses to act, the opposition parties can hope to make political gains from the executive's intransigence. Even though it is the most effective, the accountability function is the least affected by whether there is a parliamentary minority or majority. Accordingly, a strong case can be made that the accountability function is more effective under a majority parliament since opposition parties are freer to criticize without risking a potentially unwanted election.

Regardless of how it influences the government, Parliament does not control international policy. By law and the constitution, international affairs are a responsibility of the executive, and this does not change according to whether there is a majority or minority government. As a result, it must be asked why governments occasionally decide to include Parliament in international policy decisions, even though they are under no obligation to do so.

Parliamentary Vetting and Laundering

Although the executive has near total legal authority over international policy, governments face political checks on their policies and decisions. In their study of the American executive, Eric Posner and Adrian Vermeule note that "the system of elections, the party system, and American political culture constrain the executive far more than do legal rules created by Congress or the courts."[15] The same general idea holds in Canada. Whether in a majority or minority parliament, governments contend with how their policies will be received by the electorate. It is the reality of governing in a democracy, more than constitutional or legal constraints, that the executive must confront when crafting international policy.

Owing to Parliament's accountability function, governments are acutely aware that opposition parties will attempt to use the executive's policies to undermine the government's popular support. It is the opposition's responsibility to raise questions and offer critiques of the government's policies. Indeed, the opposition's use of the accountability function to criticize the executive has evolved to institutionalize the political constraints on the government's policy discretion.[16] As a corollary, the concept of ministerial responsibility has evolved to ensure that those who exercise executive authority are held to account for its use. Although the government has a near monopoly over the executive's policy powers, ministers are meant to shoulder the blame and political costs that accompany policy failures and controversy. As one PCO publication notes, ministerial responsibility "assures that Parliament may focus responsibility for the conduct of government on those of its members who hold ministerial office and who in the ultimate must personally answer to Parliament and hence the electorate for their actions and the actions of their subordinates."[17]

To lessen the political costs they face when pursuing controversial policies, and to weaken Parliament's accountability function, governments can resort to two parliamentary co-optation strategies: vetting and laundering. Vetting gives parliamentarians the opportunity to scrutinize a policy before the executive commits to it. In so doing, the executive implies, truthfully or not, that the government is open to Parliament's input. If the opposition raises particular concerns about the policy, the executive can assess how effective the opposition's attacks will be and, if necessary, adjust the policy to lessen its political costs. If no concerns are raised when the policy is initially presented, the executive can use this silence to deflect critiques that are levelled by the opposition after the policy is implemented. The government can either claim that Parliament tacitly supported the policy by not raising any concerns or that the opposition failed to provide meaningful advice when it was given the opportunity.

Parliamentary laundering is bolder. Here the executive consults Parliament in a way that is meant to imply that parliamentarians are a party to a policy decision – that is, that the government and the legislature decided the matter together. Although the decision-making authority remains with the executive, laundering makes it seem that the government's choice was contingent upon Parliament's approval or recommendations. Parliamentary laundering thus serves to sow confusion about where responsibility for the decision lies, which, in turn, complicates efforts to hold the government to account. When questioned about the decision, the government can remind critics that it consulted Parliament and secured the legislature's approval prior to acting. The executive can further claim that it acted according to the will of Parliament, despite exercising authority that is the government's alone. Opposition parties that voice their approval of a policy as a result of an executive's laundering strategy, furthermore, will be poorly placed to critique the government or hold ministers to account for the policy thereafter. Having approved the policy and being seen as sharing responsibility for it, an opposition party will have an incentive not to discuss the policy if it leads to a poor or controversial outcome.[18]

Governments have employed parliamentary vetting and laundering to protect themselves from a number of controversial international policy choices. Prime Minister William Lyon Mackenzie King's declaration that "Parliament [would] decide" Canada's entry into the Second World War was an effort to legitimize a choice that was preordained and that the executive had the authority to make itself.[19] King's government also initiated the parliamentary vetting practice of consulting Parliament prior to ratifying contentious treaties. This practice, which successive governments followed unevenly between 1926 and 1966, allowed sensitive international accords such as the North American Air Defense Command agreement and the Canada-United States Auto Pact to be given a veneer of parliamentary approval.[20]

The practice was abandoned by the government of Prime Minister Lester Pearson when opposition parties used the consultations as an opportunity to exercise Parliament's accountability function to greater effect. Special joint parliamentary committees were also established by governments to provide recommendations on difficult international policy choices. As Denis Stairs notes in Chapter 1 (this volume), in 1994, a joint parliamentary committee was established to make recommendations on Canadian defence policy. Although the government had already determined the defence policy it intended to pursue, a parliamentary committee's similar recommendations helped insulate the executive from likely criticisms.[21] While each of these efforts could be described as laudable exercises in parliamentary democracy, the benefits accrued to the executive must be acknowledged.

The Harper government used parliamentary vetting and laundering to notable effect. In 2008, the government issued its *Policy on Tabling Treaties in Parliament*. Under this policy, "all instruments governed by public international law, between Canada and other states or international organisations," are to be tabled in the House of Commons for twenty-one days after the executive has signed or agreed to the treaty but before it has been ratified.[22] Although this policy was inspired by long-standing British practice, it nonetheless serves as a parliamentary vetting process. When the executive tables treaties, the opposition's interest in debating the treaty can be assessed, as can the efficacy of any critiques that are levelled at the agreement. If the opposition chooses not to debate or oppose the treaty, the executive can ratify it and/or introduce implementing legislation (and ratify the treaty after the legislation has passed) knowing that no substantive criticisms will be offered. If a criticism is raised afterwards, it can be deflected by asking why it was not raised during the consultation period. If, on the other hand, the opposition does criticize the treaty, the executive can assess whether the argument has merit or whether the criticisms could be used to undermine the government's political standing. If so, negotiators can seek changes to the treaty text; if not, the executive can ignore the opposition. Instead of giving Parliament a significant role in treaty making, the policy's principal use is to gauge the opposition's mood and efficacy, which serves the interests of the government. For instance, the Harper government used the policy to assess Parliament's comfort with free trade agreements that were negotiated. During the Conservative minority, the policy allowed the executive to test the support of the Liberal Party for the Canada-Peru free trade accord. The government's confidence in the *Canada-Peru Free Trade Agreement*

Implementation Act, 2009 was likely eased when the Liberals signalled their tacit support for the treaty when it was first tabled.[23]

Further evidence of the policy's utility as a parliamentary vetting process is seen in its limitations. Whereas the United Kingdom has passed a statute that gives the British Parliament a partial veto over treaty ratifications,[24] the Canadian practice relies on a mere policy, one that is entirely determined by the executive. Being a policy rather than a law, the treaty-tabling practice is not binding on the executive. As the policy itself states, the treaty power remains a Crown prerogative. In addition, the policy allows for exceptions to the tabling procedure. The executive can choose to not table a treaty if the government does not feel it would be advantageous to do so. Nor is it necessary for the government to provide an explanation as to why the exception has been invoked. Consequently, if the executive believes that it would stand to lose by tabling the treaty, or if ministers feel the treaty is too important to not be ratified as is, the government can avoid giving the opposition the twenty-one days of scrutinizing that the policy prescribes.

One example highlights these points. In April 2014, the Liberal foreign affairs critic Marc Garneau questioned why the Harper government had not tabled the *Canada-United States Enhanced Tax Information Exchange Agreement*, a treaty that would allow for greater information sharing between the American Internal Revenue Service and the Canada Revenue Agency. Instead of tabling the treaty prior to introducing enabling legislation, the government had included an implementation act in its 2014 omnibus budget bill, C-31. Garneau noted that the Liberal Party had "profound disagreements" with the agreement's treatment of privacy rights and Canadian sovereignty and that these issues merited closer scrutiny and debate.[25] In his response to Garneau, the House government leader, Peter Van Loan, reminded the Liberal critic that the treaty power was a Crown prerogative and that the treaty-tabling policy was a courtesy that the executive extended to the Commons, not a legal obligation.[26] Van Loan further informed Garneau that the government had exempted itself from the treaty policy in this case.[27] Although it is hard to determine whether ministers felt that the agreement was of sufficient importance to be exempted or that a pre-legislative consultation treaty would advantage the opposition, the fact remains that tabling the treaty was easily avoided when it suited the executive.

In 2006, the Harper Conservatives initiated the practice of seeking Commons' approval of military deployments involving combat. This was a prototypical parliamentary laundering strategy. The 2008 vote requesting that the Commons approve an extension of the Canadian Armed Forces' mission in Afghanistan demonstrates how the laundering worked. With casualties mounting and an election on the horizon, the Harper government recognized that extending the mission could harm the Conservatives' electoral prospects. Obtaining the Commons' approval of the extension would offset this potential problem in two ways. First, having secured a recommendation that the mission should be extended from a panel chaired by former Liberal Cabinet minister John Manley, the Conservatives were confident that the Liberals would support an extension. Once the Liberals voted in favour of the extension, the ability of Liberal MPs to criticize the policy would be diminished. As expected, after the vote, debate about the Kandahar deployment quieted significantly, and both the Conservatives and the Liberals avoided the topic during the subsequent election.[28]

Second, the Commons vote created confusion about where responsibility for the deployment lay. Stating that Parliament approved the mission arguably masked ministers' constitutional responsibility for the decision. In a speech given shortly before the vote, Prime Minister Harper stressed that the mission was supported by both the Conservatives and the Liberals and implied that the decision was one that parliamentarians, rather than the executive, would make. As he noted when discussing the extension: "It is a clear and principled position. But it is not a Conservative position or a Liberal position. It is a Canadian position that can be supported by a majority of the elected representatives of the Canadian people."[29] While there was surely a degree of sincerity in the prime minister's statement, the benefit to the executive of clouding where the responsibility to extend an increasingly unpopular mission belonged should not be overlooked. Holding a parliamentary vote to approve the extension served this laundering purpose well.

Although the Conservative government first introduced these parliamentary vetting and laundering efforts during a minority parliament, there is no clear evidence that they are a function of that institutional context. Were these strategies predicated on a parliamentary minority, one would expect them to have been present during the Liberal minority of Prime Minister Paul Martin, and one would further expect the Conservatives to have abandoned the strategies once they formed a majority. Neither of these arguments holds. The Martin minority did not introduce a treaty-tabling policy, despite suggestions that it should. Indeed, a private member's bill that sought to give Parliament a legal role in the treaty process failed to pass during the Martin minority, with the government expressing concerns about the effect and constitutionality of the legislation.[30] The Martin government deployed the CAF to Kandahar, Afghanistan, without holding a vote in the House of Commons. Moreover, after obtaining a majority of seats in the Commons, the Harper Conservatives continued to make use of their treaty policy. Notably, Canada's free trade agreements with Honduras and South Korea, and a technical summary of the *Canada-EU Comprehensive Economic and Trade Agreement*, were tabled before Parliament under the Conservative majority government.

The practice of securing Parliament's approval of military deployment involving combat remained under the Conservative majority as well. A vote to extend Canada's military role in Libya was held shortly after the 2011 election that produced the majority Parliament. While the political constraints of governing during a minority parliament may have prompted the Conservatives to increase the legislature's involvement in international affairs with the treaty policy and military deployment votes, the distribution of seats in the Commons does not explain why the Martin Liberals did not do the same or why the Harper government continued with these practices after gaining a majority. A better explanation of the different approaches taken by the Martin Liberals and Harper Conservatives is that the Conservatives were more attuned to how consulting Parliament can benefit the executive.

Conclusion

Ministers of the Crown are constitutionally and legally responsible for international policy in Canada. Parliament has never seized the Crown's executive powers over foreign and defence policy, even though ministers are drawn from Parliament and the governing ministry must hold the confidence of the House of Commons to exercise executive authority; instead, the conventions of responsible government have evolved to ensure that Parliament holds ministers to account for their use of executive authority. Aside from implementing legislation for treaties, Parliament's ability to influence international policy largely flows from this accountability function. Whereas the recommendations of parliamentary committees are only as influential as the executive's openness to them, and threats of non-confidence measures involve risks and uncertainty for the opposition, questioning the government on the wisdom and efficacy of its policies offers Parliament the best means to illicit a reaction from the executive. Just as important, this use of Parliament's accountability function is unaffected by the dynamics of a minority or majority parliament. It rests on the willingness of the opposition parties to engage in sharp, continual criticism of the government.

Owing to the executive's legal and constitutional authorities, governments are under no obligation to involve Parliament in international policy, save for cases in which a treaty requires new legislation. Nonetheless, governments have sometimes chosen to bring international policy questions before Parliament for scrutiny or approval. The Conservative government of Prime Minister Harper was especially active in this regard. On the surface, such efforts appear to reflect a sense that expanding Parliament's role in international policy making strengthens Canada's democracy.[31] However, the political benefits the executive enjoys from selectively involving Parliament should not be overlooked. Using parliamentary vetting and laundering strategies to diminish the opposition's ability to hold the executive to account highlights the government's willingness to involve Parliament in international policy to further its own political ends. Hence, political tactics and calculations, not legal obligations, explain the increased role of Parliament in international affairs under the Harper Conservatives. It remains to be seen whether the Liberal government of Prime Minister Justin Trudeau will attempt to give Parliament legal authorities in matters of international policy or whether the Trudeau ministry will continue the vetting and laundering practices of its predecessor.

Once the political determinants of Parliament's role in international policy are appreciated, the impact of minority or majority parliaments on the legislature's influence can be better understood. Minority parliaments afford opposition parties more opportunities to exact policy concessions through the threat of non-confidence and the blocking of treaty-implementing legislation, and private members' bills that aim to constrain the government's discretion are more likely to pass under a minority government. Similarly, minority parliaments can elevate the political pressure to involve Parliament in controversial international policy decisions. Yet governments can use Parliament to their political advantage during majority parliaments as well; since the legislature's accountability function operates the same way under both minority and majority parliaments, the allure of insulating the executive from critique can be present under either arrangement. It is therefore the nature of the political challenges that governments face, rather than institutional structures, that seems to determine the executive's decision to vet or launder policy decisions through the legislature.

Notes

1. Patrick Monahan, *Constitutional Law*, 2nd ed. (Toronto: Irwin Law, 2002), 96.
2. Dennis Baker, *Not Quite Supreme: The Courts and Coordinate Constitutional Interpretation* (Montreal and Kingston: McGill-Queen's University Press, 2010), chaps. 3–4.
3. David E. Smith, *The Invisible Crown: The First Principle of Canadian Government* (Toronto: University of Toronto Press, 1995).
4. Alexander Bolt, "The Crown prerogative as applied to military operations, Canadian Armed Forces, Office of the Judge Advocate General," Strategic Legal Paper series, 2008.
5. Philippe Lagassé, "Parliamentary and judicial ambivalence toward executive prerogative powers in Canada," *Canadian Public Administration* 55, 2 (2012): 157–80.
6. The statutes that address matters of international policy are in fact numerous, particularly when laws that implement treaty provisions are taken into account.
7. Irvin Studin, *The Strategic Constitution: Understanding Canadian Power in the World* (Vancouver: UBC Press, 2014), chaps. 2–4.
8. The SCC noted at paragraph 35 that "The prerogative power over foreign affairs has not been displaced by s.10 of the Department of Foreign Affairs and International Trade Act," even though the statute provides the minister of foreign affairs with nearly all the authorities as does the prerogative.
9. *Canada (Prime Minister) v. Khadr*, 2010 SCC 3 [2010] 1 S.C.R 44 at paras. 37 and 40.
10. *New Brunswick Broadcasting Co. v. Nova Scotia (Speaker of the House of Assembly)*, [1993] 1 S.C.R. 319 at 389.
11. *Canada (House of Commons) v. Vaid*, [2005] 1 S.C.R. 667, 2005 SCC 30 at para. 21.
12. See the Federal Court case of *Turp v. Minister of Justice and Attorney General of Canada*, 2012 FC 893.
13. David E. Smith, *The People's House of Commons: Theories of Democracy in Contention* (Toronto: University of Toronto Press, 2007), 7–10.
14. Canada, House of Commons, Standing Committee on International Trade, *Report on Human Rights, the Environment and Free Trade with Colombia*, 39th Parliament, 2nd session, June 2008.
15. Eric A. Posner and Adrian Vermeule, *The Executive Unbound: After the Madisonian Republic* (Oxford: Oxford University Press, 2011), 113.
16. C.E.S. Franks, *The Parliament of Canada* (Toronto: University of Toronto Press, 1987), 143–60.
17. Canada, Privy Council Office, *Responsibility in the Constitution* (Ottawa: Ministry of Supply and Services Canada, 1993), 3.
18. For a discussion of the problem of blurred responsibility in majoritarian democracies, see G. Bingham Powell, Jr., *Elections as Instruments of Democracy: Majoritarian and Proportional Visions* (New Haven: Yale University Press, 2000).
19. Norman Hillmer and J.L. Granatstein, *Empire to Umpire: Canada and the World into the Twenty-First Century*, 2nd ed. (Toronto: Thompson-Nelson, 2008), 125–36.
20. Joanna Harrington, "Redressing the democratic deficit in treaty law making: (Re-)Establishing a role for Parliament," *McGill Law Journal* 50 (2005): 477.

21 Brian Tomlin, Norman Hillmer, and Fen Osler Hampson, *Canada's International Policies: Agendas, Alternatives, and Politics* (Toronto: Oxford University Press, 2008), 144–50.
22 Canada, Global Affairs Canada, *Policy on Tabling Treaties in Parliament*, para. 2; available at http://www.treaty-accord.gc.ca/procedures.aspx.
23 The Liberal Party did not raise concerns about the trade agreement when it was tabled and subsequently endorsed the implementing legislation when it was introduced. See Scott Brison, 20 April 2009, in Canada, House of Commons, *Debates*, 40th Parliament, 2nd session, 1550.
24 United Kingdom, House of Commons Library, *Parliament's New Statutory Role in Ratifying Treaties*, 8 February 2011.
25 Marc Garneau, 28 April 2014, in Canada, House of Commons, *Debates*, 41st Parliament, 2nd session, 1515, 1535.
26 Peter Van Loan, 5 May 2014, in Canada, House of Commons, *Debates*, 41st Parliament, 2nd session, 1525.
27 Peter Van Loan, 28 April 2014, in Canada, House of Commons, *Debates*, 41st Parliament, 2nd session, 1540.
28 Stephen M. Saideman, *Adapting in the Dust: Learning Lessons from Canada's War in Afghanistan* (Toronto: University of Toronto Press, 2016), chap. 4.
29 Stephen Harper, as quoted in CBC News, "Harper unveils new Afghan motion with 2011 end date," cbc.ca, 21 February 2008, http://www.cbc.ca/news/canada/harper-unveils-new-afghan-motion-with-2011-end-date-1.772569.
30 Canada, House of Commons, Bill C-260: *An Act Respecting the Negotiation, Approval, Tabling and Publication of Treaties*, 39th Parliament, 1st session; Dan McTeague, 18 May 2005, in Canada, House of Commons, *Debates*, 38th Parliament, 1st session, 1825.
31 J.L. Granatstein, "Going to war? 'Parliament will decide,'" *Globe and Mail*, 9 September 2009, http://www.theglobeandmail.com/globe-debate/going-to-war-parliament-will-decide/article4287580/#dashboard/follows/.

PART 2
KEY ISSUES

4

Did Minority Government Matter?

Thinking Counterfactually about the Canadian Mission in Afghanistan

JEAN-CHRISTOPHE BOUCHER AND KIM RICHARD NOSSAL

The central question of *The Harper Era* is whether the shift from minority to majority government in 2011 made a difference to the international policy of Stephen Harper's Conservative government. We examine Canada's mission in Afghanistan between 2001 and 2014, a period that spanned five parliaments. Two were majority governments: the Liberal majority under Jean Chrétien and Paul Martin (37th Parliament, 2000–04) and the majority Conservative government under Stephen Harper (41st Parliament, 2011–15). Three were minority governments: the Liberal minority under Paul Martin (38th Parliament, 2004–06) and the Conservative minority governments (39th Parliament, 2006–08, and 40th Parliament, 2008–11).

Most scholarly analyses of the structure of government and foreign policy would suggest that Canada's policies on Afghanistan should have been affected by the changing nature of government composition during this period.[1] Indeed, as the introduction to *The Harper Era* indicates, it is generally assumed that government structure – majority, minority, or coalition – affects the level of constraint on policy making, especially on questions of war and peace. As Glenn Palmer, Tamar London, and Patrick Regan argue, minority governments are always vulnerable since

> any policy disagreement may provide sufficient motivation for the opposition to bring the government down. The larger this opposition, the more

carefully the minority government may have to tread. The costs of adopting an even marginally unpopular policy may be dismissal from power, and the costs for using force may subsequently be higher for minority governments.[2]

Certainly John English (Chapter 2, this volume) would support this general conclusion: "For foreign policy," English succinctly concludes, "minority governments matter."

At first blush, it might seem that minority government played an important role in shaping Canada's mission in Afghanistan. Over the course of the mission, Canadians elected three minority parliaments in a row. If minority government mattered, we would assume that, during these parliaments, Ottawa's room for manoeuvre would have been quite limited. The government would have hesitated to embrace policies that could have precipitated a political crisis at home; instead, its policies would have been more prudent. By contrast, a majority government could have pursued an Afghanistan policy relatively free from political constraints. It could have sustained the political costs of an unpopular mission with little immediate fear of losing power.

To assess whether minority parliaments mattered to Canada's mission in Afghanistan, we look at how the mission might have evolved had there been majority governments over the course of the mission. In other words, we use counterfactual analysis to examine the degree to which decisions about Afghanistan were a function of minority government. Our counterfactual analysis proceeds by proposing two counterfactual possibilities: What would Canadian policy in Afghanistan have been had the Liberals under Paul Martin won a majority in the June 2004 election? And how would Canadian policy evolved had the Conservatives under Stephen Harper won a majority in the January 2006 election?

Our comparative counterfactual analysis shows little support for the argument that minority government had an impact on Canadian policy towards Afghanistan. In fact, from our counterfactual cases, we surmise that both Liberal and Conservative majority governments would have made similar decisions. In this context, it appears that, in the case of Canada's Afghanistan mission, minority government is neither a necessary nor a sufficient condition to explain policy decisions.

Counterfactual Analysis

We acknowledge that the methodology we have chosen for our analysis is unusual. However, counterfactual analysis has recently garnered considerable attention in political science; indeed, some scholars even argue that counterfactual reasoning should become an essential methodological tool for social scientists.[3]

Moreover, the counterfactual method has a long tradition in social science analysis. As the German sociologist Max Weber noted in 1900: "It involves first the production of – let us say it calmly – 'imaginative constructs' by the disregarding of one or more of those elements of 'reality' which are actually present, and by the mental construction of a course of events which is altered through modification in one or more 'conditions.'"[4] In other words, counterfactual analysis involves a "thought experiment" (*Gedankenexperiment*) that constructs a historically logical event that did not occur. In this sense, counterfactuals are "what if" statements developed to explore the causal explanatory power of our understanding of historical events.

Counterfactual theorizing is more than mere speculation. To be useful, counterfactuals require three protocols that are not dissimilar from those necessary to regular case studies.[5] First, the counterfactual method must concern itself with clarity – thinking clearly about causation and considering the validity of our assumptions about necessary and sufficient conditions. This method then manipulates historical events (by eliminating or introducing a specific event into the historical fabric) to assess the causal relationship between elements. Second, historical "rewrites" must be plausible. Consequently, counterfactuals must be realistic, arising from the historical context of the time and following the principle of historical consistency.[6] Third, counterfactual case selection must be logically consistent. Removing or adding a historical fact should never undercut or even reverse the relationship between cause and effect. For example, our analysis would run such a risk of logical fallacy if Canada's intervention in Afghanistan between 2001 and 2014 had affected the political environment in Canada in such a way as to *produce* minority governments in Ottawa. In such a circumstance, considering how a majority government would have acted would create a logical conundrum since it would undercut the independent variables. In our case, however, there is little empirical evidence that the mission in Afghanistan played any role at all in the elections of 2004, 2006, or 2008. On the contrary: Canada's intervention in Afghanistan was rarely mentioned during these federal elections, and all of the major political parties ignored the issue in their electoral platforms in 2004, 2006, 2008, and 2011.

Thinking Counterfactually about Canada's Afghanistan Mission

Under the three conditions of clarity, plausibility, and logical consistency, there are two possible counterfactuals that would enable us to assess the impact of minority governments on Canada's Afghanistan mission. The first posits a Liberal majority government in 2004. On 28 June 2004, the Liberals under Paul Martin won 134 ridings (155 seats were needed to form a majority government). The New Democratic Party under Jack Layton outflanked the Liberals on the left, which split the vote in key ridings. The sponsorship scandal also cost the Liberals significant votes.[7] Nonetheless, a Liberal majority was a plausible outcome. In the final days of the campaign, Harper had already cost the Conservatives the election by refusing to disavow a press release issued by the Conservative campaign that accused Martin of supporting child pornography.[8] A slightly less effective NDP or slightly better crisis management of the sponsorship scandal could well have resulted in a (slim) majority government in the 38th Parliament. This Parliament would have run until 2009, with elections likely in 2008.

The second counterfactual suggests a Conservative majority in 2006. On 23 January 2006, the Conservative Party led by Stephen Harper won 124 ridings – thirty-one shy of a majority – with more than 36 percent of the popular vote. The Conservatives made significant inroads into rural Ontario and Quebec, mostly at the expense of the Liberals. Had the Liberal brand been slightly more damaged by the Gomery Commission, or had Canadians been slightly more critical of Prime Minister Martin's ineffectual and dithering leadership, it is plausible that enough votes would have gone to the NDP (allowing Conservative candidates to benefit from the vote splitting) or to Conservative candidates that the 39th Parliament would have featured a (slim) Conservative majority. This Parliament would have run until 2011, with the next election likely in 2010.

It is important to note that our counterfactuals modify domestic variables to produce majority governments while keeping other international factors constant. Canada's capacity to single-handedly transform the international environment is limited, so we can realistically interchange minority and majority governments in Ottawa and safely assume that such a change would not have made a significant difference globally. As a result, we assume that the Afghanistan conflict would have evolved exactly as it did between 2004 and 2014, particularly the Pakistan-based Taliban insurgency that intensified in the south in early 2006 – supported and financed by elements of the Pakistan military – and the incapacity of the Afghan government to foster national reconciliation. Furthermore, we assume that Barack Obama would win the US presidency in 2008 and that his administration would refocus American policy on Afghanistan with a military surge in 2009. We also assume that the United States would withdraw most of its troops from Afghanistan in 2014.

Since we are interested in assessing the influence of government structure (minority versus majority) on foreign policy, and particularly on Canada's participation in Afghanistan between 2001 and 2014, our counterfactual creates a hypothetical policy environment that asks: How would a majority government have decided issues that were in reality taken by minority governments? In this respect, there are four key decisions to account for: the first is Paul Martin's 2005 decision to deploy a battle group in Kandahar for one year. The second is the 2006 decision by the Harper minority government to extend the Kandahar mission until 2008. The third is the 2008 decision by the Harper minority government to extend the Kandahar mission until 2011. Finally, in 2010, a Harper minority government agreed to participate in NATO's Afghanistan training mission until 2014.

A Paul Martin Liberal Majority, 2004

Would a Liberal majority government have deployed a provincial reconstruction team and a battle group to Kandahar in 2005? There is little evidence to suggest that Prime Minister Martin would have made a different decision. Martin strongly believed in reaffirming Canada's place in the world by engaging internationally. As the 2005 *International Policy Statement* proclaims:

> Now is the time to rebuild for Canada an independent voice of pride and influence in the world. It won't be easy. We will have to earn our way in defence and security. We will have to earn our way in international assistance and global commerce. And we will have to understand that we can't simply recreate what we once had. Instead, we must build today for the world of tomorrow. That is what we are dedicated to doing.[9]

The Martin government was also running budgetary surpluses that would have allowed Ottawa to invest in national defence, diplomacy, and international development assistance. To implement such an activist vision of Canada's international policy, Martin appointed like-minded individuals to key positions across government: Bill Graham became minister of national defence, Pierre Pettigrew took over foreign affairs, and General Rick Hillier was selected as the next chief of the defence staff with the clear intention of strengthening Canada's defence and security policy.[10]

It was widely recognized that Canada was committing to a dangerous mission. As Graham noted in October 2005: "I think there's no question but that the mission in Kandahar is a much more dangerous mission ... it will be more in the nature of a combat mission where they will be out looking for people who are doing exactly this type of thing to try and destabilize the country and they'll be on the lookout for them."[11] In January 2006, the Martin government signed the Afghan Compact, a five-year commitment during which Canada agreed to help the Islamic Republic of Afghanistan develop Afghan capacity and to provide assistance in rebuilding the country.[12] In other words, not only did the Martin Liberals commit Canada to a combat mission, they also created the conditions for a continued and prolonged contribution.

At the same time, however, it is highly unlikely that a hypothetical majority Martin government would have embraced a more robust policy than the minority Martin government actually did. Not only did the Canadian military not have the capacity in 2005–06 for a significantly greater combat commitment, but Martin would have had to deal with the significant sentiment within the Liberal backbench that did not fully support the Afghanistan mission.

The second decision extended the Kandahar military commitment in 2006 for at least two years. In 2006, Canada suffered extensive casualties – thirty-six Canadians, both military and civilian, died while serving in 2006[13] – and Canadian troops were confronted with a growing Taliban insurgency in Kandahar. In response to growing opposition, that September, NATO's International Security Assistance Force (ISAF) organized the first major military operation (Operation Medusa) led by Canada to destroy Taliban fortified positions in Pashmul. At the same time, public support for the intervention started to decline as Canadians began to digest the impact of the Afghanistan experience.[14] The first year of Canada's military deployment in Kandahar was particularly difficult.

Nevertheless, we can hypothesize that a Martin majority government would have renewed the mission in 2006 for several reasons. First, the Kandahar deployment was fairly fresh, and the government had already acknowledged (and expected) the setbacks. Second, key actors who made the decision to commit the CAF to Kandahar, most importantly Hillier and Graham, would have remained in place in 2006, and, if decision-making theory is correct,[15] not only would they have been disinclined to reassess policies, especially when faced with setbacks, they would also have generally been committed even more strongly to past choices. Third, the deployment to Kandahar had required reorganization and cooperation among the

Department of National Defence (DND), the Department of Foreign Affairs and International Trade (DFAIT), and the Canadian International Development Agency (CIDA), all of which had invested significant resources and political capital in the initiative. Because the decision to commit Canada to Kandahar Province, as well as the bureaucratic and organizational effort to implement this decision, created path dependency, any attempt to either default on the commitment by removing troops from Afghanistan after just one year or to deploy Canadians to another, less dangerous, province would likely have been met with strong resistance from major decision makers in Ottawa. Moreover, any withdrawal would have been contrary to Canada's Afghan Compact pledge and would have resulted in tense conversations with Washington and Brussels. Finally, even if some factions within the Liberal Party were grumbling, had Prime Minister Martin led them to a majority government he would have been able to manage the dissent. Halfway through their electoral mandate, the Liberals would have had ample room to manoeuvre in order to extend the mission for another two years and re-evaluate the Kandahar commitment before an election that would have been likely in late 2008.

The third Afghanistan policy decision involved renewing the Kandahar mission in 2008 (the Harper government extended the mission to December 2011). After two years of military presence in Afghanistan, the Canadian mission was at a low point. At home, opposition now exceeded 55 percent in most provinces (except Alberta). In addition, most of the key decision makers in 2005–06 would have probably moved on: General Rick Hillier's mandate as chief of the defence staff was coming to an end and Bill Graham would likely have either retired or taken on another portfolio. Abroad, ISAF showed clear signs of inter-allied dissension as it became obvious that some countries, including Canada, were shouldering a disproportionate share of the burden. Furthermore, Afghanistan was still far from national reconciliation and a stable security environment. Corruption and government incompetence were rampant, and the economy relied on two sources of income: development assistance and narcotrafficking.

In 2008, a Martin majority government would have been in its fourth year in power and would be contemplating whether it should decide the fate of the Canadian mission in Afghanistan before or after an election that would have to be held within a year. It seems highly plausible that a Martin majority government would have renewed Canada's commitment to Afghanistan before the impending election.

In addition, in November 2008, Barack Obama was elected president of the United States. Obama had campaigned against the Iraq war and had promised to re-engage American forces in Afghanistan,[16] creating the expectation among US allies that the Afghan war would take a turn for the better. The election of a progressive American president generated significant optimism within the rank and file of the Liberal Party and, for a brief moment, highlighted the profile of Canada's contribution to the Afghanistan mission. When Obama called for allied cooperation on Afghanistan, a majority Martin government would surely have seized the opportunity to push for the extension of the Canadian contribution. Moreover, after three years in Kandahar, Canada now had a broad knowledge of the terrain and local actors. Also, Canadian development assistance in Afghanistan was concentrated around the Kandahar Provincial Reconstruction Team (PRT) and represented a significant investment in time and money. In fact, Canada's fixation on creating a whole-of-government approach to its foreign policy engagement produced path dependence. Consequently, any change of theatre – to a different province, for example – would have required extensive readjustments. In sum, Prime Minister Martin would have considered both the domestic and international conditions of Canada's contribution to the Afghanistan intervention in 2008, and he would have renewed the mission.

Finally, let us consider the 2010 decision to withdraw from the combat operations in 2011 and pledge resources for the NATO training mission until 2014. Certainly, as we stretch the timeline of our counterfactual, our predictions must become more speculative. The 2010 decision is contingent on the assumption that the Liberal Party, still led by Martin, would have been able to keep the Conservatives in opposition in the election held in 2008–09. However, we can make a good case that external factors would have convinced a seasoned Martin government to finally put an end to the Kandahar deployment in favour of a different kind of contribution in 2011.

The situation in Afghanistan was particularly challenging in 2010, and many of those contributing to the international coalition expressed scepticism about the ability of the administration of Hamid Karzai to establish a stable state. Corruption and nepotism proliferated. Irregularities in the 2009 elections, which saw Karzai re-elected over Abdullah Abdullah, undermined the confidence of the international community. Kabul seemed powerless to control the country beyond the northern provinces and the capital itself. Moreover, many of Afghanistan's impressive economic gains were fostered by massive external subsidies and by drug trafficking.[17] At the security level, although allied forces had transitioned from a light footprint approach to a US-influenced counter-insurgency strategy, the Taliban insurgency maintained control over large parts of the territory, had access to a safe haven in Pakistan, and had local support.[18] In brief, according to most indicators, the possibility of success in Afghanistan appeared bleak in the short and medium term.

By 2010, NATO solidarity within ISAF was also stretched. Some members had already limited the size of their contributions, had imposed constraining caveats on their troops (which restricted their usefulness), or had even begun to withdraw altogether.[19] Canada, for its part, argued that it had assumed a disproportionate share of the alliance burden, in part because military commanders on the ground could "act first if necessary and then explain [their] actions later."[20] Finally, the United States was outwardly contemplating an early departure from Afghanistan and pushing for a complete transition of military operations to the government of Afghanistan by 2014. In this context, President Obama invited US allies to contribute resources to train the Afghanistan security forces. After shouldering such a heavy burden in Kandahar, Canada agreed to provide military trainers. It is reasonable to imagine that Canada would have matched the US timetable and sustained the NATO training mission until 2014.

In sum, we can safely suggest that a Martin majority government would have essentially made the same decisions as did the Martin and Harper minority governments. In the final analysis, the domestic and international conditions of Canadian policy making on Afghanistan between 2004 and 2011 exerted sufficient influence to constrain our four policy decisions of 2005, 2006, 2008, and 2010, respectively. We might also note that these choices correspond to what we know of the foreign policy priorities identified by the Liberal government in 2004–05. Those who advised Martin on foreign and defence issues strongly believed that Canada should invest resources in promoting international peace and security. In this context, NATO's intervention in Afghanistan represented the most important military undertaking of the alliance between 2001 and 2011, and it is difficult to imagine a Liberal majority government not living up to Canada's international obligations.

A Stephen Harper Conservative Majority, 2006

What would have happened had the Conservative Party finally overturned more than twelve years of Liberal rule on 23 January 2006 and achieved a majority in the House of Commons? Had this occurred, we can be fairly certain that the next election would have been held in the fall of 2010:

during the election campaign, the Conservatives had proposed introducing fixed-date elections in Canada. Accordingly, the next federal election would have been set for 18 October 2010.

As the Conservative majority government took office in February 2006, the Canadian battle group was already being deployed to Kandahar. Hence, we do not have to concern ourselves with outlining how a Harper government would have handled the decision to commit the CAF in Afghanistan in 2005. And since it is not plausible to assume a Conservative majority government in 2004, the most realistic and logical counterfactual suggests that Stephen Harper would have come to power as it happened in 2006, having committed to a one-year PRT supported by a brigade-size contingent in southern Afghanistan under ISAF. The question is whether a Harper majority would have renewed Canada's commitment to NATO in 2006. We have sufficient indications to suggest that the answer would have been yes.

First, Stephen Harper had always been a strong supporter of a robust and assertive defence policy. On numerous occasions between 2002 and 2005, the Harper-led opposition disagreed publicly with the Liberal government's approach to defence. Whether on defence expenditures, or Chrétien's decision not to participate in the Iraq war in 2003, or Martin's decision not to join the US Ballistic Missile Defense program in 2005, Harper consistently advocated a more aggressive foreign policy. Indeed, one of the first speeches he gave as prime minister reviewed the Canadian mission in Afghanistan in March 2006. Addressing Canadian troops in Kandahar, he concluded: "Friends, we have made real progress [in Afghanistan]. Your work is vital to Canada. To the free world. To the Afghan people. As you get ready to go back to work, know that I am behind you. Your government is behind you. And, most importantly, the Canadian people are behind you."[21] In sum, when the Conservatives took power in 2006, they were already fully committed to supporting Canada's intervention in Afghanistan.

Second, senior civil servants who had advised the previous Martin government on Afghanistan in 2005 would have still been in place as the Harper majority government came to power. In May 2007, the Conservative government created the Afghanistan task force in order to coordinate interagency collaboration in Afghanistan. Led by David Mulroney, this new task force operated directly from the PCO, the department closest to the prime minister. Finally, as numerous studies suggest, Canada's decision to contribute to the international stabilization mission in Afghanistan was highly influenced by allied dynamics within NATO.[22] In this context, the Kandahar decision of 2005 was a classic example of a Putnamesque two-level game.[23]

As Canada agreed to play a large role in Afghanistan in 2005, expectations increased among its allies that such a commitment would endure. Therefore, much of the internal and external pressure (and advice) Prime Minister Harper received with respect to the decision to renew Canada's existing contribution to ISAF would have pointed towards an extension.

Finally, the disarray within the Liberal Party in the wake of the 2006 election would have encouraged a majority Harper government to extend the mission. After Paul Martin resigned, different factions vied for control of the party.[24] Absorbed by a leadership campaign, the Liberal opposition would not have opposed the extension of the mission, particularly since Bill Graham, who had been the minister of national defence responsible for the 2005 decision to provide troops for Kandahar, was serving as interim leader and personally supported a mission extension.

With all of these considerations in mind, we can reasonably conclude that a Harper majority government would have renewed Canada's commitment to Kandahar but without the need for the kind of political gamesmanship that the minority Harper government engaged in between 2006 and 2008.[25] This timeframe would have allowed the CAF and other departments to make better projections in allocating their resources for Afghanistan. It also would have simplified NATO's force generation strategy for ISAF as Brussels could have expected these troops to be available for deployment. For all intents and purposes, we suggest that our counterfactual Harper majority government would have made the same decision in 2006 as did the Harper minority government.

By 2008, our counterfactual Harper majority would have been faced with the same decision as the real Harper minority: whether to renew the mission, change its parameters, or simply withdraw Canadian troops in 2009. After two years in power, a Conservative majority government would likely have been as weary of the Afghanistan mission as was the Conservative minority. Progress in Afghanistan was limited on most economic, security, and governance indicators, and the Conservatives were distressed by a generalized lack of willingness among Canada's NATO allies to provide sufficient, caveat-free resources to ISAF. In 2006, the Harper government had come to office believing that Canada needed to assume greater international responsibilities to gain influence on the world stage. Two years later, despite shouldering a disproportionate share of the alliance's burden in Afghanistan, Canada had hardly been acknowledged for its effort and sacrifice. Last, many NATO allies had begun to pull their troops out of Afghanistan, clearly indicating a desire to scale back the overall ISAF contribution by 2011.

Domestically, Prime Minister Harper would have been concerned that Canada's costly contribution to the international effort in Afghanistan could undermine his re-election prospects in October 2010. Public opinion polls showed mounting opposition to the Canadian mission. In addition, the global financial crisis of 2008 forced the Conservatives to implement budgetary restraints to which every department, including national defence, had to contribute. By October 2008, ninety-nine members of the CAF had lost their lives in Afghanistan. A report from the Office of the Parliamentary Budget Officer published in October 2008 estimated the total cost of the mission (including veterans' benefits and post-traumatic stress disorder) between $13.92 billion and $18.14 billion dollars – if it ended in 2011.[26] Finally, after several years in power, the Conservatives would have started to replace senior civil servants who had been appointed, for the most part, by the Liberals. Such changes would have likely eroded the bureaucracy's policy entrenchment on Afghanistan and given way to contrarian alternatives. In this context, although the Harper government would have been prepared to extend Canada's intervention in Afghanistan beyond 2009, it also would have been eager to set an end date.

The question remaining is whether a Harper Conservative majority would have renewed the mission for one or two years. Realistically, domestic concerns, particularly the federal elections in October 2010, suggest that a Harper majority would have opted for a two-year prolongation – for two reasons. First, the government would have preferred to defuse the question before the federal elections to avoid making Afghanistan an electoral issue that might dissuade progressive voters in Ontario, British Columbia, and Quebec, who were essential to the achievement of another Conservative majority. A one-year commitment would have brought the end of Canada's mission right around fall 2010, the worst possible time in the perspective of a government preoccupied by its re-election. The option of a two-year extension with a fixed date, for its part, would have offered a double advantage: concluding military operations in the fall of 2011 – one year after the election – and signalling to voters the conclusion of the mission and thus limiting the relevance of any debate on Canada's contribution in Afghanistan during the campaign. As an added benefit, renewing the mission for two years in 2009 would surely have exacerbated internal dissension within the Liberal opposition. As the leader of the Liberal Party, Stéphane Dion remained a critic of Canada's military commitment. Others, however, like Michael Ignatieff and Bob Rae, were strong supporters. The internal tension would have been used to good advantage by the governing Conservatives on the eve of the 2010 federal election. In short, a Conservative majority government would have likely prolonged Canada's participation in ISAF for two years and committed to ending combat operations in 2011.

The decision to participate in NATO's training mission from 2011 to 2014 was under consideration in November 2010. We acknowledge that a majority Harper government is more plausible than a counterfactual Liberal majority. Support for the Conservatives rose uninterruptedly from 2006 to 2011, due in large part to structural demographic factors.[27] Had a majority Harper government gone to the polls in October 2010 against Stéphane Dion and a Liberal electoral platform focused on curbing Canada's greenhouse emissions in the midst of a financial crisis, it is likely that the Conservatives would have increased their support in suburban Ontario and been rewarded with a second majority. The Liberals, for their part, would likely have turned to Michael Ignatieff to lead them in the October 2014 election. But Stephen Harper would have found in Ignatieff an opposition leader who was more amenable to Canada's involvement in a training mission in Afghanistan than Dion had been. With such bipartisan consensus, the government would have quickly yielded to the request from Washington and Brussels to provide much-needed troops to train and assist Afghan forces. Nevertheless, far from an open-ended intervention, Harper would have mirrored Washington's commitment by insisting on a mission deadline of 2014.

In short, considering both the domestic context and international pressures, it is highly likely that a Harper majority would have prolonged Canada's contribution to military operations in Kandahar between 2006 and 2008. Furthermore, we have strong evidence that, with federal elections set for October 2010, the Harper government would have sought to withdraw troops from combat in 2011 and, quite possibly, committed to the Afghanistan training mission as it did so.

Conclusion

Minority government, or so the argument goes, imposes a particular environment, which limits the freedom of decision makers. Policy makers are constantly aware and reminded that their position is precarious; every decision becomes tainted by the prospect of the next election. In this context, compared to majorities, minority governments are expected to make decisions that are either more prudent (in order to remain in power) or that exploit wedge issues (in order to weaken opposing parties). If this hypothesis has any merit, Canada's decade-long engagement in Afghanistan should have been influenced by successive minority governments in 2004, 2006, and 2008.

However, thinking counterfactually about how majority governments – a Liberal majority in 2004 and a Conservative majority in 2006 – might have acted on the Afghanistan file yields two sobering conclusions. First, majority governments would have made essentially the same policy choices as did the three minority governments. Consequently, it appears that the configuration of government is neither a sufficient nor a necessary condition to explain foreign policy making. In other words, minority status might have an impact on policy making, but, as our cases studies on Afghanistan suggest, such influence is not predetermined.

Second, and perhaps more interestingly, we find no indication that the two major parties would have pursued substantially different policies on Afghanistan between 2004 and 2014. To be sure, Liberals and Conservatives would likely have framed Canada's contribution differently.[28] The Liberals would have emphasized Canadian values and international responsibilities towards peace and security. The Conservatives would have focused on defending Canadians and Canada's national interests. Nevertheless, these differences would have been cosmetic rather than substantial.

In retrospect, these two conclusions suggest that the combination of domestic forces (federal election cycles, elite consensus, bureaucratic path dependency) and international pressure (the situation in Afghanistan, allied relations within NATO, US foreign policy) determined Canada's policy making towards Afghanistan, leaving little opportunity for Parliament to play an active role.

Notes

1 David P. Auerswald, "Inward bound: Domestic institutions and military conflicts," *International Organization* 53, 3 (1999): 469–504; Ryan K. Beasley and Juliet Kaarbo, "Explaining extremity in the foreign policies of parliamentary democracies," *International Studies Quarterly* 58, 4 (2014): 729–40; Sibel Oktay, "Constraining or enabling? The effects of government composition on international commitments," *Journal of European Public Policy* 21, 6 (2014): 860–84.
2 Glenn Palmer, Tamar R. London, and Patrick M. Regan, "What's stopping you? The sources of political constraints on international conflict behavior in parliamentary democracies," *International Interactions* 30, 1 (2004): 6.
3 Frank P. Harvey, *Explaining the Iraq War: Counterfactual Theory, Logic and Evidence* (Cambridge: Cambridge University Press, 2012); Richard Ned Lebow, *Forbidden*

Fruit: Counterfactuals and International Relations (Princeton: Princeton University Press, 2010); James Mahoney, Gary Goertz, and Charles C. Ragin, "Causal models and counterfactuals," in Stephen L. Morgan, ed., *Handbook of Causal Analysis in Social Research* (New York: Springer, 2013), 75–90.

4 Max Weber, *On the Methodology of the Social Sciences*, trans. and ed. Edward A. Shils and Henry A. Finch (Chicago: The Free Press of Glencoe, 1949), 173.

5 Harvey, *Explaining the Iraq War*, 24.

6 Lebow, *Forbidden Fruit*, 48.

7 Following the 1995 referendum, the Chrétien government launched a $250 million campaign to increase the federal government's visibility in Quebec. The program was dogged by allegations that it was deeply corrupt. Investigations revealed that as much as $100 million in sponsorship contracts were awarded illegally or fraudulently to Liberal friends of the Chrétien government. In an effort to blunt the impact of the scandal, Prime Minister Martin appointed a royal commission to investigate, headed by Justice John Gomery. Gomery issued the first part of his report in November 2005, prompting a motion of non-confidence that brought down the minority Martin government.

8 John Ibbitson, *Stephen Harper* (Toronto: McClelland and Stewart, 2015), 195–97. Eleven days before the vote, the Conservatives issued a press release accusing Martin personally of supporting child pornography. When Martin objected to this low blow, Harper stridently defended it. The result was an immediate overnight ten-point drop in support, from 41 percent, which would have produced a Conservative majority, to 31 percent. In Ibbitson's view, "that press release, and Harper's bitter defence of it, cost him the election."

9 Government of Canada, *Canada's International Policy Statement: A Role of Pride and Influence in the World* (Ottawa: Minister of Supply and Services, 2005), 2.

10 Janice Gross Stein and Eugene Lang, *The Unexpected War: Canada in Kandahar* (Toronto: Penguin Books, 2007); Philippe Lagassé and Joel Sokolsky, "A larger 'footprint' in Ottawa: General Hillier and Canada's shifting civil-military relationship," *Canadian Foreign Policy Journal* 15, 2 (2009): 16–40.

11 Government of Canada, *Canadian Forces in Afghanistan: Report of the Standing Committee on National Defence* (Ottawa: Minister of Supply and Services, 2007), 40.

12 North Atlantic Treaty Organization, *The Afghanistan Compact. Building on Success: The London Conference on Afghanistan* (2006), http://www.nato.int/isaf/docu/epub/pdf/afghanistan_compact.pdf.

13 Jean-Christophe Boucher, "Evaluating the 'Trenton effect': Canadian public opinion and military casualties in Afghanistan, 2006–2010," *American Review of Canadian Studies* 40, 2 (2011): 237–58.

14 Jean-Christophe Boucher and Kim Richard Nossal, "Lessons learned? Public opinion and the Afghanistan mission," in Fen Osler Hampson and Stephen M. Saideman, eds., *Canada Among Nations, 2015: Elusive Pursuits* (Waterloo: Centre for International Governance Innovation, 2015), 73–93.

15 Jack Levy, "Prospect theory, rational choice, and international relations," *International Studies Quarterly* 41, 1 (1997): 87–112.

16 "[Barack] Obama's Speech on Iraq, March 2008," *Council on Foreign Relations*, http://www.cfr.org/elections/obamas-speech-iraq-march-2008/p15761.

17 World Bank, *GDP per capita (current US$)*, http://data.worldbank.org/indicator/ NY.GDP.PCAP.CD.
18 Sten Rynning, *NATO in Afghanistan: The Liberal Disconnect* (Stanford: Stanford University Press, 2012).
19 Benjamin Zyla, *Sharing the Burden? NATO and Its Second-Tier Powers* (Toronto: University of Toronto Press, 2015).
20 David P. Auerswald and Stephen M. Saideman, "Comparing caveats: Understanding the sources of national restrictions upon NATO's mission in Afghanistan," *International Studies Quarterly* 56, 1 (2012): 73.
21 Stephen Harper, *Address by the Prime Minister to the Canadian Armed Forces in Afghanistan*, Kandahar, 13 March 2006, cited at http://www.cbc.ca/news2/background/afghanistan/pmspeech.html.
22 Stéfanie von Hlatky, *American Allies in Times of War: The Great Asymmetry* (New York: Oxford University Press, 2013); Matthew Willis, "An unexpected war, a not-unexpected mission," *International Journal* 67, 4 (2012): 979–1000.
23 Robert D. Putnam, "Diplomacy and domestic politics: The logic of two-level games," *International Organization* 42, 3 (1988): 428–60.
24 Elisabeth Gidengil, Neil Nevitte, André Blais, Joanna Everitt, and Patrick Fournier, *Dominance and Decline: Making Sense of Recent Canadian Elections* (Toronto: University of Toronto Press, 2012).
25 See Kim Richard Nossal, "No exit: Canada and the 'war without end' in Afghanistan," in Hans-Georg Ehrhart and Charles C. Pentland, eds., *The Afghanistan Challenge: Hard Realities and Strategic Choices* (Montreal and Kingston: McGill-Queen's University Press, 2009), 157–73; Stephen M. Saideman, *Adapting in the Dust: Lessons Learned from Canada's War in Afghanistan* (Toronto: University of Toronto Press, 2016).
26 Parliamentary Budget Officer, *Fiscal Impact of the Canadian Mission in Afghanistan* (Ottawa, October 2008), http://www.parl.gc.ca/pbo-dpb/documents/Afghanistan_Fiscal_Impact_FINAL_E_WEB.pdf.
27 Darrell Bricker and John Ibbitson, *The Big Shift: The Seismic Change in Canadian Politics, Business, and Culture and What It Means for Our Future* (Toronto: HarperCollins, 2013).
28 Jean-Christophe Boucher, "Selling Afghanistan: A discourse analysis of Canada's military intervention, 2001–2008," *International Journal* 64, 3 (2009): 717–33.

5
The Evolution of the Harper Government's Defence Policy
Minority versus Majority or Surplus versus Deficit?
DAVID PERRY

Did the switch from minority to majority government change the Harper government's approach to defence? In short, no. While at least one analyst initially speculated that the minority context would affect defence plans,[1] in some respects, the reverse was true. Prime Minister Stephen Harper's ambitious defence agenda was more successfully implemented during the first minority era than it was during the majority years. The journalist Paul Wells attributes the decline of Conservative effectiveness in defence policy to the prime minister's personal "enthusiasm for a heavily militarized Canada" taking a "beating in the sands of Afghanistan,"[2] while the political scientist Andrew Richter contends that the Conservatives gradually determined that rebuilding the military was "not worth the financial and political cost."[3] I find it difficult to take real issue with either suggestion, given the lack of clear evidence we have so soon after the fact.

More specifically, however, I examine the Harper government's defence record by asking whether the Conservatives' minority standing in the House of Commons affected policy in three specific areas: (1) the defence budget, (2) military procurement and defence reform, and (3) expeditionary operations. I argue that the government's approach to defence changed over time but that the number of Conservatives sitting on the government's side of the House of Commons only mattered on the margins; rather, the gap between defence ambitions and funding, the shift to austerity, changes in personnel and attitudes towards defence procurement, and emerging frustration with the Department of National Defence were the primary determinants of policy change.

As Philippe Lagassé notes in Chapter 3 (this volume), opposition parties in minority parliaments can use both the confidence and the accountability functions to constrain the government. John English (Chapter 2, this volume) adds historical evidence to this claim by demonstrating how previous minority situations have led (Liberal) governments to modify their behaviour to satisfy prospective electoral interests. Both authors maintain that opposition parties can use public criticism and the threat of non-confidence votes to force minority governments to adjust their policies.

In the case of defence, however, there is little reason to expect that Prime Minister Stephen Harper would have felt seriously threatened by his opposition since, in international relations scholar Brian Bow's words, parliamentary criticism of defence policy has typically been "relatively toothless."[4] Further, as Lagassé notes, the accountability function is arguably more effective in majority parliaments since the opposition parties are freer to critique aggressively. He also submits that the Conservatives advanced a practice of "vetting and laundering" decisions that has traditionally been effective in diminishing the opposition's accountability function. As the editors of this volume and English himself note, the historical policy shifts by minority governments were also instigated by Liberal cabinets that were sensitive to threats from the New Democratic Party to their left. Since some accounts assert that the Harper Conservatives' electoral coalition was based on capturing "centre-right Liberals," a group naturally inclined to support the government's proactive defence policy, there is little reason to suspect that the 2006–11 minority situation would have created similar opposition leverage. Moreover, as Bow explains, the accountability function is most effective when a government's handling of defence issues raises "questions about its basic competency in managing."[5] The empirical record below provides evidence that criticism along these lines may have contributed to policy changes related to defence procurement, but it also suggests that other factors were significantly more important to the broader changes in the government's overall approach.

2006–08: An Ambitious Agenda for a Minority Government

In the 2006 election, the Conservatives made two defence-related commitments. The first was material: a significant reinvestment in defence to strengthen "Canada's independent capacity to defend our national sovereignty material and security."[6] It came with a particular focus on Northern capacity but included significant force expansion, the creation of new units, and numerous equipment purchases, all of which would be supported by a $5.3 billion budgetary increase.[7] This pledge built upon the previous government's significant increase to the military budget in 2005. In combination, the measures resulted in a huge increase in the defence budget within a very short timeframe and were accompanied by sweeping plans for reinvestment.

The second commitment was symbolic. The military, and its forceful use, would become a symbol that Conservatives, if not all Canadians, "could rally around."[8] Shortly after assuming office, Prime Minister Harper publicly committed to demonstrating "an international leadership role for our country. Not carping from the sidelines, but taking a stand on the big issues that matter."[9] He framed this approach as antithetical to previous Liberal governments' mistreatment of the military. As the 2006 Conservative electoral platform's discussion of defence had made clear, "for decades, successive Liberal governments [had] undermined and under-funded Canada's armed forces."[10] The government was greatly assisted in creating this frame by its first chief of the defence staff (who was, ironically, inherited from the Liberals). General Rick Hillier had coined the evocative phrase "the decade of darkness" to describe the Canadian military's experience in the 1990s under successive Liberal governments. His refrain was used throughout the Harper era, including its last mention in the Conservatives' 2015 campaign platform, which touted their "significant investments in Canada's military following the Liberal 'Decade of Darkness.'"[11]

The newly elected Conservatives moved swiftly to implement their defence agenda. The 2006 budget delivered on the campaign promises, and in June the government announced its "Big Five" procurements: strategic airlift, tactical airlift, medium and heavy lift helicopters, medium army trucks, and joint support ships.[12] The projects received approvals in short order; contracts for airlifters were signed in 2007 and the first C17 transport aircraft was delivered that year. Concurrently, numerous "urgent operational requirements" were swiftly acquired to support the mission in Afghanistan.[13] Given the speed with which so many major purchases were advanced, if not completed, some have come to view the period between 2006 and 2008 as the most successful procurement era in recent history.[14]

Nonetheless, the government was soon forced to revise its reinvestment plans. National defence had costed the Conservative platform at between two to four times the funding it was ultimately provided.[15] This gap resulted in a significant reduction of the government's plans in 2007. Initially, the military's expansion and the establishment of new units were postponed.[16] At about the same time, defence acquisition plans began to slow as they ran into what General Hillier described as "slowly building resistance" in a bureaucracy that was jealous of the Department of National Defence's increased stature at the Cabinet table and its consequent access to resources.[17] The negative reaction was exacerbated by procurement strategies (at least for many of these early purchases) that did not rely on full, open competitions. Such "sole sourcing" expedited the acquisition process but resulted in criticism from the media and the opposition. When departmental representatives suggested a similarly accelerated approach to the purchase of unmanned aerial vehicles (UAVs) in 2007, the idea was rejected. Some accounts attribute the rejection to Cabinet concerns about the optics of yet another sole-sourced buy, while others assert that the opposition originated within the bureaucracy.[18]

In spite of the emerging procurement challenges, the government released its *Canada First Defence Strategy* (*CFDS*) in May 2008. The *CFDS* departed from previous official statements on defence by placing significantly greater emphasis on spending plans than on actual defence policy. The policy portion simply reinforced Canada's traditional roles and missions, albeit with an increased emphasis on the Arctic, while the bulk of the document provided unusually detailed descriptions of planned investments and fiscal commitments. Overall, the *CFDS* committed to replacing virtually all of the military's major fleets and to growing the military to seventy thousand full-time and thirty thousand reserve forces.[19]

The numbers in the *CFDS* were contingent on a commitment to increase the Department of National Defence's annual budget escalator (a planned annual increase) from 1.5 to 2 percent starting in 2011–12. As a result, DND was supposed to receive "stable and predictable defence funding,"[20] which would "reverse the damage done by major cuts to the defence budget in the 1990s."[21] While the plan's affordability was questioned immediately,[22] the $490 billion pledged over twenty years represented an enormous commitment to defence in both material and symbolic terms.

While these investments were occurring, as Jean-Christophe Boucher and Kim Richard Nossal note (Chapter 4, this volume), the Harper government was making active use of the military, especially in Afghanistan. Until 2011, operations in Kandahar left little capacity for other sizable activities, although, in 2006, new operations in the North and in Latin America were quietly initiated. Even though the two engagements lasted through the minority and majority eras, since one was an exercise of Canadian sovereignty and the other was low profile, neither ever attracted significant attention.[23]

The first minority government era benefitted from the unique attributes of the senior defence leadership cadre. The first minister, Gordon O'Connor, had personally written the defence section of the Conservative Party platform, was directly invested in its implementation, and therefore assumed his portfolio in 2006 with more concrete plans than did most of his newly appointed Cabinet colleagues.[24] Further, for almost two years, his plans benefitted from a close working relationship between General Hillier and his department's deputy minister, Ward Elcock. Because Elcock believed strongly in military reinvestment, he did not provide the typical bureaucratic check on the CAF's activities but, rather, worked to promote them across Ottawa. Defence analysts Joel Sokolsky and Philippe Lagassé contend that Elcock was replaced by Robert Fonberg in October 2007 to curb the military's increasingly "insatiable appetite for additional funds."[25] Fonberg's appointment thus marked a shift in the government's attitude from unwavering support for military reinvestment to increasing concern for the fiscal implications of the overall defence agenda.

During these early years, the government's minority standing in the House of Commons had little effect. Despite Conservative accusations to the contrary, the previous Liberal leader, Paul Martin, had renewed his party's support for a more robust military in 2003, and Prime Minister Harper was therefore able to merely augment Martin's $12 billion increase to the 2005 defence budget.[26] The bipartisan consensus over the need to reinvest in defence precluded significant Liberal criticism, apart from members' concerns over sole sourcing. Indeed, the 2008 Liberal campaign platform supported the Conservatives' defence investments but promised to stop the uncompetitive acquisitions process.[27] There is some evidence that opposition criticism led the Cabinet to quash a plan to direct a procurement of UAVs, which provides some support for the notion that, in at least one case, the government's minority status contributed to its change of plans. However, given General Hillier's assertion that, by 2007, the federal bureaucracy had begun to resist DND's procurement efforts, it is equally plausible that bureaucratic conflicts were the real catalyst.

2008–11: An Evolving Focus
When Stephen Harper was re-elected with another minority in 2008, his government retained the *CFDS*, but the fiscal circumstances in which it

would be pursued had changed significantly. The Great Recession had resulted in a massive, unplanned stimulus spending package, a $55 billion deficit, and cuts to defence. By 2009, public service analysts had determined that the strategy was no longer affordable, and rising, unfunded war costs exacerbated the situation. In April 2009, the government launched its first effort to reconcile the gap between the available funding and its *CFDS* commitments. That summer, DND launched a Treasury Board-mandated strategic review to identify its lowest performing activities, the money for which would be reallocated to the most significant Government of Canada priorities.[28] While this process began with the expectation that some of the reallocated resources would be directed back to defence, the 2010 budget indicated otherwise. There would be an annual, recurring cut to the department's budget of $1 billion, which lasted through 2014–15. In a move that could have undermined the Conservatives' symbolic commitment to defence had it been more aggressively reported, while the entire federal government was subjected to an operating budget freeze, DND was the only department to have its budget cut in 2010.

The Conservatives did increase the defence escalator as promised in 2011–12 and argued that DND's budget would therefore "continue to grow but more slowly than previously planned";[29] however, the net impact was a clear budgetary loss.[30] As a result, inflation-adjusted defence spending peaked in 2009–10 and declined thereafter.[31] The department responded by launching CF2020, an efficiency initiative focused on shifting resources from administration and overhead towards operational capability.[32] The impact of this shift was downplayed in the budget documents and in subsequent public statements, which stressed how much the budget had grown since 2006.[33]

While DND adjusted to the new fiscal reality, the government adapted its approach to military reinvestment. In 2008, the Conservatives had identified improving military procurement as a priority because Canada could not "afford to have cumbersome processes delay the purchase and delivery of equipment needed by our men and women in uniform."[34] By 2009, after the stimulus program was launched, the focus had shifted to re-equipping the military while concurrently obtaining domestic economic benefits from the investments. The Canadian Association of Defence and Security Industries was invited to provide recommendations on how to achieve these joint objectives, and its representatives recommended a defence industrial policy that supported critical defence sectors.[35] In the wake of the failed purchase of joint support ships and coast guard vessels in 2008, DND also initiated the National Shipbuilding Procurement Strategy, a long-term, continuous build approach to procuring ships from domestic shipyards under the decades-old build-in Canada shipbuilding policy. Announced in June 2010, this strategy aimed to procure ships for the navy and the Coast Guard, while also providing "a long-term plan that [would] create good jobs in high-tech industries across Canada."[36] By 2010, then, the domestic economic implications of procurement had risen in importance, culminating in the 2011 budget, which promised "a procurement strategy, in consultation with industry, to maximize job creation, support Canadian manufacturing capabilities and innovation, and bolster economic growth in Canada."[37]

Just as economic considerations became more prominent, trust and confidence in DND's management of procurement declined. In 2009, the Cabinet rejected DND's plan to sole-source the acquisition of search and rescue aircraft and asked the National Research Council to review the military's requirements for the aircraft.[38] In 2010, an auditor general's report found that the department had understated the developmental nature of the requirements for maritime and medium-heavy lift helicopters, presenting both to the Treasury Board as "off-the-shelf" purchases when in reality they were more risky developmental projects.[39] The July 2010 announcement that Canada would acquire F-35 fighter jets created yet more controversy.[40] The acquisition came under immediate criticism that built over time, focusing on the sole-sourced nature of the contract, the unsuitability of its capabilities, and its costs. In October the Liberal Party pledged to cancel the deal and hold a competition.[41] The Parliamentary Budget Office released its report on the F-35 in March 2011. It estimated considerably higher total costs than did DND, exacerbating an already high level of acrimony over the file.[42]

The government's failure to produce documents detailing the cost estimates for the F-35 contributed in part to its loss of a vote of non-confidence in the House of Commons, providing some support for the notion that its minority standing was meaningful. However, the F-35 issue was only one among a "flood of mini-scandals" that led to Parliament's dissolution.[43] Moreover, the criticism and vote of non-confidence did nothing to change the Conservatives' behaviour. In fact, the *only* defence commitment the Conservative Party made in its 2011 platform was to "follow through on the purchase of the F-35."[44] For the first year of its majority, it remained committed to the purchase.

In the midst of these shifting approaches to procurement and budgets, at the end of the second minority era, Prime Minister Harper initiated a major commitment of Canadian aircraft and naval forces. Canadian officials were "early enthusiastic supporters" of what began as an ad hoc coalition protecting civilians from the Muammar Gaddafi regime in Libya.[45] Canadian assets were deployed prior to NATO's assumption of command of the mission and then made significant operational contributions. As was the case in Afghanistan, they were also deployed with robust operational caveats. Canadian aircraft flew with only seven partners when engaging ground targets,[46] and the commitment of Canadian frigates went well beyond those of most allies, actively liaising with anti-Gaddafi forces.[47] The mission thus presented the first chance, aside from Afghanistan, for Prime Minister Harper to demonstrate his desire for Canada "to be seen as a muscular leader."[48] Thanks largely to the mission's initial focus on protecting civilians, not to mention its general popularity, the Conservatives could count on Liberal and NDP support through the first two House of Commons votes on Canadian deployments. As Lagassé suggests, then, it appears that the mission was thoroughly laundered and vetted. Aside from a minor controversy over its costs, the Libyan engagement faced only minor opposition criticism.

Beyond Libya, the second minority period witnessed significant changes to the Conservative approach to defence. The government pivoted rapidly from increasing the defence budget to cutting it more aggressively than it did other departments. These efforts were of course downplayed to protect the government's political narrative. At the same time, the focus on defence procurement shifted from immediately acquiring military capabilities to domestic economic considerations. In neither situation did the government's minority status appear to matter. The lack of a majority in the House of Commons was consequential when the government fell, in part because of opposition to the Conservatives' handling of the F-35 file. Yet the Cabinet remained committed to purchasing the fighter aircraft following an election in which they were a non-issue.

The 2011–15 Majority: Muscular Missions, Modest Investments
Winning a majority did nothing to stop the cuts to defence. The 2012 budget removed an additional $1.1 billion from the department on a recurring basis, although this time DND's contribution was proportional to its share of overall spending. While cutting defence put Stephen Harper in the company of many past prime ministers, the implementation of his cuts was unique. In previous eras of restraint, DND's capital program and the size of the armed forces were reduced. Between 2010 and 2015, however, both of these elements were protected (despite suggestions that cuts would be necessary to maintain the viability of the armed forces in the long term).[49]

Instead, the bulk of the reductions came from the operational accounts as training budgets and funds for maintenance, repair, and overhaul were reduced. As such, the most visible components of the Conservatives' investment in defence – a larger armed forces and ambitious capital plan – survived unscathed.

The cuts generated significant criticism amidst reports from within the military that demonstrated their significant negative impacts. The government rebuffed such concerns, however, citing its "unprecedented investments to rebuild the Canadian Armed Forces."[50] Canadian defence representatives likely faced more significant criticism at the September 2014 NATO summit in Wales, during which all of the allies committed "to reverse the trend of declining defence budgets."[51] The following March, the Parliamentary Budget Office declared DND's force structure unaffordable under current budget plans.[52]

The May 2015 budget promised to end the decline of funding for defence by pledging another increase to the escalator. If implemented in full, this policy would have eventually returned DND to the annual funding levels anticipated by the *CFDS*. In the meantime, the department contributed roughly $30 billion to deficit reduction between 2009 and 2015, and the defence budget was actually lower, adjusted for inflation, when the Harper era ended than it had been before the *CFDS* was launched.[53]

During the majority years, in spite of Conservative successes in upgrading both Canada's frigates and its surveillance aircraft, a series of procurement problems garnered increasingly strident criticism. There were delays and cost increases in shipbuilding, army projects were cancelled, and efforts to acquire maritime helicopters were stymied.[54] The F-35 file became even more contentious following a damning auditor general's report in the spring of 2012. The reaction to findings that the department had neither fully briefed officials on the consequences of their decisions nor provided full costings was "immediate and Draconian."[55] A complete review of the file was launched and its management given to Public Works and Government Services Canada (PWGSC). The lengthy review was completed in June 2014, but no decision was taken on acquiring a new fighter prior to the 2015 election. While criticism of the F-35 experience withered in 2015, the decision not to take a decision is reported to have been predicated on the government's dissatisfaction with the options presented to it and on its unhappiness with bureaucratic and military pressure to stick with the original plan.[56] In sum, the department's handling of the F-35 file created a cloud of mistrust that invigorated efforts to reform the acquisition process more generally.

In September 2012, the Conservatives appointed a successful business entrepreneur, Tom Jenkins, special adviser to the minister of public works in order to advise on such changes. His 2013 report recommended a defence industrial strategy that supported key industrial capabilities and led to the launch of the Defence Procurement Strategy in February 2014. The strategy pledged to leverage the domestic economic benefits accrued from government investments in defence, improve the timeliness of their delivery, and streamline the procurement process. The changes elevated the importance of domestic economic offsets in military procurements, which have since become evaluated components of procurement bids. The new strategy also replaced DND with PWGSC as the lead agency in the new interdepartmental procurement governance structure.[57] The initiatives designed to leverage the economic benefits of purchases advanced significantly and quickly, but little progress was made to improve the actual delivery of military equipment prior to the 2015 election.

While these procurement changes were unfolding, efforts to make DND more efficient stalled. The CF2020 process ended with the publication of the *Report on Transformation* in the summer of 2011. The document proposed sweeping reforms to achieve fiscal savings while preserving operational capability; however, due to bureaucratic resistance, only minor aspects of it were implemented. Following the 2012 budget, the PMO expressed unhappiness with DND's proposals to achieve its budget reduction and directed that the *Report on Transformation* guide its efforts to improve efficiency. Two months later, a new efficiency exercise, Defence Renewal, was launched. As of January 2015, however, only $146 million in cumulative fiscal savings were anticipated through March 2015.[58]

Since 2012, many have speculated that the *CFDS* would be formally revised, and the 2013 Speech from the Throne committed the government to doing so. The results of that effort, however, were not released prior to the 2015 federal election. While no explanation for this delay was forthcoming, aligning the defence strategy with the funding available would have been politically sensitive since the funding was inadequate to start with and had been progressively reduced. Fitting a new strategy within the available funding envelope would have required fewer planned acquisitions and reductions to the size of the military.[59] For a government that continually positioned its record of defence reinvestment against the Liberal "decade of darkness," taking such action may have proven too difficult.

Against the backdrop of reduced funding, the Canadian military was again deployed on a significant mission, this time against the Islamic State of Iraq and Syria (ISIS) militants operating in Iraq and Syria. In August 2014, the government deployed the air force to ship military supplies to beleaguered Kurdish forces and then sent Canada's Special Operations Forces on a month-long training mission to advise them. This commitment evolved into a six-month air combat mission in October. Operations in Iraq proved considerably more controversial than those in Libya: votes on the mission were opposed by both the Liberals and the NDP. The opposition preferred that the Canadian contribution be limited to humanitarian and non-combat roles.[60]

Rather than attenuating this criticism, the Conservatives actually increased it. Senior officers admitted publicly that Canadian trainers had exchanged fire with ISIS forces and were occasionally providing targeting support to coalition airstrikes. The admission was highly unusual given the traditional Canadian convention of secrecy around special operations, and no other coalition member admitted to conducting similar activities. The comments generated significant criticism and accusations of mission creep.[61] Even more controversially, when the government expanded the mission in March 2015, it extended the air campaign into Syrian airspace, joining only the United States and five Arab countries in this more aggressive posture. The Conservatives did so, it is worth noting, in spite of suggestions from the Liberal Party that its opposition to the government's policy was primarily oriented around this single facet of the operation.

The mission continued a trend evident during both the minority and majority periods of Canada's engaging militarily abroad with relatively little concern for the actions of its traditionally key allies.[62] The extension also demonstrated Prime Minister Harper's disinclination to build domestic political support for the mission. In fact, the finance minister admitted that the government intended to make the ISIS operation an election issue.[63] While the opposition was consistently critical up to October 2015, the public was significantly more supportive, at least initially, undoubtedly in part because of two terrorist attacks on Canadian soil in October 2014 that were linked to Islamist extremism.[64]

As a majority government, the Conservatives' cuts to the military initially intensified and provoked significant criticism; however, by the end of their mandate, they had promised to reinvest. Although the Conservatives faced domestic pressure because of their cuts, it is more likely that concerns expressed by NATO members and an acknowledgment that only a funding increase could forestall an unpalatable reduction in national defence capabilities generated the policy reversal. During the majority years, changes were made to defence procurement that reduced DND's management role and gave greater weight to industrial offsets. Those changes appear to have been driven at least as much by Ottawa's unhappiness with the department's administrative practices and increasing sensitivity to domestic industrial concerns as with any outside pressure. Finally, the only mission conducted fully during the majority era was arguably among Canada's most muscular. The government made no real effort to vet or launder the ISIS operation, and it adopted a role that made opposition support virtually impossible. Such conduct could be read as an indication that the Conservatives were empowered by their majority. The admission that the government's stance on the mission was electorally advantageous suggests, however, that its majority mandate was not crucial to this most muscular of stances; rather, the Conservatives intended to frame the mission against ISIS as part of their re-election narrative.

Conclusion

There was a noticeable shift in the Conservatives' approach to defence policy between 2006 and 2015, but changes in the government's standing in the House of Commons had little to do with it; rather, efforts to curb federal spending, dissatisfaction with the performance of DND, and a desire to leverage defence expenditures to generate domestic economic benefits caused the government to end its initial embrace of military reinvestment with "unprecedented passion" and to begin instead to treat defence much like previous governments.[65] Throughout, the Conservatives maintained their symbolic support for defence, a move that Kim Richard Nossal believes was intended to help "unseat the Liberals as Canada's 'natural governing party.'"[66] In a May 2015 speech reflecting on a retiring Peter MacKay's tenure as minister of national defence, Stephen Harper noted that MacKay had overseen the "re-equipping of the Canadian Armed Forces after the 'Decade of Darkness', the re-emergence of the Canadian military as a player in global security, and the restoration of the status of our men and women in uniform as members of our greatest national institution."[67] After almost a decade in power, then, the Harper government continued to define its record against the Liberal period that preceded it.

Adam Chapnick argues that the Harper Conservatives attempted to erase the foreign policy legacy of Lloyd Axworthy;[68] with respect to defence, they sought to keep a caricature of the Liberal defence legacy alive to distinguish their own approach. This motivation undoubtedly contributed to the government's unique method of cutting the defence budget as well as to its muscular international deployments. Regardless of its standing in the House of Commons, between 2006 and 2015 the Conservative Party was committed to maintaining strong symbolic support for the military even as the material support waned.

Notes

1 Martin Shadwick, "Defence and the Conservatives," *Canadian Military Journal* 7, 1 (2006): 73.
2 Paul Wells, *The Longer I'm Prime Minister: Stephen Harper and Canada, 2006–* (Toronto: Random House Canada, 2013), 391.
3 Andrew Richter, "A defense renaissance?" *American Review of Canadian Studies* 43, 3 (2013): 437.
4 Brian Bow, "Parties and partisanship in Canadian defence policy," *International Journal* 64, 1 (2008): 72.
5 Ibid.
6 Conservative Party of Canada, *Stand Up for Canada* (Ottawa: Conservative Party of Canada, 2006).
7 Conservative Party of Canada, "Conservatives will boost defence on west coast to protect Canadian sovereignty"; Conservative Party of Canada, "Conservatives call for boost to Canadian forces." Articles available through the author.
8 Wells, *Longer I'm Prime Minister*, 68.
9 Office of the Prime Minister of Canada, "Address by the Prime Minister to the Canadian Armed Forces in Afghanistan," 13 March 2006.
10 Conservative Party of Canada, *Stand Up for Canada*. The Conservatives similarly caricatured and disparaged the Liberals' approach to foreign policy. See Roland Paris, "Are Canadians still liberal internationalists?" *International Journal* 69, 3 (2014): 274–307.
11 Conservative Party of Canada, *Protect Our Economy* (Ottawa, 2015), 77.
12 Canada, Department of National Defence, "'Canada First' Defence Strategy Procurement," retrieved using the Internet Archive "Wayback Machine," https://archive.org/web/.
13 Canada, Department of National Defence, *Army Equipment for Operation ARCHER, BG–05.036* (Ottawa: 2005).
14 David Perry, *Putting the "Armed" Back into the Canadian Armed Forces* (Ottawa: Conference of Defence Associations Institute [CDAI], 2014), 5.
15 Rick Hillier, *A Soldier First* (Toronto: HarperCollins, 2009), 401.
16 David Pugliese, "Military shelves plans for expansion," *Ottawa Citizen*, 7 March 2007.
17 Hillier, *Soldier First*, 412.
18 Canwest News Service, "Tories deny trend toward increased sole-sourced contracts," *canada.com*, 20 June 2007, http://www.canada.com/story_print.html?id=5b4a6b82-860b-4dc0-bded-cb5d8b229826&sponsor=; David Pugliese, "Tories kill sole-source DND contract," *Ottawa Citizen*, 20 April 2007, http://www.canada.com/story.html?id=dea75e57-fe60-42d9-9c02-725e7e1cdd9e; Lawrence Martin, "No

competitive bidding please, we're Canadian," *Globe and Mail,* 4 January 2007; Chief Review Services, Internal Audit of Joint Unmanned Surveillance and Target Acquisition System (JUSTAS) Project (Ottawa: Department of National Defence, March 2014).
19 Canada, Department of National Defence, *Canada First Defence Strategy* (Ottawa: Government of Canada, 2008). Those commitments already represented a reduction from the plans in 2006.
20 Ibid., 3.
21 Ibid., 11.
22 Lieutenant-General (Ret'd) George Macdonald, *The Canada First Defence Strategy: One Year Later* (Calgary: Canadian Defence and Foreign Affairs Institute [CDFAI], 2009).
23 Stephen Harper, "Securing Canadian sovereignty in the Arctic," speech, 12 August 2006; Department of Foreign Affairs, Trade and Development Canada, "Canada and the Americas," http://www.international.gc.ca/americas-ameriques/index.aspx?lang=eng.
24 Hillier, *Soldier First.*
25 Philippe Lagassé and Joel J. Sokolsky, "A larger 'footprint' in Ottawa," *Canadian Foreign Policy Journal* 15, 2 (2009): 31.
26 Janice Gross Stein and Eugene Lang, *The Unexpected War* (Toronto: Viking, 2007).
27 Liberal Party of Canada, *Your Family. Your Future. Your Canada* (Ottawa: 2011).
28 Lieutenant General Andrew Leslie, *Report on Transformation 2011* (Ottawa: Department of National Defence, 2011), Annex O.
29 Department of Finance Canada, *Budget Plan 2010* (Ottawa: Government of Canada, 2010), 158.
30 David Perry, *Defence Budget 2015* (Calgary: CDFAI, 2015).
31 Minister of Public Works and Government Services Canada, *Public Accounts of Canada* (Ottawa: Government of Canada, 1970–2014).
32 David Perry, *Doing Less with Less* (Ottawa: CDAI, 2014).
33 Murray Brewster, "Conservatives' twin budgets expected to carve $2.5 billion out of DND," *National Post* 30 September 2012, http://news.nationalpost.com/news/canada/conservatives-twin-budgets-expected-to-carve-2-5-billion-out-of-dnd-report.
34 Governor General of Canada, *Speech from the Throne to Open the First Session Fortieth Parliament of Canada* (Ottawa: Government of Canada 2008), 19 November 2008, http://www.pco-bcp.gc.ca/index.asp?lang=eng&page=information&sub=publications&doc=aarchives/sft-ddt/2008-eng.htm.
35 Canadian Association of Defence and Security Industries, *Canada's Defence Industry* (Ottawa: Canadian Association of Defence and Security Industries, 2009).
36 Public Works and Government Services Canada, "Archived: Government of Canada announces national shipbuilding procurement strategy," 3 June 2010, http://news.gc.ca/web/article-en.do?crtr.sj1D=&mthd=advSrch&crtr.mnthndVl=12&nid=537299.
37 Department of Finance Canada, *Budget Plan 2011* (Ottawa: Government of Canada, 2011), 85.

38 Elinor Sloan, *Something Has to Give* (Calgary: CDFAI, 2014).
39 Office of the Auditor General of Canada, *Chapter 6: Acquisition of Military Helicopters* (Ottawa: Minister of Public Works and Government Services Canada, 2010), 2.
40 Office of the Auditor General of Canada, *Chapter 2: Replacing Canada's Fighter Jets* (Ottawa: Minister of Public Works and Government Services Canada, 2012), 35.
41 Liberal Party of Canada, *Richer, Fairer, Greener* (Ottawa: Liberal Party of Canada, 2008).
42 Tolga R. Yalkin and Peter Weltman, *An Estimate of the Fiscal Impact of Canada's Proposed Acquisition of the F-35 Lightning II Joint Strike Fighter* (Ottawa: Parliamentary Budget Office, 2011).
43 Wells, *Longer I'm Prime Minister*, 278.
44 Conservative Party of Canada, *Here for Canada* (Ottawa: Conservative Party of Canada, 2011), 16.
45 Kim Richard Nossal, "The use – and misuse – of R2P," in Aidan Hehir and Robert Murray, eds., *Libya, the Responsibility to Protect, and the Future of Humanitarian Intervention* (New York: Palgrave Macmillan, 2013), 112.
46 Stephen M. Saideman, *Afghanistan as a Test of Canadian Politics* (Waterloo: Centre for International Governance Innovation, 2012), 15.
47 David Perry, *Leading from Behind Is Still Leading* (Ottawa: CDAI, 2012).
48 David P. Auerswald and Stephen M. Saideman, *NATO in Afghanistan* (Princeton: Princeton University Press, 2014), 206.
49 Rick Hillier, interview on CTV *Power Play*, 23 September 2013.
50 David Pugliese, "Defence Minister Nicholson's office defends spending cuts," *Ottawa Citizen*, 10 June 2014, http://ottawacitizen.com/news/national/defence-watch/defence-minister-nicholsons-office-defends-spending-cuts-military-leaders-warn-cuts-having-long-term-impact.
51 NATO, Wales Summit Declaration, September 2014, http://www.nato.int/cps/en/natohq/official_texts_112964.htm.
52 Peter Weltman, *Fiscal Sustainability of Canada's National Defence Program* (Ottawa: Office of the Parliamentary Budget Officer, 2015).
53 Perry, *Defence Budget 2015*.
54 Sloan, *Something Has to Give*.
55 Kim Richard Nossal, "Late learners: The F-35 and Lessons from the New Fighter Aircraft Program," *International Journal* 68, 1 (2012–13): 178.
56 Daniel Leblanc, "Ottawa rewrites fighter jet plan with upgrades to extend CF-18 lifespan," *Globe and Mail*, 5 March 2013, http://www.theglobeandmail.com/news/politics/ottawa-rewrites-fighter-jet-plan-with-upgrades-to-extend-cf-18-lifespan/article9293289/; Steven Chase, "Ottawa to put fighter jet purchase on hold," *Globe and Mail*, 26 June 2014, http://www.theglobeandmail.com/news/politics/ottawa-to-put-hold-on-jet-fighter-purchase/article19346094/.
57 Public Works and Government Services Canada, "Defence Procurement Strategy," modified 2 December 2015, http://www.tpsgc-pwgsc.gc.ca/app-acq/amd-dp/samd-dps/index-eng.html.
58 Perry, *Doing Less with Less*, Department of National Defence, *Access to Information Request A-2015-00407* (Ottawa: 2015).

59 Philippe Lagassé, *Recapitalizing the Canadian Forces' Major Fleets* (Calgary: Canadian International Council [CIC] and CDFAI, 2012).
60 Daniel Leblanc and Kim Mackrael, "Conservative majority approves combat mission in Iraq," *Globe and Mail*, 7 October 2014, http://www.theglobeandmail.com/news/politics/house-votes-to-join-us-led-combat-mission-in-iraq/article20960695/.
61 Matthew Fisher, "'Openness' over combat with ISIS bites Harper government," *National Post*, 29 January 2015, http://news.nationalpost.com/full-comment/matthew-fisher-openness-over-combat-with-isis-bites-harper-government.
62 Justin Massie and Stéphane Roussel, "The twilight of internationalism? Neocontinentalism as an emerging dominant idea in Canadian foreign policy," in Heather A. Smith and Claire Turenne Sjolander, eds., *Canada in the World: Internationalism in Canadian Foreign Policy* (Don Mills, ON: Oxford University Press, 2013), 36–52.
63 Bill Curry, "Tories to campaign on security, economy, says finance minister," *Globe and Mail*, 6 March 2015, http://www.theglobeandmail.com/news/politics/conservatives-to-campaign-on-security-and-economy-finance-minister-says/article23332421/.
64 John Ivison, "Tories open about Iraq mission because the majority of people actually support it," *National Post*, 29 January 2015, http://news.nationalpost.com/full-comment/john-ivison-tories-open-about-iraq-mission-because-the-majority-of-people-actually-support-it.
65 Adam Chapnick, "A diplomatic counter-revolution: Conservative foreign policy, 2006-2011," *International Journal* 67, 1 (2011–12): 148.
66 Kim Richard Nossal, Stéphane Roussel, and Stéphane Paquin, *International Policy and Politics in Canada* (Toronto: Pearson, 2011), 172.
67 "For the record: Stephen Harper toasts Peter MacKay," *Macleans.ca*, 29 May 2015, http://www.macleans.ca/politics/for-the-record-stephen-harper-toasts-peter-mackay/.
68 Chapnick, "Diplomatic counter-revolution," 137–54.

6
Stephen Harper's Israel Policy

ADAM CHAPNICK

> I think Canada's an even better friend of Israel than we are.
> – YUVAL STEINITZ, ISRAEL'S MINISTER OF FINANCE, 2012[1]

As one former adviser to Prime Minister Stephen Harper noted, support for Israel was a "bedrock principle" of "the Harper Doctrine of Foreign Affairs."[2] Analysts disagree, however, on the impetus for that support. According to John English (Chapter 2, this volume), for example, Israel policy under the Harper government must be viewed through a political lens.[3] Efforts to discredit the Liberal Party's alleged support for the Jewish state during the 2004 and 2006 elections, similar accusations during a November 2009 House of Commons debate, and a 2014 fundraising campaign called *Stand with Israel* all indicate that the Conservatives pursued a politically divisive pro-Israel strategy since even before they formed their first minority government in 2006.[4] Moreover, from January 2006 onwards, they governed, in the words of one critic, like "a minority in attitude."[5]

Others dispute the claim that what some call diaspora politics drove the Harper government's thinking about Israel.[6] "There are dangers," warn scholars Brent Sasley and Tami Jacoby in their analysis of Canada's Arab and Jewish communities, in ascribing "more power to ethnic groups than they have in reality."[7] Consider also the words of the most outspoken pro-Israel foreign minister of the Harper era, John Baird (2011–15). To him, it was "a mistake to say that we are taking this position [on Israel] because of a diaspora or a community within Canada ... If you were to make a political calculus, will this get you more or less votes, if you look at my own constituency, we have 2,800 Jews. We also have 11,500 Muslims and Arabs."[8] Both Baird and his longest-serving predecessor, Lawrence Cannon (2008–11), framed support for Israel in the language of *Conservative* values, or principles: "Canada stands for what is right and good in the world," notes the governor general in the 2013 Speech from the Throne: "Our government defends Israel's right to exist as a Jewish state, the lone outpost of freedom and democracy in a dangerous region."[9] Returning to the fundamental question posed by *The Harper Era*, if the Harper government's Israel policy was principled, then the number of seats the Conservatives held in the House of Commons should never have affected Ottawa's thinking.

But just as the "minority in attitude" theory cannot entirely reconcile the Harper government's apparent disregard for Canada's fast-growing Muslim population,[10] there are also problems with the party values-based interpretation. As another contributor to this volume, Lee Berthiaume, once pointed out, if the Conservatives were genuinely motivated to support Israel, or the Israeli government more specifically, on principle, then their decision in 2010 to defy Israeli pleas not to redirect $15 million in annual funding away from the United Nations Relief and Works Agency for Palestinian Refugees in the Near East makes little sense.[11]

I therefore begin with an alternative theory: Canadian policy towards Israel between 2006 and 2015 was driven primarily by the *personal* views of Canada's prime minister.[12] The "Harper Doctrine" was based, in part, on a belief that previous governments had wrongly "gone along to get along" with Israel's critics on the world stage and, in part, on a visceral feeling that dogmatically supporting what he himself considered to be Israeli interests was simply the right thing to do: regardless of its political cost, irrespective of the number of Conservative members of Parliament seated in the House of Commons, and even sometimes without consideration for the expressed concerns of Israelis themselves. A review of Canada's Israel policy during the Harper era also indicates, however, that there were limits to the prime minister's direct influence. When he was not the primary actor, a variety of factors – including the political composition of Parliament – appears to have affected Ottawa's position. As a result, my answer to this book's central question is: it depends. When Stephen Harper determined Canadian policy towards Israel directly, as he did at the United Nations, his government's standing in the House of Commons was immaterial. When his control was constrained, as it was in response to the Israeli-Palestinian conflict, the impact of his government's political strength is less certain. And on those operational-level issues that were concerned primarily with incremental changes to the Canada-Israel relationship, like the pace of bilateral negotiations, the government's minority or majority standing played a significant role. In short, the impact of the Conservative Party's standing in the House of Commons on Canada's policy towards Israel varied depending on the extent of the prime minister's direct engagement in the specific issue under consideration.

Conservative Support for Israel: It's All about Stephen Harper
The journalist John Ibbitson suggests that Stephen Harper's "support for Israel emerged when he was a teenager and has never wavered. For Harper, Israel is a democratic Western state struggling for survival in a region of hostile and often unsavory regimes, in a world where anti-Semitism remains rife."[13] This view of Israel as personal to the prime minister has been echoed by select academics,[14] journalists at home and abroad,[15] and some fellow Conservatives.[16] Most revealing among the latter group is one witness's account of the prime minister's address to his caucus in the aftermath of the evacuation of Canadians from Lebanon in 2006. Harper made clear, Bruce Carson recalls, that it was up to Canada "to take a stand against ... the destruction of Israel." "Quite frankly," he added, "I don't believe Harper cared whether or not caucus members supported his view. This was the way it was going to be, and if you didn't like it, shut up or leave."[17]

Two years later, Foreign Minister Lawrence Cannon made a comment while accepting an international leadership award on the prime minister's behalf that was, in retrospect, revealing. "*As Prime Minister Harper reminds all of us in his cabinet,*" he said, "our position in the Middle East is not balanced – it is fair and principled."[18] That reminder might well have referred to an intervention by the Prime Minister's Office in 2006, after one of Cannon's predecessors, Peter MacKay, appeared to have (perhaps inadvertently) softened Canadian policy towards Hamas.[19] Ironically, in 2010, it appears that Cannon himself had to be reminded. Immediately after he condemned an Israeli decision to build sixteen hundred new apartments on disputed territory in East Jerusalem as "an obstacle to the prospects for peace,"[20] the PMO reframed the Canadian position in more supportive terms. The minister later issued his own statement of clarification.[21]

Contrast this official response – and the earlier reaction to MacKay's musings – with the PMO's support of one of Cannon's junior ministers, also in 2010. When Peter Kent rashly announced that "an attack on Israel would be considered an attack on Canada," a policy that could have potentially obligated the CAF to respond directly to the regular and indiscriminate barrage of Hamas rockets over southern Israel, the PMO merely noted that Kent's views reflected those of the prime minister.[22]

When John Baird succeeded Cannon as foreign minister, he, too, affirmed that, under Stephen Harper, Canada's support for Israel was not up for debate. "Not under this Prime Minister's watch," were his words.[23] And when Baird sparked outrage across the Arab world for lunching with an Israeli cabinet minister in the disputed territory of East Jerusalem,[24] the PMO refused to apologize.

Prime Minister Harper's own comments are similarly revealing.[25] Consider this statement to the Ottawa Conference on Combatting Anti-Semitism in November 2010:

> And I know, by the way, because I have the bruises to show for it, that whether it is at the United Nations, or any other international forum, the easy thing to do is simply to just get along and go along with this anti-Israel rhetoric, to pretend it is just being even-handed, and to excuse oneself with the label of "honest broker." There are, after all, a lot more votes, a lot more, in being anti-Israel than in taking a stand. But, as long as I am Prime Minister, whether it is at the UN or the Francophonie or anywhere else, Canada will take that stand, whatever the cost. And friends, I say this not just because it is the right thing to do, but because history shows us, and the ideology of the anti-Israel mob tells us all too well if we listen to it, that those who threaten the existence of the Jewish people are a threat to all of us.[26]

With Stephen Harper in charge, there was only one way to deal with Israel. Those who sympathized with his thinking, like Peter Kent or John Baird, could speak on Canada's behalf relatively freely. The rest would be corrected or ignored.

Canada and Israel at the United Nations

Like any Canadian prime minister of recent vintage, Stephen Harper exerted his greatest influence over Canada's Israel policy at the United Nations.[27] Under the Harper Conservatives, between 2006 and 2015 Canada stood by

Israel at the UN virtually unconditionally and irrespective of the views of Canadian allies, of Conservative Party members, and of the government's position in the House of Commons.

Journalists first noted the personal impact of the prime minister on a change in Canada's voting pattern at the UN Economic and Social Council in March 2006. Rather than continuing to abstain on a resolution that called on Israel to allow select Palestinian refugees to return to their homes, Canada stood alone beside the United States in opposition.[28] Two years later, the Senate Standing Committee on Human Rights, chaired by Conservative senator Raynell Andreychuk, acknowledged the deep politicization of another UN body, the Human Rights Council, but nonetheless concluded that, while "adopting honest opinions is a positive approach, ... Canada's need to use the Council as a vehicle for promoting human rights should not be lost in this balance. Canada ... should not become known as a state that is never willing to negotiate."[29] Nonetheless, hardly six months after the report was submitted, Canada stood alone at the Human Rights Council in opposition to a one-sided resolution condemning Israeli military activities in Gaza. Moreover, it even insisted on a recorded vote to shame fellow council members who might have contemplated supporting it.[30]

By August 2009, Canada had changed its vote on nine other UN General Assembly (UNGA) resolutions.[31] The trend continued once the Harper government acquired its majority. In November 2011, Ottawa opposed the Palestinian state's application for membership in the United Nations Educational, Scientific and Cultural Organization.[32] The following year, in spite of warnings that Canada's outspokenness was compromising its capacity to effect change among Israel's Arab neighbours, Minister Baird travelled to New York to personally oppose (unsuccessfully) a UNGA resolution to grant the Palestinians non-member observer status.[33] Along with the United States, Canada later refused to attend a conference in Geneva that criticized Israel's settlements policy and lobbied the UN Security Council at the end of the year to refuse to recognize Palestinian statehood without the concurrence of Israel.[34] Finally, in 2015, Canada opposed Palestinian accession to fifteen UN conventions and protocols as well as a UNGA resolution to allow the Palestinian flag to be raised at the UN's headquarters in New York.[35] In summary, between 2006 and 2015, Stephen Harper exercised direct control over Canada's voting patterns at the UN: support for Israel was unconditional, no matter the government's standing in the House of Commons.

Canada and Israel-Palestine

Canada's position on the Israel-Palestinian conflict under the Harper Conservatives is less clear-cut, and the impact, or lack thereof, of minority or majority governments is therefore inconclusive. Officially, what Ottawa calls *Canadian Policy on Key Issues in the Israeli-Palestinian Conflict* did not change substantively between 2006 and 2015. While Canada supported "Israel's right to live in peace with its neighbours within secure boundaries and recognize[d] Israel's right to assure its own security," it continued to affirm: "Israeli settlements in the occupied territories are a violation of the Fourth Geneva Convention [and] ... a serious obstacle to achieving a comprehensive, just and lasting peace."[36] Since, apart from a modest aid program to support the Palestinian people and some conditional aid to the Palestinian Authority to develop its security and governance capacity, Canada has hardly been a player in recent iterations of the Middle East peace process, it is difficult to assess the implementation of Canadian policy beyond the rhetoric of government representatives.[37] That rhetoric reveals remarkable consistency in the unflinching support of the prime minister and his foreign minister during the majority years, but it indicates that there was significantly less before then. It is tempting to suggest that the Conservatives' standing in the House of Commons must have been critical to the shift, but it is equally plausible that John Baird's personal views on Israel, and his less diplomatic approach to expressing them, were simply more in line with those of Stephen Harper than were those of his predecessors.[38]

During the minority years, Conservative ministers were much more critical of Israel in public than was their leader. Prime Minister Harper has never expressed Canada's concern over the implications of Israel's West Bank barrier, for example, but Minister MacKay did in 2007. In March 2008, it was Foreign Minister Maxime Bernier who criticized an Israeli attack on Gaza that killed 120, while the prime minister remained silent.[39] Although his prime minister did not, Lawrence Cannon expressed Canada's "strong sympathy for the predicament of innocent Palestinians in the Gaza Strip" when Israel restricted the delivery of aid to the region in 2008.[40] In 2009, when Israel announced a ten-month moratorium on settlements in the West Bank, Cannon alone indicated that it fell "short of what Canada and the international community have called for and will continue to call for."[41] In 2010, again it was Cannon, and never Harper, who expressed "Canada's concern regarding the planned expansion of Israeli settlements in East Jerusalem." "This announcement," he said, "does not advance the cause of peace in the region."[42] Indeed, when the prime minister was asked to reiterate Cannon's criticism of Israel in the House of Commons, he answered merely: "Our position on this issue is well known."[43]

In May 2011, now with a majority, Prime Minister Harper stood alone among his G8 allies in refusing to countenance an American proposal to restart Israeli-Palestinian peace negotiations on the basis of Israel's pre-1967 borders – an approach that would have been in line with official Canadian policy.[44] But this time there was greater synchronicity with the comments coming out of DFAIT. "One of the things we haven't done," the new minister, John Baird, later said, "we don't jump on the pile-on on Israel... which seems to go on, on a daily basis."[45] Throughout Baird's term, both he and the prime minister "deflected" when called upon to denounce the Israeli settlements.[46] As Harper said in his address to the Israeli Knesset, the third tenet of Canada's Israel policy under his leadership was: "we refuse to single out Israel for criticism on the international stage."[47] Even when, by the end of 2014, Palestinian leaders were questioning the Canadian prime minister's commitment to his own official policy, Harper demurred.[48]

The impact of the Conservative government's standing in the House of Commons on Israel-Palestine is therefore difficult to ascertain. At one level, Canada's official policy never changed, making the shift from minority to majority irrelevant. But the coherent allegiance of government spokespeople to that policy certainly did. Between 2006 and 2011, the rhetoric of Canada's ministers of foreign affairs was more balanced than was that of the prime minister. Post-majority, the rhetoric lined up more consistently; whether it was the new government or the new minister who made the difference, however (and whether Minister Baird was appointed because of his views on Israel or simply because Lawrence Cannon was not re-elected), is unclear.

Canada-Israel Bilateral Relations

Although it was covered extensively in the media, Israel was never the prime minister's only international concern, and the day-to-day bilateral relationship was generally outside of his immediate control. It follows that, in spite of concerted, and ultimately successful, efforts in Ottawa to expand Canadian-Israeli relations, the pace of that expansion was hardly as steady as Prime Minister Harper might have preferred. Between 2006 and 2011, Conservative efforts to increase social, economic, and military ties with Israel were unremarkable. Indeed, the level of ambition evident in the bilateral negotiations merely reflected the interests and opportunities created by the twenty thousand Canadians living in Israel and the 350,000 Jews living in Canada, many of whom retain strong personal and professional ties to Jerusalem and Tel Aviv.[49] The 2008 Declaration of Intent to enhance cooperation in the area of public safety, the deployment of leased Israeli drones to Afghanistan in 2009, and even exploratory talks launched in 2010 to expand the 1997 Canada-Israel Free Trade Agreement did little more than extend previous (Liberal) initiatives.[50]

Between 2011 and 2015, however, bilateral engagement increased to an unprecedented extent, reflective of seemingly continuous face-to-face meetings between Canadian Cabinet ministers and their Israeli counterparts. The 2008 Declaration of Intent became the Customs Mutual Assistance Agreement in December 2011, which established the necessary legal framework to deter and manage customs offences.[51] A similar memorandum of understanding signed between the Canadian and Israeli defence ministers in early 2011 led to the appointment of the first Israeli defence attaché to Ottawa in March 2012.[52] The Mutual Recognition Agreement in Telecommunications was finalized in June 2012, and the Canada-Israel Energy Science and Technology Fund was announced that October.[53] The Canadian and Israeli international development agencies signed yet another memorandum of understanding in December 2012.[54]

Canada identified Israel as a priority market in the Conservative government's 2013 *Global Markets Action Plan*, and, in January 2014, prime ministers Harper and Netanyahu launched negotiations to expand and modernize the Canada-Israel Free Trade Agreement.[55] Their announcement – which coincided with the Canadian leader's first, and only, visit to Israel and the Middle East – was followed immediately by the signing of the Canada-Israel Strategic Partnership Memorandum of Understanding, which touched on "energy, security, international aid and development, innovation, and the promotion of human rights globally."[56] That agreement, blessed as it was with the prime minister's personal approval, set the stage for a flurry of additional announcements over the next eighteen months. In March 2014, Canada and Israel agreed to work together under the framework of the Global Initiative to Combat Nuclear Terrorism.[57] In September, Canada's minister of public safety and Israel's minister of finance signed a declaration of intent to expand the Customs Mutual Assistance Agreement into a mutual recognition arrangement similar to those Canada had signed with the United States, Japan, South Korea, and Singapore.[58] In January 2015, Minister Baird and his Israeli counterpart, Avigdor Lieberman, signed a series of joint declarations and memoranda of understanding that, among other things, added Israel to Canada's Automatic Firearms Country Control List.[59] That June, the Canadian and Israeli governments announced a new $35 million Canada-Israel health research program to promote advancements in the neurosciences.[60] Finally, in July 2015, the Harper government released the text of the Canada-Israel Modernized Free Trade Agreement.[61]

That virtually all of these agreements were signed or announced by ministers, and not Prime Minister Harper himself, is critical to understanding the change of pace. Between 2006 and 2011, the government's minority status made each vote in the House critical. Ministers' foreign travel was therefore severely restricted.[62] The combination of the need for new negotiations to germinate and the inability of Canada's political representatives to leave Ottawa to facilitate or conclude the discussions inhibited rapid progress. Once the Conservatives secured a majority, however, members of the Cabinet travelled more freely, and the results followed. In summary, Stephen Harper set the tone for Canada-Israel bilateral relations at the strategic level, but he was hardly the main player operationally. As a result, the government's standing in the House of Commons played a significant role in Ottawa's efforts to promote closer bilateral cooperation.

Conclusion

In conclusion, there can be no denying that the Canada-Israel relationship grew closer under the Harper Conservatives between 2006 and 2015. The impact of the Canadian government's standing in the House of Commons on that growth, however, is less consistently clear. Canada's UN policy towards Israel appears to have been crafted by the prime minister with little regard for his electoral strength. Ottawa's response to Israeli-Palestinian conflicts did differ pre- and post-majority, but a number of factors could explain the change. Only when it comes to efforts to promote greater bilateral integration does it appear that the government's standing in the House was critical.

Notes

1 Quoted in Patrick Martin, "Baird sticks to party line – Israel's Likud party," *Globe and Mail*, 3 February 2012, http://www.theglobeandmail.com/news/world/baird sticks-to-party-line%E2%80%93israels-likud-party/article547279/.
2 Bruce Carson, *14 Days: Making the Conservative Movement in Canada* (Montreal and Kingston: McGill-Queen's University Press, 2014), 283. David Mulroney, the former foreign and defence policy adviser to the prime minister, called support for

Israel "a core interest." See his *Middle Power, Middle Kingdom: What Canadians Need to Know about China in the 21st Century* (Toronto: Allen Lane, 2015), 20.

3 See also Kim Richard Nossal, "*Primat der Wahlurne*: Explaining Stephen Harper's foreign policy," paper presented at the annual meeting of the International Studies Association, Toronto, 29 March 2014, 16; Donald Barry, "Canada and the Middle East today: Electoral politics and foreign policy," *Arab Studies Quarterly* 32, 4 (2010): 210; Jonathan Kay, "On stage at Zionism's Super Bowl," *thewalrus.ca*, March 2015; Paul Wells, *The Longer I'm Prime Minister: Stephen Harper and Canada, 2006–* (Toronto: Random House Canada, 2013), especially 57–60. Some analysts make explicit reference to Conservative efforts to court evangelical Christians through their support for Israel. See, for example, Marci McDonald, *The Armageddon Factor: The Rise of Christian Nationalism in Canada* (Toronto: Random House Canada, 2010), 11, 323; and David Rayside, "The Conservative Party of Canada and its religious constituencies," in David Rayside and Clyde Wilcox, eds., *Faith, Politics, and Sexual Diversity in Canada and the United States* (Vancouver: UBC Press, 2011), 279–99.

4 See Canada, House of Commons, *Debates*, 40th Parliament, 2nd session, 19 November 2009, http://www.parl.gc.ca/HousePublications/Publication.aspx?DocId=4240805&Language=E&Mode=1, specifically comments from Candice Hoeppner, Lois Brown, and the response by Irwin Cotler; Conservative Party of Canada (CPC), *Through Fire and Water*, YouTube video, 16 July 2014, https://www.youtube.com/watch?v=hq8MN0OBEO4. The *Stand with Israel Campaign* was also linked to the CPC Facebook page on the same day, https://www.facebook.com/cpcpcc?fref=nf.

5 Joe Clark, *How We Lead: Canada in a Century of Change* (Toronto: Random House of Canada, 2013), 103.

6 See, for example, Mark Gollom, "Harper's support for Israel: Political, philosophical or both? Personal convictions intersect with political advantage," *cbc.ca*, 7 December 2012, http://www.cbc.ca/news/canada/harper-s-support-for-israel-political-philosophical-or-both-1.1206070.

7 Brent E. Sasley and Tami Amanda Jacoby, "Canada's Jewish and Arab communities and Canadian foreign policy," in Paul Heinbecker and Bessma Momani, eds., *Canada and the Middle East: In Theory and Practice* (Waterloo: Wilfrid Laurier University Press, 2007), 200.

8 "Q&A: A conversation with John Baird," *Policy Magazine* 2, 1 (2014): 5. See also Martin, "Baird sticks to party line."

9 Government of Canada, *Speech from the Throne: Seizing Canada's Opportunity – Prosperity and Opportunity in an Uncertain World*, 16 October 2013, http://www.lop.parl.gc.ca/ParlInfo/Documents/ThroneSpeech/41-2-e.html. See also Government of Canada, "Address by Minister Cannon on behalf of Prime Minister Harper in acceptance of international leadership award," 4 December 2008, http://news.gc.ca/web/article-en.do?crtr.sj1D=&mthd=advSrch&crtr.mnthndVl=&nid=509959&crtr.dpt1D=&crtr.tp1D=&crtr.lc1D=&crtr.yrStrtVl=&crtr.kw=gaza&crtr.dyStrtVl=&crtr.aud1D=&crtr.mnthStrtVl=&crtr.yrndVl=&crtr.dyndVl=&wbdisable=true; Government of Canada, "Address by Minster Baird to the 12th annual Herzliya conference," 30 January 2012, http://www.international.gc.ca/media/aff/speeches-discours/2012/01/30a.aspx?lang=eng; Government of Canada, "Address by Minister Baird to

the American Jewish Committee," 3 May 2012, http://www.international.gc.ca/media/aff/speeches-discours/2012/05/03a.aspx?lang=eng; and Lee Berthiaume, "Canada is not a referee in the world, John Baird says," *canada.com*, 21 December 2012, http://o.canada.com/news/national/canada-is-not-a-referee-in-the-world-john-baird-says.

10 Statistics Canada, "Immigrants by major religious denominations and period of immigration, Canada, 2001," http://www12.statcan.gc.ca/english/census01/Products/Analytic/companion/rel/tables/canada/cdaimm.cfm.

11 Lee Berthiaume, "Israel urged Canadian government not to cut aid to Palestinians over UN vote: Documents," *National Post*, 9 July 2013, http://news.nationalpost.com/news/canada/israel-urged-canadian-government-not-to-cut-aid-to-palestinians-over-un-vote-documents.

12 My definition of Canadian policy towards Israel is deliberately narrow. It excludes, for example, the defunding of KAIROS and relations with Iran, both of which other analysts have linked to the Harper Doctrine. On KAIROS, see Paul Gecelovsky, "The prime minister and the parable: Stephen Harper and personal responsibility internationalism," in Heather A. Smith and Claire Turenne Sjolander, eds., *Canada in the World: Internationalism in Canadian Foreign Policy* (Don Mills, ON: Oxford University Press, 2013), 118. On Iran, see Reuters, Associated Press, and Barak Ravid, "Canada closes Iran embassy, says Tehran 'most significant threat' to world peace," *Haaretz*, 7 September 2012, http://www.haaretz.com/middle-east-news/canada-closes-iran-embassy-says-tehran-most-significant-threat-to-world-peace-1.463477.

13 John Ibbitson, "The big break: The Conservative transformation of Canada's foreign policy," *CIGI Papers* 29 (April 2014): 7. See also John Ibbitson, *Stephen Harper* (Toronto: McClelland and Stewart, 2015), 12.

14 Gecelovsky, "The prime minister and the parable," in Smith and Sjolander, *Canada in the World*, 117.

15 Mark Kennedy, "Stephen Harper's rigid support for Israel based on idea 'foreign affairs should be fought on moral grounds,'" *National Post*, 4 August 2014, http://news.nationalpost.com/news/canada/stephen-harpers-rigid-support-for-israel-based-on-idea-foreign-affairs-should-be-fought-on-moral-grounds; Michael Blanchfield, "Odd man out: How Stephen Harper changed Canada's relations with the United Nations" (Master of Journalism thesis, Carleton University, 2015); "Canada and Israel: Unlikely allies," *Economist*, 27 May 2010, http://www.economist.com/node/16231462.

16 Ezra Levant, "Stephen Harper and Israel: Not crass political calculation," *Toronto Star*, 29 May 2009, http://www.thestar.com/news/canada/2009/05/29/stephen_harper_and_israel_not_crass_political_calculation.html.

17 Carson, *14 Days*, 214.

18 Government of Canada, "Address by Minister Cannon on behalf of Prime Minister Harper in acceptance of international leadership award," emphasis added.

19 Jeff Sallot, "MacKay retreats on money for Hamas," *Globe and Mail*, 8 March 2006, http://www.theglobeandmail.com/news/national/mackay-retreats-on-money-for-hamas/article704419/; Jeff Sallot, "Canada vetoes key UN resolution on refugees," *Globe and Mail*, 11 March 2006, http://www.theglobeandmail.com/news/national/canada-vetoes-key-un-motion-on-refugees/article704765/; Barry, "Canada and the Middle East today," 198.

20 Government of Canada, "Canada concerned by settlement expansion in East Jerusalem," news release, 11 March 2010, http://news.gc.ca/web/article-en.do?m=/index&nid=517899.
21 Gollom, "Harper's support for Israel"; CBC, "Cannon condemns Israel's new settlement plan," cbc.ca, 16 March 2010, http://www.cbc.ca/news/politics/cannon-condemns-israel-s-new-settlement-plan-1.964652. See also Campbell Clark, "Baird was the man who finally put Harper's tone into Canadian diplomacy," Globe and Mail, 3 February 2015, http://www.theglobeandmail.com/try-it-now/try-it-now-politics-insider/?contentRedirect=true&articleId=22756283.
22 Stephen Chase, "An attack on Israel would be considered an attack on Canada," Globe and Mail, 16 February 2010, http://www.theglobeandmail.com/news/politics/attack-on-israel-is-an-attack-on-canada-kent-says/article1365208/.
23 John Baird, "John Baird: Why Israel holds such a special place in my heart," National Post, 20 November 2012, http://news.nationalpost.com/full-comment/john-baird-why-israel-holds-such-a-special-place-in-my-heart.
24 A move that ultimately led to a failed, but still time-consuming, Qatari effort to move the International Civil Aviation Association from Montreal to Doha. See Michael Bell, "Canada now paying the price for Baird's misstep into East Jerusalem," Globe and Mail, 6 May 2013, http://www.theglobeandmail.com/globe-debate/canada-now-paying-the-price-for-bairds-misstep-into-east-jerusalem/article11730522/; Campbell Clark, "Disgruntled Arab states look to strip Canada of UN agency," Globe and Mail, 2 May 2013, http://www.theglobeandmail.com/news/world/disgruntled-arab-states-look-to-strip-canada-of-un-agency/article11672346/.
25 See, for example, Stephen Harper, "Speech to B'Nai Brith at the Award of Merit Dinner," 18 October 2006, cited at http://nhop.ca/prime-ministers-speech-on-anti-semitism/. See also Government of Canada, "Prime Minister's speech for Israel's 60th anniversary," 8 May 2008; Government of Canada, "PM addresses the 5th Action Party of the Canadian Jewish Political Affairs Committee," 11 March 2011; Government of Canada, "PM addresses the Knesset in Jerusalem," 20 January 2014, cited at https://www.youtube.com/watch?v=Nu6UKBotdTE.
26 Government of Canada, "Statement by the prime minister of Canada at the Ottawa Conference on Combatting anti-Semitism," 8 November 2010, cited at http://nhop.ca/prime-ministers-speech-on-anti-semitism/.
27 In 2012, a document outlining Canada's official attitude towards Israel in "Multilateral Fora" – released by the Prime Minister's Office on the occasion of a visit to Canada by Israel's prime minister, Benjamin Netanyahu – was even updated to refer to "*Prime Minister Harper's* [italics added] strong stance against anti-Semitism." See Government of Canada, "Canada-Israel relations," 2 March 2012.
28 Sallot, "Canada vetoes key UN resolution on refugees."
29 Canada, Standing Senate Committee on Human Rights, Canada and the United Nations Human Rights Council: A Time for Serious Re-Evaluation (June 2008), http://www.parl.gc.ca/Content/SEN/Committee/392/huma/rep/rep13jun08-e.pdf.
30 Campbell Clark, "Canada votes against resolution," Globe and Mail, 13 January 2009, http://www.theglobeandmail.com/news/world/canada-votes-against-resolution/

article1151902/. The Japanese, South Korean, and European members of the council ultimately abstained.
31 Canadians for Justice and Peace in the Middle East, *Meeting the Challenge: A CJPME Proposal for Canada's Middle East Policy*, August 2009.
32 Government of Canada, "Canada's position on Middle East resolutions at the United Nations," 10 November 2011, http://www.international.gc.ca/media/aff/news-communiques/2011/342.aspx?lang=eng. See also Campbell Clark, "Canada protests one-sided resolutions with pro-Israel stand at UN," *Globe and Mail*, 10 November 2011, http://www.theglobeandmail.com/news/politics/canada-protests-one-sided-resolutions-with-pro-israel-stand-at-un/article4181837/; and Campbell Clark, "Canada to keep, but not hike, current UNESCO funding," *Globe and Mail*, 1 November 2011, http://www.theglobeandmail.com/news/politics/canada-to-keep-but-not-hike-current-unesco-funding/article4250681/.
33 Government of Canada, "Address by Minister Baird to United Nations General Assembly in opposition to Palestinian bid for non-member observer state status," 29 November 2012, http://www.international.gc.ca/media/aff/speeches-discours/2012/11/29a.aspx?lang=eng. On the warnings, see Campbell Clark and Patrick Martin, "Palestinians paint Canada as too extreme," *Globe and Mail*, 30 November 2012, http://www.theglobeandmail.com/news/world/palestinians-paint-canada-as-too-extreme/article5884121/.
34 Department of Foreign Affairs, Trade and Development Canada (DFATD), "Canada strongly opposes decision to convene anti-Israel conference in Geneva," news release, 16 December 2014, http://www.international.gc.ca/media/aff/news-communiques/2014/12/16b.aspx?lang=eng; Government of Canada, "Baird calls on Security Council to reject unilateral statehood bid," statement by the minister of foreign affairs, 30 December 2014, http://www.international.gc.ca/media/aff/news-communiques/2014/12/30b.aspx?lang=eng.
35 Mike Blanchfield, "Canada opposes 15 Palestinian attempts to join United Nations treaties," *Huffington Post*, 16 February 2015, http://www.huffingtonpost.ca/2015/02/16/canada-palestinian-united-nations_n_6690662.html; Associated Press, "Canada among small group of countries to oppose Palestinian flag at UN," cbc.ca, 11 September 2015, http://www.cbc.ca/news/world/palestine-flag-un-headquarters-canada-vote-1.3223774. For a general statement of Canada's voting policy, see Government of Canada, *Canadian Policy on Key Issues in the Israeli-Palestinian Conflict*, Global Affairs Canada website, last modified 24 June 2015, http://www.international.gc.ca/name-anmo/peace_process-processus_paix/canadian_policy-politique_canadienne.aspx?lang=eng.
36 Government of Canada, *Canadian Policy on Key Issues in the Israeli-Palestinian Conflict*; see also Tom Blackwell, "Conservatives have given Canada a voice in Israeli-Palestinian conflict but are we still seen as 'honest broker'?" *National Post*, 31 May 2013, http://news.nationalpost.com/news/canada/conservatives-have-given-canada-a-voice-in-israeli-palestinian-conflict-but-are-we-still-seen-as-an-honest-broker.
37 In 2014, Campbell Clark did observe that Canadian aid policy in the Middle East was evolving to reflect Prime Minister Harper's values and his understanding of the region. See Campbell Clark, "Harper sees light in Israel, amid darkness," *Globe and*

Mail, 24 January 2014, http://www.theglobeandmail.com/news/politics/harper-sees-israel-as-light-amid-darkness/article16503424/.
38 On Baird's personal views, see, among others, John Baird, "John Baird."
39 Josh Mitnick, "MacKay dodges questions on refugee issue," *Toronto Star*, 22 January 2007, http://www.thestar.com/news/2007/01/22/mackay_dodges_questions_on_refugee_issue.html; Barry, "Canada and the Middle East today," 206.
40 Government of Canada, "Statement by Minister Cannon on the situation in Israel and the Gaza Strip," 27 December 2008.
41 Government of Canada, "Canada calls for resumption of Middle East negotiations," statement by the minister of foreign affairs, 27 November 2009, http://www.international.gc.ca/media/aff/news-communiques/2009/361.aspx?lang=eng.
42 Government of Canada, "Canada concerned by settlement expansion in East Jerusalem," news release, 11 March 2010, http://news.gc.ca/web/article-en.do?m=/index&nid=517899. See also Government of Canada, "Address by Minister Cannon to Diplomatic Forum," 6 October 2010, http://www.canadainternational.gc.ca/west_bank_gaza-cisjordanie_bande_de_gaza/highlights-faits/2010-78.aspx?lang=en.
43 Harper, quoted in CBC, "Cannon condemns Israel's new settlement plan," *cbc.ca*, 16 March 2010, http://www.cbc.ca/news/politics/cannon-condemns-israel-s-new-settlement-plan-1.964652. See also Canada, House of Commons, Standing Committee on Foreign Affairs and International Trade, *Evidence*, 16 March 2010, http://www.parl.gc.ca/HousePublications/Publication.aspx?Language=E&Mode=2&Parl=40&Ses=3&DocId=4351740&File=0, specifically the dialogue between Cannon and Bob Rae; and Gollom, "Harper's support for Israel."
44 Doug Saunders, "On Israel, Harper stands alone at G8 summit," *Globe and Mail*, 25 May 2011, http://www.theglobeandmail.com/news/politics/on-israel-harper-stands-alone-at-g8-summit/article4263322/; Haaretz Service, "Lieberman thanks Canada PM for objection to 1967 borders at G8," *Haaretz*, 27 May 2011, http://www.haaretz.com/israel-news/lieberman-thanks-canada-pm-for-objection-to-1967-borders-at-g8-1.364502.
45 Baird, quoted in Tonda MacCharles, "Foreign Affairs Minister Baird says Canada's Mid-East position 'very clear,'" *Toronto Star*, 6 December 2012, http://www.thestar.com/news/canada/2012/12/06/foreign_affairs_minister_john_baird_says_canadas_mideast_position_very_clear.html; see also Blackwell, "Conservatives have given Canada a voice."
46 Canadian Press and Mike Blanchfield, "Palestinian minister praises Canada, says he won't be held 'hostage' to past words," *Canadian Press*, 19 September 2013, http://www.570news.com/2013/09/19/palestinian-minister-praises-canada-says-wont-be-hostage-to-past-words/; Mark Kennedy, "Stephen Harper heads to Middle East amid Israeli-Palestinian peace talks," *Postmedia News*, 17 January 2014, https://www.cigionline.org/articles/2014/01/stephen-harper-heads-middle-east-amid-israeli-palestinian-peace-talks.
47 Government of Canada, "PM addresses the Knesset in Jerusalem." It is worth noting that the prime minister apparently pressured Israel on its settlement policy in private. See CTV News, "Canada and Israel differ on settlement issue: Netanyahu," *CTVNews.ca*, 21 January 2014, http://www.ctvnews.ca/politics/canada-and-israel-differ-on-settlement-issue-netanyahu-1.1648442.

48 Mike Blanchfield, "Palestinians tell Canada to back Geneva Conventions' meeting on Israel," *CBC News*, 19 December 2014, http://www.cbc.ca/m/touch/politics/story/1.2879065.
49 For context and details, see Government of Canada, "Canada-Israel relations"; and Rafael Barak, "There is also innovation in Canada-Israel ties," *Hill Times*, 27 October 2014.
50 Government of Canada, "Canada and Israel sign declaration to cooperate on public safety," new release, 23 March 2008, http://news.gc.ca/web/article-en.do?crtr.sj1D=&mthd=advSrch&crtr.mnthndVl=&nid=387249&crtr.dpt1D=&crtr.tp1D=&crtr.lc1D=&crtr.yrStrtVl=2008&crtr.kw=&crtr.dyStrtVl=26&crtr.aud1D=&crtr.mnthStrtVl=2&crtr.yrndVl=&crtr.dyndVl; Jon Elmer, "Israel's new 'best friend'?," *Al Jazeera*, 29 May 2010, http://www.aljazeera.com/focus/2010/05/20105271844398 63164.html; Government of Canada, "Ministerial visit to Israel," news release, 10 October 2010, http://www.international.gc.ca/commerce/visit-visite/israel-2010.aspx?lang=eng. See also CBC News, "MacKay begins Mideast visit to Israel," *cbc.ca*, 10 January 2011, http://www.cbc.ca/news/politics/mackay-begins-mideast-visit-in-israel-1.1048953.
51 Government of Canada, "Canada and Israel sign a Customs Mutual Assistance Agreement," news release, 11 December 2011, http://itrade.gov.il/canada/canada-and-israel-sign-a-customs-mutual-assistance-agreement/.
52 Andy Levy-Ajzenkopf, "Defence chiefs deepened Canada-Israeli relationship," *Canadian Jewish News*, 19 March 2012, http://www.cjnews.com/news/defence-chiefs-deepen-canada-israel-relationship.
53 Government of Canada, "Canada reaffirms special friendship with Israel," news release, 9 April 2013, http://www.international.gc.ca/media/aff/news-communiques/2013/04/9a.aspx?lang=eng.
54 Embassy of Israel, "Canada, Israel sign foreign aid pact," 11 December 2012, http://embassies.gov.il/toronto/NewsAndEvents/Pages/Canada,-Israel-Sign-Foreign-.aspx; Sheldon Kirshner, "Canada and Israel expand relations, "*Canadian Jewish News*, 17 December 2012, http://www.cjnews.com/news/canada-israel-expand-relations.
55 Government of Canada, "Canada-Israel Free Trade Agreement expansion," 21 January 2014, http://news.gc.ca/web/article-en.do?nid=810319.
56 Government of Canada, "Canada and Israel set course for stronger bilateral relations," news release, 21 January 2014, http://news.gc.ca/web/article-en.do?nid=810299.
57 Government of Canada, "Canada and Israel reinforce cooperation on combatting nuclear terrorism," news release, 24 March 2014, http://www.international.gc.ca/media/aff/news-communiques/2014/03/24b.aspx?lang=eng.
58 Government of Canada, "Minister Blaney signals discussion with Israel on Customs Mutual Recognition Arrangement," news release, 16 September 2014, http://news.gc.ca/web/article-en.do?nid=884999&_ga=1.91939295.456584789.1414686468.
59 Government of Canada, "Canada strengthens cooperation with Israel," news release, 18 January 2015, http://www.international.gc.ca/media/aff/news-communiques/2015/01/18b.aspx?lang=eng.
60 Government of Canada, "Canada and Israel team up to explore frontiers of health research," 25 June 2015, http://news.gc.ca/web/article-en.do?nid=991359.

61 Government of Canada, *Canada-Israel Modernized Free Trade Agreement: Bringing the Canada-Israel Economic Partnership into the 21st Century*, July 2015, http://www.international.gc.ca/trade-agreements-accords-commerciaux/agr-acc/israel/canada-israel.aspx?lang=eng.

62 John Ibbitson and Joanna Slater, "Security Council rejection a deep embarrassment for Harper," *Globe and Mail*, 12 October 2010, http://www.theglobeandmail.com/news/politics/security-council-rejection-a-deep-embarrassment-for-harper/article1370239/. My own informal conversations with officials from a number of government departments confirms Ibbitson and Slater's observation of ministers' general fears of travelling abroad during the minority period.

7

Explaining Canada's Foreign Environmental Policies during the Harper Era

MICHAEL W. MANULAK

The Conservative government of Stephen Harper was widely criticized for its environmental record. In addition to developing a more restrictive communications policy for government climatologists, shutting down the National Roundtable on the Environment and the Economy, and pulling out of the United Nations Convention to Combat Desertification, the government won numerous "fossil of the year" awards for its record on climate change mitigation.[1] Under Prime Minister Harper's watch, Canada became the first country to formally withdraw from the Kyoto Protocol and was roundly criticized for its obstructive behaviour in international climate change bargaining.[2] The Harper government did not deliver on long-promised regulations for Canada's oil and gas sector and, according to Environment Canada, did not take sufficient regulatory action to meet the country's emissions reduction targets under the 2009 Copenhagen Accord.[3]

Prominent observers explain Canada's poor climate change mitigation record from 2006 to 2015 by pointing to the personal and ideological commitments of the prime minister. Stephen Harper, the argument goes, was uncomfortable with environmental issues and opposed tough regulatory action on ideological grounds.[4] Other analysts underline the impact of political factors, such as the Conservative Party's Alberta-rich political "base," in shaping Canada's climate change strategies.[5] Are these explanations persuasive? The focus of *The Harper Era* on the impact of government standing in the House of Commons on Canada's international policies provides one means of answering this question. If leading members of the Conservative government had a strong ideological or political interest in resisting cuts to Canada's greenhouse gas (GHG) emissions, then the shift from a minority to a majority government in 2011 might have led to change in Canada's foreign environmental policies. Free of parliamentary constraints, majority governments can craft measures that are closer to their true policy preferences.

I find that Canada's approach to reducing GHG emissions did not change significantly following the 2011 election. The Harper government consistently sought to align its policies with those of the United States and insisted on multilateral agreements that included all major emitters. Indeed, the international incentives facing the government in the period under study made more resolute action on climate change difficult. Factors independent of Canada's political balance therefore played a more important part in climate change policy making than did parliamentary institutions. When it comes to environmental policy, Canada's governments are more reactive to international imperatives and to Canadian resource endowments than many analysts assume.

Canada's Climate Change Mitigation Record

According to a recent Environment Canada *Emission Trends* report, Canada is unlikely to meet its Copenhagen target of reducing emissions by 17 percent below 2005 levels by 2020.[6] Canada's economy-wide emissions in 2005 were 736 megatonnes, implying a 611 megatonne target for 2020. Though Canada did reduce its total emissions by about 5 percent between 2005 and 2015, much of this progress was the result of provincial government measures, such as the closure of Ontario's coal-fired electricity plants.[7] Optimistic projections suggest that Canada may be on pace to reduce its GHG emissions by about 7 percent of 2005 levels by 2020.[8]

The Harper government adopted a sector-by-sector regulatory approach to reducing greenhouse gas emissions, focusing first on Canada's largest sectoral emitters. In the transportation sector, the government aligned its policies with those of the United States. Emissions regulations on heavy-duty vehicles, which came into effect in early 2014, were closely modelled after US regulations.[9] Rules for automobiles and light trucks will ensure that, by 2025, new cars will consume 50 percent less fuel and emit 50 percent less carbon dioxide than comparable 2008 models.[10] Given the highly integrated nature of the Canadian and American auto sectors, regulatory alignment was widely considered to be a practical approach to the issue.

Other regulatory measures were planned for the aviation and shipping sectors. These approaches were developed in multilateral fora, such as the International Civil Aviation Organization and the International Maritime Organization. Planned emission reductions in the transportation sector are expected to reduce Canada's annual emissions by about eighteen megatonnes in 2020.[11]

In June 2010, the government announced its intention to regulate carbon dioxide emissions from coal-fired power plants. Regulations sought to make emission levels from coal comparable to those generated by natural gas electricity facilities.[12] It was anticipated that the proposed regime would reduce annual Canadian emissions by 5.3 megatonnes in 2020. The proposed regulations were, however, watered down considerably. In fact, by making the regulations less stringent and extending the anticipated lifespan of existing plants, the regulations on coal will reduce emissions by about half as much as the government initially outlined.[13] Moreover, some observers argue that, by requiring new plants to meet tougher emission standards, Ottawa provided an incentive for companies to string out the lifespan of older, high polluting plants.[14] In 2020, the measures will contribute to a 0.4 percent reduction in Canada's total emissions, less than 3 percent of the gap between Canada's current emission levels and its Copenhagen target.[15] Complementary regulations were planned for the natural gas sector but were not introduced during the Harper government's tenure.

The government also announced plans to introduce regulations for the oil and gas sector, Canada's fastest-growing source of GHG emissions. According to Environment Canada, the sector is responsible for about one-quarter of Canada's emissions and is projected to contribute two hundred megatonnes to national emissions by 2020.[16] Ottawa missed several self-imposed deadlines for these regulations, even though, according to a report from Canada's commissioner of the environment and sustainable development, regulatory proposals have been available within Environment Canada since at least 2013.[17] It will be extremely difficult for Canada to meet its Copenhagen targets without introducing regulations to limit GHG emissions from oil and gas production. In December 2014, Prime Minister Harper suggested that the government might explore a carbon pricing system similar to that in place in the province of Alberta, but, again, no action was taken before the Conservatives were defeated in the fall 2015 election.[18]

In international negotiations, largely occurring under the auspices of the United Nations Framework Convention on Climate Change (UNFCCC), Canada was widely regarded as an obstructive, hesitant player. Canadian negotiators, to a large extent, aligned Canada's policies with those of the United States and insisted on agreements that were binding on all major emitters. Prior to becoming the first government to formally withdraw from its international commitments under the Kyoto Protocol, Canada's political leaders publicly doubted the efficacy of the agreement and questioned the legitimacy of an accord that did not entail emissions reductions from all of the world's largest polluters.[19] Canada refused to take on binding obligations in the second commitment period of the Kyoto Protocol, and, at a pivotal UNFCCC conference in Durban, South Africa, Canada's rumoured withdrawal from the Kyoto accord was a subject of conversation in the corridors.[20] Canada's environment minister, Peter Kent, drew the ire of leading developing countries, such as India, for his government's sharp criticisms of BASIC countries (Brazil, South Africa, India, and China). Canada's attacks were ironic, noted India's environment minister, Jayanthi Natarajan, in light of the manner in which Ottawa had "junked" the Kyoto treaty.[21]

Judged against its own standards, the Harper government's climate change policies fell short of the mark. Indeed, Ottawa's lack of progress on this file was disappointing, even to prominent members of the Conservative Party itself.[22]

Canada's Climate Change Policies: 2006–11 versus 2011–15

If the climate change policies of the Harper government were motivated by personal, ideological, or political considerations, then it is reasonable to assume that, once it formed a parliamentary majority, the government would be in a better position to implement policies that more closely reflected its true preferences. Indeed, opposition parties spoke frequently of a "hidden" Conservative agenda throughout the early 2000s, claiming that the ideologues in the Conservative Party would not be responsible stewards of the environment. Free of the need to broker support from opposition parties, it was frequently asserted, there would be a dramatic change in Canada's climate change policies. Without parliamentary pressures, regulatory action would not be forthcoming.

If a significant shift in Canada's climate change policies were to have occurred post-majority, one might have expected to see it manifested in either a weakening of the government's regulatory commitments or a retreat from its international obligations. Prima facie, the "hidden agenda" argument seems plausible. The Conservatives did weaken their proposed coal emission rules and did not finalize regulations for the oil and gas sector. Leading government officials made numerous divisive statements on environmental issues between 2011 and 2015 that further suggest a government unafraid of the immediate parliamentary ramifications of its rhetoric.[23] The Conservatives waited until after they had won a majority government to formally withdraw from the Kyoto Protocol and seemed to be relatively unconcerned that Canada was falling far short of its Copenhagen commitments.

Beneath the surface, however, the hidden agenda thesis does not seem to be justified by the evidence. For instance, regulations in the transportation sector came into effect in December 2010 and were closely aligned with regulations in the United States. Economic integration with the United States appears to have played a more important role in Canada's transportation regulations than the government's standing in Parliament. Given the highly integrated nature of the North American auto sector, it is difficult to argue that the government's minority status in Parliament provides the most compelling explanation for the stringency of Canada's emission reduction measures. Despite its majority status, furthermore, the Conservative government did considerable work on regulations for heavy-duty vehicles and engines after 2011. These policies also aligned closely with measures developed by US officials. Thus, the government did not change course in any obvious way in its transportation sector regulations after it formed a majority.

Analyzing the Conservatives' policy towards coal-burning power plants reinforces the view of the relative insignificance of the government's standing in the House of Commons. The Harper government's coal electricity regulations only set carbon dioxide emission standards for new coal plants in Canada. Older units would not have to meet the new standard until they reached the end of their "useful life." Regulations proposed in the *Canada Gazette* for stakeholder feedback in August 2011 required new coal-fired power plants to reach a performance standard of 375 tonnes of carbon dioxide per gigawatt hour (GWh) of energy produced.[24] Final regulations, published in September 2012, were weakened considerably. The performance standard was lowered to 420 t/GWh and the anticipated useful life of existing plants was extended by five years.[25] As they pertain to Canada's Copenhagen targets, the changes halved the anticipated emissions reduction in 2020 from about six megatonnes per year to three.

Do these actions constitute a significant change in electricity policy that might be attributed to the government's majority? In this case, the government's more ambitious target was released *after* its 2011 election victory. In other words, there was indeed a policy shift, but it does not appear to have been caused by the government's standing in the House of Commons.

Ottawa's failure, or unwillingness, to introduce regulations in the oil and gas sector was one of the most important areas of criticism of government policy. Again, just as was the case in the transportation and electricity sectors, there appears to have been little change in government policy after the 2011 election. In March 2008, the government noted in its *Turning the Corner: Taking Action to Fight Climate Change* policy document that it planned to develop oil and gas regulations that would toughen progressively.[26] In June 2011, Ottawa announced that it had begun work on those regulations. Since the end of 2012, government representatives set at least three public deadlines to publish the results.[27] Yet Ottawa failed to deliver on these promises by 2015. Both before and after it formed a majority in the House of Commons, then, the Harper government pledged oil and gas regulations. It did not, furthermore, back off of these promises after the 2011 election. In fact, it reaffirmed its commitment on several occasions. The government's failure to take action on emissions in the oil and gas sector therefore appears to have little to do with its standing in Parliament. Many of the government's wounds in this policy area were not inflicted by parliamentary demands.

In international negotiations, Ottawa insisted on agreements that committed all major emitters to reductions in their GHG emissions. Global climate treaties should not, the government maintained, put the Canadian economy at a disadvantage in relation to other international markets. Prime Minister Harper was particularly blunt – or "frank" – on this point.[28] His government questioned the efficacy and legitimacy of international agreements that imposed few obligations on large developing countries, such as China and India. It resisted efforts to use "historical responsibility" for the climate problem to justify more onerous burdens for wealthy countries and was a leading opponent of the environmental governance norm of "common but differentiated responsibility."[29] Agreements that imposed few obligations on large emerging markets would undermine global efforts to address the problem, Ottawa asserted.

Following the same logic, the Conservatives sought to maximize policy alignment with the United States. One significant reason for the Harper government's hostility towards the Kyoto Protocol was the fact that the United States was not subject to binding obligations. Given the high level of bilateral economic integration, tough emissions regulations could, Ottawa argued, badly disadvantage the Canadian economy vis-à-vis its southern neighbour. Canada adopted exactly the same commitments as did the United States under the Copenhagen Accord and introduced regulations for the transportation sector that are closely aligned with US policies. Prime Minister Harper publicly linked regulations in Canada's oil and gas sector to regulatory action in the United States.[30] Canada's former environment minister, Jim Prentice, has noted, furthermore, that one of the principal stumbling blocks for Canadian regulations in the oil and gas sector under his watch was a concern about the competitiveness of Canadian energy without parallel action in the United States.[31]

Although it is true that the Conservative government did not formally withdraw from the Kyoto Protocol until after it had won a parliamentary majority, the impact of this action on Canada's climate change mitigation policies was minimal. The Conservatives had frequently noted publicly the unrealistic nature of emissions reduction commitments ratified by Canada in 2002. They made no secret of their unwillingness to meet these targets when they came into office in 2006 and refused to accept obligations for Kyoto's second commitment period. Though many observers have noted the damage that Canada's repudiation of the Kyoto accord had for the country's international reputation and for the Kyoto process, the decision had little substantive effect on Canada's climate change mitigation strategies. It is also worth noting that, even though it withdrew from Kyoto, Canada maintained its membership within the UNFCCC.

Both before and after 2011, the Harper government insisted on international agreements that obligated all major emitters to cut their GHG emissions. The government consistently sought to minimize the economic risks of emissions reductions to the Canadian economy and was cautious in its assessments of promises made by other countries at the negotiating table. Governments, the prime minister remarked often, over-promise and under-deliver when it comes to emissions reductions.[32] Under Stephen Harper, Canada was unwilling to compromise its core objectives or to accept a disproportionate burden to facilitate an international agreement. Canada, leading Conservative decision makers regularly noted, contributed only 2 percent of global emissions, and, even if the government had accepted disproportionate obligations, it would not have had a major impact on the global problem.[33]

Explaining Canada's Foreign Environmental Policies

Canada's climate change policies were highly consistent under Prime Minister Stephen Harper. The easing of parliamentary constraints on the Harper government following its shift from minority to majority government status in 2011 had a minimal effect on Canada's climate change mitigation strategies. The government did not change its basic sector-by-sector approach to reducing GHG emissions, and Canadian negotiators, without fail, insisted on international agreements that entailed emission reduction obligations for all major economies. For those who emphasize the role of personal, ideological, and domestic political considerations in foreign environmental policy making, the degree of continuity in Conservative climate change policy will likely come as a surprise.

One reason for this conclusion is that Canadian governments are far more reactive in environmental policy making than many analysts assume. Such reactive behaviour is driven by two major factors: Canada's natural resource endowments and its geography. Whether or not Canada should be regarded as "an emerging energy superpower," as Stephen Harper often remarked, energy exports are an important economic driver for the Canadian economy.[34] In 2010, energy production represented about 6.8 percent of Canada's gross domestic product. Oil and gas extraction accounted for about half of that total. Other industries, such as those that provide equipment and services to the energy sector, amplify the importance of energy production. The oil and gas sector, furthermore, has the potential to play an important part in Canada's economic future. In 2013, Canada's proven oil reserves were the third largest in the world, totalling 27.6 billion cubic metres.[35]

Although the essential role of natural resource interests in foreign environmental policy making seems axiomatic, it is easily overlooked. Rather than responding in a reasonably direct fashion to ecological imperatives, states must balance a wide array of societal interests. From this perspective, it is understandable that, when contemplating cooperative measures that risk slowing economic growth and harming an important sector of the Canadian economy, Ottawa has tended to tread carefully.[36] The need to balance these two sometimes competing imperatives was manifested bureaucratically during the Harper years in the strong position of Natural Resources Canada vis-à-vis Environment Canada in climate change policy making and negotiations. The government's tough diplomacy in the environmental/natural resources realm was not, furthermore, unusual in the context of Canadian history. Whether it was through the imposition of straight baselines by the Lester Pearson government to restrict access to "Canadian" fisheries, or the Pierre Trudeau government's unilateral introduction of the Arctic Waters Pollution Prevention Bill, Canada has a history of bold, uncooperative behaviour when its resource interests are at stake.[37]

It is likely that the inability of the Conservative government to introduce oil and gas regulations – despite its stated desire to do so – was, furthermore, influenced by volatility in world energy markets. The meteoric rise of shale gas exploitation and hydraulic fracturing after 2011–12, for instance, flooded world markets with new oil and gas sources, leading to increased competition for Canadian energy exporters and to unpredictability in energy markets. The rapid drop in oil prices in the second half of 2014, moreover, was another source of uncertainty. In this context, the prime minister referred to the possibility of regulations for the oil and gas sector as "crazy economic policy."[38]

A second determinant of Canadian environmental policies is geography. It has been noted in other sources that Canada's foreign environmental policy making is driven disproportionately by its relationship with the United States.[39] High levels of ecological and economic interdependence, combined with Canada's size relative to the United States, have contributed to this reality. The impact of the United States' failure to ratify the Kyoto Protocol on the Harper government's climate change policies has already been noted. Ottawa's willingness to adopt the same emissions reduction targets as Washington at the Copenhagen climate conference further illustrates this point. In determining how to meet its Copenhagen targets, Canadian policy makers paid close attention to American actions. The toughest sectoral regulations instituted by the Harper government – those affecting the transportation sector – were modelled after regulations introduced in the United States.

An analysis of the Canadian approach to oil and gas regulation is equally illustrative. In 2010, 98.4 percent of Canadian energy exports went to the United States. Canadian crude oil accounted for about 21.5 percent of US crude oil imports and 13.0 percent of the overall US market.[40] Although the Harper government sought to diversify its energy exports, the United States remained the most important market for Canadian oil and gas. In addition to being the biggest buyer of Canadian energy, US producers are Canada's most important competitors. Hence, Ottawa was reluctant to introduce emissions rules that could negatively affect the competitiveness of Canadian energy producers.[41] Even as the Obama administration proposed new regulations for its coal sector, the Harper government resisted calls for regulatory action for Canada's oil and gas sector. It should, therefore, come as no surprise that the prime minister reportedly put out feelers to the White House about the potential harmonization of Canadian oil and gas regulations with American measures.[42]

While parliamentary constraints on the Conservative Party weakened after 2011, the incentive structure facing the government did not change. The economic importance of Canada's natural resource endowments made tough regulatory action in the oil and gas sector risky. Deep cuts to Canada's emissions were always going to be painful for certain sectors of the Canadian economy and certain elements of Canadian society. This challenge, of course, remained after the Conservatives won a majority government. The dynamism and volatility of oil and gas markets since 2011–12 only complicated matters. Furthermore, although the United States appeared to be on track to meet its Copenhagen commitments, it did not introduce significant regulations for its oil and gas sector until August 2015. The Harper government was reluctant to pursue new emission rules for this sector without commensurate US action lest it hurt Canadian oil producers. Rumoured Conservative plans for the introduction of parallel methane gas regulations for Canada's oil and gas sector after the 2015 election would seem to confirm this assessment.

At the same time, there was not a significant weakening of Canada's climate change mitigation policies. Even if the government had wanted to weaken the regulations it instituted before 2011, it would have been difficult to do so. Some analysts, moreover, claim that Ottawa's weak climate change mitigation record hurt Canada-US diplomatic relations. The government's inability to institute regulations in the oil and gas sector, argue some observers, cost Canada the "social licence" necessary to gain US approval for the Keystone XL pipeline.[43] Whether or not this view is accurate, and it is questioned in Chapter 8 (this volume) by Greg Anderson, the widespread belief that Canadian oil was "dirty" and insufficiently regulated did not ease the approval process for the controversial pipeline. Canada's continental relationship with the United States, therefore, acted as a potential external constraint on Canadian policy makers.

Conclusion

The climate change mitigation policies of the Stephen Harper government were largely consistent. The shift from a minority to a majority government in 2011 did not facilitate significant change in Canada's foreign environmental policies. The government restated its commitment to meeting its Copenhagen Accord targets and maintained its public commitment to regulating the oil and gas sector. In international fora, such as UNFCCC conferences, Canadian negotiators were unwavering in their insistence on agreements that bind all major emitters.

Canadian governments – even if they have personal, ideological, or political interests in opposing tough regulatory action – are often more reactive than some analysts assume. Canada's natural resource endowments and its integration with the United States have done much to shape its climate change policies. The basic incentive structure facing the Harper government did not change significantly between 2006 and 2015, contributing to a high degree of continuity in Canadian policy. It stands to reason, furthermore, that future governments will encounter a similar incentive structure, one that will likely act as an external driver and determinant of Canadian policy going forward.

The environmental case highlights the close linkages between multilateral and bilateral foreign policies, a major theme that emerges within this volume. Environmental policies are especially prone to this phenomenon because of the essentially local nature of many environmental problems. Even with the most global of environmental issues, continental imperatives did much to shape Canadian policy. The competitiveness of Canadian energy producers vis-à-vis the United States was a – perhaps *the* – chief policy consideration of the Harper government.

Notes

1 "Canada tagged as 'Fossil of the Year,'" CBC News, 18 December 2009, http://www.cbc.ca/news/canada/canada-tagged-as-fossil-of-the-year-1.827062.
2 Adam Vaughan, "What does Canada's withdrawal from Kyoto Protocol mean? Canada has shown that a legally binding deal does not guarantee countries won't walk away from their commitments," *Guardian*, 13 December 2011, http://www.theguardian.com/environment/2011/dec/13/canada-withdrawal-kyoto-protocol.
3 Environment Canada, *Canada's Emission Trends* (Gatineau, QC: Environment Canada, 2014), iii.
4 Jeffrey Simpson, "Harper cave on climate? Don't hold your breath," *Globe and Mail*, 15 November 2014, http://www.theglobeandmail.com/globe-debate/harper-cave-on-climate-dont-hold-your-breath/article21578278/.
5 John M.R. Stone, "Canada's approach to tackling climate change," in Ernesto Zedillo, ed., *Global Warming: Looking Beyond Kyoto* (Washington: Brookings Institution Press, 2008), 200.
6 Environment Canada, *Canada's Emission Trends*, iii.
7 Emissions from the Ontario electricity sectors have decreased by 58 percent since 2005 because of the closure of coal-fired electricity plants. Quebec and British Columbia, which rely heavily on hydroelectric power, have decreased emissions by 8.5 percent and 3.5 percent, respectively, since 2005. For details, see Environment Canada, *National Inventory Report, 1990-2012, Greenhouse Gas Sources and Sinks*

132   *Michael W. Manulak*

       in Canada: *The Canadian Government's Submission to the UN Framework Convention on Climate Change* (Gatineau, QC: Environment Canada, 2014), 9.

8 Office of the Auditor General of Canada, *Report of the Commissioner of the Environment and Sustainable Development* (Ottawa: Minister of Public Works and Government Services, 2014), 32.

9 Environment Canada, Speech for the Honourable Peter Kent, PC, MP, Minister of the Environment, "Announcement of the publication of heavy duty vehicle and engine greenhouse gas emissions regulations," Mississauga, ON, 25 February 2013, http://ec.gc.ca/default.asp?lang=En&n=976258C6-1&news=A0EEE93C-17F1-4E55-AD9D-9B60E3E9605C.

10 Environment Canada, "News release: Harper government improves fuel efficiency of Canadian vehicles," 27 November 2012, http://www.ec.gc.ca/default.asp?lang=En&n=714D9AAE-1&news=33B625CB-653E-4766-8C92-ACA551C94AB0.

11 Office of the Auditor General of Canada, *Report of the Commissioner*, 7.

12 Environment Canada, Speaking Notes for the Honourable Jim Prentice, PC, QC, MP, Minister of the Environment Announcement – "Canada shows leadership on climate change and the environment," National Press Theatre, Ottawa, 23 June 2010. See also: Environment Canada, Notes for Remarks by the Honourable Peter Kent, PC, MP, Minister of the Environment, "Canada's Environment Minister announces important step towards reducing electricity sector emissions," 19 August 2011, http://www.ec.gc.ca/default.asp?lang=En&n=714D9AAE-1&news=2E5D45F6-E0A4-45C4-A49D-A3514E740296.

13 For a discussion of changes to the planned coal regulations, see Office of the Auditor General of Canada, *Report of the Commissioner,* 9–10.

14 Jeffrey Simpson, "Canada's perpetual climate charade," *Globe and Mail*, 11 October 2014, http://www.theglobeandmail.com/globe-debate/canadas-perpetual-climate-charade/article21032688/.

15 P.J. Partington, "Who's really winning the race to end coal? A comparison of Canada and US federal regulations," *Pembina Institute*, 22 February 2013, http://www.pembina.org/blog/691.

16 Environment Canada, *National Inventory Report*, 8. Environment Canada, *Emissions Trends 2014*, iv.

17 Office of the Auditor General of Canada, *Report of the Commission*, 10.

18 "Full text of Peter Mansbridge's interview with Stephen Harper," *CBC News*, 17 December 2014, http://www.cbc.ca/news/politics/full-text-of-peter-mansbridge-s-interview-with-stephen-harper-1.2876934.

19 Tonda MacCharles, "APEC climate deal unlikely, Harper says," *Toronto Star*, 7 September 2007, https://www.thestar.com/news/world/2007/09/07/apec_climate_deal_unlikely_harper_says.html.

20 International Institute for Sustainable Development, "Durban highlights: Monday 28 November 2011," *Earth Negotiations Bulletin* 12, 524 (29 November 2011), http://www.iisd.ca/vol12/enb12524e.html.

21 Geoffrey York, "Kent defends himself against India's scorn at marathon climate talks," *Globe and Mail*, 10 December 2011, http://www.theglobeandmail.com/news/

politics/kent-defends-himself-against-indias-scorn-at-marathon-climate-talks/article4180683/.
22 Former environment minister Peter Kent has noted that he regrets his inability to reach a satisfactory agreement. See Laura Stone, "Shuffled out of cabinet – but hopefully not forgotten," *Global News*, 16 July 2013, http://globalnews.ca/news/720835/shuffled-out-of-cabinet-but-hopefully-not-forgotten/.
23 See, for example, Josh Visser, "John Baird happily admits Tories didn't like axed environment watchdog's advice," *National Post*, 14 May 2012, http://news.nationalpost.com/news/canada/john-baird-happily-admits-tories-didnt-like-axed-environment-watchdogs-advice.
24 Canada, Department of the Environment and Department of Health, "Reduction of carbon dioxide emissions from coal-fired generation of electricity regulations," *Canada Gazette*, pt. 1, vol. 145, no. 35 (27 August 2011), http://www.gazette.gc.ca/rp-pr/p1/2011/2011-08-27/html/reg1-eng.html.
25 Canada, Department of the Environment and Department of Health, "Reduction of carbon dioxide emissions from coal-fired generation of electricity regulations," *Canada Gazette*, pt. 2, vol. 146, no. 19 (12 September 2012), http://www.gazette.gc.ca/rp-pr/p2/2012/2012-09-12/html/sor-dors167-eng.html.
26 Government of Canada, *Turning the Corner: Taking Action to Fight Climate Change*, March 2008, 4, http://publications.gc.ca/collections/collection_2009/ec/En88-2-2008E.pdf.
27 Max Paris, "Oil and gas industry emission rules still not ready from Ottawa," *CBC News*, 3 July 2013, http://www.cbc.ca/news/politics/oil-and-gas-industry-emission-rules-still-not-ready-from-ottawa-1.1343855.
28 Steven Chase and Barrie McKenna, "Canada 'more frank' about climate change, Harper says," *Globe and Mail*, 9 June 2014, http://www.theglobeandmail.com/news/politics/canada-more-frank-about-climate-change-pm/article19087212/.
29 Douglas Macdonald, "Harper energy and climate change policy: Failing to address the key challenges," in Christopher Stoney and G. Bruce Doern, eds., *How Ottawa Spends, 2011-2012: Trimming Fat or Slicing Pork* (Montreal and Kingston: McGill-Queen's University Press, 2011), 131.
30 Chris Hall, "Harper offers Obama climate plan to win Keystone approval," *CBC News*, 6 September 2013, http://www.cbc.ca/news/politics/harper-offers-obama-climate-plan-to-win-keystone-approval-1.1701391.
31 Aaron Wherry, "Want a discussion about Canada's climate change policy? Here's a start: What are we going to do or not do?" *Maclean's*, 16 July 2014, http://www.macleans.ca/politics/want-a-frank-discussion-about-climate-change-heres-a-start/.
32 Simpson, "Harper cave on climate?"
33 See, for example: Stephen Harper, "Prime Minister Stephen Harper calls for international consensus on climate change," 4 June 2007, Berlin, Germany.
34 Jason Kirby, "The perils of being an energy superpower," *Macleans.ca*, 12 November 2015, http://www.macleans.ca/economy/economicanalysis/the-perils-of-being-an-energy-superpower/.

35 Natural Resources Canada, "Additional statistics on energy," last modified 4 November 2013, http://www.nrcan.gc.ca/publications/statistics-facts/1239.
36 Little evidence suggests that the government proceeded reluctantly in this area because of jurisdictional concerns. Although the federal government consulted heavily with provinces, it faced few jurisdictional obstacles to regulating sources of emissions.
37 For a discussion of these events, see Barbara Johnson, "Canadian foreign policy and fisheries," in Barbara Johnson and Mark W. Zacher, eds., *Canadian Foreign Policy and the Law of the Sea* (Vancouver: UBC Press, 1977), 65–67. See also R. Michael M'Gonigle and Mark W. Zacher, "Canadian foreign policy and the control of marine pollution," in Johnson and Zacher eds., *Canadian Foreign Policy*, 117–20.
38 Shawn McCarthy, "Harper calls climate regulations on oil and gas sector 'crazy economic policy,'" *Globe and Mail*, 9 December 2014, http://www.theglobeandmail.com/news/politics/harper-it-would-be-crazy-to-impose-climate-regulations-on-oil-industry/article22014508/.
39 Michael W. Manulak, "Multilateral solutions to bilateral problems: The 1972 Stockholm Conference and Canadian foreign environmental policy," *International Journal* 70, 1 (2015): 4–22.
40 Natural Resources Canada, "Additional statistics on energy."
41 Wherry, "Want a discussion"; Natural Resources Canada, "Additional statistics on energy."
42 Hall, "Harper offers Obama climate plan to win Keystone approval."
43 Duncan Kenyon, "The cost of losing social license," *Pembina Institute*, 6 June 2014, http://www.pembina.org/blog/the-costs-of-losing-social-licence.

8
Canada and the United States in the Harper Years
Still "Special," but Not Especially Important
GREG ANDERSON

In September 2003, the front cover of the *Economist* featured a moose sporting sunglasses along with the byline, "Canada's new spirit." The piece extolled the virtues of Canada's particular brand of social democracy, the state's sound economic management, and the growing sense of national self-confidence after generations of operating in the economic and political shadow of the United States. It was a shot in the arm for Canadians, many of whom had spent the previous two years angst-ridden over the state of the existentially important relationship with the United States. On 20 September 2001, many still recalled, President Bush had stood before a joint session of Congress and declared that "America had no truer friend than Great Britain."

Canadians were aghast at the snub. What had become of the "special relationship" that seemed to animate postwar bilateral relations?[1] What about the cultures of "exceptionalism" or "exemptionalism" that allowed Canada to wield unusual influence with American policy makers?[2] What about the postwar diplomatic culture between the two countries that underwrote it?[3] Hadn't Canadians taken in thousands of stranded airline passengers on 9/11? Didn't the two countries enjoy the longest undefended border in the world? What about all of that trade? In the years leading up to 9/11, economic integration seemed to be making the Canada-US border increasingly less relevant to the goods and people that crossed it. In the years since, the border has become more salient than ever.

Bilateral acrimony and veiled anti-Americanism characterizing the final years of the Chrétien government gave way to efforts – albeit not entirely successful – by Prime Minister Paul Martin to chart a more constructive course.[4] Canada made a substantial commitment to Afghanistan, worked assiduously on the trade-border security dynamic, and elevated relations with the United States on the government's priority list. Stephen Harper committed to go even further, regardless, presumably, of the strength of the Conservatives in the House of Commons. What's more, the number of members of Parliament from the government side was largely irrelevant since the trajectory of the Canada-US relationship had been established in the critical years before Harper became prime minister in February 2006.

Throughout his government's minority and majority years, Prime Minister Harper advanced an unusually assertive brand of Canadian foreign policy – one that could reasonably be described as a kind of muscular realism.[5] The list of supporting data points is impressive: a new commitment to Afghanistan, renewed clout in NATO, an assertive defence and security strategy at home, and numerous instances of bold stands on a range of hot-button issues from human rights to the Russian intervention in Ukraine. Yet what any of it meant for Canada-US relations remains unclear. In some areas, such as the Canadian contribution to Afghanistan, Conservative foreign policy complemented American thinking. In others, such as Canada's overt support for Israel, the Harper government likely complicated the Canada-US relationship. Yet, where Canadian foreign policy counts most – the economic and security relationship with the United States – the agenda was largely set before the Conservatives arrived. Hence, after nearly a decade of Stephen Harper as prime minister, Canada-US relations retained its "specialness," but Canada did not emerge any more important.[6]

Some scholars argue that Canada is becoming the beneficiary of an increasingly multipolar world that affords "middle" or "principal" powers greater latitude to exercise policy entrepreneurship: the relative decline of the United States as a hegemonic power, the argument goes, enables countries like Canada to chart an independent foreign policy that will ultimately reshape the norms of global order.[7] Others see a big shift in recent Canadian foreign policy as well but worry about sustainability, particularly in defence policy, where the perennial "commitment-credibility gap" could quickly re-emerge – or perhaps already has, based on David Perry's analysis (Chapter 5, this volume) – as foreign commitments are scaled back.[8]

We are undoubtedly in a period of unprecedented pluralism in international relations. Yet such analyses overstate the importance of incremental twists and turns in partnerships characterized more by continuity than by change. In 1984, Charles Doran argued that, to understand the importance of the Canada-US relationship, one had to situate it within an international context.[9] Only then could the tendency to exaggerate the impact of relatively small changes be avoided. More pointedly, to understand Canada-US relations was to understand where Canada fit within the United States' broader foreign policy agenda. In 2013, the *Economist* found Canada to be a little less "cool" than it had been.[10] However, I argue that Canada's relationship with the United States remains largely the same: special, not cool, but characterized by vast asymmetries and a divergence of interests that shape how each state conducts itself on the world stage. The United States remains Canada's most important international policy file; indeed, it is arguably Canada's only file. It follows, then, that when it comes to the Canadian-American relationship, the shift from minority to majority government in 2011 was all but irrelevant.

Doran also argues that Canada-US relations can best be understood through three analytical lenses: psycho-cultural, political-security, and trade-commercial. To begin, the stark asymmetries of power have provoked Canadian anxieties over cultural and political sovereignty. Those same asymmetries dictate how each state conceptualizes its foreign policy priorities: the United States with its diverse, global agenda, is often distracted from the bilateral, while Canada parochially focuses on its trade and commercial interests.[11]

Scholars have long noted the interdependence and intervulnerability of Canada-US relations.[12] In the context of an evolving global politics featuring US decline and an evolving post-9/11 policy environment, some have seen the United States as "vulnerable," even "dependent."[13] I propose that the unusual assertiveness of the foreign policy posture of the Harper government did little, one way or the other, to alter the trajectory of Canada-US relations; the relationship is based upon long-standing characteristics beyond the power of any single administration to change. For all of the bluster and muscularity of the Conservatives' foreign policy, Canada remains a policy price-taker in the nexus between trade and security in North America irrespective of the Canadian government's standing in the House of Commons.

Bush, Obama, and Keystone XL

The Psycho-Cultural Lens

There is already a significant body of literature that explores the often subtle differences between Canadians and Americans.[14] Anxieties over culture and hegemony, particularly among English Canadians, have regularly intensified bilateral disputes.[15] In the aftermath of 9/11, some of that attention turned to alleged divergences between the two political and diplomatic cultures. Winston Churchill once reportedly quipped that Britain and the United States were two nations divided by a common language. Indeed, Americans frequently don't give a second thought to events interpreted by Canadians as litmus tests for the health of the bilateral relationship; challenges of perception continued to plague the Harper government's management of the file.

The shock that many Canadians felt when President Bush extolled the United States' friendship with Great Britain in September 2001 gave way to a new round of angst in Canada about relations with its southern neighbour. Former ambassadors worried that the veiled anti-Americanism of Jean Chrétien had resulted in a lack of Canadian influence in Washington during the critical early days after 9/11.[16] Others questioned whether the 1990s had bred a kind of Canadian complacency that undercut the state's global identity.[17] As it reduced Canada's international footprint by withdrawing Canadian Armed Forces personnel from Europe and closing consulates worldwide, Ottawa lost its eyes and ears on the ground. The impact on relations with the United States was particularly problematic because, at the same time, Mexico was expanding its own diplomatic footprint in that country. In addition, some scholars have argued that a fundamental generational shift in each country's bureaucracies bred even more misunderstanding and potential for bilateral distrust.[18] By 2004, the diplomatic and bureaucratic disorder had become so worrisome that the Canada School of Public Service rewrote its training manual for officials posted to the United States.[19] At about the same time, the new Liberal government under Paul Martin created the Department of Public Safety, primarily to mirror the newly established US Department of Homeland Security, and then appointed Canada's first-ever national security advisor.[20]

More than a decade later, as Stephen Harper relinquished power to the Trudeau Liberals, little had changed. Canada had increased its public diplomacy efforts; it had produced maps of the United States that highlight economic activity supported by two-way trade with Canada. However, in 2013, the Harper government also eliminated funding for Canadian Studies programming, part of which supported academic outreach efforts in the United States.[21] Moreover, Ottawa's ability to interpret and understand the American political system failed again during negotiations to extend the Keystone XL pipeline. In 2008, Calgary-based TransCanada Corporation proposed to construct a twelve-hundred-mile (approximately nineteen-hundred-kilometre) oil pipeline from Hardisty, Alberta, to Steele City, Nebraska, where it would connect with the existing pipeline networks supplying US gulf coast refineries. Because the proposed pipeline would cross the US border, the president was required to issue an approval permit before construction could begin. In spite of extensive Canadian lobbying, 2015 saw President Obama's public scepticism about the project grow so great that he ultimately rejected it altogether shortly after Justin Trudeau became prime minister.

The challenges of the Keystone XL experience are indicative of the lingering lack of capacity in Ottawa and beyond to manage the differences between Canadian and American political culture.[22] TransCanada never appreciated the political backlash flowing from the 2005 US Supreme Court decision (*Kelo v. New London, CT*),[23] which conferred property expropriation rights (eminent domain) to a private developer.[24] When TransCanada began threatening Nebraska landowners with eminent domain proceedings, it managed to create an alliance between land-holders and environmentalists, each of whom had different reasons for opposing the project.[25] Similarly, the relative openness of the American political system to the insertion of stakeholder challenges affected Canadian interests at multiple levels. Specifically, the capacity of US lobbyists to delay a presidential decision on Keystone XL (or to frustrate resolution of the Mad Cow Crisis in 2003 or to shape the decades-long softwood lumber dispute) was a regular source of friction in Alberta and Ottawa.

Despite the policy differences, Stephen Harper's personal management of the US file kept the histrionics to a relative minimum by avoiding outbreaks of some of the cheap anti-Americanism expressed, if not provoked, by his immediate predecessors.[26] The Conservative prime minister generally agreed to disagree, moved on, and encouraged cooperative, collegial relations among Canadian and American officials in order to preserve a bilateral relationship that remains the envy of many other countries. Perceived slights were minimized by the countless high-level interactions among officials at fora in which Canada and the United States play major roles: Asia Pacific Economic Co-operation (APEC), the G8, the G20, the Trans-Pacific Partnership, NATO, the UN, and so on. Indeed, between 2001 and 2012, there were well over one hundred such side-bars noted in the press between Cabinet-level representatives.[27]

Stephen Harper in Afghanistan: The CAF Punched Itself Out

The Political-Security Lens

In the spring of 2003, Stephen Rosen doubted US imperial power in an article entitled "An empire, if you can keep it."[28] Applied to Canada's recent experience, such an article might read "national security policy, if you can keep it."

Virtually every assessment of record regarding how Canada became involved in Afghanistan paints a picture of bureaucratic manoeuvring – some might argue deceit – among elements of Canada's civilian and military leadership.[29] The political leadership wanted to support the American agenda, especially after Bush's "no truer friend" remark, but it never appreciated the CAF's readiness for the mission it was contemplating.[30] The military leadership spoiled for a fight as a way to assert the CAF's relevance, to rebuff European scepticism about Canada's hard power capabilities, and possibly also to hasten the provision of new kit to re-establish interoperability with its US counterparts.[31] Canada engaged enthusiastically in 2002 and, under the Conservatives, was willingly back in Afghanistan.[32] Yet, for all the bluster and chest-thumping flowing from Canada's contribution to the mission, for most of the last two decades its contribution to the United States' global agenda has in some ways resembled that of the much smaller Belgium.

Nonetheless, by virtually all accounts, the CAF proved to be an effective, reliable fighting force that performed beyond analysts' expectations. Moreover, Afghanistan placed Canada, through the CAF, in good standing with the United States – albeit awkwardly and not entirely by design.[33] One must wonder, moreover, whether that standing can be sustained, and what value there will there be in this achievement, if Canadian capabilities atrophy once more.[34]

One of Prime Minister Harper's signature initiatives during the 2005–06 federal election campaign was his pledge to "Stand up for Canada," operationalized in 2008 by the *Canada First Defence Strategy*.[35] This document

TABLE 8.1
Defence spending as percentage of GDP for Canada and Belgium

	1988	1994	1996	1998	2010	2011	2012	2013
Canada	2.0	1.7	1.4	1.3	1.2	1.2	1.1	1.0
Belgium	2.6	1.6	1.5	1.4	1.1	1.0	1.0	1.0

Source: World Bank, http://data.worldbank.org/. In 2009, 2011, and 2013, the United States spent 4.6 percent, 4.2 percent, and 4.6 percent of GDP, respectively, on defence.

emphasizes continental defence and includes a renewed commitment to shipbuilding, coastal defence, and maritime search and rescue. Also notable is its heavy emphasis on planting the Canadian flag more firmly in the far North through the basing of troops, the development of a permanent deepwater port, and the construction of new icebreaking capacity.

The Conservatives' decision not to revisit the Martin government's contentious commitment to stay out of the United States' Ballistic Missile Defense (BMD) system surprised the Bush administration,[36] but *Canada First* went some distance towards mollifying Washington after years of nagging Canada over its meagre defence spending. In May 2006, Prime Minister Harper also moved to renew and update the North American Aerospace Defense Command agreement, long a symbol of the "specialness" of Canada-US relations, and the future of which had been in doubt since the Liberals' BMD decision.[37]

Some see in Canada's national security policy under the Harper government a dramatic shift away from the country's traditional multilateral, peacekeeping approach to the deployment of Canadian forces;[38] others see the expansion of Canadian leadership on a range of issues rooted in longer-run phenomena and anchored in American decline and an increasingly pluralist global politics.[39] The CAF played a major role in the Conservatives' assertive national security strategy, yet Afghanistan has left it a spent force and rendered other elements of the security strategy meaningless.[40] Afghanistan may, therefore, prove to be an accidental aberration in Canada's postwar construction of itself as a "middle power."[41] A return to middle power internationalism would again provide Canada with the rationale to pick and choose where it wanted to engage the American agenda, possibly rekindling debates from the 1990s about drift in Canadian foreign policy.[42] It would also reinforce Doran's views about Canada's tendency to privilege vital trade and commercial interests ahead of America's emphasis on security and strategic matters.

The End of North America

The Trade-Commercial Lens

Over the last three decades, a dispute over softwood lumber has become a barometer for the state of the Canada-US relationship. One of Prime Minister Harper's first acts upon assuming office in 2006 was to sideline the dispute through October 2015 with the third major temporary settlement in the last twenty-five years.[43] Had he not done so, softwood would

TABLE 8.2
NAFTA asymmetries (in billions $US)

	1975	1987	1994	2000	2012
Canada GDP	$170	$420	$560	$770	$1,780
% of North American GDP	9%	7.9%	7.0%	6.5%	9.3%
Exports + imports as % of GDP	47%	53%	67%	85%	63%
Mexico GDP	$88	$140	$420	$581	$1,178
% of North American GDP	4.7%	2.6%	5.9%	5.2%	6.1%
Exports + imports as % of GDP	17%	33%	38%	64%	66%
United States GDP	$1,600	$4,700	$7,017	$9,764	$16,240
% of North American GDP	86%	89.3%	87.7%	88.2%	84.5%
Exports + imports as % of GDP	16%	19%	22%	26%	29%

Source: World Bank

have inhibited his broader agenda and renewed its position as a barometer for the relationship.

The Conservatives inherited a North American integration agenda in 2006 that had been transformed by the 9/11 terrorist attacks on the United States. Those attacks brought into sharp relief the existential importance of the Canada-US border to Canadian economic prosperity. More than two decades of talk about the anachronisms of borders in an integrated North America gave way overnight to their reassertion as barriers to goods and people.[44]

For a period, it certainly looked as though "security trumped trade."[45] Moreover, it appeared that Doran's views about the importance of asymmetries and the divergence in foreign policy outlooks and priorities in Canada-US relations were once again in conflict: the United States' emphasis on the *political-security* seemed to clash with Canada's focus on *trade-commercial*. The divergence of interests can, in part, be seen in Tables 8.2 and 8.3, which depict the stark asymmetries in North America's economic relationships.

Table 8.2 depicts the relative shares of North America's economic activity generated by each economy: that of the United States dwarfs those of both Canada and Mexico. Equally important is the relative economic openness of each country (exports plus imports as a percentage of GDP), or, put differently, vulnerability to changes in market access. Whereas Canada and Mexico depend on trade (exports plus imports) for more than 60 percent of their GDP, the United States is much less vulnerable. Less than one-third (29 percent) of its economy is similarly dependent. Also important is the

TABLE 8.3
NAFTA trading partners, 2012 (rank order and percentage of total)

	Canada	Mexico	United States
Exports to	United States (74.5%) China (4.3%) UK (4.1%)	United States (80.5%) Canada (3.6%) Germany (1.4%)	Canada (18.9%) Mexico (14%) China (7.2%) Japan (4.5%)
Imports from	United States (50.6%) China (11%) Mexico (5.5%)	United States (49.9%) China (15.4%) Japan (4.8%)	China (19%) Canada (14.1%) Mexico (12%) Japan (6.4%) Germany (4.7%)

Source: CIA *World Factbook.*

diversification of each country's trading partners (Table 8.3). Canada and Mexico are both heavily dependent on a single market.

The obvious implications of border closures for Canada's US market access had both the Chrétien and Martin governments scrambling to manage a rapidly changing security situation. Within weeks of the terrorist attacks, Canadian officials assembled the relics of a series of failed and/or incomplete exercises from the 1990s into the Smart Border Accords. The hope was that the agreement would enable the new imperatives of security to be balanced against a commitment to maintain the porousness of the border. The accords were expanded through the ambitious, and controversial, North American Security and Prosperity Partnership (SPP) of March 2005.[46] The SPP formally connected two historically divergent policy orientations by implicitly exchanging cooperation on security for continued market access.

Unfortunately for advocates of North American integration, the launch of the SPP proved to be the high point of trilateral cooperation on the new nexus of security and economics. The partnership looked ambitious, but it generated no new institutional mechanisms, involved no legislative oversight, placed responsibility for most of its work in the bureaucracies, and did not formally incorporate private sector or civil society input.[47] Moreover, by 2007, only one of its initial sponsors, George W. Bush, was still in office.

By 2008, all of the references to the partnership in North American Leaders' Summit (NALS) declarations had disappeared, and the SPP itself was purged from government websites the following year. In 2010, even

NALS was cancelled (Canada was to have hosted) in favour of bilateral meetings on the margins of the G20 summit in Toronto. Beginning around 2009, and lasting throughout the rest of Prime Minister Harper's time in power, NALS was undermined by the so-called "rebilateralization" of North American relations: Ottawa and Mexico City pursued issues with Washington on their own rather than in a trilateral setting. The result was the de facto end of trilateralism and the return of North American governance patterns via two separate, asymmetrical relationships.[48] Many, including some who saw it as accentuating the kind of asymmetrical power differentials Canadian multilateralism was designed to mitigate, lamented the demise of a trilateral North America.[49]

Many of Prime Minister Harper's advisors on relations with the United States, among them the former Canadian ambassador to Washington, Derek Burney, believe that Mexico is an unfortunate drag on Canadian progress with Washington,[50] an attitude that some have held at least since the early 1990s and the NAFTA negotiations.[51] Yet the Harper government's marginalization of Mexico in North American governance arguably undercut Ottawa's broader objectives in Washington. In mid-2009, and with no warning, Canada reimposed visa requirements on Mexican "visitors" under the ruse that too many of them were subsequently applying for asylum on false grounds. Five years later, a still angry President Enrique Peña Nieto cancelled a visit to Ottawa in protest. The rift with Mexico City is further indicative of how the Harper government essentially abandoned trilateralism. The NALS meetings continued, but their value increasingly resided in the opportunity for bilateral face-time with the American president.[52]

Rather than a trilateral effort to deal with the so-called "tyranny of small differences" in regulatory standards, when the Harper government lost power there were two separate regulatory harmonization processes anchored in the White House Office of Management and Budget.[53] Instead of a trilateral approach to energy and climate change, there were two separate bilateral dialogues, again housed in Washington.[54] Certainly, the progress made under the 2011 Canada-US *Beyond the Border Initiative* was genuine.[55] But it was also slow and, perhaps as a result, never became a significant part of any federal election campaign. As the initiative was launched, the prime minister announced that Ottawa would provide the Canada Border Services Agency "entry" data to the Department of Homeland Security that could be used as "exit" data for the US-VISIT program.[56] And, in March 2015, there was an agreement in principle to establish cargo "pre-clearance" facilities similar to those already used for passengers at major Canadian airports.[57]

Yet the latter announcement came with few details, and there was little additional progress prior to the October 2015 election.

Prime Minister Harper's rebilateralization of North America was problematic for several reasons. First, it represented a departure from Canada's broader approach to multilateralism and a failure to grasp the importance of institution building for small open economies. Canada undoubtedly has a special relationship with the United States that is the envy of most other countries. However, it is difficult enough to get attention in Washington without restricting one's methods of access, and much of the ongoing bilateral agenda is either handled by technocrats or mired in US domestic regulatory processes.[58] Moreover, the Conservatives' exploitation of the special relationship followed from a fundamental misreading of where Latin America, and Mexico in particular, fit in the American political system.[59] Latinos are the fastest-growing demographic group in the United States, and an increasingly potent one politically. Canada might try to ignore Mexico, but the United States can ill-afford to do the same. Moreover, the Department of Homeland Security has tended to perceive both borders similarly. To the extent that it continues to do so, Ottawa may find that its interests in Washington can best be secured in collaboration with Mexico City.

There was unquestionably significant and successful activity in Canada-US relations over the Harper era: coordination of security at the Vancouver Winter Olympics, the establishment and operation of Integrated Border Enforcement Teams, the standing up of Public Safety Canada to parallel and better coordinate with the Department of Homeland Security, an agreement to construct a new span across the Detroit River, significantly improved border wait times, and the ongoing work on the *Beyond the Border Initiative* are all examples of enhanced cooperation at all levels of government. But they are also indicative of how the stark asymmetries between the two countries have seen Canada become a bilateral "price-taker." The events of 11 September 2001 caused the policy emphases (*political-security* versus *trade-commercial*) to converge but did not fundamentally alter either country's focus. The Harper government's efforts to rebilateralize North America, efforts that were not exclusive to the Conservatives' standing in the House of Commons, only made those differences starker.

Conclusion

The Harper years were not especially transformative for Canada-US relations. Much of what has transpired fits well into the thirty-year-old frame of analysis developed by Charles Doran. The terrorist attacks of 9/11 have accentuated the intervulnerability each country confronts but have done little to alter either the starkness of the asymmetries in the relationship or the foreign policy priorities of the respective governments. Prime Minister Harper inherited a bilateral agenda dominated by border security at home and accentuated by Canada's contribution to Afghanistan abroad. The Conservatives invested heavily in both, but the impact on Canada's "special" relationship with the United States in the coming years remains uncertain. More specifically, Afghanistan became Prime Minister Harper's war when he pursued a mission extension in 2006. But Canada's capacity to maintain robust interoperability with American forces and renewed clout in NATO will depend heavily on its ability to continue to contribute robustly in the years ahead.

The more pressing significance of Canada-US relations involves the intersection of two historically divergent foreign policy agendas. The Harper government's most important initiatives took place largely out of public view: the Conservatives recast North America into a tale of two highly asymmetric bilateral relationships anchored in Washington. This outcome, however, was less transformative than it was indicative of the unique intersection of policy objectives that serve quite different goals north and south of the 49th parallel. Above all are fundamental misunderstandings about the target of Canada's highest foreign policy priority – misunderstandings that continue to complicate bilateral policy making, much as they did three decades ago. Looked at another way, in contemporary North America, Canada-US relations are too interconnected to be excessively transformed by a mere change in a Canadian political party's standing in the House of Commons in Ottawa.

Notes

1 Donald Barry, "The politics of 'exceptionalism': Canada and the United States as a distinctive international relationship," *Dalhousie Review* 60, 1 (1980): 114–37; Robert Cuff and J.L. Granatstein, *The Ties That Bind: Canadian-American Relations in Wartime from the Great War to the Cold War* (Toronto: Samuel Stevens Hakkert and Company, 1977), 151–63; Charles Doran, *Forgotten Partnership: Canada-US Relations Today* (Baltimore: Johns Hopkins University Press, 1984), 21–25, 74–84; Geoffrey Hale, *So Near Yet So Far: The Public and Hidden Worlds of Canada-US Relations* (Vancouver: UBC Press, 2012), 14.
2 Edelgard Mahant and Graeme S. Mount, *Invisible and Inaudible in Washington* (Vancouver/East Lansing: UBC Press/Michigan State University Press, 1999), 14.
3 Brian Bow, *The Politics of Linkage: Power, Interdependence, and Ideas in Canada-US Relations* (Vancouver: UBC Press, 2009), 11–16; Christopher Sands, "The changing of the guard," *International Journal* 60, 2 (2005): 483–96.

4 Brian Bow, "Anti-Americanism in Canada, before and after Iraq," *American Review of Canadian Studies* 38, 3 (2008): 354.
5 See Colin Robertson, "Harper's world view," *Policy Options* (October 2011): 76–80.
6 I thank Joseph Jockel and Joel Sokolsky for this phrase. They have applied it (and the title of this chapter) to Canadian defence policy more specifically.
7 John Kirton, "Vulnerable America, capable Canada: Convergent leadership for an interconnected world," *Canadian Foreign Policy Journal* 18, 1 (2012): 133–44.
8 Robert W. Murray and John McCoy, "From middle power to peacebuilder: The use of the Canadian Forces in modern Canadian foreign policy," *American Review of Canadian Studies* 40, 2 (2010): 171–88; Joseph Jockel and Joel Sokolsky, "Canada and the war in Afghanistan: NATO's odd man out steps forward," *Journal of Transatlantic Studies* 6, 1 (2008): 100–15.
9 Charles Doran, *Forgotten Partnership: Canada-US Relations Today* (Baltimore: Johns Hopkins University Press, 1984), 1.
10 "Uncool Canada," *Economist*, 19 November 2013, http://www.economist.com/news/21589156-moose-loses-its-shades-uncool-canada.
11 Doran, *Forgotten Partnership*, 85–108; 109–38; 139–77.
12 Robert Keohane and Joseph Nye, Jr., *Power and Interdependence* (New York: Longman, 1977); Doran, *Forgotten Partnership*, 53;
13 Kirton, "Vulnerable America"; Stephen Clarkson, *Dependent America: How Canada and Mexico Construct US Power* (Toronto: University of Toronto Press, 2012).
14 Will Kymlicka, "Being Canadian," *Government and Opposition* 38, 3 (2003): 357–85; Sarah Song, "What does it mean to be an American?" *Daedalus* 138, 2 (2009): 31–40; Michael Adams, *Fire and Ice: The United States, Canada, and the Myth of Converging Values* (Toronto: Penguin, 2003).
15 See James McIlroy, "The international implications of the Canada-United States magazine dispute," *Journal of World Intellectual Property* 2, 6 (1999): 1031–51; Andrew M. Carlson, "Country music television dispute: An illustration of the tensions between Canadian cultural protectionism and American entertainment exports," *Minnesota Journal of Global Trade* 6 (1997): 585.
16 See Bow, *The Politics of Linkage*, 6–16; Sands, "Changing of the guard."
17 Andrew Cohen, *While Canada Slept: How We Lost Our Place in the World* (Toronto: McClelland and Stewart, 2011).
18 Sands, "Changing of the guard," 483–96; Bow, *Politics of Linkage*, 6–16.
19 Jeff Heynen and John Higginbotham, "Advancing Canadian interests in the United States: A practical guide for Canadian public officials," *Canada School of Public Service Action-Research Roundtable on Managing Canada-US Relations* (Ottawa: Canada School of Public Service, 2004), 1–86.
20 Andrew Brunatti, "The honest counselor: The role of the national security advisor to the Canadian prime minister," *Paterson Review* 9 (2008): 55–70.
21 See John Meisel and John Graham, "It's hard to understand Canadian studies cuts," *Globe and Mail*, 12 July 2012, http://www.theglobeandmail.com/globe-debate/its-hard-to-understand-canadian-studies-cuts/article4408869/.
22 See Greg Anderson, "A dubious disbelief," *Policy Options* (September 2012): 1–5.

23 Daniel Cole, "Why Kelo is not good news for local planners and developers," *Georgia State University Law Review* 22 (2005): 803–56; Gideon Kanner, "Kelo v. New London: Bad law, bad policy, and bad judgment," *Urban Lawyer* 38, 2 (2006): 201–35.
24 By 2009, forty-three states had engaged post-Kelo reform legislation to curb eminent domain. See Ilya Somin, "The limits of backlash: Assessing the political response to Kelo," *Minnesota Law Review* 93, 6 (2009): 2100–78.
25 See Somin, "Limits of backlash," 2100–78.
26 Robertson, "Stephen Harper's management of the Canada-US relationship," *Policy Options* (1 April 2012), http://policyoptions.irpp.org/magazines/harpers-foreign-policy/stephen-harpers-management-of-the-canada-us-relationship/. See also Bow, "Anti-Americanism in Canada," 350.
27 Author's calculations.
28 Stephen Rosen, "An empire, if you can keep it," *National Interest* 71 (spring 2003): 51–61.
29 Janice Gross Stein and Eugene Lang, *The Unexpected War: Canada in Kandahar* (Toronto: Viking, 2007), 40–51, 230–45; Jockel and Sokolsky, "Canada and the war in Afghanistan," 102–06.
30 Patrick James, *Canada and Conflict* (Oxford: Oxford University Press, 2012), 6–22.
31 Robertson, "Stephen Harper's management."
32 Stein and Lang, *Unexpected War*, 230–45; Jockel and Sokolsky, "Canada and the war in Afghanistan," 107–08.
33 Jockel and Sokolsky, "Canada and the war in Afghanistan," 113.
34 Ibid., 109–10.
35 Government of Canada, *Canada First Defence Strategy* (Ottawa: Department of National Defence, 2006), 4.
36 Kim Richard Nossal, "Defense policy and the atmospherics of Canada-US relations: The case of the Harper Conservatives," *American Review of Canadian Studies* 37, 1 (2007): 25, 30; Stein and Lang, *Unexpected War*, 121–27, 152–77; James, *Canada and Conflict*, 92–96.
37 See Joseph Jockel and Joel Sokolsky, "Special but not especially important," in Greg Anderson and Christopher Sands, eds., *Forgotten Partnership Redux: Canada-US Relations in the 21st Century* (Amherst: Cambria Press, 2011), 149–67, esp. 145–61.
38 James, *Canada and Conflict*; Murray and McCoy, "From middle power to peacebuilder," 171–88. See also Tom Keating and Robert W. Murray, "Mutual constitution or convenient national interest? The security strategies of Canada and the United States since 1991," *Canadian Foreign Policy Journal* 20, 3 (2014): 247–58.
39 Kirton, "Vulnerable America," 133–44.
40 Nossal, "Defense policy," 23–34.
41 See Adam Chapnick, "The Canadian middle power myth," *International Journal* 55, 2 (2000): 188–206; and Andrew Fenton Cooper, Richard Higgott, and Kim Richard Nossal, *Relocating Middle Powers: Australia and Canada in a Changing World Order* (Vancouver: UBC Press, 1993).
42 Fen Osler Hampson and Dean F. Oliver, "Pulpit diplomacy: A critical assessment of the Axworthy doctrine," *International Journal* 53, 3 (1998): 379–406; Kim Richard Nossal, "Foreign policy for wimps," *Ottawa Citizen*, 23 April 1999; Joe Jockel and Joel Sokolsky, "Lloyd Axworthy's legacy," *International Journal* 56, 1 (2000–01): 1–18.

43 See Canada-United States Softwood Lumber Agreement, 12 September 2006, http://www.international.gc.ca/controls-controles/softwood-bois_oeuvre/other-autres/agreement-accord.aspx?lang=eng. See also Greg Anderson, "Can someone please settle this dispute: Canadian softwood lumber and the dispute settlement mechanisms of the NAFTA and WTO," *World Economy* 29, 5 (2006): 585–610; Greg Anderson, "The Canada-US softwood lumber dispute: Where politics and theory meet," *Journal of World Trade* 38 (August 2004): 661–99.

44 See Greg Anderson, "Securitization and sovereignty in post-9/11 North America," *Review of International Political Economy* 19, 5 (2012): 711–41; Maureen Molot, "The trade-security nexus: The new reality in Canada-US economic integration," *American Review of Canadian Studies* 33, 1 (2003): 27–62; Robert Pastor, *The North American Idea* (Oxford: Oxford University Press, 2011); and Robert Pastor, *Toward a North American Community* (Washington, DC: Institute for International Economics, 2001).

45 Paul Cellucci, *Unquiet Diplomacy* (Toronto: Key Porter Books, 2005), 131–46.

46 See Greg Anderson and Christopher Sands, "Negotiating North America: The Security and Prosperity Partnership," *Hudson Institute White Paper* (Washington, DC: Hudson Institute, 2007); Jason Ackleson and Justin Kastner, "The Security and Prosperity Partnership of North America," *American Review of Canadian Studies* 36, 2 (2006): 207–32; Pastor, *North American Idea*.

47 Anderson and Sands, "Negotiating North America"; Ackleson and Kastner, "Security and Prosperity Partnership."

48 Robert Pastor, "The future of North America: Replacing a bad neighbor policy," *Foreign Affairs* 87, 4 (2008): 84–98; Pastor, *North American Idea*.

49 Pastor, *North American Idea*, 156; Stephen Clarkson, *Does North America Exist? Governing the Continent after NAFTA and 9/11* (Toronto: University of Toronto Press and Woodrow Wilson Center Press, 2008); Isabel Studer and Carol Wise, *Requiem or Revival: The Promise of North American Integration* (Washington, DC: Brookings Institution Press, 2007); Jeffrey Ayres and Laura Macdonald, *North America in Question: Regional Integration in an Era of Economic Turbulence* (Toronto: University of Toronto Press, 2012).

50 See Derek Burney and Fen Hampson, "Six reasons the 'Three Amigos' summit died," *Globe and Mail*, 16 January 2015, http://www.theglobeandmail.com/globe-debate/six-reasons-harper-postponed-the-three-amigos-summit/article22485818/.

51 Maxwell Cameron and Brian Tomlin, *The Making of the NAFTA: How the Deal was Done* (Ithaca: Cornell University Press, 2000), 63–68.

52 One small exception at the 2014 NALS in Toluca, Mexico, was the effort to harmonize all trusted traveler programs (NEXUS, SENTRI, Global Entry) into a single, unified operation.

53 Canada-US: Beyond the Border: A Shared Vision for Perimeter Security and Economic Competitiveness, the Regulatory Cooperation Council; US-Mexico: High Level Regulatory Cooperation Council.

54 Canada-US: The Clean Energy Dialogue; US-Mexico: Bilateral Framework on Clean Energy and Climate Change.

55 See Beyond the Border Implementation Report 2012, http://actionplan.gc.ca/sites/eap/files/media/legacy_files/pdfs/beyond_border_report_en_final.pdf. In perhaps the ultimate testament to the lack of impact of the shift from minority to majority,

the initiative was negotiated largely in the minority period but then was concluded and, in part, implemented after the 2011 election. There is no evidence that the Harper government's strategy was affected by its stronger position in the House of Commons post-2011.

56 See *Entry/Exit Information System Phase I Joint Canada-United States Report* http://www.cbsa-asfc.gc.ca/btb-pdf/eeis-ponerep-sdes-rappun-eng.html.
57 See Public Safety Canada, "Canada and the United States sign historic preclearance agreement," 16 March 2015, http://news.gc.ca/web/article-en.do?nid=950429.
58 See Hale, *So Near Yet So Far*.
59 It is worth noting that the Harper government also cut all funding to the Canadian Foundation for the Americas in the 2011 budget.

9

The Harper Government's Approach to Energy
Shooting Itself in the Foot
MONICA GATTINGER

When the Conservative Party of Canada formed a minority government in 2006, newly minted prime minister Stephen Harper famously touted Canada as an "emerging energy superpower." Close to a decade on, although the government had increased its standing in the House of Commons, Canada was less an energy superpower than a country with an energy "super problem." When the Conservatives returned to the polls in October 2015, the Keystone XL pipeline extension was just weeks away from being rejected outright by the Obama administration; Canadian energy resource companies had yet to secure access to tidewater for export to international markets; and community, Indigenous, environmental, and interregional opposition to energy projects of various descriptions had become increasingly fierce, polemic, and intractable. In this chapter, I explore how this state of affairs came about. In particular, I examine the Harper government's policy objectives and style on the energy file between 2006 and 2015 in the context of whether the shift from minority to majority government had a significant impact. The government's primary aim was to secure access to international markets for Canadian energy resources, but it did not make that happen in either the minority or the majority years – not because of a lack of appetite for Canadian energy in global markets but because of political opposition domestically and internationally. I argue that the government's policy style, which can be characterized as non-consultative, unilateral, and at times even combative vis-à-vis environmental non-governmental organizations, provinces, Indigenous communities, and the general public – and which does not appear to have been affected at all by the shift from minority to majority – stymied realization of its primary policy aim. All told, between 2006 and 2015, the Harper government shot itself in the foot when it came to energy, irrespective of whether it held a minority or majority of seats in the House of Commons.

This chapter has two sections. The first provides a brief "primer" on energy in Canada. It describes the complexity of contemporary energy policy making and rapid transformations in the North American energy marketplace that are having significant impacts on Canadian energy development. The second details the Harper government's approach to energy, paying particular attention to its policy aims and style, and noting the lack of discernible shifts in approach in the transition from minority to majority status.

A Primer on Energy Policy and Markets

Contemporary Energy Policy Making: Making a MESS of Energy Policy

Energy policy making is becoming ever more challenging for governments.[1] They must attend to four imperatives that have progressively layered onto one another over time. Each is complex and multifaceted in its own right, and addressing all four simultaneously is extraordinarily challenging. The first imperative deals with energy markets. Beginning in the 1970s, Western industrialized countries focused on liberalizing energy markets with a view to strengthening their efficiency and competitiveness. In Canada, liberalization in oil and gas began in the 1980s and included deregulating prices, introducing competition into the upstream and downstream energy systems, liberalizing trade through the Canada-United States Free Trade Agreement, and functional unbundling within firms to create open, non-discriminatory access to their services and facilities.[2] In electricity, a wave of liberalization began in the 1990s, with many provinces introducing competition into power generation and wholesale/retail sales.[3]

The second imperative emerged in the 1980s and 1990s with reference to the environmental impact of energy development (exploration, production, transportation/transmission, and consumption). The environmental imperative comprises everything from biodiversity and ecosystem health to climate change, land use and remediation, and water quality and diversion. Given that environmental impacts spill over political borders, many of these issues have been the subject of international agreements, such as the 1994

United Nations Framework Convention on Climate Change. In Canada, all levels of government have developed policies to address the environmental impacts of energy, including, for example, federal regulations for coal-fired electricity generation, British Columbia's carbon tax, and Quebec's cap-and-trade program with California (and now, it appears, Ontario).

The third imperative is energy security. Since Canada is a net energy exporter, security tends to be understood less in terms of disruptions to energy supply (although eastern regions of the country depend on foreign oil imports) and more in terms of vulnerability to price spikes. Following the terrorist attacks of 9/11, the concept of energy security broadened to include security of critical energy infrastructure (i.e., the physical and cyber-security of pipelines, nuclear facilities, refineries, etc.). The concept of energy security also expanded in 2003 as a result of the largest electricity outage in North American history, during which 50 million Canadians and Americans lost power. Protection of critical energy infrastructure has likewise heightened as a result of hacking efforts targeting energy firms and critical energy infrastructure in Canada and the United States, some allegedly by the Chinese military.[4]

The fourth imperative facing energy policy makers pertains to social acceptance – or frequently lack of acceptance – of energy development. In the post-9/11 era, public opposition to energy projects of various descriptions has become far more frequent, high profile, and intense. It has also grown in scope from opposition that can be characterized as NIMBYism (not in my backyard) to far more challenging forms of principled opposition to energy development, captured neatly by the acronyms BANANA (build absolutely nothing anywhere near anything) and NOPE (not on planet earth). Principled opposition is often focused on hydrocarbon development and is rooted primarily in concerns over climate change. It can rarely be addressed by conventional policy, regulatory, and proponent responses (compensating affected parties, project relocation, etc.).

Taken together, these four imperatives (market, environment, security, and social acceptance) – the energy "MESS" – comprise the complex and challenging terrain energy policy makers must navigate in the twenty-first century. The question for governments is what kind of MESS they will make of energy policy: a mess in the sense of disorder and disarray (i.e., uncoordinated, ill-conceived policies) or a mess in the sense of a "mess hall," a place where people come together to meet their shared needs (i.e., policy that identifies socially acceptable balance-points between market, environment, and security imperatives)?

Transformations in the North American Energy Marketplace

To assess the Harper government's approach to energy it is also essential to appreciate the backdrop of rapid and widespread change in the North American energy marketplace. Since the mid- to late 2000s, the energy picture in North America has been transformed by the capacity to profitably develop the continent's massive reserves of unconventional oil and gas (shale/tight oil and shale gas) through hydraulic fracturing and horizontal drilling. According to a 2013 report of the US Energy Information Administration, proved oil reserves in the United States stand at 25 billion barrels, but the country possesses close to ten times that – 220 billion barrels – in technically recoverable resources.[5] The potential in natural gas is also striking: the US possesses 305 trillion cubic feet of proved reserves and over 2 quadrillion (2,000 trillion) in technically recoverable resources. For Canada, the change in picture is less dramatic for oil, given the country's long-standing proved (over 170 billion barrels) and technically recoverable unconventional reserves (320 billion barrels), largely in the oil sands.[6] Canada's potential in unconventional gas is substantial: the country has 70 trillion cubic feet of proved gas reserves, with another 1 to 2 quadrillion technically recoverable.[7]

The so-called "shale revolution" is generating significant impacts on Canada-US energy relations. The United States is on its way to becoming a net gas exporter and therefore no longer a heavy importer from Canada. In oil, although the United States will continue to be a net importer, import volumes are on the decline. Washington cut its oil imports in half between 2006 and 2012, and a 2013 Citigroup report predicted it could eliminate oil imports from the Middle East and hostile suppliers by 2018.[8] In gas, the US Energy Information Administration projects a decline in net gas imports from Canada out to 2040.[9] All told, the shale revolution is calling into question the size and viability of the US appetite for Canadian energy going forward.

It is no accident that recent years have also seen multiple pipeline proposals and liquefied natural gas project proposals coming forward to carry Canadian energy to international markets beyond North America. Not only would such projects secure new markets for Canadian energy, they could also fetch higher prices for the product. Increased oil and gas production in the United States has put downward pressure on the prices of both commodities. This new normal has been especially challenging for the oil sands, which tend to have a higher break-even point than lighter oil from shale formations. The United States may also be shifting from consumer to competitor for Canadian gas, although shale gas production in northeastern British Columbia has yet to secure infrastructure along the west coast for export.[10] The shale revolution is projected to ultimately decrease US electricity imports from Canada as well.[11]

These market dynamics are generating powerful incentives for oil and gas producers to gain access to international markets beyond North America. The main options for oil are east to eastern Canadian and export markets (TransCanada's Energy East pipeline and Enbridge's Line 9 reversal), and west to British Columbia's coast for export to Asia (Kinder Morgan's Trans-Mountain pipeline and Enbridge's Northern Gateway pipeline). For gas, the focus is on a large number of liquid natural gas (LNG) export proposals in British Columbia.[12]

Remarkably, none of these major projects had gone forward by October 2015, and, in every instance, the reason was a lack of social acceptance and support – something that was not due to the Harper government's lack of trying. Indeed, one of its main policy objectives was to secure market access for Canadian energy resources. Why did these projects not prove to be "no brainers" (as Prime Minister Harper famously quipped early in his first mandate when referring to the Keystone XL pipeline)? The next section addresses this question.

Shooting Itself in the Foot

Beginning when it came to power in 2006, and irrespective of the Conservative Party's standing in the House of Commons over the next nine years, the Harper government's policy interventions focused first and foremost on the market imperative of the energy MESS: securing and maintaining "market access" for Canadian energy exports. The environmental imperative of energy policy making appears to have taken a backseat to this economic objective both at home and abroad. Likewise, the government did not place great emphasis on the security imperative. It is with regard to the last "S" of the energy MESS – social acceptance – that the government encountered the most difficulty. Its policy style tended towards unilateralism – a style that is far from a "mess hall" approach to energy. This approach stymied the realization of its market access policy aims.

Energy in the Harper Minority Governments, 2006–08, 2008–11

Energy did not occupy as prominent a place in the Conservative agenda before 2011 as it did afterwards – but the subsequent increase in emphasis does not appear to have been related to the shift from minority to majority status in the House of Commons; rather, market transformations were critical. The shale revolution and its impacts were not fully under way until the latter half of the government's minority era, so the focus on market access was not initially as sharp as it was to become. Much of the federal government's policy attention was focused instead on responding to the global financial crisis of 2007–08 and the ensuing Great Recession of 2008–09. That said, the Conservatives did engage with energy, primarily through their support for the oil sands, their stance on climate change, and their efforts to work with the Obama administration on energy and the environment.

The Conservative Party platform for the 2006 federal election, *Stand Up for Canada*, centred mainly on accountability, written as it was in the wake of the "sponsorship scandal" that plagued Paul Martin's Liberal government. Energy was only mentioned once, and this in connection with the environment: the Conservatives committed to develop a "made-in-Canada" plan to reduce GHG emissions, criticizing the Liberal government, which, they said, "sign[s] ambitious international treaties and send[s] money to foreign governments for hot air credits, but can't seem to get anything done to help people here at home."[13]

In May 2006, the new government made good on this commitment when Rona Ambrose, minister of the environment and chair of the United Nations Framework Convention on Climate Change meetings in Bonn, Germany, shocked delegates and many Canadians when she stated that Canada would not meet its Kyoto GHG reduction targets.[14] She called for the second post-2012 phase of the Kyoto Protocol to use voluntary targets, establish lengthier deadlines, and include exceptions for Canada's resources.[15] Two months later, the government's support for the market imperative of energy policy making was further underscored when Prime Minister Harper touted Canada as an "emerging energy superpower" in a speech to the Canada-United Kingdom Chamber of Commerce. "We are a stable, reliable producer in a volatile, unpredictable world,"[16] he said. Indeed, "industry analysts are recommending Canada as 'possessing the most attractive combination of circumstances for energy investment of any place in the world.'"[17] In 2007, the government's *Turning the Corner* plan pledged a 20 percent reduction in Canada's 2006 GHG levels by 2020. The new target was critiqued for halving the country's original Kyoto commitment.[18]

When the government went back to the polls in 2008, its election platform paid greater attention to energy. The Conservatives committed to transforming Canada into a "clean energy superpower" by supporting pipeline development in the North, prohibiting the export of bitumen to countries with comparatively lower environmental standards, investing in biofuels and renewable energy, and aiming to have 90 percent of Canadian electricity generated by non-emitting sources like nuclear, hydro, and wind.[19] The Conservatives also pledged to establish a cap-and-trade system in North America between 2012 and 2015. This final commitment was ultimately reversed in the wake of the global financial crisis and recession, which knocked cap-and-trade off the policy agendas of both the United States and Canada.

The Harper government appeared to be looking to work with the United States on energy and climate, but this interest in bilateral collaboration was not initially reciprocated. When the United States elected Barack Obama president in fall 2008, climate change was high on his agenda but direct cooperation with Canada on the file was not. Indeed, the Harper government tried to engage the Obama administration in an energy security/climate change deal at the prime minister's first meeting with the newly inaugurated president,[20] but it was unsuccessful. Instead, the meeting produced the far less ambitious Clean Energy Dialogue, which committed "senior officials from both countries to collaborate on the development of clean energy science and technologies that will reduce greenhouse gases and combat climate change."[21] As to putting a price on carbon, the United States moved ahead with seemingly little reference to Canada, prompting the head of the National Roundtable on the Environment and the Economy to urge Ottawa to act quickly so as to avoid getting caught up in American environmental protectionism.[22] In June 2009, the Conservatives announced that they planned to develop a cap-and-trade system, presumably one that would be similar in approach to the US plan given the countries' highly integrated and interdependent economies.

In the aftermath of the global financial crisis, bilateral energy conflicts emerged between Canada and the United States over development of the oil sands, which have been criticized for having a heavier environmental footprint vis-à-vis conventional oil (higher GHG emissions, water usage, damage to the boreal forest, production of tailings ponds, etc.). Increasingly, the Canadian government found itself facing mass protests and high-profile advertising campaigns against the oil sands – referred to as the "tar sands" or "dirty oil" by opponents. American politicians, including Barack Obama himself, also began to make pronouncements against "dirty oil." Policy and legislation against the oil sands began to create real headaches for the Harper government. Specifically, federal legislation prohibiting the US government from purchasing fuels that produce more emissions than conventional oil, a resolution by the US Conference of Mayors against the use of oil sands fuel for municipal vehicles, and the development of low carbon fuel standards in California threatened future Canadian economic prosperity. Although the Harper and Alberta governments noted that GHG emissions from the oil sands were comparable to those of conventional oil producers who exported to the United States, opposition to the oil sands did not dissipate. Pressure on the Obama administration to reject the proposed extension of the Keystone XL pipeline was potent, relentless, and ultimately effective.

Energy in the Majority Harper Government, 2011–15
The Conservatives' third term in government saw energy rise substantially on policy and political agendas, but the change does not appear to have been driven by the shift from minority to majority; rather, it was controversy over energy projects and failure to "get shovels in the ground" that focused government attention on the sector. Opposition to the Keystone XL pipeline was increasingly joined by opposition to other major oil pipeline projects: Enbridge's Northern Gateway pipeline (which would extend from Alberta to the west coast); Kinder Morgan's TransMountain pipeline (which would expand an existing pipeline into British Columbia); Enbridge's Line 9 pipeline reversal (which, instead of carrying imported crude from Montreal to Sarnia, would now transport western Canadian crude through Ontario and Quebec); and TransCanada's Energy East pipeline (which would construct new pipelines and convert and expand an existing natural gas pipeline to carry crude oil from Alberta to refineries in Quebec and New Brunswick for Canadian and international markets). Opponents ranged from local communities and landowners; to city mayors and council members; to Indigenous leaders and communities; to local, national, and international environmental NGOs; and to individual citizens. Mass protests were mounted and, in the case of the TransMountain project, which received partial regulatory approval, a number of individuals sought to prevent the company from proceeding with seismic testing and were arrested in the process.

The Harper government's response to this opposition, which also included provincial premiers expressing concern over projects crossing through their jurisdictions, seems to have been to double down on its primary policy objective of securing market access for Canadian energy. It rolled out a suite of policy measures, some aspects of which addressed opponents' concerns and others of which intensified opposition. The concept of Responsible Resource Development, for example, was first unveiled in Budget 2012. The government noted: "Canadians will only reap the benefits that come from our natural resources if investments are made by the private sector to bring the resources to market. Yet those who wish to invest in our resources have been facing an increasingly complicated web of rules and bureaucratic reviews that have grown over time, adding costs and delays that can deter investors and undermine the economic viability of major projects."[23]

To capitalize on the opportunity and address the challenges, the government committed to streamlining the regulatory review process for major projects by reducing duplication between federal and provincial environmental assessment regimes, decreasing the time it takes to process applications, strengthening protection of the environment, and enhancing consultation with Indigenous peoples in environmental assessments.[24] The Conservatives promised to provide additional funding to the Major Projects Management Office, which it established in 2007 to coordinate federal review processes with the aim of shortening timelines. The government established measures to strengthen tanker safety and increase pipeline safety inspections. It altered the regulatory framework governing the National Energy Board: specifically, by requiring that applications rejected by the board come to Cabinet for review and possible reversal, it left the fate of pipeline proposals directly in the hands of the prime minister. Finally, the government approved the $15 billion acquisition of energy giant Nexen by the Chinese National Offshore Oil Company in a move that, some argued, placed market imperatives (in this case foreign direct investment from a Chinese state-owned enterprise) above security considerations.[25]

Over time, additional measures were added to the Responsible Resource Development initiative, including measures for marine oil spill prevention and response, timely regulatory reviews (including additional funding for participants in the process), increasing absolute liability to $1 billion for oil and gas companies operating offshore, and establishing more favourable tax treatment for direct investments in the LNG sector. The focus on market access continued to anchor the government's approach, with Budget 2014 noting: "About 98 per cent of Canada's crude oil exports and 100 per cent of our natural gas exports are to the United States. Exporting only to the US market has resulted in significantly lower Canadian crude oil prices relative to global benchmarks in recent years. This is significantly reducing the value of Canadian exports and gross domestic product."[26] In addition, in the wake of the tragic train derailment in Lac Mégantic in 2013, which saw train cars loaded with oil from the Bakken shale formation explode in a massive fireball on the town's main street, killing close to fifty people and devastating the community, the federal government worked in tandem with the United States to strengthen railcar safety.

The Conservatives' efforts were regularly critiqued by their opponents for privileging the economy over the environment, notably when it came to amendments to the *Canadian Environmental Assessment Act* and to reductions in the timelines of regulatory approval processes. Moreover, on the climate change front, as Michael Manulak notes (Chapter 7, this volume), the government was criticized for dragging its feet. Rather than developing a comprehensive plan, the Conservatives appear to have adopted a piecemeal approach, committing, for example, to meet US tailpipe emissions standards, putting in place regulations for the coal-fired power sector, and investing in carbon capture and sequestration projects in Saskatchewan and Alberta. Their GHG emissions reduction commitment announced in May 2015 did target a 30 percent reduction in emissions from 2005 levels by 2030; however, that objective was less ambitious than the American pledge because regulations for the oil sands – Canada's fastest-growing source of emissions – were not included and because the government was not on track to meet its prior climate commitments.[27]

What's more, the government's policy style rubbed many of its opponents (and possible allies) the wrong way. Its approach can be characterized as unilateral rather than consultative, combative rather than conciliatory, and autonomous rather than collaborative. To be fair, the Harper government exercised leadership, but its leadership style was often counterproductive. Instead of working with industry, other governments, civil society, and Indigenous groups to identify balance-points between market, environment, and security imperatives that garner social acceptance, the government seems to have predetermined where the balance-points lay and pursued its objectives in a fashion that invited conflict.

With regard to the Keystone XL pipeline, as noted above, between 2006 and 2015, the government was a staunch supporter, making regular trips to Washington and other US locations to lobby in favour of the Obama administration's approval. As Greg Anderson notes (Chapter 8, this volume), the fashion in which it did so, however, sometimes poked a stick in the eye of the US administration. This was most apparent when Prime Minister Harper stated before a business audience in New York that Canada would not "take no for an answer."[28]

The government was also unwilling to engage with the provinces on questions of energy. While provincial governments had been collaborating since the first Harper mandate to develop a national energy strategy, the federal government expressly chose not to participate.[29] Nor did it intervene in provincial disputes over energy matters, including one between the premiers of British Columbia and Alberta over the Northern Gateway pipeline, during which BC premier Christy Clark laid out a number of environmental, social, and fiscal conditions for her province's support.[30]

Indigenous peoples expressed disappointment that the government did not do more to consult their communities on energy projects. The brief "fly-in" of a number of ministers to British Columbia on the Northern Gateway project was emblematic of that approach. Stewart Phillip, grand chief of the Union of BC Indian Chiefs, once said of the government's style: "Everything they've done has been unilateral without any discussions."[31]

But it was towards non-governmental opponents of energy development – environmental NGOs in particular – that the Conservatives were the most combative. These groups seemed to be perceived as illegitimate actors advancing unreasonable policy positions in the public sphere. The government appears to have taken pains to demonize them and to portray them as solely responsible for opposition to energy project development. The apogee of this position was a 2012 "open letter" from the minister of natural resources, Joe Oliver, published in the *Globe and Mail* and posted on the ministry's website. The text begins: "Canada is on the edge of an historic choice: to diversify our energy markets away from our traditional trading partner in the United States or to continue with the status quo." It continues: "Unfortunately, there are environmental and other radical groups that would seek to block this opportunity to diversify our trade. ... These groups threaten to hijack our regulatory system to achieve their radical ideological agenda. They seek to exploit any loophole they can find, stacking public hearings with bodies to ensure that delays kill good projects. They use funding from foreign special interest groups to undermine Canada's national economic interest."[32]

In addition, the passage of Bill C-51, the *Anti-Terrorism Act, 2015*, generated significant opposition because it included provisions that some fear will be used to clamp down on individuals or groups protesting the approval or construction of energy projects. Leaders of some of Canada's major environmental NGOs (like John Bennett, the executive director of the Sierra Club of Canada) feel they were painted as terrorists simply for holding views counter to those of the government.[33] The Canada Revenue Agency's "blitz" to audit the advocacy activities of organizations holding charitable status also left many in the environmental community feeling there was a chill on advocacy in the country.[34]

This negative, combative approach seemed to extend to climate change policy writ large, whereby the government increasingly distanced itself from putting a price on carbon that would apply across the country, be it through a cap-and-trade system – which, it must be recalled, the Conservatives were committed to early on in their first mandate – or a carbon tax. Indeed, when Liberal Party leader Stéphane Dion campaigned on a proposal to establish a carbon tax in the 2008 federal election, Prime Minister Harper referred to it as an "insane" idea that would "screw everybody," just like the National Energy Program of 1980 (ably recalled by John English in Chapter 2, this volume).[35] In 2014, in the wake of the substantial drop in oil prices, the prime minister declared that it would be "crazy" to establish climate regulations on the oil and gas sector in such a challenging economic climate; moreover, when accused of privileging the economy over the environment, he conceded: "We are just a little more frank about [doing it], but that is the approach that every country is seeking."[36] Paradoxically, this combative and minimalist stance on climate change mitigation appears to have stymied the government's market access objectives: in the absence of a forum to make meaningful progress on climate change, many environmental NGOs blocked oil sands pipeline projects during the regulatory process.[37]

Conclusion – A Glimmer of Change in the Harper Government's Policy Style: Too Little Too Late?

When Stephen Harper touted Canada as an emerging energy superpower in 2006, the world appeared to be Canada's energy oyster: energy prices were strong, demand in the United States was steady, emerging economies were growing ever thirstier for the kinds of energy resources Canada possesses, and large projects to get the country's energy resources to market were in the offing. Nearly a decade later, the landscape had changed substantially: the shale revolution called into question the size and viability of the US market for Canadian energy, and the sector faced seemingly intractable opposition to just about every major energy project on the table – including the Northern Gateway and TransMountain pipelines that had already received partial or full regulatory approval. Industry insiders even began to talk about "democratic risk" when it came to investment decisions in the Canadian energy sector.

To be fair, transformations in North America's energy markets and politics would challenge any government, but the Conservatives' approach between 2006 and 2015 tended to exacerbate political conflict around energy and, paradoxically, stymied the attainment of its market access objectives. There is no question the government exercised leadership – the question is whether it was the right kind. Addressing the market, environment, security, and social acceptance imperatives of contemporary energy policy requires that governments make a MESS of energy policy in the sense of a mess hall: collaborative, consultative efforts bringing together governments, industry, and civil society to identify balance-points between market, environment, and security imperatives that garner social acceptance.

In the lead-up to the 2015 election, however, there were glimmers of a shift in style.[38] The appointment of Greg Rickford as the minister of natural resources in March 2014 seemed to herald a somewhat more productive approach. The minister engaged effectively with the American secretary of energy, Ernest Moniz. Secretary Moniz even held a consultation session on the United States' quadrennial energy review in Ottawa – the only such session held outside of the United States. The two also signed a memorandum of understanding on science and technology collaboration. And then, in May 2015, along with their Mexican counterpart, they founded the North American Energy Ministers' Working Group on Climate Change and Energy.[39]

The government also made greater efforts to better engage Indigenous communities in the energy sector, most notably with the appointment of Doug Eyford as its special federal representative on West Coast energy infrastructure. Eyford's December 2013 final report underscored that the government must build effective relationships with Indigenous peoples through engagement that addresses their concerns and challenges. In addition, Natural Resources Canada became more engaged on matters of social acceptance and, specifically, in terms of how to strengthen public confidence in energy development. The department began working on this front internally and with the provinces, territories, and non-government initiatives.

Nonetheless, in October 2015, the government still had some serious catching up to do, work that it will be up to the Liberal government of Justin Trudeau to complete. Indigenous leaders and communities still felt that they continued to be inadequately consulted on energy, and Ottawa remained distant from the provinces' national energy strategy discussions. On climate change, the Harper government's approach – notably its aversion to putting a price on carbon – remained inadequate in the view of many environmental NGOs. Indeed, in this context, it is difficult to imagine how the Conservatives could have ever attained their market access objectives.

In sum, between 2006 and 2015, during both the minority and majority years, instead of getting shovels in the ground, the Harper government seemed to shoot itself in the foot.

Notes

1 For a more fulsome discussion of the energy policy MESS framework, see Monica Gattinger, "Canada-United States energy relations: Making a MESS of energy policy," *American Review of Canadian Studies* 42, 4 (2012): 460–73.
2 André Plourde, "The changing nature of national and continental energy markets," in G. Bruce Doern, ed., *Canadian Energy Policy and the Struggle for Sustainable Development* (Toronto: University of Toronto Press, 2005), 51–82.
3 Ibid.
4 David Sanger, David Barboza, and Nicole Perlroth, "Chinese army unit is seen as tied to hacking against US," *New York Times*, 18 February 2013, http://www.nytimes.com/2013/02/19/technology/chinas-army-is-seen-as-tied-to-hacking-against-us.html?_r=0.
5 United States Energy Information Administration (US EIA), *International Energy Statistics*, Petroleum and Natural Gas Reserves, 2013, http://www.eia.gov/cfapps/ipdbproject/IEDIndex3.cfm. Note that "technically recoverable resources" refers to probable, possible, and speculative reserves so this must be interpreted with caution.
6 Ibid.
7 Ibid.
8 Lawrence Soloman, "Fight jihad, stop carbon taxes," *Financial Post*, 21 February 2013 (last updated 22 February), http://business.financialpost.com/2013/02/21/lawrence-solomon-shale-means-security/.
9 US EIA, *Annual Energy Outlook 2013 Early Release Overview*. Report No. DOE/EIA-0383ER, 2013 (Washington, DC: United States EIA, 2012).
10 Jonathan S. Drance and Brandon Mewhort, "BC LNG: The path to first gas," *Canadian Energy Law Blog*, Stikeman Elliott LLP, 22 May 2015, http://www.lexology.com/library/detail.aspx?g=6bdea4ac-8eae-4166-8e69-c85e5deb274c.
11 US EIA, *Annual Energy Outlook 2013*.
12 Drance and Mewhort, "BC LNG."
13 Conservative Party of Canada, *Stand Up for Canada: Conservative Party of Canada Federal Election Platform 2006* (Ottawa: Conservative Party of Canada, 2006), 37.
14 Bill Curry, "Opposition parties to force Tories to meet Kyoto targets," *Globe and Mail*, 16 May 2006, http://www.theglobeandmail.com/news/national/opposition-parties-to-force-tories-to-meet-kyoto-targets/article18162531/.
15 Ibid.
16 Stephen Harper, *Address by the Prime Minister at the Canada-UK Chamber of Commerce*, London, 14 July 2006, as cited in Stephen Harper, "Harper's Index," *The Dominion*, 21 October 2007, http://www.dominionpaper.ca/articles/1491.
17 Ibid. The analyst in question is Henry Groppe. See David J. Deslauriers, "Oil forecasting legend paints dire energy picture," *Hard Assets*, 6 June 2005, http://www.resilience.org/stories/2005-06-06/energy-headlines-june-6-2005-part-two.

18 Matthew Bramley, "Far from turning the corner: Canada's Conservative government has substantially shifted its position on climate change, but is its policy response too timid, too complex and likely to be superseded?" *Carbon Finance*, 20 June 2008, http://www.pembina.org/op-ed/1661.
19 Conservative Party of Canada, *The True North Strong and Free: Stephen Harper's Plan for Canadians* (Ottawa: Conservative Party of Canada, 2008), 23.
20 Shawn McCarthy, "Ottawa swoops in with climate-change offer," *Globe and Mail*, 6 November 2008, http://www.theglobeandmail.com/news/world/ottawa-swoops-in-with-climate-change-offer/article17973912/.
21 The White House, Office of the Press Secretary, *Press Availability by President Obama and Prime Minister Harper of Canada*, Ottawa, 19 February 2009.
22 Tom Ford, "Inaction on climate change backfires," *Winnipeg Free Press*, 25 May 2009, http://www.winnipegfreepress.com/opinion/analysis/inaction-on-climate-change-backfires-45974802.html.
23 Canada, Ministry of Finance, *Jobs, Growth and Long-Term Prosperity: Economic Action Plan 2012* (Ottawa: Her Majesty the Queen in Right of Canada, 2012), 88.
24 Ibid, 92.
25 Terry Glavin, "Scrutinizing Canada's pipeline to Beijing," *National Post*, 29 January 2012, http://news.nationalpost.com/full-comment/terry-glavin-scrutinizing-canadas-pipeline-to-beijing.
26 Canada, Ministry of Finance, *The Road to Balance: Creating Jobs and Opportunities* (Ottawa: Her Majesty the Queen in Right of Canada, 2014), 142.
27 Shawn McCarthy, "Ottawa commits to 30 percent cut in GHGs but no regulations for oil sands," *Globe and Mail*, 15 May 2015, http://www.theglobeandmail.com/news/national/ottawa-commits-to-30-per-cent-cut-in-emissions-but-not-for-oil-sands/article24453757/.
28 Susana Mas, "Harper won't take no for an answer on Keystone XL: PM touts benefits of proposed pipeline to business leaders in New York," *CBC News*, 26 September 2013. http://www.cbc.ca/news/politics/harper-won-t-take-no-for-an-answer-on-keystone-xl-1.1869439.
29 See Monica Gattinger, "A national energy strategy for Canada: Golden age or golden cage of energy federalism?" in Loleen Berdahl, André Juneau, and Carolyn Hughes Tuohy, eds., *Canada: The State of the Federation* (Montreal and Kingston: McGill-Queen's University Press, 2015, 36–69).
30 Ibid.
31 Mark Hume, "BC First Nations leaders still oppose Northern Gateway pipeline," *Globe and Mail*, 9 June 2014, http://www.theglobeandmail.com/news/british-columbia/bands-still-oppose-northern-gateway/article19087205/.
32 Joe Oliver, "An open letter from the Honourable Joe Oliver, Minister of Natural Resources, on Canada's commitment to diversify our energy markets and the need to further streamline the regulatory process in order to advance Canada's national economic interest," Ottawa, Natural Resources Canada, 9 January 2012, http://www.nrcan.gc.ca/media-room/news-release/2012/1/1909.
33 John Bennett, "Remarks to the panel: Energy and natural resources," 2015 Policy Conference of the Political, International, and Development Studies Student Association, University of Ottawa, 1 March.

34 Voices, *Canadian Charities and the Canada Revenue Agency*, 1 May 2015, http://voices-voix.ca/en/facts/profile/canadian-charities-and-canada-revenue-agency.
35 CBC News, "PM: Dion's carbon tax would 'screw everybody,'" 20 June 2008, http://www.cbc.ca/news/canada/pm-dion-s-carbon-tax-would-screw-everybody-1.696762.
36 Les Whittington, "Stephen Harper says economy trumps climate action," *Toronto Star*, 9 June 2014, http://www.thestar.com/news/canada/2014/06/09/stephen_harper_says_economy_trumps_climate_action.html.
37 Positive Energy, "Positive Energy: Building a Path to Social Acceptance and Support for Energy Development," inaugural conference of the Positive Energy Project, co-chaired by the University of Ottawa's Collaboratory on Energy Research and Policy and the University of Western Ontario's Energy Policy and Management Centre, Ottawa, 4–5 March 2015.
38 It is worth noting that most of the observable shifts in the government's behaviour captured in this chapter coincided with the year or so leading up to a federal election, not with the actual results.
39 Barry Cohen, "US, Canada, Mexico create working group on climate change and energy," *PowerNewsWire*, 28 May 2015, http://powernewswire.com/stories/510546746-u-s-canada-mexico-create-working-group-on-climate-change-and-energy.

10

Canadian Aid Policy during the Harper Years

STEPHEN BROWN

To what extent did the Conservative government's majority status in 2011–15 affect its development assistance policy? That is the question that I seek to answer. To do so, I review the record of Stephen Harper's government over three time periods: an initial phase of minority government (2006–08), characterized by inertia, during which the government took few initiatives of its own; a more proactive phase of minority government (2009–11), when the government made some bold changes; and the period during which the Conservatives held majority status in the House of Commons (2011–15), when they intensified some of their previous initiatives and established some new ones.

Ultimately, majority status had little impact on the Harper government's foreign aid policy. Rather than 2011, the year 2009 is a more accurate turning point in Canadian aid policy, for it was then that the government undertook bold new initiatives, including adopting new focus countries and themes, making prominent linkages to the extractive sector, and downgrading its relationship with Canadian development non-governmental organizations. Such initiatives multiplied over time, continuing after 2011, with a deepening of commercial self-interest and the abolition of the Canadian International Development Agency. However, they were not significantly affected by the government's majority status. Some, in fact, broadly followed global trends, such as the rise and fall of security considerations in aid programs – nowhere more evident than in Afghanistan – and the increased commercialization of aid.

Initial Inertia: 2006–08

During its first few years in power, the Harper government paid scant attention to foreign aid. It took few new initiatives related to international development and contented itself mainly with pursuing policies inherited from the Liberal governments of Jean Chrétien and Paul Martin. In public pronouncements on aid, Conservative politicians and government officials emphasized the government's commitment to doubling aid to Africa and overall aid spending, omitting the fact that these were actually promises made under the Liberals.[1] The Harper government did achieve both of these targets within the promised timeframe. Figure 10.1 illustrates the trend in Canadian official development assistance (ODA), both overall and to Africa, expressed in constant US dollars to facilitate comparison.[2] The Harper government also initially pursued reforms to its foreign aid program in line with the development chapter of the *International Policy Statement*, issued by the Liberals under Paul Martin, including focusing bilateral aid on twenty-five priority countries identified by them.[3]

Nonetheless, the Conservative government did announce some changes to aid policy. The first ones, made in 2007, were relatively minor: aiming to

FIGURE 10.1
Canadian official development assistance, 1993–2014

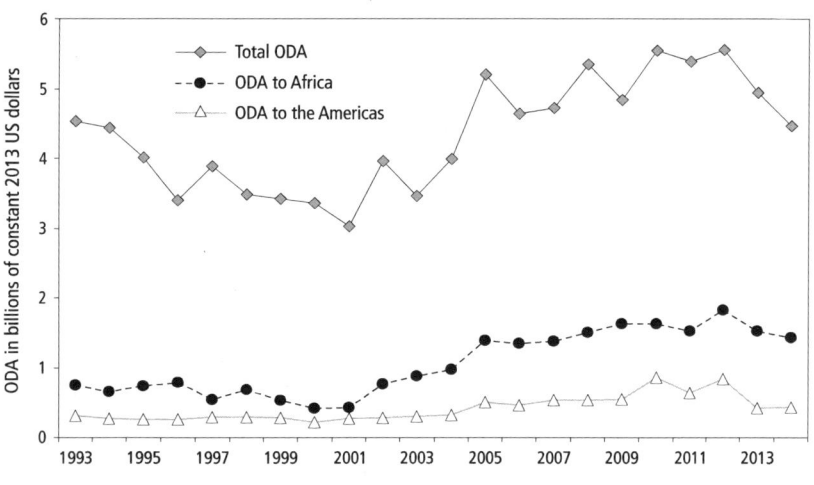

Source: OECD, Query Wizard for International Development Statistics, https://stats.oecd.org/qwids/.

be "among the largest five donors in core countries of interest" and promising to "put more of our staff in the field."[4] These new goals were not met, however, as the number of countries "in which top five bilateral donor status was achieved" remained in the eight to twelve range by the government's own calculation, depending on the year,[5] whereas it had already been eleven in 2004–05.[6] The government also balked at the high cost of decentralizing staff, which was at odds with its commitment to reduce overhead.

Also in 2007, Prime Minister Harper made a surprise announcement at the Heligendamm G8 summit that Canada would henceforth place greater emphasis on the Americas, appearing to break with the donor consensus – and with Liberal practice – to prioritize the poorest continent, Africa. Though widely interpreted as Canada abandoning Africa, this did not turn out to be the case (as can be seen in Figure 10.1 above). Moreover, despite a new Americas Strategy, aid to this region did not rise much until 2010. However, the new rhetoric did signal some changes to come regarding Latin America and the Caribbean (discussed below).

The biggest change in development policy during this period was the prioritization of Afghanistan and, specifically, Kandahar, where Canada assumed responsibility for the Provincial Reconstruction Team in 2005, while the Liberals were still in power. The Conservatives, however, dedicated vast new resources to Afghanistan for military, diplomatic, and development purposes, ramping up foreign aid from US$124 million in 2005 to a high of $400 million in 2007, albeit dropping down to the $220 to $285 million range for the next four years.[7] Between 2001 and 2012, Canadian ODA to Afghanistan totalled more than CAD$2 billion, constituting CIDA's largest program ever.[8]

None of the initiatives described above appears to be linked to the Harper government's minority status in 2006–08. Unlike in 2005, when the NDP forced the Liberals to increase the foreign aid budget as a condition for supporting the minority Martin government's budget,[9] no opposition party took such steps to "force" the Harper minority government to meet the Liberals' commitments to increase ODA. The rhetorical shift to the Americas was certainly not meant to please opposition parties. However, in the case of Afghanistan, the Conservatives enjoyed and perhaps even co-opted Liberal support for the mission, appointing former Liberal Cabinet minister John Manley to head the Independent Panel on Canada's Future Role in Afghanistan, which duly recommended increased involvement. As Jean-Christophe Boucher and Kim Richard Nossal observe (Chapter 4, this volume), nothing suggests that the Afghanistan policy, as opposed to the strategy to adopt it, responded to the government's minority status.

One policy change, however, certainly was facilitated by the Conservatives' minority status in Parliament: the passage of the 2008 *Official Development Assistance Accountability Act*, which legislated that the central focus of aid was to be poverty reduction and that aid must "contribute[] to poverty reduction; take[] into account the perspectives of the poor; and [be] consistent with international human rights standards."[10] It was presented by Liberal backbencher John McKay and enjoyed strong support from the NDP and other opposition parties. Surprisingly for a private member's bill, especially one that the government initially opposed, it passed – with unanimous support – though only after its provisions were watered down to gain Conservative support and prevent the Senate from blocking its passage. In the end, the legislation proved rather toothless; the government claimed that it was already compliant with the law's basic principles, and no changes were made to Canada's development program.[11]

Seizing the Initiative: 2009–March 2011

Starting in 2009, the Canadian government took a more proactive role in foreign aid, introducing numerous new policy initiatives. In February, it made one of its boldest moves: it announced that CIDA would henceforth spend 80 percent of its bilateral aid in twenty "countries of focus," and it officially included alignment with Canadian foreign policy objectives as a criterion for country selection. In whittling down its list from the Martin government's twenty-five priority countries, the Harper government conspicuously cut a number of low-income African states, notably francophone ones (e.g., Burkina Faso and Benin), and added middle-income countries in the Americas, including ones with which Canada was seeking closer trade relations (such as Peru and Colombia). These actions were in line with the emphasis on the Americas heralded by Prime Minister Harper in 2007, though the impact on aid played out differently from country to country.[12]

Simultaneously, the Conservatives replaced the Martin government's five priority sectors with three priority themes: food security, children and youth, and sustainable economic growth, in addition to three cross-cutting themes – namely, gender equality, environmental sustainability, and governance. These themes – like the priority sectors that had preceded them – were specific enough to give the impression of focus, while broad enough to accommodate any project that the government wanted to support.

The following year, at the 2010 G8 summit in Muskoka, Ontario, Prime Minister Harper announced a signature initiative on maternal, newborn, and child health (MNCH). Though the government claimed the Muskoka

Initiative, as it was dubbed, fell within its theme of "children and youth," it appears to have been more of an afterthought, an "announceable" for the summit for which Canada could claim international leadership. At that point, many other countries were already quite active in the area, and the Harper government's attempt to seize the initiative was not well received among fellow donors, not least because the Canadian government explicitly excluded abortion services, even where these were legal, and downplayed the importance of contraception in ensuring maternal health. As a result, in the words of David Black, "Canadian leadership aspirations on MNCH have been constrained by the paucity of followership."[13]

In 2009, the government untied all food aid and promised to untie all other assistance by 2013 – that is to say, it no longer required that goods and services be procured in Canada (which was often more expensive and, in the case of emergency assistance, much slower). This decision was in keeping with the donor consensus on aid effectiveness and with what most European donors had already done. The government presented the untying of aid, like the "focus on focus" (fewer countries and themes), as part of its "Aid Effectiveness Agenda."

This agenda also included a greater emphasis on measurable results – or "real results," as successive development ministers often preferred to refer to them. The prominence accorded to visible results introduced a bias in favour of short-term measurable outputs rather than long-term transformation, which aid experts have shown to undermine aid effectiveness.[14] The fetishization of visible outcomes attributable to Canada was epitomized by the announcement of three signature projects in Afghanistan – adopted in response to the Manley Commission's report (see above) – whose results and the sustainability thereof actually proved disappointing, especially the much-touted Dahla Dam and irrigation system in Kandahar.[15]

The whole-of-government approach was a further component of the Harper government's rhetorical emphasis on aid effectiveness, building on the Martin government's 3-D initiative, bringing together development, defence, and diplomatic efforts to better achieve Canada's international policy goals. Though theoretically such collaboration among government departments can be more effective, joining together is only beneficial for development if sustainable poverty alleviation is the overarching goal (or at least one of them). Using aid for counterinsurgency purposes does not typically meet developmental aims. It follows that cross-departmental collaboration failed to produce sustainable results in Afghanistan, although it could ultimately prove to be more effective elsewhere, such as in Haiti.[16]

The emphasis of the government's aid effectiveness agenda, in fact, did not match international understandings of effectiveness, which focused on the recipient country's ownership of the development process, donor alignment with national priorities (as opposed to Canada setting its own), and harmonization among donors (rather than signature projects). Instead, the Canadian approach prioritized accountability to Canadians, which entailed greater bureaucracy and risk-aversion, thereby reducing CIDA's ability to implement innovative and timely programs on the ground. In fact, other than the elimination of tied aid, during this period the measures taken by the Harper government in the name of aid effectiveness had no positive impact on effectiveness and, indeed, sometimes yielded a negative one – for example, by causing aid volatility and unpredictability.[17]

Also starting in 2009, CIDA's relationship with development NGOs deteriorated significantly. First KAIROS, then Alternatives, the Canadian Council for International Co-operation, and several other respected organizations had their CIDA funding radically cut or eliminated. The reasons provided seemed spurious, and a pattern soon emerged: the NGOs appeared to be targeted for their public criticisms of Canadian international policies, especially with regard to Israel/Palestine and the activities of Canadian mining companies. In 2010, CIDA reformed the way it funded NGOs, eliminating the mechanism based on unsolicited proposals and making them respond to calls for proposals, emphasizing the need to work primarily on the Canadian government's priority countries and themes – treating them more as contractors and less as development actors in their own right, with legitimate priorities of their own. Again, the government presented its underlying motivation as improving effectiveness, but the effect was the opposite, because it undermined the NGOs' work in their actual areas of expertise.[18]

Finally, in 2010, the government achieved the commitment of doubling aid. It consequently decided to cap the "international assistance envelope" at CAD$5 billion as part of a fiscal austerity/budget balancing exercise. This presaged the subsequent cutting of ODA (discussed below).

None of the initiatives outlined above can be attributed to the minority status of the Harper government. If anything, the boldness of some of these moves would be more likely to occur under a majority government, given the objections they engendered. None of them was ever voted on or even seriously debated in Parliament, except the defunding of KAIROS. More controversial than the decision not to fund the NGO's proposal were the circumstances under which it was made. An access-to-information request by the media revealed that the various levels of approval at CIDA and the Department of Foreign Affairs and International Trade had all strongly endorsed the KAIROS project proposal, including CIDA's president and the minister herself. However, someone had inserted the word "NOT" in the approval statement above Minister for International Cooperation Bev Oda's signature, thereby reversing its meaning. Oda initially told a parliamentary committee in December 2010 that she had not added the "NOT" and did not know who had. However, after the affair refused to die, Oda finally admitted in March 2011 that she had in fact instructed her chief of staff to amend the document to reverse her decision – and make it seem like the other signatories had agreed with her negative assessment. The speaker of the House of Commons found her in contempt of Parliament – the first time for a Cabinet minister in Commonwealth history – for having lied about it. However, the opposition parties voted a motion of non-confidence in the government, leading to the dissolution of Parliament before it could formally confirm the ruling. The KAIROS scandal did not bring down the government on its own (a similar controversy dogged the government regarding spending estimates) and the Conservatives would probably have fallen anyway soon afterwards (the Liberals, NDP, and Bloc Québécois had all indicated that they would vote against the budget). Thus the government's minority status did not affect aid policy, but aid policy – or, more specifically, one funding decision – played a role in the fall of a government that was possible only because it lacked a majority.

Majority Rules, May 2011–15

When Stephen Harper returned to power with a majority government, he reappointed Bev Oda as minister for international cooperation. In so doing, he signalled that, regardless of his government's new majority, Canadian aid policy would continue along the same path as it had since 2009. In many ways, it did just that. The government continued, at least initially, to emphasize the rhetoric of aid effectiveness, stress the importance of focus and "real results," increase funding to MNCH, and cut funding to a growing list of critical NGOs. Some of these trends were amplified, such as the government's fractious relationship with development NGOs, worsened by the lack of any new general calls for proposals after 2011. The lack of new funding for NGOs pushed many of them to the brink of bankruptcy. In 2012, the government also abolished Rights and Democracy, an arm's-length institution created by Parliament in 1988 to promote human rights and democratic development. The North-South Institute, Canada's only think tank focused exclusively on development issues, dissolved itself in 2014 when the government decided to cut off its funding.

Continuity with the past did not prevent the government from taking new initiatives. One of the first was the increased emphasis on the role of the private sector. Following the May 2011 elections, the Conservatives gained a majority of seats on parliamentary committees and therefore held more sway over their agendas. In 2012, the House of Commons Standing Committee on Foreign Affairs and International Development issued a report, *Driving Inclusive Economic Growth: The Role of the Private Sector in International Development*, recommending greater use of foreign aid to support the private sector and often conflating Canadian multinationals with small and medium enterprises in developing countries.

During this period, the government drew particular attention to Canadian mining companies and their contributions to development abroad. In September 2011, for instance, Oda announced new financing for NGOs collaborating with Canadian mining companies in Burkina Faso, Ghana, and Peru, working mainly in communities affected by the mines.[19] Concurrently, Ottawa announced a $20 million Andean Regional Initiative for Promoting Effective Corporate Social Responsibility, also aimed at people living near extractive operations. In 2013, the government approved $25 million to establish the Canadian International Institute for Extractive Industries and Development, later renamed the Canadian International Resources and Development Institute. In 2014, Minister of International Development Christian Paradis announced the Extractives Cooperation for Enhanced Economic Development Program, which would contribute up to $25 million per year for an unspecified number of years in order to "expand Canada's involvement in the extractive sector in Africa."[20] Though the Harper government never issued any sort of policy paper on international development, Gabriel Goyette describes the emphasis on the extractive sector as a "new de facto Canadian aid policy."[21]

In their public statements, successive development ministers – namely, Oda (who resigned in 2012), Julian Fantino (2012–13), and Christian Paradis (2013–15) – frequently mentioned the importance of the private sector with regard to development. They increasingly emphasized how aid should benefit Canada's trade interests and Canadian corporations. For instance, when Oda was asked about how Canada's trade and foreign policy interests could diverge from development goals, she replied, "I really don't separate them."[22] Her successor, Fantino, went so far as to argue that, in its development policies, the Canadian government has "a duty and a responsibility to ensure that Canadian interests are promoted" and that "Canadians are entitled to derive a benefit" from Canadian foreign aid.[23] Paradis also frequently spoke of the importance of the private sector in development, including in the delivery of humanitarian assistance. The increased commercialization of Canadian aid mirrored its decreased securitization – that is to say, its waning association with security interests – especially after Canadian troops withdrew from Afghanistan, and Canadian ODA to that country was cut accordingly: from a peak of US$400 million in 2007, Canadian aid to Afghanistan dropped to $89 million in 2014.[24] The commercialization trend continued in 2015, when the government announced a "Development Finance Initiative" to be housed within Export Development Canada (EDC) that would encourage Canadian companies to invest in developing countries. Though the government claimed the initiative would "raise people out of poverty and put them on the road to prosperity," past experience has failed to demonstrate that such endeavours are effective ways to reach that outcome – and it remained unclear whether the initiative's $300-million capitalization would be taken from the aid budget.[25]

Having frozen aid in 2010, the government proceeded to cut expenditure, reducing it from its highpoint of US$5.6 billion in 2012 to $4.2 billion in 2014 – a 24 percent drop in just two years, which left the budget lower (in constant dollars) than when Stephen Harper became prime minister in 2006 (see Figure 10.1). In 2014, ODA fell to 0.24 percent of Canada's gross national income, also less than the 0.29 percent ratio in 2006, when the Harper Conservatives were first elected.[26] Moreover, the cuts were actually about twice as large as those foreseen in successive federal budgets due to hundreds of millions of dollars that were allowed to lapse and therefore returned to the government's central coffers. Despite the aid cuts, the Harper government ramped up its spending on MNCH, reaching a total of CAD$2.85 billion between 2010 and 2015.[27] The growing proportion of funds dedicated to MNCH and mining-related activities, as well as humanitarian assistance, meant that – especially in the context of declining overall budgets – significantly less money was available for other development goals and sectors.

The biggest change to the development landscape under the Harper majority government was the abolition of CIDA in 2013 and the transfer of its functions to the expanded and newly renamed Department of Foreign Affairs, Trade and Development. The move was first contemplated during the 2006 transition, but at the time it was deemed too bureaucratically cumbersome.[28] According to Minister of International Cooperation Fantino, the motive of the merger was to "enhance coordination of international assistance with broader Canadian values and objectives, and to put development on equal footing with trade and diplomacy."[29] Indeed, by then, policy coherence had outgrown the limits of a 3-D, or whole-of-government, approach and had become a justification for the abolition of a separate aid agency. There remained the question around what objectives aid policy would cohere: Would they be narrowly conceived self-interested goals, such as commercial interests, or would policy coherence marshal a broader range of resources to respond to the challenges of global poverty and inequality? The first indication of the overarching priority came with the 2013 release of DFATD's *Global Markets Action Plan* – discussed in more detail by Christopher Kukucha (Chapter 12, this volume) – which mentions aid only as part of a desire to "leverage development programming to advance Canada's trade interests."[30] Concomitantly, the government's emphasis on aid effectiveness faded.

The merger was followed by a few aid-related initiatives. The most prominent was a new list of priority recipients announced in 2014, brought back to twenty-five countries as it was under the Martin government. The revisions to the list added several francophone African countries, some of which had been on the 2005 list but were then dropped in 2009 (Benin and Burkina Faso), and they reflected the interests of Canadian mining companies in several resource-rich countries, such as Mongolia, Myanmar, and the Democratic Republic of the Congo. Minister of International Development Paradis also tried to improve relations with NGOs, releasing in early 2015 the new Civil Society Partnership Policy, which promised to reverse some of the least popular changes under Oda, including the elimination of responsive funding. However, the new policy did not produce any visible results before the Conservatives lost power in October 2015.

To what extent can the Harper government's development policies in 2011–15 be attributed to its majority status? It is hard to identify any that would not have been possible under a minority government. Only the federal budgets and CIDA's absorption into DFAIT required legislation and, therefore, a debate in Parliament, but even this controversial merger had widespread opposition support, especially among the Liberals. Perhaps, though, under a minority government, the Conservatives would not have abolished CIDA, as they did, as part of a massive omnibus bill. Indeed, while it is possible that the government had greater confidence in its ability to reorganize the bureaucracy as a majority, it is just as likely that seven years of governance experience – and not the Conservatives' standing in the House of Commons – played a greater role. Similarly, cuts to the aid budget would not have been a salient enough issue for the opposition parties to bring down a minority government.

Conclusion

To return to the question posed in the introduction of this chapter: To what extent did the Conservative government's majority status in 2011–15 affect its international development assistance policy? The pithy answer is, "not much." As noted by Philippe Lagassé (Chapter 3, this volume), the government does not need to involve Parliament in its international policy. Under the Harper Conservatives, Parliament – whether under a minority or a majority government – played a minor role in setting aid policy, other than passing the relatively toothless 2008 *ODA Accountability Act* and rubber-stamping annual budgets, along with issuing a few committee reports in line with government policy preferences. If one were to identify a pivotal year in the Harper government's aid policy, it would be 2009, not 2011, as it was in the former year that the government began a series of initiatives that continued past 2011, with most enduring through 2015. The changes that the Conservatives implemented after 2011, such as the cutting of the aid budget and the abolition of CIDA, could almost as easily have been enacted under a minority government.

Starting in 2009, the Harper government gained interest and self-confidence in international affairs, including development. The Conservatives stopped operating under the inertia of previous policies, inherited from the Liberals, and put in place many of their own (including new themes and priority partners) as well as placing greater emphasis on the private sector and, especially, the extractive industry. Overall, opposition to their initiatives, whether from parliamentarians, NGOs, academics, or the media, proved meek and ineffective, allowing the Conservatives to push their increasingly aggressive agenda. Some of the changes and reversals, including increasing emphasis on the private sector and decreasing involvement in Afghanistan, should not be interpreted through the lens of Canadian politics alone as they are part of broader trends among Western donors. Others, such as the use of the rhetoric of policy coherence to promote self-interest, are also part of truly global trends, which characterize many "emerging" aid providers (such as China, India, and Brazil) as well.

Notes

1 The Martin government's 2005 federal budget promised "an increase of $3.4 billion over the next five years for international assistance with the goal of doubling assistance by 2010–11 from its 2001–02 level" (which the Chrétien government had pledged to do when it signed the 2002 Monterrey consensus) and to "double aid to Africa by 2008–09 from its 2003–04 level." See Canada, Department of Finance, *The Budget Plan, 2005* (Ottawa: Finance Canada, 2005), 21.

2 When calculating in constant US dollars, to take into account inflation and currency fluctuations, total aid did not actually double. In the case of aid to Africa, the government achieved the doubling goal only by using a lower figure for the base year and by allocating to Africa funds that were not previously assigned to a specific region. For further information on the regional allocation of aid and how it is calculated, see Stephen Brown, "Canadian aid to Africa," in Yiagadeesen Samy and Rohinton Medhora, eds., *Canada Among Nations, 2013: Canada-Africa Relations – Looking Back, Looking Ahead* (Waterloo, ON: Centre for International Governance Innovation, 2013), 183–85.

3 For a discussion of this document, see Stephen Brown, "'Creating the world's best development agency'? Confusion and contradictions in CIDA's new policy blueprint," *Canadian Journal of Development Studies* 28, 2 (2007): 213–28.

4 Canada, Department of Finance, *The Budget Plan, 2007* (Ottawa: Finance Canada, 2007), 262.

5 Foreign Affairs, Trade and Development Canada (DFATD), "International Assistance Commitments," 17 October 2014, http://www.international.gc.ca/department -ministere/open_data-donnees_ouvertes/dev/international_assistance_commitments -engagements_matiere_internationale.aspx?lang=eng. Note that the government calculation is of bilateral donors only, whereas the commitment referred to all donors, for which the number of countries would be lower.

6 See discussion in Stephen Brown, "CIDA under the gun," in Jean Daudelin and Daniel Schwanen, eds., *Canada Among Nations, 2007: What Room to Manoeuvre?* (Montreal and Kingston: McGill-Queen's University Press, 2008), 91–107.

7 Figures expressed in constant 2013 US dollars and taken from OECD, *Query Wizard for International Development Statistics*, http://stats.oecd.org/qwids/, extracted 10 February 2016.

8 DFATD, *Synthesis Report: Summative Evaluation of Canada's Afghanistan Development Program, Fiscal Year 2004-2005 to 2012-2013* (Gatineau, QC: Foreign Affairs, Trade and Development Canada, 2015), 18, 36. For a more in-depth discussion of Canadian aid to Afghanistan, see Stephen Brown, "From Ottawa to Kandahar and back: The securitization of Canadian foreign aid," in Stephen Brown and Jörn Grävingholt, eds., *The Securitization of Foreign Aid* (Basingstoke, UK: Palgrave Macmillan, 2016): 113–37. See also Boucher and Nossal (Chapter 4, this volume).

9 CBC News Online, "Liberal-NDP budget deal," 24 June 2005, http://www.cbc.ca/ news2/background/budget2005/liberal-ndp-deal.html.

10 Canada, *Official Development Assistance Accountability Act, 2008*, sections 2 and 4 (Ottawa: Justice Canada, modified 27 April 2015), http://laws-lois.justice.gc.ca/ eng/acts/O-2.8/FullText.html.

11 See the discussion in Canadian Council for International Co-operation, *A Time to Act: Implementing the ODA Accountability Act – A Canadian CSO Agenda for Aid Reform* (CCIC: Ottawa, 2010).
12 See Laura Macdonald and Arne Ruckert, "Continental shift? Rethinking Canadian aid to the Americas," in Stephen Brown, Molly den Heyer, and David R. Black, eds., *Rethinking Canadian Aid* (Ottawa: University of Ottawa Press, 2014), 125–42.
13 David R. Black, "The Muskoka Initiative and the politics of fence-mending with Africa," in Medhora and Samy, *Canada Among Nations, 2013*, 243. See also Stephen Brown and Michael Olender, "Canada's fraying commitment to multilateral development cooperation," in Hany Besada and Shannon Kindornay, eds., *Multilateral Development Cooperation in a Changing Global Order* (New York: Palgrave Macmillan, 2013), 166–70.
14 See Frank Vollmer, "Debating 'visibility' and its effects on the effective delivery of Official Development Assistance: Diagnosis, justification and possibilities," *Information Development* 30, 4 (2014): 298–312.
15 See DFATD, *Synthesis Report*, 29 and 46, as well as the discussion in Brown, "From Ottawa to Kandahar," in Brown and Grävingholt, *Securitization of Foreign Aid*.
16 DFATD, *Synthesis Report*; Stephen Baranyi and Anca Paducel, "Whither development in Canada's approach toward fragile states?" in Stephen Brown, ed., *Struggling for Effectiveness: CIDA and Canadian Foreign Aid* (Montreal and Kingston: McGill-Queen's University Press, 2012), 108–34.
17 Stephen Brown, "Aid effectiveness and the framing of new Canadian aid initiatives," in Duane Bratt and Christopher J. Kukucha, eds., *Readings in Canadian Foreign Policy: Classic Debates and New Ideas*, 3rd ed. (Don Mills, ON: Oxford University Press, 2015), 467–81.
18 For further information and analysis on the new funding mechanism, see Stephen Brown, "CIDA's new partnership with Canadian NGOs: Modernizing for greater effectiveness?" in Brown, *Struggling for Effectiveness*, 287–304.
19 See Stephen Brown, "Undermining foreign aid: The extractive sector and the re-commercialization of Canadian development assistance," in Brown, den Heyer, and Black, *Rethinking Canadian Aid*, 277–95; and Dragana Bodruzic, "Promoting international development through corporate social responsibility: The Canadian government's partnership with Canadian mining companies," *Canadian Foreign Policy Journal* 21, 2 (2015): 129–45.
20 Christian Paradis, "Address by Minister Paradis: The World Bank Event on the Africa Mining Vision and the African Minerals Development Centre," 3 February 2014, http://www.international.gc.ca/media/dev/speeches-discours/2014/02/03b.aspx?lang=eng.
21 Gabriel C. Goyette, "Charity begins at home: The extractive sector as an illustration of changes and continuities in the new de facto Canadian aid policy," in Brown, den Heyer, and Black, *Rethinking Canadian Aid*, 259–75.
22 Quoted in Elizabeth Payne, "Foreign aid gets down to business," *Ottawa Citizen*, 27 January 2012, A3.
23 Quoted in Kim Mackrael, "Fantino defends CIDA's corporate shift," *Globe and Mail*, 3 December 2012, http://www.theglobeandmail.com/news/politics/fantino-defends-cidas-corporate-shift/article5950443.

24 Figures expressed in constant 2013 US dollars and taken from OECD, *Query Wizard for International Development Statistics*, http://stats.oecd.org/qwids/, extracted 10 February 2016.
25 Government of Canada, *Budget Plan 2015: Chapter 4.2 – Strong Communities*," 21 April 2015, http://www.budget.gc.ca/2015/docs/plan/ch4-2-eng.html. In placing the initiative at EDC, the government ensured that the *ODA Accountability Act* would not apply. See James Munson, "New aid package isn't bound by Conservatives' own accountability law," *iPolitics.ca*, 8 May 2015, http://ipolitics.ca/2015/05/08/new-aid-package-isnt-bound-by-conservatives-own-accountability-law/. It would also benefit from EDC's exemption from access-to-information laws.
26 Figures expressed in constant 2013 US dollars and taken from OECD, *Query Wizard for International Development Statistics*, http://stats.oecd.org/qwids/, extracted 10 February 2016.
27 Government of Canada, "The Muskoka Initiative: Background," 18 December 2014, http://mnch.international.gc.ca/en/topics/leadership-muskoka_background.html.
28 Derek Burney and Fen Hampson, "So long, CIDA: Bringing aid to centre stage at DFAIT," *iPolitics*, 1 April 2013, http://ipolitics.ca/2013/04/01/so-long-cida-bringing-aid-to-centre-stage-at-dfait/.
29 DFATD, "Today, the Honourable Julian Fantino, Minister of International Co-operation issued a statement following the release of Economic Action Plan 2013," 21 March 2013, http://www.acdi-cida.gc.ca/acdi-cida/ACDI-CIDA.nsf/eng/ANN-321154018-R3R?OpenDocument.
30 DFATD, "Global Markets Action Plan," 12 September 2014, http://international.gc.ca/global-markets-marches-mondiaux/plan.aspx?lang=eng.

11
The Shaping of a Conservative Human Rights Policy in the Harper Era

DAVID PETRASEK AND REBECCA TIESSEN

The Conservative government under Stephen Harper claimed to pursue a "principled" foreign policy, one that promoted human rights and democracy. In fact, its policies in this area were highly selective: the Conservatives ignored certain human rights issues or the human rights record of certain countries, while vigorously pursuing others. Further, the government's choices on these matters appear in many cases to have been ideologically driven, leading to equivocation and inconsistency in its concern for human rights abroad. This, in turn, weakened the impact of the few well-intentioned initiatives that were pursued.

The Harper Era in Canadian Foreign Policy poses the question of whether there were clear differences in foreign policy between the first two Conservative minority governments, from 2006 to 2011, and the last majority government, from 2011 to 2015. As Philippe Lagassé notes (Chapter 3, this volume), since most foreign policy remains firmly within the control of the executive, there is no obvious reason why a majority in Parliament should give the prime minister greater freedom to pursue his or her own foreign policy priorities, unshackled by the need for parliamentary approval. This may be especially so as regards the promotion abroad of human rights. Although Canada's concern for human rights abroad generates much media attention, a decision regarding which approach to take is unlikely to lead to a non-confidence motion in the House of Commons (as, for example, might be the case with a major new trade deal or a decision to send troops abroad). Further, most human rights initiatives would not require substantial new funding that would demand or attract significant parliamentary oversight.

However, in examining the Conservatives' record, one does see that their distinctive approach was more pronounced during the period of majority government. Although a new direction was evident in the first two minority terms in office (2006–11), it became *increasingly* so over time. The years 2009 and 2010 marked a pivotal moment for a particular branding of Conservative human rights rhetoric, and this brand was given full expression in the majority government from 2011 to 2015 with the appointment of John Baird as foreign minister.[1] Baird spoke out regularly in defence of a particular Conservative vision of how Canada should be promoting human rights abroad. Nevertheless, it is doubtful that Baird's ramping up of the rhetoric resulted from the Tories' strengthened position in Parliament. In 2009–10, a new approach was already clear when human rights issues were given short shrift in the government's signature aid initiative regarding maternal, newborn, and child health. Indeed, taking office in 2006, the Conservatives pointed in a new direction on human rights. Finding their stride, as it were, they simply marched more forcefully on their chosen path, and especially so once they were in a majority position. As regards the latter period, it may simply be attributable to the zeal and visibility Baird brought to the job.[2]

We provide an overview of the key features of the Conservative government's approach to promoting human rights abroad. This is a wide-ranging subject. Space constraints do not permit us to treat fully the Conservative record across the entire range of human rights concerns;[3] rather, in drawing out the essentials of their approach, we choose a number of areas that are, we believe, indicative of the broader picture: international human rights concerns that were newly introduced, or given an added or different emphasis, by the Conservatives. These areas include maternal and newborn health, and ending child, early, and forced marriage. We also look at the Conservative policy on particular human rights issues, including the International Criminal Court (ICC) and the ratification of new human rights treaties, and its record in speaking out on human rights issues in the Middle East.

A New Direction

Since the late 1970s, *all* Canadian governments have claimed to emphasize the promotion of human rights in their foreign policies.[4] Some have done so more seriously than others, of course, but none has questioned such advocacy as a legitimate, and indeed priority, foreign policy goal. In this context, it was no surprise that when the Conservative government was elected in 2006 it promised to pursue a "principled" foreign policy, promoting human rights and democracy.

It is also the case that, over the past forty years, in promoting human rights abroad, different Canadian governments, and indeed different foreign ministers, have given different emphases to distinct human rights issues.[5] It would be naïve to imagine these choices were made in a completely non-partisan manner. No doubt, under most governments the question of electoral advantage at home has to some degree factored into decisions on the defence of human rights abroad. However, what distinguishes the Harper government, as Christopher Kukucha notes (Chapter 12, this volume) with reference to international trade, is the degree to which it emphasized that it was taking a new approach to human rights, suggesting repeatedly that it was breaking with the past. And indeed, unlike what Kukucha finds in his analysis, in several respects, including the issues it championed – and those it did not – this new, deeply ideological approach was evident to observers both at home and abroad.

Key features of the Conservative approach mimicked American neoconservative thinking on the promotion of human rights. What were these signature features of the Conservative approach? It was marked by a strong rhetorical commitment to promoting human rights and democracy, alongside a pronounced (and unapologetic) selectivity in doing so.[6] The vehemence with which human rights abuses were denounced in some countries stands in sharp contrast to the near total silence on abuses elsewhere.

The approach also had as its hallmarks scepticism regarding multilateral efforts to protect human rights via the UN, taking sides unreservedly with Israel against criticism of its human rights record, a waning interest in and support for the ICC, and downplaying human rights and gender equality in aid programs aimed at improving the situation of women and girls worldwide. Finally, the Conservative approach emphasized principles that reflect socially conservative, "family" values, which played out in key priorities; the maternal health initiative, which falls short on sexual and reproductive rights, is one such example.

First Steps

Turning to the way in which policies developed, the Conservatives' approach was already apparent during the first minority era. Almost immediately on taking office, they suggested that their response to authoritarian regimes would be more principled. The clear implication, of course, was that previous governments had somehow been too accommodating of dictatorships. For example, in opposition, prominent Conservatives, including Stephen Harper and Jason Kenney, had been vocal critics of the Chinese government's human rights record. Once he assumed office in 2006, Prime Minister Harper made no special effort to reach out and establish a dialogue with the Chinese. Perhaps as a result, the Chinese president, Hu Jintao, refused to meet Harper at an APEC summit in Vietnam in November 2006. In reply, Harper said: "I think Canadians want us to promote our trade relations worldwide, and we do that, but I don't think Canadians want us to sell out important Canadian values .... [t]hey don't want us to sell that out to the almighty dollar."[7] This belief that the Conservatives were different, more principled, and would not be so accommodating of dictatorships, seemed to be genuinely held. Yet it bears little relation to the historical record. Previous Progressive Conservative and Liberal governments regularly spoke out about or voted at the UN to condemn authoritarian regimes. Of course, under the Liberal governments of Jean Chrétien and Paul Martin, there were concerted efforts to increase trade with China, and one result might have been less vocal criticism of China's human rights record. But the Conservatives' policy too would soften considerably on China. Nevertheless, Prime Minister Harper's insistence on a new, principled stance would, as discussed below, strengthen over time.

A second early shift concerned Israel, and the prime minister's apparent reluctance to criticize in any way Israeli actions that might raise questions regarding its adherence to international human rights and humanitarian law. Soon after taking office, Prime Minister Harper described the Israeli attack on and invasion of Lebanon in the summer of 2006 as a "measured response" to Hezbollah's action in seizing Israeli soldiers as hostages[8] – this despite the clear evidence of disproportionate attacks by Israel that prompted a massive population displacement.[9] Similar pronouncements from the government marked the reaction to the short but deadly war between Hamas and Israel from December 2008 to January 2009.[10]

The Pace Quickens
After their second minority election victory, the Conservatives' particular approach to human rights became more pronounced. In 2009–10, they took steps to reject what they perceived as Liberal-era institutions and discourse, and to move away from a long-pursued Canadian commitment to promoting gender equality in international fora.

The International Centre for Human Rights and Democratic Development (Rights and Democracy) had, for twenty-five years, received public funds to promote human rights with the support of all political parties (indeed, it was established under the Progressive Conservative government of Brian Mulroney in 1988 and was first directed by former leader of the New Democratic Party Ed Broadbent). In 2009, the Conservatives appointed a new chair to the board of the organization, a person who was openly hostile to the funding the institution had provided to both Israeli and Palestinian human rights groups.[11] This move led to internal controversy and the eventual closure of the institution in 2012. Also in 2009, the prime minister reportedly insisted that the Department of Foreign Affairs and International Trade cease all references to signature Liberal foreign policy initiatives in the human rights field, including "human security" and the Responsibility to Protect.[12]

On women's rights and gender equality, there were also important policy changes in the period preceding the 2011 election. They included an official shift in language from "gender equality" to "equality between women and men" in 2009 and the announcement in 2010 of the Muskoka Initiative on Maternal, Newborn, and Child Health. The "erasure of gender in Canadian foreign policy" applied to individuals and gendered institutions and practices alike;[13] thus, the shift in language limited discussions of systemic oppression and structural inequality that might be perceived as being more political in nature. The change was further problematic given that the internationally recognized terminology is linked to Canada's pioneering role in promoting gender equality at the international level in the 1970s and 1980s.[14] The language was not abandoned permanently, as references to gender equality returned to official foreign affairs website material and official speeches by 2013. But the temporary shift had reverberating effects on policy commitments, including the decision to prioritize MNCH.

The MNCH initiative was introduced in Muskoka, Ontario, during the 2010 G8 Summit. It soon became the Conservatives' leading international aid commitment. Building on the 2000 Millennium Development Goals' inclusion of targets for improved maternal and newborn health, the Muskoka Initiative promised a suite of programs directed at improving services for pregnant women. However, it left out, on the part of Canada, funding for legal abortion facilities and only provided limited support for sexual and reproductive health services. Despite great potential for the MNCH initiative to highlight and address human rights issues, it was limiting in its near-exclusive focus on providing clinicians and clinics rather than addressing root causes of women's maternal health challenges. For example, it failed to consider gender inequality at the household level in terms of access to and control of resources that prevent women from receiving neo-natal health care results in empty clinics. A lack of consultation with local organizations specializing in gender equality in designated countries diminished the potential for a human rights and equality-centred program for women in need of maternal health care.

In Full Stride

In 2011, having received a majority mandate from the Canadian public, the Conservatives began to articulate their new and "principled" approach with greater vigour. Shortly after the 2011 election, Prime Minister Harper reaffirmed Canada would no longer go along with the consensus in multilateral fora simply to get along; Canada would "take pretty clear stands."[15] In a speech at the Conservatives' annual conference in June 2011, Harper stated emphatically that Canada would "no longer [try to] please every dictator with a vote at the United Nations." He continued: "And I confess that I don't know why past attempts to do so were ever thought to be in Canada's national interest."[16] This point of view was repeated frequently by both the prime minister and Foreign Affairs Minister John Baird from 2011 onwards.

Under Baird, the key features of the Conservative approach were given greater emphasis: hostility towards the UN and its human rights program, uncritical support for Israel, a regressive stance on women's and girls' rights, and increased selectivity in singling out countries. Long-standing Canadian support for the ICC also changed to indifference and even hostility.

On the question of selectivity, it should first be noted that the Harper government did regularly criticize human rights abuses in many countries, raising these issues both bilaterally and in multilateral fora. No doubt, there were often principled reasons for doing so. For example, the prime minister took a strong position in demanding that the Sri Lankan government investigate and punish credible allegations of war crimes committed in 2009, when the Sri Lankan army defeated the Liberation Tigers of Tamil Ealam (LTTE). When it failed to do so, he refused to attend the Commonwealth Heads of Government Meeting in Sri Lanka in November 2013.[17] However, the principled positions it may have taken with regard to human rights abuse in some countries were overshadowed by the obvious selectivity it applied elsewhere.

Consider the Conservative government's singling out of Iran for criticism, and its relative silence with regard to the human rights records of Iran's rivals in the Gulf. The emphasis on the human rights situation in Iran was hardly new. Previous Canadian governments had also been outspoken regarding human rights in Iran. Under Liberal governments, Canada first led the process of condemning Iran in the UN General Assembly in 2003 and continued to condemn Iran's human rights record at the UN annually thereafter. However, over time, and with the eventual decision to break off diplomatic relations with Tehran in September 2012, Canada's antagonism towards Iran certainly became more pronounced. At the same time, however, Minister Baird was noticeably mute with regard to the human rights situation in other Gulf countries. For example, in the face of widespread protests and instability in Bahrain from 2011 onwards, with credible evidence of arbitrary arrests, unfair trials, torture, ill-treatment, and undue restrictions of free expression and assembly, Baird was publicly silent, even in the official statements concluding his two visits to the country.[18] In a March 2013 visit to Qatar and the United Arab Emirates, during which each of these states was maintaining or even tightening repressive rule, Baird did not publicly raise the issues of democracy or freedom, and he barely mentioned human rights.[19] Similarly, while criticizing the Iranian record on religious freedom and women's rights, he made almost no criticism of the human rights record of the Saudi government.[20]

The selective approach vis-à-vis Gulf states was also evident in relation to the Conservative government's decision to speak out in defence of the rights of lesbian and gay persons. Though Prime Minister Harper lobbied President Yoweri Museveni of Uganda in an effort to thwart the passing of a private member's bill in Uganda's Parliament that further criminalized homosexuality,[21] no such action or statements were made concerning similar laws and ongoing persecution of sexual minorities in Saudi Arabia and other Gulf states.

This selective approach was particularly marked in relation to the Israeli-Palestinian conflict, where increasingly, and especially under Foreign Affairs Minister Baird, the government drew back from any public condemnation of Israel in relation to human rights (Adam Chapnick [Chapter 6, this volume] discusses this story in depth). It is striking to note, however, that although no *official* change in Canadian policy was made regarding the illegality of the Israeli occupation and continuing settlement expansion, it was a policy that neither Baird nor Harper publicly endorsed, including during visits made both to Israel and to the Palestinian Territories. This selective approach was so marked that concern to defend Israel from criticism coloured even the government's view on Palestinian abuse of human rights. Thus, when the Palestinian Authority sought to accede to numerous UN human rights treaties – which would result in greater scrutiny of *Palestinian* policy – Foreign Minister Baird objected,[22] simply on the grounds that it gave greater international recognition to the Palestinian Authority (and thus likely facilitated the eventual Palestinian accession to the ICC).[23]

Regarding the ICC, Canada had been instrumental in the negotiation of the Rome Statute leading to its establishment, and Canada's advocacy for international justice enjoyed cross-party support. Yet enthusiasm for the court waned between 2006 and 2015. In 2013, for example, after a UN commission of inquiry – and many NGO reports – had decried ongoing war crimes in Syria, the Swiss government led an initiative to petition the UN Security Council to refer the situation to the ICC. Over sixty countries signed on, including virtually all of Canada's European allies, but Ottawa initially would not commit.[24] Canada did, finally, lend its support in 2014, when the French presented a draft resolution on Syria to the Security Council (it was vetoed by the Russians and Chinese). But that resolution, controversially for many, made clear that nationals of states not party to the ICC would be exempt from the investigation.[25] Similarly, at the November 2013 Assembly of State Parties to the ICC, the Harper government threatened to break an established consensus by demanding a "zero growth" budget for the organization, and it only backed down after considerable pressure was brought to bear by other states.[26]

The Conservatives' waning support for the ICC was likely influenced by the increasing interest on the part of the Palestinian Authority in acceding to the Rome Statute, a possibility denied it before it was recognized by the UN General Assembly as a non-member observer "state" in November 2012. When the Palestinians did finally formally seek accession to the Rome Statute in January 2015, Baird strongly criticized the move.[27] Indeed, he threatened repercussions and did not distance himself from comments made by the Israeli foreign minister, who threatened to ask Israel's allies, including Canada, to stop funding the ICC.

From 2011 until 2015, the distinct paternalistic and ideological approach to "saving mothers" also continued. In 2014 at a summit in Toronto, the Harper government pledged an additional $3.5 billion to promote maternal health programming from 2015 through 2020.[28] The ongoing failure to include much-needed services such as abortions and sexual and reproductive health care reinforced the Conservatives' ideological positioning on women's rights.

A particular brand of paternalism also played out in the speeches by Minister Baird on child, early, and forced marriage (CEFM). While the anti-CEFM campaign resulted in few financial commitments and programmatic priorities, it became a touchstone for the Conservatives in their rhetorical commitment to protect girls both at home and around the world. Specifically, Ottawa positioned itself in a highly protective role for girls facing early and forced marriage, employing a particular language around its "disgust" for such "barbaric" practices. As such, the Conservatives claimed to be "speaking up for," and thereby speaking for, these girls.[29] Thus, the instrumentalization of the girl child, cast in highly vulnerable terms in foreign policy discourse, served a highly partisan and ideological agenda. The rhetoric of paternalistic sentiments around protecting "vulnerable girls" evoked an emotional response that blinded Canadians to the lack of tangible programs to support them. Baird's speeches on CEFM highlighted the value of education for girls and the importance of keeping girls in schools to prevent early marriage. Yet Canada's financial commitment to education around the world under the Conservatives was limited; moreover, schools may be the very place where girls experience sexual violence. Without a commitment to addressing gender equality and education for boys and men on women's and girls' rights, efforts to improve the situation for girls will yield negligible results, at best.

Nonetheless, focusing on maternal health and vulnerable girls is highly strategic. The Harper government successfully shifted the rhetoric from gender equality to the protection of women and girls as victims of violence in highly essentialist terms.[30] Such "motherhood statements," quite literally in the context of the MNCH initiative, struck a chord with an important political constituency in Canada from which the Conservatives counted on support. The platitudes of "saving mothers and girls" allow Canadians to feel good about their country's commitment to important issues while minimizing the real work – the human rights strategies – necessary to make a sustained impact in the lives of those who are highly disadvantaged and/or marginalized.

Finally, the distinct Conservative approach to human rights, strengthening over time, is evident in the way Ottawa interpreted Canada's international human rights treaty commitments. Prior to 2006, Canada routinely ratified

UN human rights treaties and new protocols.[31] During the Conservative government's time in office, however, only one of six new UN human rights treaties and protocols was ratified – in March 2010, Canada ratified the Convention on the Rights of Persons with Disabilities. No serious steps were taken to ratify protocols strengthening supervisory procedures for the treaties on disability rights, children's rights, and the prevention of torture or inhumane treatment, nor to ratify a treaty outlawing forced disappearances. Nor did the Conservative government sign the Arms Trade Treaty, an agreement the UN adopted in April 2013 that places restrictions on the transfer of weapons to states where they might be used in the commission of human rights abuses.

In the initial period of minority government there was a certain ambiguity with regard to the government's position on these treaties. For example, in 2009, during the UN Human Rights Council's Universal Periodic Review process, Canadian representatives claimed that Canada was considering signing and ratifying the Optional Protocol to the UN Convention against Torture (OP-CAT).[32] In 2013, at the next review, the position had changed, and the Harper government indicated that it had no plans to sign or ratify any of the outstanding human rights treaties.[33]

It is important to point out that, with the notable exception of the United States (which is loath to ratify any human rights treaties), most of Canada's allies have moved to ratify these new agreements. All European states have signed or ratified OP-CAT, as have Australia and New Zealand. Numerous others have signed or ratified the protocol to the children's rights treaty and the Convention on Enforced Disappearances. Most strikingly, all of Canada's European allies, Australia, New Zealand, *and* the United States have signed and/or ratified the Arms Trade Treaty. With the election of a Liberal government in 2015, it is likely that Canada will sign and ratify this last treaty, and there is hope that ratification of other treaties will be considered actively.

As a UN member state, and through its existing obligations under other UN human rights treaties, Canada is already subject to periodic reviews, scrutiny, and visits by various UN bodies charged with monitoring states' treaty obligations. Between 2006 and 2015, Conservative ministers and members of Parliament were nonetheless openly critical of UN scrutiny of Canada. They did not simply disagree with the findings of the UN bodies, they also questioned the right of such bodies to examine Canada's record, along with their impartiality in doing so. For example, when a UN expert on the right to food came to Canada, Jason Kenney, then the minister of citizenship and immigration, described the visit as "completely ridiculous."

The minister of health added that it was "insulting" that a UN representative might investigate the food security challenges facing Canada's Indigenous peoples. Other UN experts were also roundly condemned.[34]

Conclusion

It might be argued that the underlying rationale for the pursuit of one human rights priority over another is irrelevant. If the government sees electoral advantage in, for example, ending CEFM, so be it. It is certainly an issue demanding greater attention. A problem arises, however, because partisanship at home is noticed abroad, thus undermining the government's claim that it is raising concerns as a matter of principle. Moreover, the politicization of human rights advocacy is also unhelpful when it comes time for policy implementation. Improvements in human rights take time, certainly longer than the usual election cycle. Real advances on issues like eliminating child marriage require a generation. A true, strategic commitment to such issues would therefore necessitate building cross-party support so that it would continue to be prioritized over successive governments.

Furthermore, the human rights priorities established by any one government must reflect international agreements to which Canada is party. Focusing on women's and girls' rights, for example, is indeed within those national and international obligations. However, shifting the discourse away from rights, as in the case of the MNCH initiative or the CEFM statements, and narrowing in on charitable approaches around a limited understanding of needs suggests a government "off track" in relation to Canadian commitments and international obligations. This is further evidenced in the ambivalence the Conservatives showed towards the ICC and towards Canadian support for and full participation in the UN human rights regime.

Early on, the Conservatives signalled a new approach to human rights. After winning their second minority, they began to implement policies that back-tracked from long-standing Canadian commitments to women's rights and gender equality. Foreign Minister Baird's "stamp" on several human rights issues in the 2011–15 period reinforced this direction and gave full expression to a Conservative agenda that asserted high principles but that, in practice, was profoundly partisan.

Notes

1 See Stephen Brown (Chapter 10, this volume) for further discussion of the significance of the year 2009 for other important international policy priorities and changes.

2 Baird's own influence on policy, as opposed to the fact that he served as foreign minister in a majority government, is also cited by Adam Chapnick (Chapter 6, this volume) as a reason for particular positions.
3 For example, the Conservatives' indifferent approach to international concern over missing and murdered Indigenous women (and men) in Canada is worth examining, but it is not covered here.
4 See, for example, Andrew Lui, *Why Canada Cares: Human Rights and Foreign Policy in Theory and Practice* (Montreal and Kingston: McGill-Queen's University Press, 2012), for a book-length assessment of both realist and constructivist explanations of the attention given to human rights in Canadian foreign policy.
5 Consider the differences in both style and substance that Lloyd Axworthy and John Manley brought to the portfolio – both serving their terms as foreign minister under Prime Minister Jean Chrétien.
6 For a somewhat different assessment, see Hugh Segal (Chapter 15, this volume).
7 "Won't sell out on rights despite China snub: PM," *cbc.ca*, 15 November 2006, http://www.cbc.ca/news/world/won-t-sell-out-on-rights-despite-china-snub-pm-1.570708.
8 Michael Byers, "Harpers' unmeasured support for Israel," *Tyee*, 19 July 2006, http://thetyee.ca/Views/2006/07/19/Israel/.
9 See Human Rights Watch, "Why they died: Civilian casualties in Lebanon during the 2006 war," 19, 5 (2007), https://www.hrw.org/reports/2007/09/05/why-they-died.
10 Peter Kent, then a junior foreign minister, blamed the deaths of children at a school attacked by the Israeli Defence Forces entirely on Hamas, without any clear evidence that they were at or near the school when it was attacked. See Aaron Wherry "Apparently Peter Kent has the conch," *Macleans.ca*, 7 January 2009, http://www.macleans.ca/politics/ottawa/apparently-peter-kent-has-the-conch.
11 Haroon Siddiqui, "Stephen Harper's home-grown human rights problem," *Toronto Star*, 24 January 2010, http://www.thestar.com/news/canada/2010/01/24/siddiqui_stephen_harpers_homegrown_human_rights_problem.html.
12 Jeff Davis, "Liberal-era diplomatic language killed off," *Embassy*, 1 July 2009, http://www.embassynews.ca/news/2009/07/01/liberal-era-diplomatic-language-killed-off/37788?absolute=1.
13 Rebecca Tiessen and Krystel Carrier, "The erasure of 'gender' in Canadian foreign policy under the Harper Conservatives: The significance of the discursive shift from 'gender equality' to 'equality between women and men,'" *Canadian Foreign Policy Journal* 21, 2 (2015): 95–111.
14 Rebecca Tiessen, "Gender equality and the 'two CIDAs': Successes and setbacks between 1976 and 2013," in Stephen Brown, Molly den Heyer, and David R. Black, eds., *Rethinking Canadian Aid* (Ottawa: University of Ottawa Press, 2015), 195–209.
15 Kenneth Whyte, "In conversation – Stephen Harper," *Macleans*, 5 July 2011, http://www.macleans.ca/general/how-he-sees-canadas-role-in-the-world-and-where-he-wants-to-take-the-country-2/.
16 Paul Wells, "Why Harper wants to take on the world," *Maclean's*, 15 July 2011, http://www.macleans.ca/authors/paul-wells/why-harper-wants-to-take-on-the-world/.
17 David Carment and Joseph Landry (Chapter 13, this volume) are less generous in their assessments of the government's actions, suggesting that the strong stand on Sri Lanka was driven by a desire to win Tamil votes.

18 Admittedly, Foreign Minister Lawrence Cannon did initially demand respect for human rights when protests erupted in Bahrain in early 2011, and he issued several statements calling on the government to investigate alleged human rights abuse, respect due process rights, and so on. See "Statement by Minister Cannon on situation in Bahrain," 18 February 2011, http://www.international.gc.ca/media/aff/news-communiques/2011/069.aspx?lang=eng. See also "Statement by Minister Cannon on situation in Bahrain," 16 March 2011, http://www.international.gc.ca/media/aff/news-communiques/2011/108.aspx?lang=eng; and "Minister Cannon condemns ongoing violence in Yemen, Bahrain and Syria," 21 March 2011, http://www.international.gc.ca/media/aff/news-communiques/2011/113.aspx?lang=eng.
19 David Petrasek, "Going along to get along – John Baird's Mideast tour," *CIPS Blog*, 5 April 2013, http://www.cips-cepi.ca//going-along-to-get-along-john-bairds-mideast-tour/.
20 The only exceptions were mildly worded expressions of concern at one point over protests in Bahrain and over the case of the Saudi blogger, Raif Badawi, sentenced to one thousand lashes. See David Petrasek, "As nuclear talks progress, Baird's concern for human rights in Iran rings hollow," *CIPS Blog*, 10 November 2013, http://www.cips-cepi.ca//on-human-rights-baird-leaves-a-troubled-legacy/; and David Petrasek, "On human rights, Baird leaves a troubled legacy," *CIPS Blog*, 3 February 2015, http://www.cips-cepi.ca//as-nuclear-talks-progress-bairds-concern-for-human-rights-in-iran-rings-hollow/.
21 Marc Epprecht and Stephen Brown, "Queer Canada? Canadian policy towards international lesbian, gay, bisexual, transgender and intersex rights," in Rebecca Tiessen and Stephen Baranyi, eds., *Omissions and Obligations: Canada's Ambiguous Actions on Gender Equality* (Montreal and Kingston: McGill-Queen's University Press, forthcoming). See also Edward Jackson, Ian Smillie, and Stephen Brown, "Lesbian, gay, bisexual and transgender rights: A call for Canadian leadership," mcleodgroup.ca, March 2013, http://www.mcleodgroup.ca/wp-content/uploads/2013/02/LGBT-March.pdf.
22 Foreign Affairs, Trade and Development Canada (DFATD), "Baird calls on Palestinians, Israelis to re-commit themselves to Kerry peace initiative," 3 April 2014, http://www.international.gc.ca/media/aff/news-communiques/2014/04/03a.aspx?lang=eng.
23 David Petrasek, "Canada makes Palestinian human rights a pawn in Mid-East peace talks," *CIPS Blog*, 10 April, 2014, http://www.cips-cepi.ca//canada-makes-palestinian-human-rights-a-pawn-in-mideast-peace-talks/.
24 David Petrasek, "Why has Canada given up on justice in Syria?" *Globe and Mail*, 23 January 2013, http://www.theglobeandmail.com/globe-debate/why-has-canada-given-up-on-justice-in-syria/article7656847/.
25 Washington insisted that this exemption be included not only in the event that American forces might become involved in Syria but also because Israel's forces are present in Syrian territory through their occupation of the Golan Heights. See Mark Kersten, "The ICC in Syria: Three red lines," *Justice in Conflict*, 9 May 2014, http://justiceinconflict.org/2014/05/09/the-icc-in-syria-three-red-lines/.
26 Coalition for the ICC, *Report of the 12th Session of the Assembly of States Parties*, 20–28 November 2013, http://www.iccnow.org/documents/asp12_report.pdf, 23–24.

27 DFATD, "Canada concerned by dangerous action by the Palestinian authority," 1 January, 2015, http://www.international.gc.ca/media/aff/news-communiques/2015/01/01a.aspx?lang=eng.
28 Mike Blanchfield, "PM Harper pledges $3.5 billion to extend maternal, child health initiative to 2020," *Toronto Star*, 29 May 2014, http://www.thestar.com/news/canada/2014/05/29/pm_harper_pledges_35_billion_to_extend_maternal_child_health_initiative_to_2020.html.
29 John Baird, "Stop child marriage: Canada speaking up for girls," *Toronto Star*, 3 July 2014, http://www.thestar.com/opinion/commentary/2014/07/03/stop_child_marriage_canada_speaking_up_for_girls.html; and DFATD, "Canada leads UN effort to stop child, early and forced marriage," 24 October 2013, http://www.international.gc.ca/media/aff/news-communiques/2013/10/24a.aspx?lang=eng.
30 Rebecca Tiessen, "Gender essentialism and Canadian foreign aid commitments in fragile states and crisis-affected communities," *International Journal* 70, 1 (2015): 84–100.
31 The only exception was the 1990 International Convention on the Protection of the Rights of Migrant Workers, but no major developed country has ratified this treaty.
32 Report of the Working Group on the Universal Periodic Review, Canada, Addendum: Views on conclusions and/or recommendations, voluntary commitments and replies presented by the State under review, A/HRC/11/17/Add.1, 8 June 2009, http://www.upr-info.org/sites/default/files/document/canada/session_4_-_february_2009/ahrc1117add.1canadae.pdf.
33 Report of the Working Group on the Universal Periodic Review, Canada, Addendum: Views on conclusions and/or recommendations, voluntary commitments and replies presented by the State under review, A/HRC/24/11/Add.1 General Assembly Distr.: General, 17 September 2013, http://www.ohchr.org/EN/HRBodies/UPR/Pages/CASession16.aspx.
34 See an open letter to Prime Minister Harper signed by several Canadian human rights groups, criticizing the government's open contempt for the UN expert, 30 May 2012, http://www.amnesty.ca/sites/amnesty/files/canadaletterpmonsr30may12.pdf; Colleen Kimmett, "Human rights groups blast Tories' reaction to UN envoy," *Tyee*, 30 May 2012, http://thetyee.ca/Blogs/TheHook/Federal-Politics/2012/05/30/Tory_Reaction_UN_Envoy/.

12

Canada's Incremental Foreign Trade Policy

CHRISTOPHER J. KUKUCHA

Prime Minister Stephen Harper framed the aggressive expansion and deepening of Canada's international trade relationships as one of his government's greatest achievements.[1] Under the Conservative Party's minority and majority governments, Canada successfully completed, or pursued, trade pacts with over a dozen partners, including India, South Korea, the European Union, Singapore, the Dominican Republic, Ukraine, and Turkey. It also published reports detailing the need to increase ties with existing, emerging, and non-traditional markets. I argue, however, that Canada continues to practise a form of trade policy that is unique neither to the Harper era nor to the particular standing of any governing party in the House of Commons. Internationally, Canada has played a role in the incremental expansion of a global trade system based on the transfer of capitalist norms and rules, usually in the form of multilateral institutions but also in the form of regional and bilateral frameworks. These efforts tend to be modest due to agendas dominated by major economic powers and Canada's long-standing commitment to its own economic self-interest. Domestically, the factors contributing to incrementalism, including the form and practice of Canadian federalism related to the negotiation, ratification, and implementation of international commitments, as well as Canada's own internal trade regime, are similarly unrelated to the government's standing in the House.

Evaluating Change

Under Stephen Harper's leadership, the Conservatives published two policy documents related to international trade, one each from their minority and majority governments. The first, *Seizing Global Advantage: A Global Commerce Strategy for Securing Canada's Growth and Prosperity*, called for greater engagement in global value chains, securing access to international markets, and expanding foreign direct investment. In the pursuit of these goals the thirteen-page document noted the importance of international trade agreements, the evolution of the North American Free Trade Agreement (NAFTA), foreign investment protection agreements, air service agreements, and science and technology partnerships. Specific targets for trade policy included an expansion of trade promotion, especially through the Trade Commissioner Service, and focusing on markets in the Americas (Brazil, Mexico, the United States, and Latin America), Europe, the Middle East, and the Asia-Pacific (China, India, Japan, and Korea).[2]

In 2013, the now majority Harper government released the *Global Markets Action Plan: The Blueprint for Creating Jobs and Opportunities for Canadians through Trade*. This report was an extension of Ottawa's new focus on "economic diplomacy," which was announced immediately after the 2011 election.[3] The *Global Markets Action Plan* promised to extend the *Global Commerce Strategy* by targeting a larger list of emerging markets in the Asia-Pacific, Latin America and the Caribbean, the Americas, the Middle East, Africa, and Turkey. Twenty-four trading partners that offered specific opportunities for Canadian suppliers were mentioned explicitly, as were another thirty-six states with already established ties to Canadian producers. Once again, the Trade Commissioner Service was tasked to expand opportunities in these markets. Unlike the earlier report, however, the *Global Markets Action Plan* included an enhanced discussion of trade policy. It not only emphasized trade agreements but also highlighted the need for an "agile and adaptable trade strategy" focused on a range of specific sectors.[4]

Although the *Global Markets Action Plan* was hailed as a new direction in trade policy, and might therefore be considered by some as evidence of a shift in policy between minority and majority governments, like the *Global Commerce Strategy*, it was vague on specifics. In fact, both documents supported efforts to *broaden* and *deepen* Canada's foreign trade relations. *Broadening*, or identifying new priority trading partners, should have led to an expansion of negotiated agreements. In the years following 2013, however, only two trade agreements were signed and ratified, the 2015

Canada-Korea Free Trade Agreement (CKFTA) and the Canada-Honduras Trade Agreement (2014), and negotiations for both began during the Liberal governments of Jean Chrétien. The 2009 agreement with the European Free Trade Association, not to be confused with the later Canada-European Union Comprehensive Economic and Trade Agreement (CETA), also began with Chrétien in 2000.

Other ongoing, or recently concluded, negotiations also predate the Harper era. CETA was actually a continuation of the failed 2006 Canada-EU Trade and Investment Enhancement Agreement (TIEA), and talks with Guatemala, Nicaragua, El Salvador, Singapore, the Caribbean Community, and MERCOSUR were also originally Chrétien-era initiatives. Moreover, most of the Harper-driven negotiations began during minority governments. Talks with the Dominican Republic opened in 2007; India, Morocco, Turkey in 2009; and Ukraine in 2010. The only ratified agreements brought into force during the Harper era that were initiated by the Conservative minority governments were with Colombia and Peru (started in 2007) and Panama and Jordan (opened in 2008). Three more, with Japan, Thailand, and the Trans-Pacific Partnership (TPP), all launched in 2012, were undertaken during the majority period. Canada was also invited into, and did not initiate, already well-established regional TPP negotiations. As a result, it is impossible to link a broadening of trade agreements solely to the Harper majority or minority periods.

Deepening is more difficult to measure and, as a result, more difficult to assess in the context of a shift from minority to majority. Both documents make specific reference to providing support for Canadian businesses and to liberalizing markets. It is clear that the intent is to provide support through the Trade Commissioner Service. Liberalization, on the other hand, is referred to without any clear measure of progress, as though signing agreements will simply provide Canadian businesses with greater access to goods and new markets. This assumption has led some observers, like trade policy analyst Michael Hart, to conclude that the Canadian government continues to pursue a mercantilist trade policy reflective of an era of international trade and investment that no longer exists and that is incompatible with a contemporary world of evolving supply chains and rapidly changing trade and investment patterns. Hart's solution is to proactively remove domestic barriers – restrictive procurement practices, inefficient subsidies (including supply management), costly regulatory measures, and anti-dumping and countervailing practices – in advance of bilateral, regional, or multilateral negotiations.[5]

I suggest that the deepening of trade commitments must be judged on the basis of whether it represents *significant* or *incremental* change. *Significant* change would include a transformational alteration to Canada's current trade commitments similar to Hart's recommendations: a long-term, if not permanent, liberalization of markets as well as institutional reforms related to the rules and norms of trade policy, typically codified in international agreements. Changes would have to directly affect policy outcomes, as opposed to simply altering already existing patterns of interaction. While there are no universally accepted measures, signs of significant change might include: (1) commitments to national treatment and Most Favoured Nation status, especially related to traditionally protected sectors of the Canadian economy; (2) clear language requiring signatories to open access to markets; (3) greater transparency, which allows trade barriers to be properly identified for the purpose of their removal in future negotiations; (4) the adoption of negative lists in those negotiations; and (5) the liberalization of already existing positive lists.[6]

Incremental change, on the other hand, would reflect minor shifts in policy, closely associated with existing rules and norms. It would represent a consistency of interaction tied to the practices of well-established international institutions and agreements. Measures pointing to incremental change would include Hart's observations of current Canadian practices as well as: (1) consistent and specific exclusions or reservations in trade agreements; (2) placing the onus on governments, and in some cases on businesses and workers, to prove they meet a specific aspect of an agreement (this is difficult, expensive, and time consuming); (3) a reliance on positive lists; and (4) sending issues to committees for "further work and clarification."

International Considerations and Canadian Incrementalism

Historical Precedents

In the immediate post-Second World War period, Keynesian principles of state intervention were widely, if imperfectly,[7] adopted to manage and rebuild the capitalist economy through multilateral trade and financial institutions known collectively as the Bretton Woods system. By the 1970s, however, motivated by the ongoing decline of the United States as an economic power, Washington turned its back on Bretton Woods. President Richard Nixon imposed a 10 percent surcharge on imports, implemented wage and price controls, and announced what amounted to an end to the gold standard. Twenty years later, the expanded membership of the European Union and its decision to establish a monetary union to increase the efficiency of trade and investment further reinforced these changes.

In the aftermath of the Cold War, the remnants of the Bretton Woods system continued to struggle on the trade side, partly due to ongoing divisions between and among Western economic powers but also because of changes stemming from an evolving, somewhat unstable, multipolar system. Specifically, most investment and trade now flowed between Europe, North America, and East Asia, while the rest of the world experienced increasing inequality and poverty. The significant economic growth of China also created challenges for the traditionally Western-based focus of trade rules and agreements. The pursuit of liberalization within the World Trade Organization (WTO) has consequently stalled, reflective of conflicting priorities between North and South, and developed and developing economies. As a result, the legitimacy of the WTO as a means of transferring Western capitalist rules and norms to the East and South has declined. For the United States (and indeed Canada as well), the lack of progress has inspired the pursuit of a series of bilateral trade agreements and an ongoing attempt to transfer Western norms outside of the WTO, exclusive of developing countries and China.

In this context, there have been limited opportunities for Canada to play an activist role in creating an innovative international trading system over the last six decades. Within the General Agreement on Tariffs and Trade (GATT) Canada's role often focused more on "procedural notions of order than substantive content," especially in matters related to foreign trade policy.[8] Canada also pursued its own economic objectives in other regional and bilateral frameworks, including the 1965 Auto Pact with the United States and the pursuit of what became known as the Third Option.[9] The shift between bilateral/regional and multilateral fora continued in the 1980s with Prime Minister Pierre Trudeau's *Royal Commission on the Economic Union and Development Prospects for Canada*, which culminated in the negotiation of the 1988 Canada-US Free Trade Agreement (CUSFTA) by Brian Mulroney's Progressive Conservative government. All of this occurred as the Uruguay Round of GATT negotiations began in 1986, and CUSFTA was expanded to include Mexico in NAFTA in 1994. Like the United States, Canada, under the Liberal Chrétien government, and then the Harper Conservatives, also used bilateral solutions to bypass the WTO.

Throughout all of these changes is a remarkably consistent record of Canada's pursuit of its own self-interest. As Michael Hart notes, Canadians have earned a well-deserved reputation as "chiselers."[10] Arguably, the only times in the post-Second World War period when the government's standing in the House of Commons has had a tangible effect on trade policy took place during the negotiations of CUSFTA and NAFTA. As at least one observer has suggested, only a majority government could provide the Cabinet and caucus with the unity and political will required to pursue these comprehensive agreements.[11] Similarly, if Canada had any desire to initiate significant domestic sectoral reform it would come during a majority government; instead, however, during the Uruguay Round, Ottawa sought to liberalize trade in grain and red meats but was not willing to expose its dairy and poultry sectors.[12] CUSFTA's Chapter 6 of exempted provinces from altering technical standards and procedures, and Chapter 7 preserved provincial marketing boards and farm income stabilization and price support programs. Chapter 12 also excluded key regional sectoral interests, such as the export of logs and unprocessed east coast fish. And Chapter 13 excluded government procurement and financial services. Six years later, NAFTA contained a wide range of exclusions, including government procurement, energy-related services, subsidies, and financial services. It also largely excluded agriculture and failed to address the contentious issue of alcohol and provincial liquor boards.[13]

The Harper Minority and Majority Governments

The Harper government's similar disinclination towards multilateralism in foreign trade dealings was, in part, a reflection of Ottawa's limited fiscal, bureaucratic, and diplomatic resources, but it was also a tactical shift in the Conservatives' approach to securing, and maintaining, a majority government. As other chapters in this book demonstrate, foreign policy could be used to rally domestic constituencies through polarizing policies. In the case of international trade, and especially agriculture, the Conservative government defined the national interest not only in economic terms but also on the basis of "the governing party's electoral calculus – the seats lost and gained as a result of a trade policy agreement."[14] The important thing to remember, however, is that the declining multilateral engagement of the Harper Conservatives was consistent with international trends that were well under way before 2006.

In sum, the Harper Conservatives pursued bilateral and regional trade agreements at an aggressive pace, but any analysis of their effectiveness, and thus any assessment of the impact of minority or majority government on policy outcomes, must consider the end state. Are these agreements innovative ways of managing international trade and liberalizing markets or are they merely an extension of an older, deeper approach to Canadian foreign trade policy? Has the pursuit of Canadian self-interest, what Hart refers to as the mercantilist approach, resulted in broader, but not deeper, trade relations?

As already noted, the Canada-Korea agreement is arguably less a Conservative achievement than the much delayed outcome of a previous Liberal initiative. The only challenge facing Stephen Harper's trade negotiators was ensuring that any contemporary deal was consistent with subsequent Korean pacts negotiated by the United States and the European Union. Some might still argue that the completion of the Korean agreement represents significant change, especially with reference to tariff barriers. South Korea, for example, agreed to remove duties from 98.2 percent of its tariff lines on Canadian products. In return, Canada would remove 97.8 percent of duties on its tariff lines. On closer inspection, however, it is clear that the Chrétien, and then Harper, government maintained a commitment to Canadian interests. In terms of alcohol, provincial purchasing, pricing, and distribution practices are excluded and protection for the terms "Canadian whisky" and "Canadian rye whisky" is provided.[15] The accord also applies much of the already existing WTO Agreement on the Application of Sanitary and Phytosanitary Measures as well as the WTO's Agreement on Technical Barriers to Trade. Further, access to service providers is consistent with terms under already existing US and European agreements, both of which followed the WTO's General Agreement on Trade in Services (GATS) and, as ever, Canada maintained sovereign control over natural resources, "public services" such as health, public education, and other social services. Finally, provincial, territorial, and municipal procurement projects are not included in the CKFTA.[16] If, moreover, there was no substantive change from previous Canadian initiatives, there is little reason to assume that the Conservatives' standing in the House mattered.

CETA also has its foundations in previous Liberal trade negotiations. Nonetheless, some aspects of the agreement do appear to represent a progressive Conservative trade policy willing to embrace significant change, especially related to procurement. The agreement, for example, allows EU suppliers unprecedented access to federal, provincial, Crown corporation, utilities, and MASH (municipalities, academic institutions, school boards, and publicly funded health and social services entities) procurement projects. Not only are provinces included, but the extent of the liberalization is significantly "deeper" and includes (admittedly limited) access to utilities procurement, which represents approximately $1 billion annually in the Canadian market.[17] Provincial and territorial mass transit contracts are also part of the final agreement. Moreover, sub-federal governments were added to Annex II of Canada's commitments to the WTO's Revised Agreement on Government Procurement in 2014.[18]

CETA, however, is hardly the radical shift that some make it out to be. It provides for exclusions relating to health care, Canadian airport and port authorities, research and development, "sensitive" goods involved with security and policing, and public-private partnerships in services and utilities. Moreover, procurement bidding thresholds generally do not exceed already existing commitments in the WTO and Buy American Agreements. Other areas of the agreement also follow previously negotiated rules and norms. The practices of provincial liquor boards related to listing, quotas, and purchasing, previously the focus of a number of Canada-EU disputes, remain largely intact.[19] Sanitary measures and technical barriers generally extend already existing commitments under the WTO's sanitary and phytosanitary agreement as well as the Canada-EU Veterinary Agreement, both of which are sensitive to provincial areas of jurisdiction.[20] Although press coverage focused on the likelihood of higher imports of EU cheese,[21] CETA does not dramatically extend agricultural obligations beyond existing WTO and NAFTA commitments with regard to the outright exclusion of poultry and eggs. Finally, CETA does not broadly alter existing limitations on licensing and qualification requirements tied to labour mobility, even if the agreement does provide a framework to negotiate future liberalization in specific occupations where both parties have similar objectives.[22]

When examining the Korea and CETA agreements, two of the most often referenced accomplishments of the Harper era, it is difficult to see significant change and therefore also difficult to make any distinction between the work of the minority and majority governments. Both agreements are tightly linked to the priorities of other international economic powers and the well-entrenched and largely non-partisan historical practice of protecting Canadian sectoral interests. Although Prime Minister Harper formally announced a new focus on economic diplomacy following his party's majority victory in 2011, Conservative policy did not result in a broadening or deepening of Canada's foreign trade policy in any significant manner.

The Domestic Context of International Trade

Canadian Federalism

Canadian federalism and trade rules within Canada's internal market further reinforce the incremental nature of Canada's foreign trade policy. For much of the history of GATT, foreign trade policy was the exclusive responsibility of the federal government. Negotiations focused solely on tariffs, which are not a provincial responsibility. As negotiations shifted to services, labour mobility, technical standards, and procurement, however, they began to intrude directly on the jurisdiction of Canadian provinces, territories, and, in some cases, municipalities.

For the most part, the evolving role of the provinces in Canadian foreign trade policy reflected the resilience of Canadian federalism. In constitutional terms, provinces have a degree of international legitimacy not often granted to sub-federal actors in other federations. The intrusion of international agreements into domestic areas of jurisdiction, however, also created pressure on the federal government to ensure the compliance of provinces and territories to negotiated commitments. Ottawa responded to these developments by adopting consultative mechanisms during the Tokyo Round of GATT (1973–79), which evolved into the Committee for the Free Trade Agreement, the Committee for North American Free Trade Negotiations, and culminated in the ongoing Federal/Provincial/Territorial Committee on Trade (C-Trade).[23] In all cases, provincial access to the negotiating table was granted to meet concerns related to the implementation of international agreements and in response to international trade disputes involving provinces. Whether the governing federal party was in a minority or majority position in the House of Commons was irrelevant.

The CETA experience was fundamentally different. For the first time, provincial and territorial governments were directly involved in international trade negotiations. Their involvement was a response to a specific request by the European negotiators. The Europeans were concerned about the reliability of the provincial governments as implementers of a new agreement based on their experiences in previous trade disputes with Canada, especially related to alcohol and beef, not to mention the failure of earlier Canada-EU Trade and Investment Enhancement Agreement negotiations. The solution, offered by Ottawa and eventually agreed to by the European Union, was to have provinces and territories "at the table" for certain elements of the negotiations relevant to specific sub-federal issues of jurisdiction. Those elements included services, procurement, monopolies, technical barriers to trade, investment, labour and environmental issues, and state-owned enterprises.[24] It is important to note, however, that "direct" participation was limited even in those formal sessions. Representatives would only talk if asked to do so by the Canadian negotiator at the table, and this did not happen frequently.[25] Although sub-federal representatives were at certain tables, it was ultimately federal officials who negotiated for Canada during both the minority and majority periods.

In the aftermath of CETA, neither the provinces nor the territories were granted a consistent role in the TPP negotiations and bilateral discussions with India. Several provincial and territorial representatives did participate in preliminary negotiations and regular ministerial TPP meetings in Singapore in 2013 and 2014, but provincial officials were never directly "in the room" as they were for the CETA talks. It is also unlikely that direct sub-federal participation in negotiations will occur under Justin Trudeau's Liberal government. Ottawa is open to further provincial involvement but not within a CETA context. The expense and cost for the provinces and territories to attend negotiations is also prohibitive. Ultimately, engagement will likely continue on an ad hoc basis dependent on the issues being negotiated. The provinces and territories will also continue to meet with the federal government within the existing C-Trade consultative process.

Sub-federal involvement in bilateral negotiations with India is less significant and is likely to continue to remain so. The provincial and territorial governments submit their views in much the same manner as with other negotiations, but there is no sub-federal presence at actual meetings and formal talks. Most issues on the table, primarily tariffs, fall under federal jurisdiction, and India has a small negotiating team, limiting the range of topics to be discussed at any one time. Finally, the difficulty and expense in getting a large number of provincial and territorial officials to Delhi is a further deterrent.[26]

So how does federalism contribute to the incremental nature of Canadian foreign trade policy and thereby, implicitly, limit the impact of a change in the government's standing in the House of Commons? Put simply, federal negotiators must always be sensitive to issues of sub-federal implementation. Historically, there is a long legacy of sub-federal governments protecting sectors crucial to regional and provincial political economies that has nothing to do with minority or majority governments at the federal level. The evidence is clear from the exclusions noted earlier in this chapter and also in previous GATT trade disputes related to Ontario's pricing and distribution of wine and beer.[27] During the Uruguay Round of WTO negotiations Canada's refusal to accept American proposals to alter Article 2.2 of the Agreement on Subsidies and Countervailing Measures was also directly tied to provincial agricultural subsidy programs. Other provincial priorities have included Article 11, relating to the investigation of subsidy complaints, and Article 8.2, which protects exemptions for regional development programs. Similar examples exist in NAFTA's treatment of services. Annex I of NAFTA, for example, excluded provincial health care measures in existence prior to 1994. Ottawa also aggressively protected NAFTA's Social Service Reservation as it related to provincial health care.

More recently, the government of Newfoundland and Labrador initially limited its role in Canadian foreign trade policy to that of an observer in CETA negotiations due to concerns related to provincial implementation. The province ultimately engaged in the negotiations as a full participant in March 2011 but still made it clear that it would not support any agreement unless it fully reflected Newfoundland and Labrador's interests. Indeed, in January 2015, disappointed by the results of the federal government's negotiations, Newfoundland and Labrador announced its intention to withdraw from all existing Canadian trade agreements, including those still under negotiation. At the core of this decision was the province's claim that Ottawa failed to follow through on a commitment to provide $280 million of a $400 million compensation fund for having pledged to eliminate minimum processing requirements for fish plants in the European negotiations.[28] The Harper government's reluctance to address supply management issues during TPP negotiations, due to concerns of opposition from dairy farmers in Ontario and Quebec, is another example of ongoing subfederal influence.[29] In fact, the Conservative position on agriculture, as noted throughout, remained remarkably consistent in both the minority and majority settings. When the text of the TPP was revealed during the 2015 election campaign, the Harper government promised over $4 billion in compensation to the dairy industry as well as support for processor modernization and market development.[30] There is nothing, then, to suggest a shift away from incremental change in the agricultural sector.

Canada's Internal Trade Regime
Finally, Canadian foreign trade policy is also influenced by internal trade agreements regulating Canada's domestic economy. In addition to the national Agreement on Internal Trade (AIT), signed in 1994 under a majority Liberal government, a number of regional and provincial agreements were concluded during the Harper minority regimes, including, but not limited to, the Atlantic Procurement Agreement (APA, 2008), the Ontario-Quebec Trade and Co-operation Agreement (TCA, 2009), the New Brunswick-Nova Scotia Partnership Agreement on Regulation and the Economy (PARE,

2009), and the Alberta, British Columbia and Saskatchewan New West Partnership Trade Agreement (NWPTA, 2010). Internal trade rules, then, have evolved for decades and continue to change. These developments have served as a catalyst for greater liberalization, albeit asymmetrically across policy areas, in Canada's internal market. What is interesting, and what reinforced Prime Minister Harper's incremental approach to trade policy, is that provinces – and not Conservative minority and majority governments – drove many of these changes. These provincial agreements also limited the scope of issues that could be addressed in international negotiations, again regardless of the federal government's political standing.

Procurement is a good example. As noted above, sub-federal governments were historically excluded from international procurement agreements. When negotiating federal commitments, however, Ottawa had to be aware of existing domestic rules and norms in this policy area so as to ensure some level of consistency between them and subsequent international commitments. Adding the provinces and territories to CETA and the WTO further reinforced this reality. To make matters more complicated, procurement is an area of internal trade that is consistently evolving. The AIT, for example, has undergone significant transformation since 1995, introducing extensive new areas of procurement, most notably in the MASH and Crown corporation sectors, and adding a number of exclusions and exceptions, especially in terms of procurement by MASH entities, Crown corporations, and entities of a commercial or industrial nature.

Procurement commitments in the Ontario-Quebec TCA are similar to those in the AIT. Indeed, the TCA explicitly adopted the AIT's terms of reference in its Article 9.3 (*Scope and Coverage*) and 9.4 (*Applicable Rules*).[31] Like the AIT, the TCA also includes a complaint process and a procurement coordinating committee. The APA, on the other hand, which includes New Brunswick, Nova Scotia, Newfoundland and Labrador, and Prince Edward Island, has lower bidding thresholds than any other internal agreement in Canada.[32] Nonetheless, exemptions outlined in Article 4 of the APA are identical to those listed in the AIT.

The significant difference between these internal agreements and the NWPTA is the latter's broad adoption of negative lists. The AIT, TCA, and APA include negative lists but rely heavily on positive ones, especially in areas related to procurement thresholds. In contrast, the negative list approach is obligatory as per Parts II (A) and (B) of the NWPTA unless otherwise indicated. As a result, all government entities in all sectors are covered by the procurement obligations of that agreement with the exception of non-government entities that exercise authority delegated by law, many of which are listed in Part V of the NWPTA. Bidding thresholds in the form of positive lists are also included in the NWPTA. Most exclusions in all domestic trade agreements, including the NWPTA and the AIT, are consistent with international exclusions.[33] Such exclusions, moreover, limit the flexibility of any Canadian federal government, again regardless of its standing in the House.

Conclusion

One of the purposes of this chapter is to challenge the assertion of the former Conservative government of its broader and deeper foreign trade policy. The evidence presented here suggests that Canada's international trade regime evolved incrementally over decades and, indeed, through both the Harper government's minority and majority years. Specifically, historic and current international trade agreements, the form and practice of Canadian federalism, and Canada's internal trade regime all reflect already well-established practices, rules, and norms that establish constraints under which any federal government, regardless of its political strength, will make foreign trade decisions. International and domestic Canadian trade agreements have liberalized Canada's economy but in a manner that still places a heavy emphasis on reservations and exclusions, positive lists, and rules reflecting hybrids of positive and negative lists. Finally, much of the attempted liberalization that has occurred has targeted areas of sub-federal jurisdiction, making provincial and territorial governments more important to Canada's international conduct, again regardless of the federal government's parliamentary standing.

Ultimately, Canada has broadened its international commitments since 2006, but many of the Harper-era trade negotiations were either tied to previous Liberal governments or represented linkages with less than dominant trading partners. The agreements that do exist also fail to significantly deepen Canada's trade relations. Finally, and in contrast to earlier negotiations of CUSFTA and NAFTA, most of these efforts began during minority governments. This last point reinforces the limited and consistent ambition of such discussions, in spite of claims of a new era of economic diplomacy.

Notes

1 Prime Minister of Canada, "Prime Minister Stephen Harper highlights government's 2012 achievements," http://news.gc.ca/web/article-en.do?nid=713619.

2 Government of Canada, *Seizing Global Advantage: A Global Commerce Strategy for Securing Canada's Growth and Prosperity* (Ottawa: Minister of Public Works and Government Services Canada, 2009).

3 John Ibbitson, "Tories new foreign-affairs vision shifts focus to economic diplomacy," *Globe and Mail*, 27 November 2013, http://www.theglobeandmail.com/news/politics/tories-new-foreign-affairs-vision-shifts-focus-to-economic-diplomacy/article15624653/.

4 Government of Canada, *Global Markets Action Plan: The Blueprint for Creating Jobs and Opportunities for Canadians Through Trade* (Ottawa: Minister of Public Works and Government Services Canada, 2013).

5 Michael Hart, *Breaking Free: A Post-Mercantilist Trade and Productivity Agenda for Canada* (Toronto: CD Howe Institute, 2012).

6 Negative lists, which were a cornerstone of NAFTA, are used with the specific intent of liberalizing markets and call for the non-discriminate movement of all goods and services, unless specifically *excluded* in a transparent list of reservations, annex, or appendix. Positive lists, on the other hand, only extend coverage where issues are voluntarily *included* by signatories, usually in a schedule, annex, or appendix.

7 Differences between Great Britain and the United States during this period often took the form of American protectionism, usually articulated by the US Congress, which refused to endorse the International Trade Organization.

8 Tom Keating, *Canada and World Order: The Multilateralist Tradition in Canadian Foreign Policy*, 3rd ed. (Don Mills, ON: Oxford University Press, 2013), 9.

9 The Third Option is an economic strategy that seeks to diversify Canada's foreign trade by opening up or expanding markets primarily in Europe.

10 Michael Hart, *Fifty Years of Canadian Tradecraft: Canada at the GATT, 1947-1997* (Ottawa: Centre for Trade Policy and Law, 1998), 67.

11 Daniel Gagnier, "Majority or minority government: A personal perspective," *Policy Options* (October 2011): 38–40.

12 Hart, *Fifty Years of Canadian Tradecraft*, 177.

13 Michael Hart, *A North American Free Trade Agreement* (Ottawa: Centre for Trade Policy and Law/Institute for Research on Public Policy, 1990); and Stelios Loizides and Gilles Rheaume, *The North American Free Trade Agreement: Implications for Canada* (Ottawa: Conference Board of Canada, 1993).

14 Grace Skogstad, "Supply management, Canadian federalism and trade negotiations," *Federal News* 4, 2 (2013): 1–6.

15 Government of Canada, *Canada-Korea Free Trade Agreement: Creating Jobs and Opportunities for Canadians, Final Agreement Summary* (Ottawa: Public Works and Government Services Canada, 2014), 27–28.

16 Ibid., 30–45.

17 Christopher J. Kukucha, "Internal trade agreements in Canada: Progress, complexity and challenges," *Canadian Journal of Political Science* 48, 1 (2015): 204–08.

18 David Collins, "Globalized localism: Canada's procurement commitments under the CETA," 23 February 2015, http://papers.ssrn.com/sol3/papers.cfm?abstract_id=2568629.

19 Government of Canada, *Opening New Markets in Europe, Creating Jobs and Opportunities for Canadians: Technical Summary of Final Negotiated Outcomes, Canada-European Union Comprehensive Economic and Trade Agreement – Agreement in Principle* (Ottawa: Public Works and Government Services Canada, 2013), 7.
20 Ibid., 11. An exchange of letters did take place, however, on the issue of beef exports, with both sides agreeing to further consultations on this historically sensitive SPS issue.
21 Jason Fekete, "Canada's dairy farmers 'angered and disappointed' by EU trade deal that would double cheese imports," *National Post*, 16 October 2013, http://news.nationalpost.com/news/canada/dairy-farmers-angered-by-reports-canada-close-to-eu-trade-deal-that-would-allow-more-cheese-imports.
22 Government of Canada, *Opening New Markets in Europe*, 13.
23 Christopher J. Kukucha, *The Provinces and Canadian Foreign Trade Policy* (Vancouver: UBC Press, 2008).
24 Stéphane Paquin, "Federalism and the governance of international trade negotiations in Canada: Comparing CUSFTA with CETA," *International Journal* 68, 4 (2013): 545–52.
25 Grace Skogstad, "International trade policy and the evolution of Canadian federalism," in Herman Bakvis and Grace Skogstad, eds., *Canadian Federalism: Performance, Effectiveness, and Legitimacy*, 3rd ed. (Don Mills, ON: Oxford University Press, 2012), 203–22.
26 Canadian government official, personal interview with the author, 24 March 2014.
27 Douglas M. Brown, "The evolving role of the provinces in Canadian trade policy," in Douglas M. Brown and Murray G. Smith, eds., *Canadian Federalism: Meeting Global Economic Challenges?* (Kingston: Queen's University Institute of Intergovernmental Relations, 1991), 101–06.
28 Sue Bailey, "Newfoundland and Labrador says it won't participate in ongoing trade talks," *Globe and Mail*, 19 January 2015, http://www.theglobeandmail.com/news/politics/newfoundland-and-labrador-says-it-wont-participate-in-trade-agreements/article22519888/.
29 Barrie McKenna, "Harper's game risks losing billions in trade," *Globe and Mail*, 6 March 2015, http://www.theglobeandmail.com/report-on-business/harpers-game-risks-losing-billions-in-trade-from-trans-pacific-partnership/article23318168/.
30 Government of Canada, "Government of Canada delivers new programs for supply management sector," 5 October 2015, http://news.gc.ca/web/article-en.do?nid=1017899.
31 Although it has a lower MASH bidding threshold for construction, set at $100,000.
32 For MASH entities, levels are set at $25,000 for goods, $50,000 for services, and $100,000 for construction. Crown corporations, on the other hand, have lower thresholds of $10,000 for goods and $50,000 for services.
33 Kukucha, "Internal trade agreements in Canada," 195–218.

13

Diaspora and Canadian Foreign Policy
The World in Canada?
DAVID CARMENT AND JOSEPH LANDRY

> Just as we have been in the forefront of creating a multicultural society, so too could we be at the forefront of thinking through how to create a foreign policy that can respond to that reality.
> – JENNIFER M. WELSH, "CANADA'S FOREIGN POLICY: DOES THE PUBLIC HAVE A SAY?"[1]

> Kenney notes the Conservatives won 24 of 25 suburban Toronto ridings: "Without the support of the ethnic communities, we could never have done that." The Conservatives estimate that they captured 42 per cent of the country's ethnic vote last election – more than 30 per cent of their total vote, and more than any other party. "I have no intention of stopping now."
> – ALEC CASTONGUAY, "THE INSIDE STORY OF JASON KENNEY'S CAMPAIGN TO WIN OVER ETHNIC VOTES"[2]

Diaspora Politics in a Distinctly Canadian Context

Between 2006 and 2015, when Prime Minister Stephen Harper's Conservative Party led both minority and majority governments, diaspora politics produced a troubling mix of outcomes, giving rise to invidious comparison, special pleading, and behind-the-scenes lobbying. Conservative politicians and members of Cabinet showed favouritism towards some groups at the expense of others, developed special diaspora initiatives with sizable budgets, and compromised Canada's international standing for the sake of votes at home. Even more troubling, Stephen Harper's approach to diaspora politics eroded civil society by encouraging Canadian voters to organize along ethnic lines.[3]

The following analysis assumes implicitly that securing votes among diaspora groups, and specifically among new Canadians, was helpful in pushing the Conservatives to a majority. Indeed, it appears that among those ridings with disproportionate immigrant populations won by the Conservatives for the first time in 2011, there were sizable and important shifts in their favour.[4] It is also important to note that shifts in policies towards Ukraine, China, and India – the subjects of three more detailed case studies below – did occur as the government transitioned from a minority to a majority. At the same time, however, as we demonstrate, changes in Conservative policy were just as likely to come from policy adjustments reflective of a government adapting to events outside of both its control and the Canadian electoral cycle.[5]

Irrespective of their standing in the House of Commons, as either a minority or a majority government, the Harper Conservatives, through the pursuit of a diaspora political agenda, opened up the country to exploitation by other states seeking to disrupt Canada's internal affairs. Previous Canadian governments understood, rightly, that Canada's security needs rest on policies that advance the interests of many diverse groups, not just a few. Nevertheless, the Harper government repeatedly supported narrowly defined ethnic nationalism.[6] Privileging the positions of one ethnic group over another invites these groups to bring disputes from their countries of origin into Canadian politics.

Such populism compromised the durability of traditional Canadian civic nationalism and risked further long-term damage to Canada's national identity.[7] The uncertainty surrounding the long-term durability of that identity arguably makes diaspora politics the most important Canadian international policy issue of the twenty-first century. Consider, for example, that at least 6 million Canadians are foreign born and twice that are second- or third-generation immigrants who maintain ties to their homeland; moreover, many of Canada's new immigrants come from fragile states where economies are weak, minorities are at risk, and human rights violations and open conflict are common.[8]

Between 2009 and 2014, the largest sources of immigrants to Canada were Asia and the Middle East. Since then, Africa's diaspora has delivered the fastest-growing immigrant population in Toronto while China's has done so for Vancouver.⁹ This concentration of immigrant populations in specific parts of Canada's urban centres makes diaspora groups critical to national elections on a riding-by-riding basis. Yet it is only in the twenty-first century that immigration-based electoral politics has emerged strongly in a large number of Canada's cities. This influence can readily be seen in the changing nature of parliamentary representatives, who have never been more ethnically diverse.¹⁰

As the Conservatives worked unremittingly to court diasporas from regions of the world deeply immersed in conflict, we saw simultaneously the emergence of a more conservative Canadian society that complemented the Harper government's broader political agenda. If previous generations of immigrants brought in their suitcases issues such as human rights, democracy, and the like, more recently we have seen different kinds of interests at play: commercial success, perhaps at the expense of human rights, the rule of law, and social justice.¹¹ For example, new immigration laws gave greater influence to employers to screen and select applicants based on their business qualifications while at the same reducing benefits to refugees coming from war-torn countries.¹²

Yet, in spite of this radical shift, the influence diaspora groups brought to bear during the Harper era is difficult to measure. Some foreign policy choices closely converged with the agendas of particular diaspora communities but others did not – a disconnect that does not appear to have been based on the balance of power in the Lower House. Indeed, conditions under which diaspora politics held sway were usually calculated behind the closed doors of the Prime Minister's Office. Policies were chosen because they were thought to generate the greatest support for the Conservative Party. The outcomes of these policies, however, can play out in the public sphere because federal ridings are often contested by representatives of a targeted ethnic group.¹³

The decision to pander and cater to diasporas proved to be a delicate and difficult balancing act. For one thing, the Harper government took ethnic outbidding to extreme and unnecessary levels simply to win votes at home. Especially disturbing were instances in which diaspora pandering converged with the government's ideological orientation, creating and reinforcing a nested policy agenda that appealed to a narrow political base at home while serving no core Canadian interests abroad or, worse, generating hostility with homeland governments. Canada's confrontational rhetoric on Iran, the purpose of which was to appease a Jewish political base, for example, led ultimately to the closure of Canada's embassy in Tehran – a reckless decision that, as David Petrasek and Rebecca Tiessen note (Chapter 11, this volume), dramatically limited Canada's influence.[14] Similarly, confrontations with Russia over its involvement in the Ukraine crisis led to sanctions that not only hurt Canadian businesses but also resulted in a lack of Canadian leverage and influence with Russia.[15]

For another, there is the problem of satisfying a domestic constituency while simultaneously maintaining good relations internationally with Canada's allies, trading partners, and aid recipients. Consider, for example, the recognition of the Armenian genocide (to Turkey's great displeasure); severed relations with Iran (much to the chagrin of the Iranian business community in Canada); support for "the Republic of" Macedonia (to Greece's annoyance); and outreach to Canadian Tamils (to Sri Lanka's constant irritation).[16]

Finally, differences within Canadian diaspora communities could be acute when the government courted a particular faction for its perceived sympathy to the Conservative Party at the expense of others within that same group. For example, the former immigration minister, Jason Kenney, who kept his responsibilities for multiculturalism through both the minority and majority eras, actively involved himself in supporting privileged and extremely contentious political points of view within ethnic communities.[17] His actions risked compromising Canada's multicultural traditions in order to build support for the Conservative government's agenda.[18]

To be clear, in Canadian politics, electoral size, while important, is not the ultimate determinant of an effective and influential diaspora community. Some groups are simply better organized, more cohesive, and have access to greater resources than do others, generating an unevenness in outcomes and perceptions of favouritism.[19] On the one hand, there is the "black box" of influence-peddling and lobbying, and the largely undocumented impact that certain groups have with regard to courting individual members of Parliament, influencing constituency dynamics, and shaping the selection of candidates to run for elections.[20] On the other hand, there was the Harper government's "slice-and-dice" approach to policy making, which parsed the political landscape in terms of carefully orchestrated political handouts to constituencies based on demography and ethnicity.[21] Consider the circumstances surrounding a Conservative private member's bill to recognize 30 April as a national day commemorating the exodus of Vietnamese refugees and their acceptance in Canada after the fall of Saigon to North Vietnamese communist forces. The bill provoked Vietnam's ambassador to

Canada, To Anh Dung, to respond: "If passed, this bill will have an adverse impact on the growing bilateral relations between our two countries. Despite claims of being non-political, this bill clearly incites national hatred and division, not unity."[22]

The exponential increase in catering to diaspora groups spawned an ethical debate across the country. How far can a party go with such a strategy? And what are the implications of taking diaspora politics to its logical conclusion? What the future may portend for a Canada under the grip of diaspora politics is not hard to see. Imagine a memorial for every ethnic group that was ever victimized by a past ideology, the defunding of non-governmental organizations who stand in the way of a particular diaspora group's homeland agenda, or members of former terrorist organizations now declared legitimate members of Canadian society.

But diaspora politics is a two-way street. While the manipulation of diaspora communities to meet Conservative ends was arguably more extensive than ever before in Canadian history, so, too, were efforts by diaspora groups to impose their particular interests on Canada's international policy agenda. This "push" side of diaspora politics poses new challenges, especially since the rise of cheap and ubiquitous telecommunications, social media, instantaneous money transfer, and air travel, coupled with financial liberalization, have enabled members of Canada's diaspora communities to connect to their homelands instantaneously. These new ways of communicating have both created opportunities for growth and investment, and opened old wounds that can prove hard to heal.[23]

Diaspora lobbying and pressure tactics lead to more selective, but not necessarily better, foreign policy choices that can create confusion regarding where Canada really stands.[24] Such confusion was evident in both the minority and majority eras. For example, two respected non-governmental organizations working out of the Middle East, Mada al-Carmel and KAIROS International, suffered significantly under the Conservatives, a theme explored in more detail in Stephen Brown's discussion of Canadian aid (Chapter 10, this volume). The 2010 decision by the government-funded International Development Research Centre (IDRC) to cut more than $700,000 in grant money to Mada al-Carmel fuelled tensions with Palestinians and weakened Canada's presence and influence in the Middle East. The NGO ultimately contested the cut in court, and it was later revealed that an Israeli group, NGO Monitor, had approached the Conservatives with concerns prior to the government's decision. Observers noted that, afterwards, David Malone, then president of the IDRC, believed that the Crown corporation had little choice but to cut Mada al-Carmel's funding.[25] Former minister of international cooperation Bev Oda's intervention to cancel some $7 million worth of funding to Kairos (see Brown, Chapter 10, this volume), carried a similar message.[26]

Also during the minority era, Jason Kenney, then minister of immigration, once stated that Canada acted against its own interests in listing the LTTE, or Tamil Tigers, as a terrorist organization.[27] That Kenney made this announcement at a meeting of Tamil Canadians to a closed ethnic press is indicative not only of the controversy such a statement would create in the mainstream media but also of the kind of narrow casting of policy choices that was a crucial part of the Conservative diaspora politics playbook. It was subsequently revealed that remnants of the Tamil separatist movement in Canada had worked their way into the Conservative Party apparatus.[28]

Cast into a similar situation during the majority period, during a 2012 visit to India, Prime Minister Harper was asked by the Indian government to denounce Sikh aspirations for a separate state, something he would not do. Instead, he stated: "The government of Canada, and I believe the vast majority of Canadian people, including the vast majority of Indo-Canadians, have no desire to see the revival of old hostilities in this great country." He also noted that Sikh advocacy for a separate state of Khalistan is not illegal in Canada. His foreign minister at the time, John Baird, was more unequivocal: Canada's Conservative government would do "everything it [could] possibly do, under the law, to combat radical extremism."[29] Baird's statement was poorly received in the Sikh community.

Finally, in the spring of 2015, the Harper government announced it would support the construction of not one, but two victims' memorials in Ottawa. The first, a memorial to the victims of the Holocaust, was to be built across from the War Museum, and the second, a memorial to victims of communism, would be located in a small park across from the Supreme Court of Canada. While the former was developed mostly unopposed, a great deal of debate arose over the latter's purpose and merits.[30] For many critics, it served as little more than a vote-buying exercise, playing off of the feelings of victimization on the part of select diaspora groups.[31]

Cases in Detail: Ukraine, India, and China

There are a number of additional notable cases that illustrate both the "push" and the "pull" of diaspora politics under the Harper government. Consider, for example, the 2006 controversial handling of the evacuation of thirteen thousand Canadians from war-torn Lebanon; the 2014 deployment of over

450 Canadian observers to the Ukrainian parliamentary elections; and the decision to take a leading humanitarian relief role in at least two states – Haiti (2010) and the Philippines (2013) – with large diaspora communities, all of which together once more indicate that diaspora politics bridged the minority and majority eras.

We now explore three particular cases – the situations in Ukraine, India, and China – in more detail. Canada is home to one of the largest Ukrainian diaspora communities in the world. Since the history of Ukrainian mass migration to Canada dates back to the 1890s, the majority of Canada's Ukrainian population was born in Canada. Their long history in Canada makes the Canadian Ukrainian Congress and Canada Ukraine Foundation particularly effective in their international advocacy efforts, and events in Ukraine during the Harper era increased the salience and intensity of their activity. For example, in 2010, during the minority years, the Canadian Ukrainian diaspora sent 115 election monitors to preside over Ukraine's presidential election.[32]

Four years later and now in the majority era, as political tensions escalated following Russia's 2014 annexation of the Crimean peninsula, both the Canadian government and the Ukrainian diaspora intensified their advocacy. Foreign Affairs Minister John Baird visited Ukraine in early 2014, signalling the government's strong intent to be politically active in the country as Russian-backed rebels attacked in the east. With a diaspora population of over 1.2 million (compared to 500,000 of Russian descent) mostly located in the Prairies, an area of strong Conservative government support, it made political sense for members of the Harper government to respond aggressively. Not only could they appeal to the Conservative base, they could also court the increasing numbers of youth of Ukrainian origin who have moved to urban areas across the country and who therefore represent potential swing votes in closely contested urban ridings, particularly in the Greater Toronto Area. While most keen observers of Canadian foreign policy will realize that Canada has little recourse with regard to Russian actions in Crimea specifically and eastern Ukraine more broadly, most Canadians, including most Conservative voters, lacked such depth of understanding and relied instead on the bold headlines that proclaimed Prime Minister Harper's repeated rebukes of Russian president Vladimir Putin.[33] Such actions played well politically in a climate of fear, regardless of whether this climate was generated in a minority or a majority context.

The Indian case was generally less politically charged. Sikhs from India were the first to immigrate to Canada, settling in British Columbia in the late 1890s. Because of Canada's restrictive immigration policy, the number of migrants of Indian origin remained low until Ottawa instituted a points system in 1967, at which point Indians quickly became the second largest group of immigrants after the Chinese.[34] Indeed, since the late 1990s, approximately twenty-five to thirty thousand Indians have arrived each year. Canada is now home to close to 1 million Indo Canadians, with the vast majority living in the Vancouver and Toronto regions.[35] In addition, unlike with the Ukrainian diaspora population, the majority are foreign born.

Sikhs make up about one-third of the Indian diaspora population in Canada, whereas in India they only account for about 2 percent of the population. As is the case in many diaspora communities, there tends to be a generational divide over maintaining traditional cultural practices such as religious festivals and other customs. Generally, the first generation keeps such traditions alive while subsequent generations tend to eschew them and more readily adopt Canadian cultural norms. Such adaptation is facilitated by the similarities between Canadian and Indian political cultures. Both states abide by parliamentary, federalist, and democratic systems of governance; both share a common British heritage; and both promote multiculturalism at home and peace and security abroad.[36] Despite the obvious potential for a strong Indo-Canadian bilateral relationship, however, the links between Canada and India remain underdeveloped.[37]

Throughout both the minority and the majority government eras, the Conservatives attempted to bridge this gap and, in so doing, to make inroads into urban voters of Indian origin. Their minister of state for multiculturalism, Tim Uppal, was the first Turban-wearing Sikh minister in Canada and played a prominent role in his government's efforts to build appeal among Indian voters. In April 2015, the newly minted Indian prime minister Narendra Modi – a controversial figure at home and abroad – visited Canada and met with both political and business leaders to spur investment in his country.[38] While global business leaders praised Modi's efforts, social justice advocates and other critics protested his previous actions, which include accusations of substantial human rights abuses.[39] Despite the protests, Modi remained popular among the large and well-organized Indian diaspora in Canada, and Prime Minister Harper appeared with him multiple times for carefully calibrated speeches and photo-ops. There can be little doubt that the Conservative Party saw a political opportunity and seized it as it provided a springboard from which the prime minister could illustrate his dedication to furthering ties with India in spite of a lack of progress since 2006. Ottawa also announced improvements to the tourist visa process for Canadians planning to visit India, a change designed to appeal to youth of Indian descent who might not have retained their parents' citizenship. These overtures illustrate how diaspora politics can play out in practice, regardless of the standing of the government in the House of Commons, and provide insight into important questions that arise from treating groups with special interests more favourably than others.

Finally, China has historically been one of the leading sources of newcomers to Canada; indeed, since 1998, it has often been the number one source. In 2013, over 13 percent of all new immigrants to Canada came from China, and Canada is home to close to 1.5 million Chinese Canadians.[40] In addition, the numbers of temporary workers and international students of Chinese origin have significantly increased in recent years, and many will end up staying in Canada or returning in the future. Needless to say, this population represents a critical voting bloc.

As Kim Richard Nossal and Leah Sarson note, the Harper government began its relationship with China on the wrong foot. However, after realizing that "people to people links across the Pacific" presented an electoral advantage, it quickly reversed course.[41] Indeed, as Jason Kenney proudly observed, in 2011, the Conservatives fielded more Chinese Canadian electoral candidates than any other party. Kenney also personally advocated that the government issue an apology for the old Chinese head tax, which had extensively limited Chinese immigration and family unification in the late nineteenth and early twentieth centuries (1885–1923);[42] spear-headed the Community Historical Recognition Program – a $13.5 million project to celebrate and commemorate historical Canadian achievements that greatly benefitted Chinese communities in Vancouver and Toronto; and increased his number of carefully planned appearances in the Chinese community on culturally significant holidays.[43] There were, of course, other factors (such as the global financial crisis and avoiding marginalization in the Asia Pacific region) that stimulated and added to this policy reversal; however, according to Nossal and Sarson, since the shift was evident "by the time that the Conservatives won a majority in 2011," there is little reason to believe that the government's standing in the House of Commons made a difference.[44]

From Politics to Policy: The Search for Coherence

As these three cases illustrate, diaspora politics and diaspora policy are different animals, occasionally working together, sometimes at odds with one another. To date, there remains no official and comprehensive Canadian government diaspora policy. There was the leaked document on building support for the Conservative agenda entitled *Breaking Through: Building the Conservative Brand in Cultural Communities*, but the Harper government showed no interest in developing a formal organization or institutional capacity that would actively represent diaspora interests. This decision was somewhat surprising, considering that many of Canada's largest migrant-sending countries – including the Philippines, India, and Mexico – have all formally institutionalized their diaspora communities into their foreign policies and have created specific organizations to advance their interests. The United States also has several well-funded and active government-sanctioned diaspora organizations with global reach and influence.

Why did the Conservatives choose a different approach? First, one might consider the lack of parliamentary experience in dealing with the evolution of diaspora politics. The China case seems to support this conclusion, but it hardly justifies continued inaction over nine years of Conservative government. The fact that diaspora communities possess specific cultural and political knowledge that has not yet reached Canada's mainstream policy-making community cannot, therefore, be explained by inexperience alone.

Historically, linkages between Canada's diaspora communities and Canadian economic prosperity focused on immigrant retention, including why people moved to Canada; the specific contributions of diaspora communities to Canada (e.g., economic, cultural, social, political); and the nature of these new immigrants' relationships to their home countries. Only recently has the federal government considered questions of how diaspora communities can be engaged both in Canada and abroad on trade, development, and security issues. It follows that the creation of closer and more formal linkages between diaspora groups and an independent government body could serve as an inventory of expertise on cultural, social, economic, and political environments around the world. There is nothing to suggest, however, that the Harper government wanted such an independent, and thus non-partisan, arm's-length body to come to fruition.

A third explanation could be that Canada's long-standing embrace of an official policy of multiculturalism has made the task of articulating a single national interest much more complex. Nonetheless, this challenge also presents a, thus far, missed opportunity. The *Canadian Multiculturalism Act* is intended to "preserve and enhance the multicultural heritage of Canadians while working to achieve the equality of all Canadians."[45] A coherent policy towards Canada's diaspora communities could sanction diaspora groups' political activities while simultaneously encouraging them to maintain their heritage and identity independently of political affiliation and at arm's-length from Canada's political parties. There are a number of similar policy initiatives in play around the world that are explicitly aimed at developing relationships between home countries, host countries, and diaspora communities. Examples include the establishment of flexible citizenship laws and residency requirements, improved visa access and political rights, portable pensions, accessible social services, and tax incentives for investment.

These observations suggest that effective diaspora-based interventions must recognize the complexity of the policy environment. In the Canadian context, contemporary policies have tended to focus on immigration flows, including temporary foreign workers programs and security issues. It would be more effective to think not just about Canadian immigrants and permanent residents but also about second-generation immigrants who are interested in contributing to their home countries' development – and about the implications of their contributions for Canadian policies towards developing countries. For example, over the last number of years, the importance of diaspora groups to consolidating stability and peace, and the security implications of diaspora communities for host and home countries in general, have received broad media coverage and increasing attention by policy makers, academics, diaspora members, and practitioners in the fields of trade, development cooperation, international relations, migration politics, and security.[46]

New Canadians also stimulate trade and investment because the information advantages they hold reduce the transaction costs of entry into home markets. For the banking and investment sector, diaspora connections are important to overcoming obstacles to resource transfer. Economic studies on diaspora communities focus on the various strategies that such groups have used to promote bilateral trade, including the development of networks through personal connections, knowledge translation, and the provision of insight into the operations and culture of the foreign market.[47] Harnessing diaspora communities effectively, therefore, serves both the Canadian market and economic development abroad.

Regrettably, the positive effects of diaspora communities on trade and diplomacy, not to mention their economic, social, and political benefits to multicultural host societies, have often been overshadowed by concerns over the threat of "homegrown" terrorism, "sleeper cells," and the creation and fermentation of so-called "parallel societies" within Canada. Most research, however, shows that the integration of new Canadians increases their capacity to participate positively. In other words, while it may be true that members of diaspora communities utilize host country freedoms to lobby for political and partisan aims in their countries of origin, such activity does not always bring overt conflict to host states such as Canada. [48]

New Canadians with diaspora connections are also now recognized as key drivers of development through remittances, the transfer of human and social capital, and direct support for democracy processes and peacebuilding in fragile states.[49] Diaspora communities can bring to light the intricate challenges facing development programs in their members' homelands and can provide valuable insight into priority areas and culturally sensitive issues that Canadian programs may be ill-trained to address.[50]

Finally, Canada's policies on investment, tourism, health, the environment, and technology have all worked to encourage highly skilled foreign-born workers to become Canadian citizens. Indeed, immigrants now account for more than 70 percent of Canada's labour force growth.[51]

Conclusion

The nature of any diaspora community's relationship with the rest of Canada, its national contributions, and its linkages with its members' homeland depend in large part on the ability of these communities to integrate into Canada and to gain access to national, provincial, and municipal programs and services. Although not all diaspora communities in Canada arrive economically underprivileged, many of those fleeing conflict homelands do. Added to this is the difficulty many new immigrants from developing countries face trying to be politically and economically involved with their homelands while at the same time establishing a home in Canada. Their influence in both locations risks becoming undermined by a lack of time and resources.

Nonetheless, as the main source of growth for Canada's population, the importance of immigrants in Canada will only continue to increase. Since its inception, Canada has always been shaped by diaspora communities, but today's diaspora groups are truly transnational populations in a position to influence both home and host governments, shape their security, and influence trade, development, and investment policy preferences.

Diaspora politics therefore deserves a special place in any discussion on Canada's foreign policy because it occupies a kind of "grey zone" of political propriety. Politicians have an ethical duty to avoid getting caught up in the agendas and partisan interests of specific ethnic groups and in seeing that perceptions of favouritism do not invite internal conflict. Behind-the-scenes lobbying can damage the Canadian democratic process. It follows that the Harper government's approach to instrumentalizing ethnic constituencies for political gain – an approach that characterized both the minority and majority eras – risked creating unevenness in outcomes and inequality in access. Moreover, there is a paucity of evidence that catering to specific groups strengthens Canada overall.

Efforts should be made to immunize new Canadians against partisan manipulation. Amending the *Multiculturalism Act* to ensure the non-partisan independence of community organizations would be a good first step. Creating a federally funded arm's-length diaspora office would be another. These steps would reflect an understanding that participation in democratic institutions is fundamentally distinct from the short-term and self-interested partisan agendas of political parties. An official diaspora policy might also generate reciprocity among groups and encourage them to cooperate on specific agendas. To this end, Canada needs better and more coherent policies specific to the Canadian context. The benefits that diaspora communities bring to this country must be sufficiently documented, strategized, and made policy relevant independently of political interests.

Coming back to the theme of *The Harper Era*, one cannot be certain that the standing of the government in the House of Commons mattered to diaspora politics during the Harper era. However, it is clear that diaspora politics did matter to the government's standing in the House of Commons. Diaspora politics was an essential ingredient in the Harper's government's pursuit of power as both a minority and a majority.

Notes

1 Jennifer M. Welsh, "Canada's Foreign Policy: Does the public have a say?" Dal Grauer Lecture, Vancouver, British Columbia, 15 September 2007. Unpublished paper.
2 Alec Castonguay, "The inside story of Jason Kenney's campaign to win over ethnic votes," *Maclean's*, 2 February 2013, http://www.macleans.ca/news/canada/welcome-to-my-world/.
3 "Building a trusting relationship between the government and immigrant communities has fast become Kenney's priority. Six to 10 times per year, his team organizes 'friendship days' on the Hill, where leaders from cultural communities – spiritual leaders, heads of community centres, presidents of ethnic chambers of commerce, etc. – can arrange to meet ministers of their choosing. 'It gives a chance for the communities to be heard at the highest level in Ottawa, and they appreciate the

gesture," says Agop Evereklian, who was Kenney's chief of staff from 2008 to 2010 and, until recently, chief of staff to former Montreal mayor Gerald Tremblay." Ibid.

4 Joe Friesen and Julian Sher, "How courting the immigrant vote paid off for the Conservatives," *Globe and Mail*, 3 May 2011, http://www.theglobeandmail.com/news/politics/how-courting-the-immigrant-vote-paid-off-for-the-tories/article578608/.

5 The shift from minority to majority might have been more important in other cases, such as the creation of the Office of Religious Freedom, but, for reasons of space, that story is beyond the scope of this chapter. See David Carment, "Religious freedom? This office is about ethnic votes," *Globe and Mail*, 21 February 2013, http://www.theglobeandmail.com/globe-debate/religious-freedom-this-office-is-about-ethnic-votes/article8901119/.

6 Diaspora politics is seductive and populist. For example, John Baird pursued a vitriolic and aggressive policy on Iran and worked with and funded the Munk Centre to help destabilize the Iranian regime through social media. See David Carment and Ariane Sadjed, "Old enemies, new technology," *Opencanada.org*, 12 December 2014, http://opencanada.org/features/old-enemies-new-technology/. For an alternative perspective, see Adam Chapnick (Chapter 6, this volume).

7 See the 2014 special issue of *Canadian Foreign Policy Journal* for a critical review of foreign policy under Stephen Harper: *Canadian Foreign Policy Journal* 20, 2 (2014).

8 Canada's diaspora connections are increasingly relevant for a variety of reasons, including Canada's changing demographic profile, declining fertility rates, shifts in priority immigrant countries, and transformations in refugee processing and acceptance rates. According to data from the *National Household Survey on Immigration and Ethnocultural Diversity in Canada*, in 2011 more than 20 percent of the total population in Canada was foreign-born. See http://www12.statcan.gc.ca/nhs-enm/2011/as-sa/99-010-x/99-010-x2011001-eng.cfm.

9 One might infer, therefore, that contemporary Canadian immigration trends are not shaped by any government's standing in the House of Commons.

10 Concerns over so-called "imported conflicts" remain high on the list of security threats for many Western countries, including Canada. Canada, like other aid donors, is also under increasing pressure to generate more effective aid programs and innovative solutions to reverse these impacts and to stabilize war-torn societies. See, for example, Laura Payton, "Ethnic riding targeting key to Conservatives' 2011 victory," *cbc.ca*, 23 October 2012, http://www.cbc.ca/news/politics/ethnic-riding-targeting-key-to-conservatives-2011-victory-1.1142511; and the special issue of *Canadian Foreign Policy Journal* 17, 2 (2011), entitled "Brain circulation and diasporic tourism in the Caribbean."

11 John Ibbitson, "Conservatives changed the nature of Canadian immigration," *Globe and Mail*, 16 December 2014, http://www.theglobeandmail.com/news/politics/how-conservatives-changed-the-nature-of-canadian-immigration/article22101709/.

12 These changes would alter the profile of the kind of immigrants coming to Canada. See Ratna Omidvar, Global Diversity Exchange, "Ten immigration stories to watch," 1 January 2015, http://www.globaldiversityexchange.ca/ten-canadian-immigration-stories-to-watch-in-2015/.

13 Castonguay, "Inside story"; Bryn Weese and David Akin, "Kenney staffer resigns after 'unacceptable' gaffe," *thedailyobserver.ca*, 4 March 2011, http://www.thedaily observer.ca/2011/03/03/kenney-staffer-resigns-after-unacceptable-gaffe-4.

14 OpenCanada Staff, "John Mundy on the embassy closure, diplomacy from a distance, and the nuclear threat," 22 May 2013, https://opencanada.org/features/john-mundy -on-the-embassy-closure-diplomacy-from-a-distance-and-the-nuclear-threat/.

15 Margo McDiarmid, "Arctic Council tensions threaten environment as Canada exits chair," *cbc.ca*, 24 April 2015, http://www.cbc.ca/news/politics/arctic-council-tensions -threaten-environment-as-canada-exits-chair-1.3045975.

16 In 2009, Tamil Canadians filled the streets of Toronto and Ottawa to protest against what they called a genocide and to support intervention and a demand for an immediate ceasefire. In response, the Canadian government merely threatened to boycott the forthcoming Commonwealth Heads of Government Meeting in Colombo and draw down the already relatively small aid program of $20 million.

17 In 2008, Jason Kenney established the Community Historical Recognition Program, with a $13.5 million budget. Its role was to finance commemorative projects and erect statues to honour key historical figures. Italian, Jewish, Indian, and Chinese communities have all profited from it. See Castonguay, "Inside story."

18 "Read the Tory ethnic-outreach strategy," *Globe and Mail*, 3 March 2011, http:// www.theglobeandmail.com/news/politics/read-the-tory-ethnic-outreach-strategy/ article632554/.

19 See, for example, Sami Aoun, "Muslim communities: The pitfalls of decision-making in Canadian foreign policy," in David Carment and David Bercuson, eds., *The World in Canada: Diaspora, Demography, and Domestic Politics* (Montreal and Kingston: McGill-Queen's University Press, 2008), 109–22.

20 There is an increasing openness to inviting such groups to lobby on foreign-policy issues, and it is expected that there will be an increase in their influence on the foreign-policy agenda – even if or when the groups are not yet formally organized. Consider the cases of Haiti and Jamaica, for example. Canada has long claimed to have a "special" relationship with both of these countries; language, geography, economics, and political considerations have all played a role in the formation and evolution of these relationships. Canada has repeatedly looked to civil society organizations in both island states.

21 Susan Delacourt, *Shopping for Votes: How Politicians Choose Us and We Choose Them* (Toronto: Douglas and McIntrye, 2013).

22 Joan Bryden, "Obscure Senate bill infuriates Vietnam, sparks diplomatic spat with Canada," *Globe and Mail*, 5 December 2014, http://www.theglobeandmail.com/news/ politics/obscure-senate-bill-infuriates-vietnam-sparks-diplomatic-spat-with-canada/ article21966166/.

23 As an example of the former, consider India's prime minister Narendra Modi's visit to Canada in 2015, in which he staked out a strategy of diaspora investment in India's infrastructure by engaging these groups directly in a cross-Canada tour. Stephen Harper was consistently at his side. In the latter instance, consider the decision by the Toronto Symphony Orchestra, under pressure from anonymous donors, to cancel performances by Ukrainian pianist Valentina Lisitsa, who openly criticized the Ukrainian government on social media.

24 Prime Minister Harper was keen to sign a number of bilateral trade deals in which diaspora politics played out favourably, despite the relatively meagre economic gains: free trade agreements with Ukraine, the Philippines, and Israel are notable examples.
25 Patrick Martin, "Arab-Israeli group takes Canadian agency to court over terminated funding," *Globe and Mail*, 1 July 2010, http://www.theglobeandmail.com/news/world/arab-israeli-group-takes-canadian-agency-to-court-over-terminated-funding/article1215647/; "Prof. Steinberg radio interview about Mada al-Carmel," 3 August 2010, *NGO Monitor*, http://www.ngo-monitor.org/article/prof_steinberg_on_galei_zahal_radio.
26 A 2015 CBC story indicated that the Harper government was threatening to use hate speech laws to deter Canadian organizations and individuals, including church groups and student bodies, advocating a boycott of Israeli goods. See Neil Macdonald, "Ottawa cites hate crime laws when asked about its 'zero tolerance' for Israel boycotters," *cbc.ca*, 11 May 2015, http://www.cbc.ca/news/politics/ottawa-cites-hate-crime-laws-when-asked-about-its-zero-tolerance-for-israel-boycotters-1.3067497.
27 Michelle Zilio, "Canada acted against its own interests," *iPolitics*, 11 February 2013, http://ipolitics.ca/2013/02/11/canada-acted-against-own-interests-in-listed-ltte-as-terrorist-group-kenney/. See also Ira de Silva, "Canada overtaking pro-LTTE groups," 24 February 2013, http://www.island.lk/index.php?page_cat=article-details&page=article-details&code_title=73401.
28 Anthony Reinhart, "'Tories' bid to win over South Asians opens party to Tamil Tigers' remnant," *Globe and Mail*, 5 March 2011, http://www.theglobeandmail.com/news/politics/tories-bid-to-win-over-south-asians-opens-party-to-tamil-tigers-remnant/article576456/?page=all.
29 Steven Chase and Kim Mackrael, "On Sikh separatism, Harper in India defends freedom of expression," *Globe and Mail*, 8 November 2012, http://www.theglobeandmail.com/news/world/on-sikh-separatism-harper-in-india-defends-freedom-of-expression/article5085143/.
30 Roy MacGregor, "New victims of communism memorial in Ottawa a looming disaster," *Globe and Mail*, 30 January 2015, http://www.theglobeandmail.com/news/national/new-victims-of-communism-memorial-in-ottawa-a-looming-disaster/article22730797/; Andrew Cohen, "Communism memorial a monumental folly," *Ottawa Citizen*, 10 March 2015, http://ottawacitizen.com/opinion/columnists/communism-memorial-a-monumental-folly.
31 Carment and Sadjed, "Old enemies."
32 Hila Olyan and Phoebe Smith, "Diasporas: A policy review prepared for the Privy Council Office," April 2011, http://www4.carleton.ca/cifp/app/serve.php/1357.pdf.
33 A small number of Ukrainian Canadians have gone to fight for Ukraine, supported and funded by the Ukrainian diaspora; some fighters have extreme right-wing affiliations. See Mark MacKinnon, "Bypassing official channels, Canada's Ukrainian diaspora finances and fights a war against Russia," *Globe and Mail*, 26 February 2015, http://www.theglobeandmail.com/news/world/ukraine-canadas-unofficial-war/article23208129/.
34 Soodabeh Salehi, "Building bridges: The role of the Indian diaspora in Canada – Literature review," December 2007, http://archives.cerium.ca/IMG/pdf/Building_

Bridges-_The_Role_of_the_Indian_Diaspora_in_Canada_Literature_Review_-2.pdf.

35 Statistics Canada, "Ethnic origins, 2006 counts, for Canada, provinces and territories – 20% sample data," last modified 10 June 2010, http://www12.statcan.ca/census-recensement/2006/dp-pd/hlt/97-562/pages/page.cfm?Lang=E&Geo=PR&Code=01&Table=2&Data=Count&StartRec=1&Sort=3&Display=All&CSDFilter=5000.

36 Reeta Chowdhari Tremblay, "Canada and India: Broadening and deepening relationship," in Asia Pacific Foundation of Canada, ed., *Canada in Asia: Foreign Policy Dialogue Series, 2003-2004* (Vancouver: Asia Pacific Foundation of Canada, 2003).

37 See the proceedings of a special, IDRC-sponsored "Canada-India Diaspora Workshop" held at Carleton University, spring 2014, http://carleton.ca/india/cu-events/canada-india-diaspora-event/.

38 Kim Mackrael, "Indian PM Modi to meet with pension funds, banks during visit to Canada," *Globe and Mail*, 7 April 2015, http://www.theglobeandmail.com/news/politics/indian-pm-modi-to-meet-with-pension-funds-banks-during-visit-to-canada/article23818565/.

39 Iain Marlow and Andrea Woo, "Indian PM Modi attracts protesters at BC stop," *Globe and Mail*, 16 April 2015, http://www.theglobeandmail.com/news/british-columbia/large-crowds-in-vancouver-await-modi-on-final-leg-of-canadian-visit/article23996857/.

40 Citizenship and Immigration Canada, "2014 Annual Report to Parliament on Immigration," last modified 31 October 2014, http://www.cic.gc.ca/english/resources/publications/annual-report-2014/.

41 Kim Richard Nossal and Leah Sarson, "About face: Explaining changes in Canada's China policy, 2006–2012," *Canadian Foreign Policy Journal* 20, 2 (2014): 151. See also Mary Young and Susan Henders, "Other diplomacies and the making of Canada Asia relations," *Canadian Foreign Policy Journal* 18, 3 (2012): 375–88.

42 Ibid., 157.

43 Castonguay, "Inside story."

44 Nossal and Sarson, "About face," 146. Nossal and Sarson do concede that the relationship deepened during the majority era, but they attribute these changes, at least in part, to the personality of Minister John Baird (150).

45 Government of Canada, *Canadian Multiculturalism Act, 1988*, http://laws-lois.justice.gc.ca/eng/acts/C-18.7/ (emphasis added).

46 Brandon Lum, David Carment, Yiagadeesen Samy, and Milana Nikolko, "Diasporas, remittances, and state fragility" *Ethnopolitics* 12, 2 (2012): 201–18.

47 Maurice Bitran and Serene Tan, *Diaspora Nation: An Inquiry into the Economic Potential of Diaspora Networks in Canada* (Toronto: Mowat Centre, September 2013). See also D.W. Brinkerhoff and S. Taddesse, "Recruiting from the diaspora: The local governance program in Iraq," in Jennifer M. Brinkerhoff, ed., *Diasporas and Development: Exploring the Potential* (Boulder, CO: Lynne Rienner, 2008), 67–87; Anita Singh, "The diaspora network of ethnic lobbying" *Canadian Foreign Policy Journal* 18, 3 (2012): 340–57.

48 John Monahan et al., *The Perception and Reality of "Imported Conflict" in Canada* (Toronto: Mosaic Institute, 2014); Mosaic Institute and Walter and Duncan Gordon Foundation, *Tapping Our Potential: Diaspora Communities and Canadian Foreign Policy* (Toronto: Mosaic Institute and Walter and Duncan Gordon Foundation, 2011).
49 See David Carment, Dacia Douhaibi, and Milana Nikolko, "Canadian foreign policy and Africa's diaspora," in Rohinton Medhora and Yiagadeesen Samy, eds., *Canada Among Nations 2013: Canada-Africa Relations – Looking Back, Looking Ahead* (Waterloo: Centre for International Governance Innovation, 2013), 71–78.
50 J.M. Brinkerhoff, "Diaspora philanthropy in an at-risk society: The case of Coptic orphans in Egypt," *Non-profit and Voluntary Sector Quarterly* 37 (2008): 411–33; J.M. Brinkerhoff, "Creating an enabling environment for diasporas' participation in homeland development," *International Migration* 50 (2009): 75–95.
51 Immigration Watch, "Labour shortage," n.d., http://www.immigrationwatchcanada.org/background/research/immigration/labour-shortage/.

PART 3
ADDITIONAL PERSPECTIVES

14

Minority Report

Covering Canadian Foreign Policy in a Minority and Majority Government

LEE BERTHIAUME

In the long history of the Parliamentary Press Gallery, it was an extraordinary act of defiance. The date was 23 May 2006, and Prime Minister Stephen Harper was set to start a press conference in his Parliament Hill office when about two dozen journalists turned and walked out. The prime minister, newly elected to power only four months earlier, had been about to announce $40 million in humanitarian and military assistance for Darfur. But it wasn't the topic of the press conference that had prompted the journalists to leave.

Relations between the gallery and Harper's staff had started to fray shortly after the election, when the latter ended the long-standing practice of saying when Cabinet would meet. Journalists were then barred from waiting outside the cabinet room to ask ministers questions. Next came the surprise decision to ban reporters and news cameras from the runway at CFB Trenton during repatriation ceremonies for Canadian soldiers killed in Afghanistan. Now Harper's staff had said journalists would no longer be allowed to ask questions during photo ops in the Prime Minister's Office. Even worse, they would begin choosing which reporters could ask questions during future press conferences. It was the last straw.

A few weeks later, I joined a small foreign policy newspaper in Ottawa called *Embassy*. The closest I'd gotten to federal politics during my short career to that point was covering the 2004 election for the *Peterborough*

Examiner. The tense standoff between the Parliamentary Press Gallery and the PMO meant nothing to me.

I knew only a smidgen more about foreign policy. I'd seen first-hand during sixteen months in Cambodia how even the smallest, impoverished country was tugged this way and that by the competing interests of China, Japan, Australia, the United States, and France. And I'd witnessed the difficulties facing South Africa after apartheid and the brutality of the Mugabe regime during a year in southern Africa. But otherwise my knowledge was rudimentary.

In the following nine-plus years of Conservative rule, during which I continued to cover Canadian foreign policy for *Embassy*, the Postmedia newspaper chain, and, most recently, the *Ottawa Citizen*, Canada saw six foreign affairs ministers, fought in three wars, and held three federal elections. And while one thing that didn't change was the Conservative government's desire to control information and circumvent the media when it came to foreign affairs (and pretty much everything else), the shift from a minority to a majority government in 2011 made that task all the easier. The question now is whether things will change under Justin Trudeau's Liberals, who promised more openness and a better working relationship with the media before winning their own majority government.

In the Beginning ...

When I joined *Embassy* in June 2006, the Conservative government was less than six months into its first minority mandate. I recall one of the first things that struck me in my new position: not only was foreign policy not a priority for the new government, it didn't appear to actually have one.

As a number of chapters in this collection mention, the Conservatives had been elected on a largely domestic agenda. Their platform had mentioned expanding free trade and investing more money into the Canadian Armed Forces. But foreign policy received only a token mention, with vague allusions to "true Canadian values" and Canada's "national interests." Prime Minister Harper did hint at his eventual foreign policy priorities early in his mandate. During his fourth week in power, he scolded Hamas, appointed an ambassador to Washington, and spoke to Ukrainian president Viktor Yushchenko, Colombian president Alvaro Uribe, and Palestinian leader Mahmoud Abbas. But these were isolated events that went largely unexplained and were easily overlooked as the government moved on its real priorities, which included passing the *Accountability Act* into law, cutting the goods and services tax, and introducing the universal child care benefit.

It was hard to blame the Conservatives for focusing on the home front. Paul Martin had invested a great deal of time and energy in his international policy statement, but the much-ballyhooed paper didn't keep his Liberals in power. And in this uncertain time, when an election was always around the corner, it was all about votes. The downside, however, was that everything was in limbo when it came to foreign affairs. Officials in then foreign affairs minister Peter MacKay's office as well as the department would quietly tell me there was little to no direction coming from on high. This problem persisted in some foreign policy areas for years.

For example, in August 2006 I attended the International AIDS Conference in Toronto. One of the speakers was Josée Verner, who at the time was international development minister. Ministers and officials were rarely available to the media, so this was a rare opportunity to ambush her. My question was whether the Conservative government would continue the Martin government's plan to focus the bulk of Canadian foreign aid on twenty-five least-developed countries. "We are looking at where it can be more effective," Verner said. "We are working on that."[1] In fact, as Stephen Brown (Chapter 10, this volume) notes, it would take another two and a half years before the Conservatives revealed their new foreign aid policy, which focused Canadian aid on twenty countries and included a shift from several low-income African states to middle-income trading partners in the Americas.

Further complicating matters was a hub-and-spoke communications management system implemented by the PMO and the PCO shortly after the Harper Conservatives came to power. All interview requests, questions, and speeches went through the PMO and the PCO, better known as the Centre. The results were devastating. Unless the Centre thought a request was a priority, everything took days if not weeks to work through the bottleneck. Even then, most interview requests were denied and most questions were answered with prepared lines that had only passing relevance to the original query. It got to the point at which I would call ministers' offices or departments with questions not because I expected an answer but, rather, because I was obligated to give them an opportunity to respond to some criticism or other. And my interview requests slowly petered out as vague promises produced no results.

From time to time, frustration over this system among public servants created opportunities for journalists. In January 2009, for example, a disgruntled official leaked to us details of the government's aforementioned shift in Canadian foreign aid from Africa to Latin America. When the government realized we were trying to confirm the list, it hurriedly announced the change without first notifying the affected countries.

However, for the most part, political and departmental officials were scared of speaking even off the record. The Centre was merciless with those who spoke out of turn. And no one wanted to be held responsible for sparking a controversy that would bring down the government. So most kept their mouths shut. Indeed, it seemed the only person allowed to speak freely was Prime Minister Harper. In July 2006, he called Israel's bombing of Lebanon a "measured" response to Hezbollah's abducting two Israeli soldiers. In November, he said Canada wouldn't sell out to the "almighty dollar" when it came to championing human rights in China.

These were significant statements from a Canadian prime minister. But, as with almost everything else, they came with little explanation or broader context. This meant having to rely on outsiders to analyze and interpret the comments. A refined form of tea-leaf reading, perhaps, but tea-leaf reading nonetheless. Even when the government did begin to announce more substantive foreign policy directions later on, such as the Americas Strategy and a new free trade agenda in 2007, there was often little accompanying explanation. Officials remained off limits and canned lines continued to replace substantive information.

Looking back, it seems the idea was to shift Canadian foreign policy without sparking controversy. And some of the changes were significant. The Americas Strategy, for example, represented a concerted shift from multilateralism to regionalism. The government also ended automatic appeals for clemency for Canadians on death row abroad, overhauled the refugee system, and cut funding to Canadian aid groups. As David Carment and Joseph Landry explain in detail (Chapter 13, this volume), the government also used foreign policy to court specific ethnic groups. Such a strategy wasn't new to Canadian politics. The Liberals, for example, refused to follow the United States and Great Britain in listing Sri Lanka's Tamil Tigers as a terrorist group because Canada is home to the largest Tamil population outside South Asia. But the Conservatives took the practice to new heights. There was the unwavering support for Israel, of course, but also formal recognition of the Armenian genocide and the Holodomor in Ukraine. There was also criticism of Vietnam's communist government, Vladimir Putin's Russia, and Japan's use of so-called comfort women during the Second World War. Each of these prompted strong reactions from respective countries, including friends and allies such as Japan and Turkey. But they also appealed to key voter blocs in Canada: Ukrainians, Armenians, Chinese,

South Koreans, and Vietnamese who had fled that country's communist regime.

To ensure the initiatives garnered maximum attention with their intended voter groups, the Conservatives launched a dramatic and sustained campaign that side-stepped the mainstream press and troublesome Parliamentary Press Gallery and instead engaged directly with relevant ethnic media organizations. "The Harper government also has a whole team in the Prime Minister's Office working on connecting with ethnic media across the country," *Embassy* reported in March 2011. "The so-called 'regional communications advisers' in Toronto, Vancouver and Montreal coordinate teleconferences and roundtables with the ethnic press, often leaving the mainstream media in the dark and clueless about these initiatives."[2]

While the government's communications strategy created significant frustrations, it was also an exciting time to be covering federal politics. With the ever-present threat of an election, no one knew what the prime minister or government would do next. For example, Prime Minister Harper chose the middle of the 2008 election to announce Canada would definitively end its combat mission in Afghanistan in 2011. Separately, the Liberals and NDP presented their own alternate foreign policy proposals at different times throughout the minority years. But, like the government, their shifting interests and constant watch on the polls meant that nothing was ever certain.

In April 2007, for example, the NDP helped defeat a Liberal motion that would have had Canada announce its plan to withdraw all troops from Afghanistan in February 2009. The NDP said it opposed the motion because it wanted the troops out immediately, but some believed it didn't want to be upstaged by the Liberals. Eleven months later, with the Manley panel having given them the necessary political cover, the Liberals turned around and supported extending the Afghanistan mission until December 2011. Interestingly, twenty Liberal MPs were absent from the vote.

The Fog of War

As Jean-Christophe Boucher and Kim Richard Nossal note (Chapter 4, this volume), the Conservatives' first two years in power had coincided with the bloodiest fighting the Canadian military had seen since Korea. Nearly sixty soldiers died and another 260 were wounded in Afghanistan as Canadian forces fought pitched battles with the Taliban, including during Operation Medusa in September 2006. The government had initially embraced the Afghan war; Stephen Harper's first foreign trip as prime minister was to

Kandahar in March 2006, where he pledged that Canada wouldn't "cut and run." But behind the bravado was an apparent fear the war could become a political liability.

One of the Conservatives' first acts in government was the aforementioned decision to bar journalists from repatriation ceremonies at CFB Trenton. While the decision was partly rescinded following anger from some families of the fallen, it was still emblematic of the government's desire to crack down on bad news about the mission. Indeed, the government's strategy was to put the best spin on the war at all times. This involved highlighting successes while refusing to reveal, discuss, or acknowledge problems and challenges. That it had a willing partner among senior bureaucrats and military officers made things even more difficult for the press. The result was that the government and officials used the same canned lines over and over, which the media promptly ignored; instead, reporters filled the news vacuum with whatever nuggets they could uncover, even if that meant some insignificant issues got blown out of proportion.

In January 2008, there came hope things were about to change. The prime minister had unexpectedly tapped former Liberal minister John Manley to head a blue-chip panel that would study the conditions for extending Canada's war in Afghanistan. Manley's appointment was strategically brilliant. There was never any doubt that he would recommend an extension, and his involvement gave the Liberals the political cover they needed to jump on board. But the panel also had some pointed findings about how the mission had been conducted to date.

"To put things bluntly," the panel's report read, "governments from the start of Canada's Afghan involvement have failed to communicate with Canadians with balance and candour about the reasons for Canadian involvement, or about the risks, difficulties and expected results of that involvement." The panel concluded: "This information deficit needs to be redressed immediately in a comprehensive and more balanced communication strategy of open and continuous engagement with Canadians." Among its recommendations was "franker and more frequent reporting on events in Afghanistan."[3]

The government promised to act. Quarterly reports were created to provide regular updates on the military, diplomatic, and development aspects of Canada's mission in Afghanistan. It wasn't long, however, before those reports also became little more than propaganda. The more lasting and important result was the establishment of a special Cabinet committee on Afghanistan, which saw regular updates about the war from ministers and departmental officials. It also played a key role in the Afghan detainee scandal.

Digging Deep

The small committee room in Parliament's West Block was crowded with journalists and political aides when a previously unknown diplomat named Richard Colvin walked through the door and into Canadian history on 18 November 2009. Over the next ninety minutes, Colvin would testify that the Canadian military had knowingly handed Afghan detainees over to torture during the early part of Canada's combat mission in Kandahar in 2006 and 2007. He said most of the Afghans had been innocent of any wrongdoing.

"Many were just local people: farmers, truck drivers, tailors, peasants, random human beings in the wrong place at the wrong time," he said at one point. "In other words, we detained, and handed over for severe torture, a lot of innocent people."[4] Colvin said he was initially ignored when he tried to raise concerns with senior officials at Foreign Affairs and National Defence that the detainee transfers might make Canada and the military complicit in war crimes. Then, when *Globe and Mail* journalist Graeme Smith started poking around in early 2007, the makings of a cover-up began. Colvin was told to shut up and stop causing problems. If he had to report something, he was to pick up the phone and avoid leaving a paper trail.

Colvin's testimony blew apart the Conservative government's repeated assertions – echoed by Canadian military commanders and others – that there were no credible reports of Afghan detainees having been tortured after being transferred from Canadian custody. The government responded by attacking Colvin's credibility. But three weeks later, the chief of the defence staff, General Walter Natynczyk, admitted that the Canadian Armed Forces had indeed witnessed at least one detainee being beaten by Afghan police in June 2006.

The revelations were devastating to the government. After two years of denials, there was suddenly the very real possibility that the Canadian military had been complicit in war crimes in Afghanistan – and that Conservative ministers had lied to Parliament about it. In the House of Commons on 10 December 2009, opposition parties passed a resolution requiring the government to release forty thousand pages of uncensored documents related to the treatment of Afghan detainees. Faced with having to either produce the documents or risk being found in contempt of Parliament, which would have triggered an election, Prime Minister Stephen

Harper took a third path. On 30 December 2009, he prorogued Parliament for the second time in a year.

Looking back, the minority years were a golden age for the parliamentary committee system. With a majority of members on every committee, opposition parties were able to call ministers and departmental officials to testify in a quasi-judicial setting on any topic. And they took full advantage of that opportunity. Would Colvin have been called to testify if the Conservatives had owned a majority government and, thus, had more members on the House of Commons committee? Would the committee have even agreed to study the detainee issue in the first place? Would a resolution requiring the release of uncensored documents have passed in the House of Commons? Would the prime minister have at any point faced losing a confidence vote over the issue? The probable answer to each of those questions is no. Thus there is a very real possibility that the story, which emerged following dogged reporting by the *Globe and Mail*'s Smith, and which made headlines for years, would have died long before it reached such a stage.

The Afghan detainee scandal wasn't the only topic to go before committee. There was also Bev Oda's tortured explanation about who inserted a handwritten "NOT" to cut an NGO's funding after public servants recommended it be extended, and the parliamentary budget officer Kevin Page's relentless criticisms of the cost of the F-35. There were sharp debates over the prime minister's decision to exclude abortion from his maternal and child health initiative, the impacts a free trade agreement with Colombia would have on that country's human rights situation, and the Kyoto Protocol. Unsurprisingly, many of the most controversial studies were prompted by media reports. Those studies, in turn, often generated and advanced media reports. Indeed, the media and parliamentary committees in those days had an almost symbiotic relationship.

Majority Rules

They just wouldn't answer the question: How much was it going to cost? It was October 2014 and Canada was at war again. The Conservative government was sending Canadian fighter jets, surveillance planes, and a refuelling aircraft to Iraq to bomb Islamic State forces from the sky for the next six months, while several dozen special forces troops helped the Kurds on the ground. But how much was it all going to cost? The Conservative government refused to say.

Did Canadians care? The government claimed the majority of Canadians supported the mission. They were probably right. But it was still a question worth asking. The government had promised to be open with Parliament about the mission. Taxpayers deserved to know how their money was being spent. The Canadian Armed Forces were already making do with less. And, if the majority of Canadians were truly in favour of the mission, as the Conservatives claimed, there was no reason to hide the information.

It wasn't until the following February that the government revealed that it expected the war in Iraq to cost $122 million. The information wasn't willingly released but came out through the Treasury Board's estimates process, which required that the figures be reported to Parliament. By then, Canada had already been at war for months.

Four years earlier, on 4 May 2011, the Conservative government had won its coveted majority. Though Canada had lost its bid for a Security Council seat the year before and was engaged in two wars, in Afghanistan and in Libya, the election was largely devoid of foreign policy. In the aftermath, there was a palpable hope that having a majority government would mark a fresh start in relations between the Conservatives and the media, particularly the Parliamentary Press Gallery. "Having just won a solid majority government, will Prime Minister Stephen Harper change his style?" *Globe and Mail* columnist Jeffrey Simpson asked two weeks after the election. "Will he ease up on his desire to control so much, to be so stingy with information, to be so relentlessly partisan?"[5] The post-minority era did see some changes, but it is difficult to say how much of that had to do with the switch to a majority government and how much had to do with experience and personalities.

Unlike many of his predecessors to the foreign affairs portfolio, John Baird was one of the Conservatives' most powerful and influential ministers. Not by coincidence, the members of his staff were among the more open, engaged, and experienced. Having a background conversation with them was much easier than doing so with other ministerial staff. But, while off-the-record chats were easier to arrange, most things on the record still had to flow through the Centre. Meanwhile, Question Period remained little more than partisan theatre, parliamentary debates became little more than chest-beating, and most ministers and officials were still largely unavailable for interviews.

Perhaps the most significant change was that parliamentary committees became largely uncontroversial as the Conservatives around each table used their majority to steer clear of contentious issues or topics that could cause the government embarrassment. The Veterans Affairs Committee, for example, refused to look at government cuts to Veterans Affairs Canada (VAC) staffing or at the contentious decision to close nine VAC regional offices in January 2014. The Commons' defence committee, meanwhile, spent the first eight months of the war against ISIS studying continental defence. This was despite questions about the war's cost, what Canadian soldiers were doing in northern Iraq, and how one of those soldiers was killed by friendly fire in March 2015.

The government also adopted an even more stringent communications approach to the war against ISIS than it did to the war in Afghanistan. There were occasional technical briefings with a high-ranking officer, but these were usually devoid of much detail and included a good deal of cheerleading. Journalists were also forbidden from interviewing or taking pictures of Canadian military personnel participating in the mission. This policy ended a long-standing tradition, dating back to Canada's earliest military endeavours, and applied even to soldiers who were embarking in Canada and their families. Meanwhile, the government stepped up its efforts to side-step the mainstream media and the Parliamentary Press Gallery. The PMO used Twitter to announce new Cabinet ministers during the July 2013 shuffle before telling journalists. And the PMO launched a weekly propaganda video called *24/7*.

Even aspects of foreign policy the government should have had no problem touting, or might have wanted to actually promote, were difficult to cover. Throughout the fall of 2014, for example, I had wanted to write about the non-military aspects of Canada's involvement in Iraq and the fight against the Islamic State. I was particularly interested in what was being done to address the disenfranchisement of Sunni Muslims in Iraq and Syria, which had contributed to ISIS's rise in the region. But my requests for information and interviews were repeatedly ignored or rebuffed. Meanwhile, Minister Baird was strongly pushing for the adoption of digital diplomacy and the elimination of early childhood marriage. Yet requests to interview him on both were unsuccessful. And the US military became a better source of information about some joint training exercises and operations than the CAF. The result was big holes in what Canadians knew about their country's activities and positions on the world stage, including many good news stories.

In this information vacuum, journalists learned to go to other sources: Order Paper questions, reports to Parliament, budget estimates, the Parliamentary Budget Office, and access-to-information requests. In each case, however, the government gradually imposed its control. Order Paper questions, reports to Parliament, and budget estimates became devoid of substance. The Parliamentary Budget Office and Access to Information requests were blocked with regularity. (Sometimes it seemed the only way to get a real answer about the government was from the auditor general, which is why his reports on the F-35, for example, had such a huge impact.) This undoubtedly spared the government some bad press. But it also meant media organizations would often seize on anything that did slip through – including what, with a bit of explanation or context, would have been non-stories – and play it big.

Journalists also learned to do whatever they needed to get answers from the government. Visits by foreign officials, for example, became one of the few occasions the Parliamentary Press Gallery had to ask the prime minister a question. That meant Prime Minister Harper was often asked about some domestic issues while the foreign guests looked on awkwardly. The practice even followed the Canadian prime minister abroad. On 21 May 2013, I travelled with Harper as he visited Peru and Colombia to discuss Canada's joining the Pacific Alliance. Just before leaving Ottawa, revelations had emerged that Harper's chief of staff, Nigel Wright, had given Senator Mike Duffy $90,000. Harper had addressed the Conservative caucus that morning to say he was "not happy" but that the government would have to move on.[6] He did not take questions from the media, who'd been invited to listen, and the speech was widely panned as an attempt to sweep the whole affair under the rug. The next day, Harper and Peruvian president Ollanta Humala appeared in the gorgeous government palace in Lima to announce several agreements. The surprise wasn't that Canadian media used their two questions in the following press conference to ask about Duffy but, rather, that a Peruvian journalist asked about it as well. If Harper had addressed the issue in Ottawa, it could be argued, there is a chance he might have actually taken a question on relations with Peru.

The More Things Change ...
On 15 October 2015, Liberal leader Justin Trudeau held a press conference in Montreal. At one point, Trudeau was asked about the resignation of campaign co-chair Dan Gagnier after it was revealed he had provided advice to an oil pipeline company on how to lobby a new government. The issue had dogged the Liberals for several days, and the journalist hadn't finished asking the question before party supporters on stage with Trudeau began to groan. "Hey!" Trudeau scolded them. "We have respect for journalists in this country. They ask tough questions and they're supposed to. OK?" He then took the reporter's question. Afterward, the incident was widely reported

and contrasted with Harper's own lackadaisical intervention when Conservative supporters heckled reporters earlier in the election campaign.[7] Four days later, Canadians gave the Liberals a majority government.

Trudeau was elected on a promise of doing government differently. And there is reason for optimism. The Liberal platform included pledges to: strengthen the *Access to Information Act* and parliamentary committees; provide more information about how taxpayer dollars are spent; and empower the Parliamentary Budget Office, officers of Parliament, and backbenchers, among other things. Taken together, this would represent a dramatic improvement to the government's openness and transparency. Meanwhile, in the aftermath of the 19 October 2015 election, many have debated the degree to which the Conservatives' unprecedented level of control and secrecy contributed to their demise. That it did so seems to be an agreed upon fact. The Liberals have no doubt listened and will learn from that experience.

Yet optimism must be tempered with caution. In the months leading up to October 2015, I heard various members of the Parliamentary Press Gallery hoping for a minority government after the next election. "Why?" I would ask. Invariably the answer went back to the government having less control. That the Liberals won a majority means they ultimately have all the same powers as did the Conservatives. Meanwhile, it's always easier to complain when in opposition than when in government, where the temptation to exert control can become difficult to resist. After all, one only has to remember that the Conservatives also promised more openness and accountability before coming to power. And what's good for the goose ...

Notes

1 Verner, quoted in Lee Berthiaume, "Tories haven't disavowed Liberal foreign aid policy," *Embassy*, 23 August 2006, http://www.embassynews.ca/news/2006/08/23/tories-havent-disavowed-liberal-foreign-aid-policy/32406.
2 Anca Gurzu, "How diaspora politics are beginning to drive Canada's foreign policy," *Embassy*, 16 March 2011, http://www.embassynews.ca/news/2011/03/16/how-diaspora-politics-are-beginning-to-drive-canadas-foreign-policy/39996.
3 John Manley, Derek H. Burney, Jake Epp, Paul Tellier, and Pamela Wallin, *Independent Panel on Canada's Future Role in Afghanistan* (Ottawa: Minister of Public Works and Government Services, 2008), 20, 38.
4 Richard Colvin, quoted in Associated Press, "Transcript: Explosive testimony on Afghan detainees," *Globe and Mail*, 18 November 2009, http://www.theglobeandmail.com/news/politics/testimony-on-afghan-detainees/article4215493/.

5 Jeffrey Simpson, "Stephen Harper could relax now, but will he?" *Globe and Mail*, 18 May 2011, http://www.theglobeandmail.com/globe-debate/stephen-harper-could-relax-now-but-will-he/article624759/.
6 Mark Kennedy, "Stephen Harper accused of evasion in Senate expense scandal," *Ottawa Citizen*, 21 May 2013, http://o.canada.com/news/national/stephen-harper-speaks-to-restless-caucus-over-senate-expense-scandal.
7 National Post Staff and Canadian Press, "'Hey! Hey!' Trudeau berates his own supporters who tried to shout down reporter's question," *National Post*, 15 October 2015, http://news.nationalpost.com/news/canada/canadian-politics/hey-hey-trudeau-berates-his-own-supporters-who-tried-to-shout-down-reporters-question.

15

Foreign Policy and the Senate

Microscope and Telescope in Turbulent Times

HUGH SEGAL

In any analysis of the Senate perspective on the foreign policy changes brought about under the Harper government's tutelage, it is important to position the role and status of the Senate accurately and to parse the kind of role Senate deliberations have played in foreign policy discussions and other debates overall. Here, both undue self-reverence or structurally unfounded castigation are equally unhelpful. As Canada's unelected Upper House, the Senate's impact on foreign policy development and articulation is neither central nor seminal. On occasion, as in the vote against the Canada-United States Free Trade Agreement prior to the 1988 election, it can be a prelude to a larger national and electoral debate. Or consider one matter of particular controversy when, in 1990, the Senate killed bill C-43, the proposed legislation attempting to criminalize abortions after the Supreme Court struck down the existing law. Also on occasion, its studies and committee work can precipitate greater debate and policy change. But the core lack of democratic legitimacy justifiably constrains its influence and role. That being said, there are events at the margins where work done in the Senate, usually on a bipartisan basis (there are only two major political parties currently represented in the Senate), and hence irrespective of the governing party's standing in the Lower House, can generate a different debate and become one of a series of events that actually changes aspects of our foreign policy.

Beginning in 2006, the articulation of Canadian foreign policy by the Harper government was thematically coherent along several core premises:

- The old Pearsonian "honest broker" stance, which necessitated a "going-along-to-get-along" even-handedness between 1963 and 2006 was deemed by the new federal government to be out of date and unproductive.
- Canada has a series of foreign policy imperatives that reflect core Canadian values, to wit – democracy, the rule of law, human rights, gender equality, freer trade, and global stability.
- Our global networks and our military capacity (however limited) must be better deployed in support of these core values and in support of traditional Canadian interests like free trade, humanitarian engagement, and unity with our most significant allies.
- The utility of all of our international memberships and underlying financial commitments needs to be measured against these values and interests.

Such relatively straightforward thematics would, of necessity, have different stakeholders reacting in different ways. The usual "striped pants" set, made up of older diplomats now in academe and many colleagues who were shaped by, and helped shape, the traditional Liberal and Progressive Conservative foreign policy and diplomatic posture, did not like what they saw and said so openly and with some genuine sense of loss and betrayal.

Traditional corporate and non-governmental organization clients of the former Canadian International Development Agency lamented any change in the approach to international development assistance. Devotees of the largely mythical "Pearson in Suez" peacekeeping heroic innovation narrative were deeply troubled by Canada's moving away from the duplicity (to be fair, some would say even-handedness) of serial abstentions on anti-Israel resolutions at the UN and elsewhere to a more clearly pro-Israel stance, which Adam Chapnick (Chapter 6, this volume) describes in some detail. Setting aside nuance for precision and clarity has to discourage those who believe, with some justification, that the multi-layered texture of international diplomacy holds important opportunities for middle powers seeking to have influence and impact. It was my own conclusion, from the vantage point of the Senate, that, throughout the 2006–14 period during which I served, and thus during both minority and majority regimes, being on the right side of an issue (i.e., consistent with Canadian values and interests) was more important to the Harper government than any unique role for Canada in the sort-out of any negotiation or crisis.

Aspects of this dialectic are well represented by work in the marketplace of ideas, op-eds, conferences, and a compelling book entitled *Getting Back in the Game: A Foreign Policy Playbook for Canada*.[1] In it, Paul Heinbecker, a respected foreign policy practitioner and diplomat, argues from the perspective of a lost "golden age." While this aspirational view is understandable, it is surely relevant that, in diplomatic histories written outside of Canada or by non-Canadian practitioners, reference to the alleged Canadian golden age seem not to appear. Nevertheless, the estimable and always thorough Mr. Heinbecker (whom I very much admire despite our disagreements) makes his case very plainly:

> In my career, I have served as Prime Minister Brian Mulroney's chief foreign policy adviser and speechwriter, and I have written foreign-policy speeches for Prime Minister Pierre Trudeau, Secretaries of State for External Affairs Mark MacGuigan and Joe Clark, and for Ambassadors Allan Gotlieb and Derek Burney. As the "political director" of the Department of Foreign Affairs and Trade, I have advised Lloyd Axworthy on Canada's human security agenda. I have served as Canada's political minister in our embassy in Washington, ambassador to Germany, and Permanent Representative to the UN in New York. The last assignment brought me into close contact with John Manley and Prime Ministers Jean Chrétien and Paul Martin.
>
> I have seen from inside Ottawa and from the diplomatic front lines what we, Canadians, are capable of doing when we have the vision, the self-confidence, and the will to make a difference. Sadly, I do not believe we have been living up to our potential ... We can be, and – in our own interests – should be, an effective and responsible global player ...
>
> I believe that Canadians want their country to exercise its own judgment, to do good and well, both. That is my aspiration for Canada too. I intend this book to be an antidote to the pinched vision and curtailed ambition I see in contemporary foreign policy and to the unique Canadian blend of self-deprecation and self-satisfaction evident in so much public commentary about it. I do not hanker after a lost golden age.[2]

While the debate on various foreign policy issues in the Middle East, Afghanistan, or Asia would be joined on occasion by opposition or independent senators' speeches or questions, this was not especially frequent between 2006 and 2014, nor did it appear to me to be based on the strength of the governing party in the Lower House. And, unlike the United Kingdom's House of Lords, where the Foreign and Commonwealth Office had a designated spokesperson on the government side – usually someone with foreign policy expertise or experience – all questions to the government on foreign policy (as well as any other questions) could only be answered by the government leader in the Senate. These answers are given from a massive briefing book that covers all possible questions relating to all government departments. This process ensures a level of engagement that is "over lightly" and the usual repetition of "talking points" used by parliamentary secretaries or ministers in the elected House of Commons.

The most fundamental area for debate, policy innovation, or substantive engagement in the Senate centres on the work of the standing senate committees on foreign affairs and international trade, national security and defence, and special committees such as that on anti-terrorism. The motions establishing the terms of reference for these committee reports are debated in the Senate, as are the reports themselves, and the ratification of international treaties. It is in the content of these reports and the ensuing debate that matters of substance are engaged in the Upper House – often with significant impact and genuine depth. Understanding these many reports, rather than focusing on the standing of the Conservatives in the House of Commons, is the best way to assess a Senate perspective on foreign policy during the Harper era.

An Activist Agenda

The genuine constraints of legitimacy and relevance between the years 2006 and 2014 (when I left the Senate), with which the Senate's engagement on foreign policy might be framed, did not mean a lack of thoughtful discussion. A cursory listing of areas of foreign policy in which the committees of the Senate (in this case, the Standing Committee on Foreign Affairs and International Trade and the Standing Committee on National Security and Defence) engaged is quite extensive. Indeed, going back through the records of Parliament, I note at least fifteen significant reports from the foreign affairs committee, on issues ranging from softwood lumber, to development assistance, to free trade, to the Commonwealth, to cluster munitions, and at least four more from the Standing Committee on National Security and Defence, including reviews of Afghanistan, the Arctic, and the future of Canada's primary reserve. In no case, it is further worth noting, do I detect any trends shaped by the results of the 2011 election of a majority Conservative government.[3]

It is important to understand the dynamic of how committees operate in the Senate. The agenda is established by the committee's steering committee, usually composed of the chair and one senator from each of the two parties.[4] The party with the majority on the committee (and the opposition Liberals held this majority until shortly after the 2011 federal election)[5] were in control of setting the committee's agenda as they determined the choice of the chair, which gave them two of the three steering committee members. For five years after Mr. Harper was invited to form a government in 2006, the opposition held a majority on all Senate committees, including those dealing with foreign affairs and international trade and national security and defence. What this underlines is important in capturing the value and impact of Senate reports:

- they usually represent a bipartisan agreement on the agenda;
- their recommendations represent a bipartisan consensus; and
- they are reflective of few if any substantive instances of parties ramming their own partisan policy biases through at the expense of consensus.

So we have not only inquisitive foreign policy activism but also a wide range of witnesses with different and often critical input on bills and issues other than those of the government du jour. In this mix as well are the many Canada-"name of country/region/organization" parliamentary associations.[6] These membership groups, for which members of Parliament and senators sign up and pay a membership fee (out of their own funds), are not without influence. The relationships developed and the common issues under discussion often provide the "soft diplomacy" network that allows for behind-the-scenes compromise necessary for country-to-country cooperation.

Regular trips abroad, usually facilitated by parliamentarians in the host country, foreign ambassadors, and/or our own missions in those countries, constitute a form of "parliamentary diplomacy" that builds awareness, deepens impact, and produces better informed parliamentarians on a host of bilateral issues. Moreover, unlike the situation depicted by Chapnick in his chapter on Israel (Chapter 6, this volume), senators' travel is not necessarily restricted by the government's, or opposition's, standing in the House of Commons. No government will fall if a senator misses a vote.

The Canada-NATO Parliamentary Association connects Canadian parliamentarians with their counterparts in all of NATO's twenty-eight member countries. Regular conferences on issues like Russian adventurism, cyber-warfare, women in defence and security, the terrorist threat, and so on produce opportunities for linkage and learning. Each association has more than one MP or senator from various parties, and their meetings across the spectrum of parliamentary associations produce annual elections for chairs, co-chairs, and so on. Membership in these associations is sought after by MPs and senators, often based on their own areas of interest but also for the opportunity of informative Parliament-funded travel and networking. Election to the association executive is a stamp of approval by peer colleagues in Canada. Moreover, when larger assemblies, like the Commonwealth Parliamentary Association, elect Canadian members to the helm, they demonstrate significant trust in Canada's Parliament and parliamentarians. Still, because the Senate party whips are the final authorities on who is allowed to travel, this eagerness to participate is to their advantage. Even in the Senate, there are no instruments that are left completely unused in the maintenance of party discipline.

As there are very few standing committees of the House or Senate that are "joint" (having both senators and MPs sitting on the same committee), parliamentary associations often produce valuable opportunities for representatives of both Houses to work together. So the activism in reports and the collaboration implicit in that activism and the joint work on bi-national and joint associations becomes the key point of influence in the dynamics between the Upper House and Canada's foreign policy. The role of Canadian parliamentarians on the Canada-China Legislative Association – throughout both the minority and majority government years – was not unimportant in the mellowing out of the initial stance on Canada-China dynamics. And because unelected members of the Upper House retain much of the parliamentary institutional memory, they are sources of abundant information on what was successful in the past and are knowledgeable regarding what problems were encountered and which mistakes were made. In foreign policy, duplicating mistakes from the past is the most serious mistake a government can make.

Anticipation and Reaction to Events

While it is fair to conclude that unanticipated crises tend to dominate the foreign policy agenda of most democracies, a careful look at almost thirty Senate reports between 2006 and 2014 originating from both the foreign affairs and international trade committee and the national security and defence committee implies a mix of reaction and constructive anticipation.

The report on Canadian aid to sub-Saharan Africa in 2007 (which began during a Liberal minority government) reflected both a deep-seated interest in Africa and a better understanding of the dynamics of CIDA's engagement across the region. As I only arrived in the Senate in 2005 after my appointment by the governor general at Prime Minister Paul Martin's recommendation, much of the research and testimony preceded me. There were members of the committee like Senator Raynell Andreychuk, who had served with great distinction as a Canadian high commissioner in Africa before serving at home in the courts of Saskatchewan and being appointed to the Senate by Prime Minister Brian Mulroney. Prominent Liberal members like Roméo Dallaire (Quebec) and Mobina Jaffer (British Columbia) had their own unique Africa experiences. Senator Dallaire, aside from his military role for the UN in Rwanda, had been appointed by Prime Minister Martin as a special envoy to Sudan along with Senator Jaffer during her time in government. Senator Pierre Claude Nolin also had extensive experience as chair of the Canada-NATO Parliamentary Association and, like Senator Andreychuk, held international posts to which he had been elected by parliamentary colleagues from other countries. Senator Pierre Debané was a former minister for CIDA. Senator Serge Joyal was a former Trudeau-era minister. Senator David Tkachuck headed the Canada-Japan Parliamentary Association.

In contrast, the committee hearings into the "Lebanon extraction" after the 2006 outbreak of hostilities between Hezbollah and Israel, stranding fifty thousand Lebanese Canadians in Lebanon (fifteen thousand of which were ultimately evacuated), was a reaction to the dynamics of the extraction and a desire by the Senate to learn from the events. What went well? What went less well? How could "best practices" be framed for the future from the experience? Many of the committee's recommendations were adopted by the then minority government.

Often committees consider private legislation that has been passed by the House of Commons and has proceeded to second reading in the Senate. C-293, a private member's bill to broaden the accountability of CIDA to the international development community in Canada (discussed in more detail by Stephen Brown [Chapter 10, this volume]) is one example. It was prepared by John McKay (Liberal MP, Scarborough-Guildwood), who was active on the development assistance file and keen to increase the accountability of both the CIDA minister and CIDA officials to a broad community. Up until then, there had been no separate statute defining the role and purposes of CIDA – simply one line in the act establishing the agency. A full statute would have established performance norms and provided for regular review by parliamentarians in both places.

Consideration of trade agreements, usually a detailed role for the Senate (Canada-Peru 2009), as well as anticipatory committee inquiries (i.e., Canada-Russia [2010] and India-Canada [2010]), can be constructive in terms of intent and recommendations. The same can be said about the Brazil-Canada Report in May 2012 and the Charter of the Commonwealth Report in April 2012, wherein the committee was discharging the "open public consultation" on the charter that had been proposed at the Commonwealth Heads of Government Meeting in Perth in the fall of 2011. A careful look at the recommendations of these reports, none of which was shaped, in my view, by the government's standing in the House, promotes further insight into the foreign policy preferences being addressed by the Senate over this period.

Senate Committee Recommendations: Purposes and Impact

Here are three examples of recommendations (numbers one, two, and four) emanating from the 2007 report on sub-Saharan Africa submitted by the Standing Senate Committee on Foreign Affairs and International Trade:

1. The Government of Canada should develop a coherent and comprehensive international policy on Africa and, in so doing, reorient existing policy on Africa to devote significantly greater attention to generating economic and employment opportunities for African people.
2. Given the failure of the Canadian International Development Agency (CIDA) in Africa over the past 38 years to make an effective foreign aid difference, the Government of Canada should conduct an immediate review of whether or not this organization should continue to exist in its present non-statutory form. If CIDA is to be abolished, necessary Canadian development staff and decision-making authority should be transferred to the Department of Foreign Affairs and International Trade. If CIDA is to be retained, it should be given a stand-alone statutory mandate incorporating clear objectives against which the performance of the agency can be monitored by the Parliament of Canada ...
4. The Government of Canada should completely redesign its foreign aid program in Africa by: Concentrating all bilateral development aid on countries in Sub-Saharan Africa that are aggressively undertaking economic and political reforms to (a) improve governance; (b) develop their private sectors and create a favourable investment climate; and (c) realize their economic growth and employment prospects. The government

should develop precise, new aid-qualifying criteria based on the above list of preconditions, and with the help of internationally recognized indices of country performance, appropriately revise the Canadian International Development Agency's existing list of focus countries. Any country that does not satisfy these criteria, or that graduates from aid-recipient status, should receive zero official development assistance from Canada.[7]

In February 2007, when this report was released, it encompassed a retrospective look at Canadian aid to sub-Saharan Africa over the course of four decades. The committee heard from more than four hundred witnesses and determined that Africa was the only continent in the world that had not benefitted from global growth and that no amount of outside aid would assist in its future. African growth had to come from within, not without, and the international community's assistance had to begin with the promotion of good governance and the building of economies on the African continent. The committee made sixteen substantial recommendations, but it was recommendation two (above) that garnered the attention of the public and the media. It was not the intention of the committee to focus on one area of "failure" but, rather, to provide concrete suggestions for improvement. Nonetheless, on 18 February 2007, the *National Post* declared: "Senators call for CIDA to be disbanded."[8]

While the committee expressed frustration at the media fixation on only one of sixteen recommendations, in 2013, as Brown notes in greater detail, CIDA was brought under the foreign affairs umbrella completely, and the Department of Foreign Affairs, Trade and Development was established.[9] Whether this move has improved the funding and assistance of Canada to developing countries is an issue for continued debate.

The Senate and the Afghanistan Dialectic

In 2008, the Independent Panel on Canada's Future Role in Afghanistan's report was released. As Jean-Christophe Boucher and Kim Richard Nossal note (Chapter 4, this volume), this independent task force was commissioned by Prime Minister Harper during the minority government period and included Pamela Wallin, Derek Burney, Paul Tellier, and Jake Epp. It was chaired by John Manley, a former Liberal foreign minister and deputy prime minister, and its job was to ascertain what Canada should do at the expiry date of its first Afghanistan commitment in 2011. Afghanistan was a deployment and commitment inherited from the Chrétien government.

Wallin and Burney were former Canadian diplomats; Tellier was a former clerk of the Privy Council. Generally speaking, and perhaps because of the absence of the NDP from the chamber, the Senate was supportive of continuing Canadian involvement in a combat role as part of NATO's overall support for the Afghan government and response under Article 5 of the North Atlantic Treaty. On 5 March 2008, I made the following statement in the Chamber:

> Honourable senators, I rise today to recognize and thank the members of the Independent Panel on Canada's Future Role in Afghanistan ...
>
> The value and worth of the final report, its recommendations and insights are a testament to the quality and tenacity of the individuals involved. They took personal risks and worked tirelessly to provide parliamentarians and, more important, the Canadian public with a clear and eminently understandable assessment of the situation and challenge that currently prevails in Afghanistan.
>
> Their no-nonsense evaluation of Canada's contribution now and in the future, our accomplishments to date and the vital steps we must take on an ongoing basis provide a solid Canadian even-handedness to the most complicated of situations, which in turn has provided Canada, Canadians and our NATO allies with a road map to move forward.
>
> This non-partisan report did not take sides. It was equally critical of all the major players: the government in Afghanistan and its tolerance of corruption; NATO partners and their up-until-now unwillingness to share the burden more extensively in the South; the demand that was issued in the report for another 1,000 forces to complement Canadian operations in the South; and in its criticism of the Canadian government for not providing franker and more frequent updates to Canadians as to our successes and progress in Afghanistan.
>
> This frank assessment was our wake-up call. We were not unaware of our difficulties; however, the Manley report succeeded in "un muddying" the waters for us all.
>
> Those of us in day-to-day politics who pride ourselves on being current and able to form knowledgeable opinions owe much to the Manley panel members who, while otherwise engaged with more than full careers, accepted the call and took up the challenge of their mission. Thanks to them and their hard work, the opinions on the Hill and the opinions of the Canadian public are definitively more informed, more reasonable and more focused on the complicated topic that is Afghanistan.

The effects of the report have been positive on all sides. Her Majesty's Loyal Opposition in the other place took this report to heart, did not dismiss it out of hand and suggested thoughtful amendments which were, in part, taken up by the government. The Liberals should be commended for recognizing the validity and common sense of the recommendations as set out by the Manley panel, as should the government. The panel sought a Canadian solution, not a Conservative or a Liberal solution.

As a government and as a country we are more understanding of our role in Afghanistan, our successes thus far, where improvement and support are needed, and the reality of our role going forward.

All of us, including the troops in the field, owe a debt of gratitude to Messrs. Manley, Burney, Epp, Tellier and Ms. Wallin for their work.[10]

While the Senate's foreign affairs committee offered no detailed analysis of Afghanistan, this was not the case for the National Security and Defence Committee. In 2010, the committee released its own interim report: *Where We Go from Here: Canada's Mission in Afghanistan*. The conclusion of this report, agreed to by all members of the committee in a non-partisan fashion, states:

> If there is a recurring theme to what witnesses have told us, it is that the job in Afghanistan is not done and that Canadian troops should stay in some capacity. With the surge of NATO forces now underway, gains are at last being consolidated instead of lost. That surge of forces is importantly fighting alongside soldiers of the Afghan National Army. Ultimately, this fight against the Taliban is their fight. It will be a key part of Canada's legacy in Afghanistan that Canadian soldiers helped prepare them for this fight. Based upon the evidence, testimony, and suggestions we have heard; upon our deliberations; and given our concern for our nation's standing among its allies, this Committee believes and recommends that Canada's important and highly-valued contribution to the development of the leadership, training and mentoring of the Afghan National Army and the Afghan National Police must continue beyond 2011, and that Parliament should, at its earliest opportunity, give careful consideration to the question of the role of the Canadian Forces in Afghanistan after 2011.[11]

Reports on Russia, Turkey, and on the Canadian Armed Forces Reserves, which together straddled the minority and majority government periods, while not revolutionary in their conclusions, had an element of prescience about coming foreign policy challenges. And this is relevant to a consideration of the Senate's role.

Conclusion: Neither Mirror nor Echo Chamber

The avid debate on the role of the Senate that began before Confederation is unlikely to abate any time soon. Failed efforts at constitutional reform of the Senate (over twenty since Confederation) and Supreme Court decisions on such reforms underline the discomfort Canada and Canadians feel towards an unelected chamber with legislative powers and prerogatives that are largely parallel to those of the elected House of Commons.

On a host of important foreign policy issues between 2006 and 2015, through both minority and majority periods of Conservative governance, the Canadian Senate was a testing ground for new ideas and different solutions and departures. It was also a place for closer examination of the instruments of foreign policy, of development and trade facilitation, and a harbinger of some areas of change and innovation. Laws addressing nuclear terrorism and Canada's adherence to the Seoul Treaty were first introduced in the Senate, as were criminal code amendments regarding travelling abroad for the purpose of supporting terrorism.

Some have suggested that the Senate's role in foreign policy was that of an echo-chamber or bull horn for the government of the day, a suggestion that would imply at least a tenuous line between the Senate's behaviour and the parliamentary strength of the governing party. That suggestion is, on balance, both simplistic and unfair. Its role is more about taking a deeper and broader look at where foreign policy is headed and how the instruments of foreign policy are actually operating. A mirror or bull horn would not be appropriate symbols of Senate engagement with the foreign policies of the government that came into power in 2006 – a telescope and microscope would be substantially more apt.

This ability to look more deeply and, simultaneously, more broadly, regardless of the governing party's standing in the "other House," is underlined by the number of former ministers, academics, businesspeople, NGO leaders, diplomats, and the like who find themselves appointed to Senate seats, not to mention the provincial ministers and federal and provincial public servants, former military, and police who join its ranks. Perspective, experience, and institutional memory matter in foreign policy and diplomacy – three attributes found in greater abundance in the Senate than in the Commons, media, or public service. None of this, of course, negates the undemocratic nature of the Senate's overall standing. But together these elements produce a relevance at the margins of Canadian foreign policy debate and discussion that should not be underestimated. Those who seek to maintain a strident status quo in foreign policy shaped by nostalgia or special interest, as well as those who seek radical ideologically driven foreign policy change (from the far right or the far left), ignore the Senate's role and capacities at their political and policy peril. The period of 2006–14 offers ample evidence of this.

Notes

1 Paul Heinbecker, *Getting Back in the Game: A Foreign Policy Playbook for Canada* (Toronto: Key Porter, 2010).
2 Ibid., 11–12.
3 All of the reports of Senate committees can be found at http://www.parl.gc.ca/SenCommitteeBusiness/default.aspx?parl=39&ses=1&Language=E.
4 The fact that the New Democratic Party, which formed the opposition in the House of Commons in 2011, is not represented in the Senate reinforces the relative unimportance of parliamentary elections to Senate business.
5 Note again that it was not the election itself but, rather, the retirement of a number of Liberal senators and their replacement by new appointments by Prime Minister Stephen Harper throughout the 2006–11 period that caused the change. When it comes to the power of senatorial appointments, the governing party's majority or minority standing in the House of Commons is, for all intents and purposes, irrelevant.
6 These include: Canada-Africa Parliamentary Association; Canada-Europe Parliamentary Association; Canadian Delegation to the Organization for Security and Co-operation in Europe Parliamentary Assembly; Canadian Branch of the Assemblée parlementaire de la Francophonie; Canadian Branch of the Commonwealth Parliamentary Association; Canadian Group of the Inter-Parliamentary Union; Canadian NATO Parliamentary Association; Canadian Section of ParlAmericas; Canada-China Legislative Association; Canada-France Inter-Parliamentary Association; Canada-Japan Inter-Parliamentary Group; Canada-United Kingdom Inter-Parliamentary Association; Canada-United States Inter-Parliamentary Group; Canada-Germany Inter-Parliamentary Group; Canada-Ireland Inter-Parliamentary Group; Canada-Israel Inter-Parliamentary Group; and the Canada-Italy Inter-Parliamentary Group, to name just a few.
7 Standing Senate Committee on Foreign Affairs and International Trade, "Overcoming 40 years of failure: A new road map for sub-Saharan Africa," February 2007, http://www.parl.gc.ca/Content/SEN/Committee/391/fore/rep/repafrifeb07-e.pdf.
8 *National Post* staff, "Senators call for CIDA to be disbanded," *National Post*, 18 February 2007, http://www.nationalpost.com/story.html?id=c63974a5-00f3-43b5-b5ed-6f2ed1df4125.
9 Whether the government's transition from minority government, when it received the report, to majority, when it integrated CIDA into Foreign Affairs, affected the

decision that created the merger is debatable, but that change certainly had no effect on the Senate deliberations.

10 Hugh Segal, 5 March 2008, in Senate of Canada, *Debates*, 39th Parliament, 2nd session, vol. 144, issue 39, http://www.parl.gc.ca/Content/Sen/Chamber/392/Debates/039db_2008-03-05-e.htm.

11 Standing Senate Committee on National Security and Defence, "Where we go from here: Canada's mission in Afghanistan," interim report, June 2010, http://www.parl.gc.ca/Content/SEN/Committee/403/defe/rep/rep04jun10-e.pdf.

16

Concluding Thoughts

The Prime Minister of the Few

NORMAN HILLMER

Stephen Harper was prime minister for just short of a decade, putting him in the top rank of Canadian leaders in length of service. He had instinctively strong ideas about the world from his first day in office. Yet the prime minister and his international policies remain a puzzle. Sir Wilfrid Laurier's creative compromises with the British Empire, the diplomatic nationalism of Mackenzie King, the Pearsonian internationalism of post-1945 Liberal governments, Brian Mulroney's tilt towards North America and its explicit link to global activism – none of these was precisely drawn or rose to the level of doctrine, but each was carefully balanced, easy to comprehend, and well within the conventions of national politics. Prime Minister Harper was different from his predecessors, but how different, and in what ways? What combination of principles, politics, and the personal drove him and his government? What interests and what values? To what extent did foreign policy evolve or change between 2006 and 2015? And how differently, if at all, did the Harper government behave once it had the certainty of a majority of seats in the House of Commons? These, the last more explicitly than the others, are this book's questions.

Parliamentary majorities allow prime ministers and their teams to be themselves, while governing without a majority is of necessity a time for caution. That's the conventional wisdom, and there is experience to back it up. The Joe Clark government discovered in the Christmas season of 1979 that minorities can be brought down, unexpectedly and cruelly. Clark and his political friends had wrongly proceeded on the assumption that the opposition parties would not dare vote them out of office.[1] The lesson is clear. Minorities are wise to whisper and walk softly. A measure, even if unpopular, of a government sure of its support in the House of Commons can slide safely into law or practice; in a minority situation, every action or reaction is potentially controversial, and what raises the ire of the other side of the House risks crisis and defeat.

It follows that there ought be a substantial separation between two Stephen Harpers: the prudent prime minister who governed without a parliamentary majority from 2006 to 2011 and the assertive prime minister who emerged unfettered after the 2011 election gave him ample elbow room to do as he and his colleagues wished. Harper might have been giving notice of just such a difference when, his majority finally achieved, he was very public about the role his Canada meant to take as "a meaningful contributor" on "the right side" in the "struggle between good and bad" in a "dangerous world." His government would be tested in "those big moments where everything's at stake" and would not be found wanting. The Harper resolve was not "to go along and get along with everyone else's agenda" and "to please every dictator with a vote at the United Nations." His government knew "where our interests lie, and who our friends are, and we take strong, principled positions in our dealings with other nations – whether popular or not."[2]

However forcefully stated, these were not new thoughts. The experts who contribute to *The Harper Era* make little distinction between the earlier and the later Harper governments. Philippe Lagassé gets in a first word, and, although he doesn't quite say that minority parliaments are irrelevant, he comes close. What is crucially important, he rightly says, is that international policy is the bailiwick of the executive no matter the state of the House of Commons. Parliament can have an influence, particularly by holding the government's feet to the fire, but, in a minority situation, the opposition must exercise its capacity for leverage with discretion or risk unintended consequences – at the worst defeat in an election caused by its own actions. In addition, the executive is much more likely to use Parliament to give the government policy legitimacy than to change course because the legislature wills it. This, for Denis Stairs, is a shame. He agrees that governments do not need to involve Parliament more in what they do and decide internationally, but he thinks that they ought to do so for the sake of better policy, public education, and their own credibility.

Stairs reminds readers that there are hundreds of foreign policies bouncing around in the body politic but that Parliament might be thought to have a heightened interest in the ones given over to peace, war, and security, residing as they do at the pinnacle of state responsibility. Jean-Christophe Boucher and Kim Richard Nossal test the assumption that minority parliaments limit a government's freedom of movement when the stakes are at their highest. Their case study is the Afghanistan conflict, the signal international policy endeavour of the Harper era, around which so many resources and so much rhetoric gathered. The authors convincingly portray a leader who entered the office of prime minister as a fiery advocate of a robust defence policy and a foreign policy that was more aggressive than that of his Liberal predecessors – a leader, in other words, predisposed to vigorously carrying on Canada's commitment to the Afghan conflict. This Harper's government immediately did. As time went on, the domestic and international forces that eased his original decision conspired to make further commitments more difficult. He nonetheless made those commitments, more tentatively it is true, despite his minority standing in the House of Commons. Boucher and Nossal cannot imagine that the Harper government would have acted differently had its parliamentary circumstances been more secure.

To Afghanistan David Perry adds the Libyan mission in 2011 and the campaign against the Islamic State beginning in August 2014, noting the government's affection for the military as an instrument of its principled foreign policy and a potential vote-getter. Perry stipulates, however, that the Harper record of material support of the Canadian Armed Forces is uneven and that it was at its most vigorous during the government's first minority mandate. Defence spending as a percentage of the country's gross domestic product has been in decline for years, and, indeed, the military has seldom been a high priority for any government since the 1950s. The bright light that the Harper agenda once shone on defence has dimmed.

Human rights are temptingly fertile ground for governments that celebrate their principles. David Petrasek and Rebecca Tiessen have the government barging into the rights business from the start, its rhetorical comfort level steadily increasing and reaching a peak during the majority years after 2011. From his position in the Senate, which he is quick to admit is not a central foreign policy actor, Hugh Segal saw the consistency and "theoretical coherence" of Harper foreign policy purpose, in which human rights were identified as a key Canadian value and "being on the right side" of such issues was standard operating procedure.

Petrasek and Tiessen excoriate a human rights approach that disdains the United Nations and its programs, downgrades the International Criminal

Court, heaps condemnation on certain countries while ignoring abuse in others, and pays insufficient attention to institutions and strategies that would build commitment and impact over time. Both Petrasek-Tiessen's and Stephen Brown's development assistance chapters point to the cramped vision of the Conservatives' maternal health program, which denied funding for legal abortions and put sexual and reproductive health services in the shade. Brown, too, finds next to no constraints in minority governing, concluding that bold initiatives, notably in the commercialization and politicization of aid policy, tumbled forth well before the 2011 election.

Nowhere is the claim of elevated principle more striking than in Harper's policy towards Israel. There seemed little doubt about the sincerity of the prime minister's views on the subject, aligning, as they did, perfectly with his sense of what was right and wrong in the world. He believed, and acted vigorously on the belief, that Israel is a beleaguered outpost of freedom and democracy surrounded by hostile neighbours and threatened with extinction. Adam Chapnick's chapter demonstrates, however, that Harper's insistences did not extend to every aspect of Canadian policy – not preventing, in the minority years, Cabinet ministers from criticizing Israel's treatment of Palestinians and not altering the long-standing Canadian official statement of opposition to Israeli settlements as an obstacle to lasting peace in the region. Perhaps it was useful to have things both ways, or perhaps Chapnick exposes confusion in the ranks. Perhaps both. The prime minister probably did not care since the Jewish community knew where he stood and made life difficult, as Liberal leader Michael Ignatieff discovered on his way to political oblivion, for anyone who wished to attempt more nuance.[3] Chapnick does not place great weight on electoral politics in his analysis of the Israel file. Other authors in this collection do, with David Carment and Joseph Landry broadening out the discussion into an attack on the partisan diaspora politics that they identify as blatantly characteristic of all of the Harper Conservative governments.

Stephen Harper promised interests as well as principles, and, in 2006, he took steps to stabilize a Canadian-American relationship that had deteriorated under recent Liberal governments. Harper and US president George W. Bush talked the same muscular talk, and they collaborated on the Afghanistan campaign, the war on terror, and softwood lumber.[4] From the beginning, the prime minister also put distance between himself and the United States, and Barack Obama's Washington returned the favour after the 2008 American election.[5] Greg Anderson's chapter highlights cooperation rather than conflict. Anderson totes up the many places where, and times when, the two countries cooperated in the Harper era, the "special relationship" having a life of its own, whatever the nature of the governments that happened to be in power. The Harper government pushed Mexico to one side, and Anderson questions whether the all-but-abandonment of North American trilateralism is in the best interests of a healthy long-term Canada-US relationship. Some Ottawa insiders and media outsiders would also have Canada move the United States aside since it is a spent force. Such predictions have been made before. They were wrong then and they are wrong now.

The trade, environment, and energy chapters of this book further engage Harper government conceptions of hard interests. Christopher Kukucha reports on the aggressive pursuit of international trade agreements, but seldom at the expense of domestic producers and consumers. Michael Manulak's account of Ottawa's environmental policies, a failure even when measured against its own stated aims, takes account of the risks that tough regulatory measures pose to the Canadian bottom line, particularly if the United States does not move in lockstep. Monica Gattinger points to the paramountcy of the economics of market access in the energy field. She notes Harper's early and unsuccessful attempts to cooperate with the United States in the linking of climate change to energy security and the escalating opposition to the Alberta oil sands that complicated bilateral and domestic politics. The government turned people who disagreed with it into enemies, and this made the achievement of its goals more difficult. The three scholars agree that policy making was not sensitive to the balance of forces in Parliament, although it is clear that electoral considerations played into the way that interests were calculated.

The Harper Era almost always gives the opposite impression, but minority parliaments can make a difference. The first evidence of this came after the election of 1921, when Mackenzie King's Liberals won only 117 out of the 245 available House of Commons seats. The country was badly divided, the economy was in recession, war debt had piled up, and the King government and its inexperienced leader had no great mandate to wield and little room for manoeuvre when it came to domestic policy. So the prime minister instead moved into the area of external relations, exploiting the fact that more than half of his members of Parliament were from anglo-sceptic Quebec and that the other side of the House was dominated by Progressives – a new group of MPs that, in its own way, was suspicious of the world.

Very early on in his premiership, King set off on a mission to Washington, making it clear that he wanted to do international business separately from

Britain and its empire. His government signed a treaty with the United States on its own, the first time in Canada's long history that had been done, and declared that the great issues of peace and war were the concern of the Canadian Parliament. At the Imperial Conference of 1923, King made all kinds of trouble, insisting that Canada had a right to as much control over its foreign policy as it had in the realm of domestic affairs, and as much right to complete self-government as the United Kingdom itself. He stopped there, short of independence from Great Britain, but he was promising to isolate a bruised populace from the world's troubles, binding up the wounds that Quebec had sustained during the First World War, and assuring Canadians that their international destiny would be decided by them alone.[6]

John English's chapter amplifies the argument that minority parliaments can count for a great deal. Lester B. Pearson and the Liberals won elections in 1963 and 1965 but never had a majority in the House of Commons. Pearson came to power as a supporter, and to some extent because he was a supporter, of the United States and the introduction of nuclear weapons into Canada. But he joined in with the left's critique of the United States and its war in Vietnam. That did not deliver him from his minority, but it did bring him Pierre Trudeau. Without the Pearson minority predicament, and the need to demonstrate resistance to an American empire about which doubts were rapidly growing, Canadians would never have known Trudeau, who shaped modern Canada and saved it from being broken apart by an independent Quebec.

Trudeau's foreign policy sputtered and led many lives. The vociferous opponent of nationalism in all its forms indulged in it himself when confronted with his own minority Parliament from 1972 to 1974. Like Pearson, he needed the support of the New Democratic Party, and, as in the 1960s, Vietnam and American dominance were sticking in the Canadian craw. Trudeau's Liberals denounced the United States' Southeast Asian war, and economic nationalism blossomed with the establishment of the Foreign Investment Review Agency and the creation of Petro-Canada as a federal government-owned energy company. Trudeau feared an exodus of voters in the direction of the NDP more than he feared Calgary, or Wall Street, or Washington. English does point out that Stephen Harper's circumstances were not Pearson's or Trudeau's. The left offered no foreign policy menace or opportunity for Harper. He could with impunity look to conservative Canada, where clenched fists, Israel's survival, and a particular slant on human rights had a potent appeal.

Stephen Harper's policies are frequently described as a big break with the past,[7] but major departures in Canadian foreign policy are rare. Pierre Trudeau tried one after 1968, but he finished up looking very much like his predecessor. Harper proclaimed that he would restore Canada's lustre in the world, but that sounded suspiciously like Prime Minister Paul Martin's pledge to restore the country to a role of pride and influence.[8] Harper's was not the first government to have an external policy that was consciously based upon internal impulses, to practise selective multilateralism, to promote human rights enthusiastically, or to exhibit (to use Manulak's phrase) "bold, uncooperative behaviour" when crucial interests were thought to be at risk. The way ahead in Canadian foreign policy is often what has gone before.

Canadian governments are not autonomous creatures. They operate under an accumulation of subterranean limitations. Secondary powers react more often than they act. Kukucha puts it well with respect to tradecraft: "historic and current international trade agreements, the form and practice of Canadian federalism, and Canada's internal trade regime all reflect well-established practices, rules, and norms that establish constraints under which any federal government, regardless of political strength, will make trade decisions." Manulak underlines Canada's dependence on natural resources and its interdependence with a United States many times more powerful. Anderson refers to the "starkness of the asymmetries" in a Canada-US relationship that is nonetheless not easily damaged or transformed, such are the tenacious connections of diplomacy and necessity built up over decades. Boucher and Nossal illustrate the importance of Canada's international obligations as a partner to the United States and as a member of the North Atlantic Treaty Organization in policy making on Afghanistan. Carment and Landry speak of the significant pressures exerted by influential diaspora groups. Gattinger paints the cluttered landscape of energy imperatives that a government must run with lest it be overrun by them. More evidence, in other words, that the shape of parliaments does not drive international policy – or drives it very little.

Our authors search for concrete shifts of policy that distinguish the early Harper governments from the later. They are hard to find. The Harperites were a secretive clan, and it is, at any rate, difficult to extract the cause of a particular effect from a complex of factors, especially when only a few government records are as yet available to scholars or the media. The parliamentary resistance to Stephen Harper's international policy was also generally weak, so the opposition did not make the most of its opportunities to press for influence. Yet even the doubters agree that a parliamentary minority can encourage different political behaviour. It did so when Afghanistan policy took its twists and turns. First the Liberals, in 2010, favoured a continuation of the military operation, and then they were against it, and the government took notice.[9] Nor should the definition of Parliament's impact be drawn too narrowly. It is clear that, once they had a majority at their back, Harper and his team proceeded with a confidence and determination that an inexperienced and outnumbered government did not have from 2006 to 2011.

Lee Berthiaume's chapter is significant testimony from a close observer of the Stephen Harper era. Having watched events unfold day by day from *Embassy* magazine and the Parliamentary Press Gallery, Berthiaume remembers the unpredictable minority Harper parliaments as substantially different from that of the majority years. With an election possible at any time, the government had to keep its eye on the opposition. The Liberal-NDP advantage in numbers was notable in parliamentary committees, where issues were aired and the government held to account. Minority thinking might also have played a part in the decision to keep a tight grip on the public service and the flow of information to the media – a practice that continued with a vengeance after 2011.

The luxury of a majority gave Harper a foreign minister on whom he could rely. From 2006 to 2011, John Baird had been moved from portfolio to portfolio as need arose and troubleshooting competence was required. Meanwhile, the *Globe and Mail*'s John Ibbitson complained that a succession of minority governments and short-lived ministers "left our foreign policy in a shambles and our foreign service paralysed." On the great issues before the international community, "on anything that matters, Canada has nothing to say. When we do speak, nobody listens."[10] Once the Harper majority was in place, the prime minister was free to send Baird to foreign affairs. Canada had a consistent, often angry, and always busy, presence on the international stage. Baird paraded Conservative values unabashedly, championed the military, blasted Iran, and backed Israel to the hilt, writes journalist Campbell Clark, while being "prepared to look uncouth to prod Canadian business deals abroad ... He doesn't mind if others think he's too coarse for diplomatic sensitivities. Sometimes, he revels in it."[11] In foreign policy, talk and tone are vital, and Baird matched Harper's mouth and mood perfectly.

Stephen Harper came to the premiership unschooled in foreign policy and in the world outside Canada. He modelled himself on successful prime ministers, it is said, and the most successful of all was Mackenzie King.[12]

Harper and King became prime minister in their mid-forties, at almost exactly the same age. Yet compare their resumes. By 1921, King had travelled the world, worked productively in the United States, attained a doctorate from Harvard, and been a Cabinet minister. Harper had none of those credentials or anything like them when he won his minority victory in 2006.

But Harper's lack of knowledge and experience was no impediment to certitudes about Canada's role and responsibility in the world. He knew intuitively what he thought and wanted to achieve. The prime minister's international vision began, Roland Paris explains, with a belief in "an enduring Manichean struggle between the forces of good and evil, and the transformative and redemptive potential of this struggle." He placed Canada in the centre of the maelstrom as a "courageous warrior" that had defeated tyranny and oppression in the grand-historical conflicts that had defined the country and the world. Now that he had the responsibility, he would take up the crusade, never allowing his country to descend into the muck of moral relativism and flabby compromise. He misunderstood, perhaps deliberately, what his Liberal and Progressive Conservative predecessors had done to preserve Canada's freedoms and went out of his way to demean their achievements.[13]

Pierre Trudeau criticized Lester Pearson's internationalist helpful fixing, but he learned from experience that it wasn't so bad after all. Harper's staple views of the world around him and Canada's place in it did not change or evolve as time went on and global affairs unfolded in unexpected ways. He was unshakeable. "One step at a time," he liked to say of his tactics, and he could be flexible at the margins, but the strategy was steadfast, radical, and revolutionary, nothing less than the stamping out of the Liberal past, the transformation of Canadians' understanding of themselves, and the manoeuvring of the country into a Conservative century.[14] The combative Harper style was the man himself.

The Harper decade is over, and the era of another Trudeau has begun, full of promise (and promises) that foreign policy will revert to the sunnier ways of its pre-2006 self. During the 2015 election campaign, six university scholars warned of the dangers of such thinking. First of all, they reminded their readers, the international system does not bend to Canada's will. The opposite is almost always sure to be the case, and the insecure world of the early twenty-first century will not yield up the "alleged glories" of simpler days. Second, a changed Canadian society is more likely now than in the past to hold to the Conservative view that law and order must be strictly maintained abroad as at home, by force if need be. Third, Harper's world is difficult to dismantle because he made it so, particularly through a reduced tax base that restricts the policy investments of the future.[15] There is truth in these claims, at least the first and third of them, but a return to an admittedly imperfect liberal internationalism was a certainty from the moment that Justin Trudeau became prime minister. He pledged a foreign policy that engaged constructively with the world, knowing that it, not Harperism, was in the mainstream of Canadian politics as they have been practised since the Second World War.

Stephen Harper was markedly different from the Canadian leaders who came before him. Perhaps his narrow victory in 2006 reinforced an instinct to govern from a bunker on behalf of Canadians who thought as he did. Even with a majority Parliament, he continued to rule as if he represented an aggrieved minority. Harper foreign policy specialized in the mean-spirited, the negative, and the divisive, trespassing against long-standing habits of Canadian diplomacy. Beyond or beneath the scowl, which frequently substituted for policy itself, there was a contradiction between aim and execution. Trade led all agendas, but the alliances and institutions that had previously smoothed the country's path received confused attention – and inattention. The United States, Canada's indispensable ally, was held at arm's length. Deep cuts in international and defence spending clashed with the Harper assertion that "if you don't have the capacity to act you are not taken seriously."[16] Principles too showily advertised fell before the inevitability of crass politics.

One searched in vain for evidence that the government had become more comfortable with the world, or that the world had become more comfortable with it. Stephen Harper stayed where he had begun, rock solid in his convictions, the prime minister of the few.

Notes

1 Jeffrey Simpson, *Discipline of Power: The Conservative Interlude and the Liberal Restoration* (Toronto: Personal Library, 1980), 113–14.
2 Kim Richard Nossal, "The Liberal past in the Conservative present: Internationalism in the Harper era," and Jean-Christophe Boucher, "The responsibility to think clearly about interests: Stephen Harper's realist internationalism, 2006-2011," both in Heather A. Smith and Claire Turenne Sjolander, eds., *Canada in the World: Internationalism in Canadian Foreign Policy* (Don Mills, ON: Oxford University Press, 2013), quotations on 22 and 60–61.
3 Michael Ignatieff, *Fire and Ashes: Success and Failure in Politics* (Toronto: Random House Canada, 2013), 78.
4 Stephen Azzi and Norman Hillmer, "The unquiet times of United States-Canada relations in the era of the George W. Bush presidency," paper delivered at the Twelfth

Presidential Conference of the Peter S. Kalikow Center of the Study of the American Presidency, "The George W. Bush Presidency," Hofstra University, New York, 25 March 2015. Revised version forthcoming in *Diplomacy and Statecraft* (March 2017).

5   Paul Wells, *The Longer I'm Prime Minister: Stephen Harper and Canada, 2006–* (Toronto: Random House Canada, 2013), 241–48; "I thought we were friends," *Maclean's* cover, with editorial, 28 November 2011, 4–5; Campbell Clark, "How Ottawa left US Ambassador Bruce Heyman out in the cold," *Globe and Mail*, 18 March 2015, http://www.theglobeandmail.com/news/politics/how-ottawa-left-us-ambassador-bruce-heyman-out-in-the-cold/article23514669/.

6   Norman Hillmer and J.L. Granatstein, *Empire to Umpire: Canada and the World into the Twenty-First Century* (Toronto: Nelson, 2008), 77–89.

7   John Ibbitson, "The Harper doctrine, in black and white," *Globe and Mail*, 13 June 2011; Joe Clark, *How We Lead: Canada in a Century of Change* (Toronto: Random House Canada, 2013), chap. 6; Adam Chapnick, "Middle power no more? Canada in world affairs since 2006," *Seton Hall Journal of Diplomacy and International Affairs* 14, 2 (2013): 102.

8   Hillmer and Granatstein, *Empire to Umpire*, chap. 10 (Trudeau), and 332–35 (Martin-Harper).

9   Kim Richard Nossal, "*Primat der Wahlurne*: Explaining Stephen Harper's foreign policy," paper delivered at annual conference of the International Studies Association, Toronto, 29 March 2014, 8 and 15.

10 John Ibbitson, "As Obama bestrides the world stage, Canada has nothing to say," *Globe and Mail*, 4 February 2009. Ibbitson later wrote of the increasing "coherence and competence" of the government's foreign policy during the majority years. See his "The big break: The Conservative transformation of foreign policy," *CIGI Papers* 29 (April 2014): 13.

11 Campbell Clark, "John Baird's Canada: No longer content to 'go along just to get along,'" *Globe and Mail*, 10 August 2012, http://www.theglobeandmail.com/news/national/john-bairds-canada-no-longer-content-to-go-along-just-to-get-along/article4475191/.

12 On Harper and King, see Wells, *Longer I'm Prime Minister*, 292–93.

13 Roland Paris, "Are Canadians still liberal internationalists? Foreign policy and public opinion in the Harper era," *International Journal* 69, 3 (2014): 281–86. Grounding his analysis in good empirical research, the author answers the question in his title in the affirmative.

14 Ibid., 283–84, 300, and 305.

15 Stéphane Roussel, Jean-Christophe Boucher, Stéfanie von Hlatky, Thomas Juneau, Kim Richard Nossal, and Jonathan Paquin, "We can't turn back the clock on Canada's foreign policy," *Globe and Mail*, 27 September 2015, http://www.theglobeandmail.com/news/politics/we-cant-turn-back-the-clock-on-canadas-foreign-policy/article26556228/.

16 Quoted in Adam Chapnick, "A diplomatic counter-revolution: Conservative foreign policy, 2006-2011," *International Journal* 67, 1 (2011–12): 146.

Contributors

Greg Anderson is associate professor of political science at the University of Alberta.

Lee Berthiaume is an award-winning journalist who has covered Canadian foreign policy on Parliament Hill since 2006.

Stephen Brown is professor of political science at the University of Ottawa.

Jean-Christophe Boucher is assistant professor of political science at MacEwan University.

David Carment is professor of international affairs at Carleton University.

Adam Chapnick is deputy director of education at the Canadian Forces College and professor of defence studies at the Royal Military College of Canada.

John English is director of the Bill Graham Centre on Contemporary International History at Trinity College at the University of Toronto.

Monica Gattinger is chair of the University of Ottawa's Collaboratory on Energy Research and Policy and associate professor at the School of Political Studies.

Norman Hillmer is professor of history and international affairs at Carleton University.

Christopher J. Kukucha is professor of political science at the University of Lethbridge.

Philippe Lagassé is associate professor and the Barton Chair at the Norman Paterson School of International Affairs at Carleton University.

Joseph Landry is a PhD candidate at the Norman Paterson School of International Affairs at Carleton University.

Michael W. Manulak is a fellow at the Balsillie School of International Affairs.

Kim Richard Nossal is a professor in the Centre for International and Defence Policy at Queen's University.

David Perry is a senior analyst at the Canadian Global Affairs Institute.

David Petrasek is associate professor in the Graduate School of Public and International Affairs at the University of Ottawa.

Hugh Segal is former chair of the Senate Committee on Foreign Affairs and International Trade, the Special Committee on Anti-Terrorism, and member of the Senate Committee on National Security and Defence. He is currently the Fifth Master of Massey College at the University of Toronto, chairs the NATO Association of Canada, and is a senior fellow at the Munk School of Global Affairs and the Canadian Global Affairs Institute.

Denis Stairs is professor emeritus in political science at Dalhousie University and a senior fellow with its Centre for Foreign Policy Studies.

Rebecca Tiessen is associate professor at the School of International Development and Global Studies at the University of Ottawa.

Index

Abbas, Mahmoud, 232
Abdullah, Abdullah, 80
Access to Information Act, 242
access-to-information requests, 172, 240–41
Accountability Act, 232
accountability, Conservative Party emphasis on, 156. *See also Accountability Act*; *Official Development Assistance Accountability Act*
Afghan Compact, 78–79
Afghan detainee scandal, 18, 237–38
Afghan National Army, 254
Afghanistan: Afghanistan task force (PCO), 82; Cabinet committee on, 236–37; Canadian commitment to, 74–75, 136, 140–41, 146, 235–36, 239, 246, 252, 254, 260, 265; caveats to deployment of troops, 96; cost of mission, 84; corruption, 79–80, 253; Dahla Dam, 171; death of Canadian soldiers, 84, 231, 235; Harper's extensions of mission in, 3–4, 9–10, 12, 66, 83–85, 146, 235–36, 253, 254, 265; government, 76, 79–80, 253; interagency collaboration in, 82; irrigation system, 171; narcotrafficking, 79–80; opposition to Canadian mission, 84; Senate review of, 247; Taliban insurgency, 76, 78, 81, 235, 254; US presence in, 76–77, 80–81, 261; withdrawal from, 175, 235. *See also* official development assistance, Afghanistan; NATO, training mission in Afghanistan; war crimes
Africa: need for comprehensive international policy on, 251; official development assistance, 251–52; source of immigrants, 211–12; trade ties with, 196. *See also* CIDA
Agreement on Internal Trade (1994), 205–7
Agreement on Subsidies and Countervailing Measures. *See* GATT, trade disputes
aid effectiveness agenda, 171–73, 176–77
air service agreements, 196
Alberta: carbon capture and sequestration projects, 160; carbon pricing system, 123; conflict with federal

government, 50, 139; Conservative political base, 121, 216; NWPTA, 206; oil sands, 158, 262; pipelines from, 139, 158, 161
Alternatives (NGO), 172
Ambrose, Rona, 156
Americans for Democratic Action, 46
Andean Regional Initiative for Promoting Effective Corporate Social Responsibility, 174
Andreychuk, Raynell, 109, 250
anti-Americanism, 42, 44, 136, 138–39
anti-Israel rhetoric, 108
Anti-Terrorism Act (2015), 161
apartheid, 232
Arab-Israeli War, 50
Arctic Waters Pollution Prevention Bill, 128
Armenian genocide, 213, 234
Arms Trade Treaty (UN), Conservative refusal to sign, 190
Asia Pacific Economic Co-operation (APEC), 139, 184
Asia-Pacific, Canadian trade with, 196
Atlantic Procurement Agreement (2008), 205–6
Australia, 190, 232
Auto Pact (Canada-US), 45, 63, 199
Automatic Firearms Country Control List, 113
Axworthy, Lloyd, 33, 100, 185, 192n5, 246

Bahrain, 187, 193n18
Baird, John: environment minister, 9; foreign affairs minister, 15, 182, 187–88, 191, 215, 239–40, 265; pro-Israel stance, 105–106, 108–11, 187–88; promoter of Conservative values, 5, 15, 106, 182, 186, 189, 265; use of social media, 6, 223n6; visit to Ukraine, 216
Belgium, 140
Benin, 170, 176
Bennett, John, 161

Bernier, Maxime, 110
Berthiaume, Lee, 106
bilingualism, 41, 44, 48. *See also* Royal Commission on Bilingualism and Biculturalism
biodiversity, 152
bitumen exports, 156
Black, David, 171
Bloc Québécois, 3, 173
Bomarc missiles. *See* nuclear weapons, acquisition of
Bow, Brian, 90
Bratt, Duane, 9
Brazil, 124, 177, 196, 251
Breton, Albert, 52
Bretton Woods system, 198–99
British Columbia: carbon tax, 153; Chinese immigrants, 218; hydroelectric power emissions, 131n7; Indian immigrants, 216; pipelines through, 155, 158, 161; shale gas production, 155. *See also* New West Partnership Trade Agreement
Broadbent, Ed, 185
Bryden, Penny, 43
Burkina Faso, 170, 174, 176
Burney, Derek, 144, 246, 252, 254
Bush, George W., 135, 138, 140–41, 143, 261
Buy American Agreement, 202

Cadieux, Marcel, 44, 46
Cambodia, 232
Canada 21 Council, 33
Canada Border Services Agency, 144
Canada First Defence Strategy, 13–14, 92–94, 97–98, 140–41
Canada Pension Plan, 41
Canada Revenue Agency, 65, 161
Canada School of Public Service, 138
Canada Ukraine Foundation, 216
Canada-EU Comprehensive Economic and Trade Agreement (CETA), 67, 195; Chrétien initiative, 197, 201;

Index

exclusions, 202; negotiations, 15, 203–6
Canada-EU Trade and Investment Enhancement Agreement (2006), 197, 203
Canada-EU Veterinary Agreement, 202
Canada-Honduras Trade Agreement (2014), 197
Canada-Israel Energy Science and Technology Fund, 112
Canada-Israel Free Trade Agreement, 112–13
Canada-Israel health research program, 113
Canada-Israel Strategic Partnership Memorandum of Understanding, 112
Canada-Korea Free Trade Agreement (2015), 197, 201–2
Canada-United Kingdom Chamber of Commerce, 156
Canada-United States Enhanced Tax Information Exchange Agreement, 65
Canada-US Free Trade Agreement (1988), 152, 199–200, 207, 244
Canada-US relations, 5, 13–14, 154, 262, 264; border security, 135–36, 142–46; Clean Energy Dialogue, 157; culture of exceptionalism, 135–36, 145, 262; deterioration of, 17; economic integration, 129–31, 135, 138, 142–44; memorandum of understanding on science and technology collaboration, 163; political-security analysis, 140–42, 145; prioritization of, 17, 261; psycho-cultural analysis, 137–39, 146; railway safety, 28–29; trade-commercial analysis, 141–45; US-VISIT program, 144. *See also* Chrétien, Jean; Diefenbaker, John; Martin Jr., Paul; Pearson, Lester B.; Trudeau, Pierre
Canada-US Softwood Lumber Agreement (2006), 13

Canadian Armed Forces: Conservative support for, 18, 97, 140, 232, 239; hard power capabilities, 140, 146; joint training exercises with US, 240; Liberal support for, 18, 49, 140; repatriation ceremonies, 231, 236; special operations forces, 99, 238; withdrawal from Europe, 138. *See also* Afghan detainee scandal
Canadian Association of Defence and Security Industries, 94
Canadian Coast Guard, 95
Canadian Council for International Co-operation, 33, 172
Canadian Environmental Assessment Act, 160
Canadian flag, 41, 44
Canadian Foundation for the Americas, 150*n*59
Canadian International Development Agency (CIDA), 79, 167, 170, 245; abolition of, 175–77, 251–52; accountability of, 250; Afghanistan, 169; engagement in Africa, 249–52; funding cuts, 172–73, 176. *See also* official development assistance
Canadian International Institute for Extractive Industries and Development. *See* Canadian International Resources and Development Institute
Canadian International Resources and Development Institute, 174
Canadian Multiculturalism Act, 219, 222
Canadian national interest: Harper as defender of, 3, 86, 90, 161, 200; Pearson's view of, 48; Trudeau's view of, 48; values as basis of, 5, 86, 106, 232, 245, 259–60
Canadian sovereignty, 14, 65, 90, 93, 137, 141, 263
Canadian Studies programming (in US), funding cuts, 138
Canadian Ukrainian Congress, 216

Canadian War Museum, 215
Cannon, Lawrence, 106-8, 110-11, 193*n*18
cap-and-trade program, 153, 157, 162
carbon pricing system, 123, 157, 162-63
carbon tax, 153, 162
Caribbean Community, trade with, 169, 196-97
Carson, Bruce, 10, 107
Castonguay, Alec, 210
CF2020, 94, 98
CFB Trenton, 231, 236
Chapnick, Adam, 100
Charter of Rights and Freedoms, 26
child, early, and forced marriage, 182, 189, 191, 240
China, 177, 232; communist regime, 47, 49; environmental issues, 124, 126; human rights record, 17, 184, 234; shift in policies towards, 211; source of immigrants, 212, 218; trade with, 184, 196, 199
Chinese head tax, 218
Chinese National Offshore Oil Company, 159
Chrétien, Jean: appeals to NDP, 51; development assistance, 168, 178*n*1; foreign policy, 5, 32, 73, 82, 184, 246, 252; relations with US, 136, 138, 143; trade negotiations, 197, 199, 201
Churchill, Winston, 138
Cité Libre, 45
civic nationalism, 211
Civil Society Partnership Policy, 176. *See also* non-governmental organizations
Clark, Campbell, 265
Clark, Christy, 161
Clark, Joe, 4, 7, 246, 258
climate change: antipathy towards Quebec, 17; concerns about, 152-53; hidden Conservative agenda, 124-25; link to energy security, 157, 262; mitigation strategies, 121-22, 124, 127, 129-30, 156-57, 162-63;

obstructive behaviour, 121-22, 160, 162; political factors, 121, 124, 128, 131; trilateral approach, 144
coal-fired electricity: closure of plants (Ontario), 122, 131*n*7; regulation of emissions, 123-26, 153, 160; US regulation of, 129
Cold War, 9, 41, 44, 48, 199
Colombia: development assistance, 170; free trade with, 15, 61, 197, 238; Harper's visit to, 241
Colvin, Richard, 237-38
Commonwealth Heads of Government Meetings: Colombo, 186, 224*n*16; Perth, 251
Community Historical Recognition Program, 218, 224*n*17
Conference of Defence Associations, 33
Connally, John, 52
conscription crisis, 31, 263
Constitution Act, 1867, 57
Cooper, Andrew F., 4
Copenhagen Accord (2009), emissions reduction targets, 121-23, 125-26, 129-30
counterfactual methodology, 75
Creighton, Donald, 44
Criminal code amendments, 255
criminalization of abortion (Bill C-43), 244
criminalization of homosexuality, 187
Crown prerogatives, 58, 65. *See also* foreign policy, executive responsibility
Cuba, 47
Cuban missile crisis, 40*n*1
cyber-warfare, 248

Dallaire, Roméo, 250
Darfur, 231
Davey, Keith, 46
Debané, Pierre, 250
defence policy: Arctic, 12, 14, 90-92, 141, 247; assertiveness of, 82, 96, 99, 141; coastal defence, 14, 94, 141;

Index

commitment-credibility gap, 136; continental security, 14, 141, 240; Martin government, 77; procurement strategies, 12, 89–98, 100; review of, 32–33, 39–40, 64, 94; shipbuilding, 95, 141
Defence Procurement Strategy (2014), 98
defence spending: cuts, 12, 84, 93–101, 140, 239, 260, 267; increases, 12, 77, 90–93, 96, 99, 232; Liberal "decade of darkness," 91, 98, 100.
democracy, 5, 62, 64, 68, 106, 221, 245, 261; promotion of, 9, 181, 183, 187. *See also* participatory democracy; social democracy
Democratic Republic of the Congo, 176
Department of Foreign Affairs and International Trade, 79, 111, 173, 185, 233, 251; merger with CIDA, 175–76
Department of Foreign Affairs, Trade and Development, 6; coordination of official development assistance, 176, 252; legislation establishing, 58
Department of National Defence, 78, 84, 90, 92–94
Department of Public Safety, 138, 145
diaspora networks: economic impact, 219–21; influence on government policy, 216–22; need for arm's length diaspora office, 219, 222; political activities of, 220–22; security concerns, 211, 220–21, 223*n*10
diaspora politics: dangers of, 211, 213–14; favouritism, 15–16, 210–14, 218, 222; immigration-based electoral politics, 212–13, 216–18, 222, 234; lobbying, 210, 213–15, 221–22, 224*n*20, 264; voting along ethnic lines, 16, 211, 222, 234
Diefenbaker, John, 4, 7–8, 40*n*1, 44, 46; relations with US, 42
digital diplomacy, 6, 240
Dion, Stéphane, 51, 84–85, 162
Dominican Republic, trade agreement with, 195, 197

Doran, Charles, 137, 141–42, 145
Douglas, Tommy, 44–46
Duffy, Mike, 241
Dung, To Anh, 214

Eayrs, James, 7
economic diplomacy, 15, 196, 202, 207
economic nationalism, 49, 263
Economist, 135, 137
ecosystem health, 152
El Salvador, 197
Elcock, Ward, 93
electricity, non-emitting sources, 157
Embassy, 231–32, 265
eminent domain. *See* Keystone XL
Emission Trends, 122
Enbridge: Line 9 reversal, 155, 158; Northern Gateway pipeline, 155, 158, 161–62
Energy East, TransCanada pipeline, 139, 155, 158
energy policy: Conservative priorities, 155, 160–61; four imperatives, 152–53; unilateralism, 151–52, 155, 158, 160–63
energy sector: access to international markets, 151, 154–56, 158–59, 161–63; drop in oil prices, 129–30, 154, 162; economic importance, 13, 128, 162, 262; energy security, 153, 157, 262; environmental impact, 152–53; Indigenous communities and, 151–52, 158–61, 163; interventionist approach, 50, 52; oil and gas sector regulations, 121, 124, 126, 129; oil sands, 154, 156–57, 160, 162; opposition to projects, 14, 151, 153, 155, 157–58, 160, 162–63; price deregulation, 152
energy superpower, Canada as, 14, 128, 151, 156, 162
Environment Canada, 121, 123, 128
environmental policy: consistency of, 127–28; economic considerations, 126–28, 130, 155, 162, 262; Harper's

views on, 121-22, 124, 128, 131; Major Projects Management Office, 159; multilateral agreements, 13, 122-24, 126-28, 130-31; political considerations, 121-22, 124, 128, 131, 262; regulatory review process, 159-62, 262
Epp, Jake, 252, 254
ethnic nationalism, 211
European Common Market, 7, 198-99
European Free Trade Association, 197
Export Development Canada, 175
Extractives Cooperation for Enhanced Economic Development Program, 174
Eyford, Doug, 163

F-35 fighter aircraft, 60, 95-97, 238, 241
Fantino, Julian, 174-75
federal elections: 1921, 262; 1965, 46; 2004, 75-76; 2006, 3, 12, 75, 140, 156; 2008, 12, 51, 75, 162, 235, 261; 2011, 13, 16, 75, 248; 2015, 10, 98, 138, 242
Federal/Provincial/Territorial Committee on Trade (C-Trade), 203-4
federalism, 195, 202-4, 207, 264
First World War: French-English tensions, 31; secret treaties, 7, 35. *See also* conscription crisis
Fonberg, Robert, 93
food security, 170, 190-91
foreign aid. *See* official development assistance
foreign investment, 49, 159, 196
foreign investment protection agreements, 196
Foreign Investment Review Act, 49, 52
Foreign Investment Review Agency, 50, 52, 263
foreign policy: assertiveness of, 4, 82, 136-37, 141, 259, 266; "big break," 5, 19n10, 264; Canada as honest broker, 108, 245; Conservative priorities, 232, 245, 261; executive responsibility, 26-27, 34-35, 56-59, 62, 181, 259; golden age, 246; interplay with domestic policy, 27-28, 31, 52, 86, 200, 202, 205; multiplicity of, 27, 259; oversimplification of analyses, 37, 261; path dependence, 79-80; political considerations, 57, 100; public consultation, 33-34, 38-39; whole-of-government approach, 80
foreign policy review, 11, 32-33, 39-40, 49. *See also International Policy Statement*
"fossil of the year" award, 121
fragile states, 211, 221
France, 232
Fraser Institute, 50
free trade agenda, 232, 234, 245, 247

G20 Summits, 139, 144
G8 Summits, Heligendamm, 14, 169; Muskoka, 170, 185
Gaddafi, Muammar, 96
Gagnier, Dan, 241
Garneau, Marc, 65
gender equality, 18, 170, 183-86, 189, 191, 245
General Agreement on Tariffs and Trade (GATT): Tokyo Round, 203; trade disputes, 204-5; Uruguay Round, 199-200, 204
Ghana, 174
Gillespie, Alastair, 49
global financial crisis, 12, 51, 84-85, 156-57, 218
global identity, damage to, 138, 211
Global Initiative to Combat Nuclear Terrorism, 112
Global Markets Action Plan (2013), 15, 112, 176, 196
global trade system, 195-97
Globe and Mail, 51, 161, 237-39, 265
Gomery Commission. *See* sponsorship scandal
goods and services tax, 232
Gordon, Walter, 44-46
Gotlieb, Allan, 246

Goyette, Gabriel, 174
Graham, Bill, 77-79, 83
Grant, George, 44
Gray, Herb, 49
Great Recession, 94, 156-57
Greece, 213
greenhouse gas emissions, 85; oil and gas sector, 123-24, 126-27, 129-30; policy alignment with US, 13, 122-23, 125-27, 129-31, 157-58; reduction targets, 121-23, 126-28, 130, 156, 160; transportation sector, 122-23, 125-27, 129, 160
Guatemala, 197

Haiti, 171, 224n20; humanitarian aid to, 216
Hamas, 107-8, 184, 232
Hammarskjöld, Dag, 41
Harper, Stephen: leadership skills, 9, 16, 18; personal beliefs, 16, 18, 264, 266-67; populism, 51, 211; rebilateralization of North America, 144-45, 200. See also Israel, Harper's views on
Hart, Michael, 197-99, 201
hate speech laws, 225n26
Head, Ivan, 50
Heeney, Arnold, 42
Heinbecker, Paul, 246
Hezbollah, 13, 184, 234, 250
Hillier, Rick, 77-79, 91-93
Honduras, free trade agreement with, 67
horizontal drilling, 154
House of Commons Standing Committees: Defence, 240; Foreign Affairs and International Development, 174; International Trade, 61. See also parliamentary committees
Hu Jintao, 184
Humala, Ollanta, 241
human rights, 5, 245, 264; abuses, 15, 183, 186, 190, 193n18, 211, 217; international standards, 170, 184; international treaties, 182, 189-91; "principled" policy, 10, 15, 136, 181-84, 186, 191, 260; promotion of, 173, 181-83, 185, 264; selectivity of Conservative policy, 15, 17, 181-84, 186-89, 191, 238, 260, 263; Senate standing committee on, 109
human security, 18, 185, 246
hydraulic fracturing, 129, 154
hydrocarbon development, 153

Ibbitson, John, 10, 107, 265
Ignatieff, Michael, 84-85, 261
Immigration: impact on urban centres, 212; influence of business interests on, 212; maintenance of cultural practices, 217; percentage of Canadian population, 221, 223n8; percentage of labour force, 221; security issues, 220; Sikh population in Canada, 216-17; sources of, 211-12
immigration reform, 41
Imperial conference (1923), 263
incrementalism, 195, 198-99, 202, 204-7
Independent Panel on Canada's Future Role in Afghanistan, 66, 169, 171, 235, 252-54; appointment of, 6, 236; criticism of government communication strategy, 236
India: emerging aid provider, 177; Harper's visit to, 215; improved tourist visa process, 218; lack of emissions reduction targets, 124, 126; shift in policies towards, 211, 217-18; Sikh separatism, 215; source of immigrants, 216-17, 219; systems of governance, 217; trade agreement with, 195-97, 204, 251
Integrated Border Enforcement Teams. See Canada-US relations, border security
intellectuals, disdain for, 8-9
International AIDS Conference, 233
International Centre for Human Rights and Democratic Development. See Rights and Democracy
International Civil Aviation Organization, 123

International Criminal Court, 182–83, 186, 191, 260; Assembly of State Parties (2013), 188; Rome Statute, 188
International Development Research Centre, 214
International Maritime Organization, 123
international peace and security, 28, 31, 81, 86, 100
International Policy Statement, 77, 168, 233
international trade, 15; Canada's dependence on, 142; formal agreements, 197–99, 262, 264; influence of internal trade, 205–7, 264; liberalization of, 152, 197–201, 206–7; mercantilist policy, 197, 201; negative lists, 198, 206–7, 208n6; position on agriculture, 200, 205; positive lists, 198, 207, 208n6; protected sectors, 200–2, 204–7; provincial involvement in negotiations, 202–7
internationalism, 141
Iran: Canadian opposition to US negotiations, 17; end to Canadian diplomatic relations, 187, 212–13, 223n6, 265; human rights record, 187
Iraq War (2000s): Chrétien's position on, 82; Obama's position on, 80
Iraq War (2014): air combat mission, 99, 238; cost of, 238–40; non-military initiatives, 99, 240; opposition to military role in, 99; special operations forces, 99, 238
Islamic State of Iraq and Syria (ISIS): Canadian deployment against, 6, 98–100, 240, 260; Kurdish forces, 99; rise of, 240. *See also* Iraq War
Israel: Attack on Gaza, 110; Canadian support for, 105–7, 136, 183, 185–88, 234, 245, 265; criticism from NGOs, 172; Customs Mutual Assistance Agreement, 112; defence forces, 192n10; diaspora politics and, 105–6; Harper's views on, 13, 51, 106–11, 113, 184, 261, 263; illegality of occupation and expansion, 187, 261; Mutual Recognition Agreement in Telecommunications, 112; settlements policy, 261; Stand with Israel fundraiser, 105; West Bank, 110–11
Israeli-Palestinian conflict, 107, 110–11, 113, 187

Jacoby, Tami, 105
Jaffer, Mobina, 250
Jamaica, 224n20
Japan, 232; comfort women, 234; trade with, 196–97
Jay, John, 34
Jenkins, Tom, 98
Johnson, Lyndon, 42, 45–47
Jordan, trade with, 197
Joyal, Serge, 250

KAIROS, defunding of, 172–73, 214–15, 238
Karzai, Hamid, 80
Kennedy, John F., 42, 44–45
Kenney, Jason, 184, 190–91, 213, 215, 218, 224n17
Kent, Peter, 108, 124, 192n10
Kent, Tom, 41–43
Keynesian principles of state intervention, 198
Keystone XL: Canadian push for pipeline extension, 14, 17, 138–39, 155, 160; eminent domain, 139; US views on pipeline extension, 13, 130, 139, 151, 158
Kinder Morgan, TransMountain pipeline, 155, 158, 162
King, William Lyon Mackenzie: contrast with Harper, 265–66; diplomatic nationalism, 258; independent foreign policy, 263; minority government (1920s), 7–8, 51, 262; role of Parliament in foreign policy, 31, 34, 63
Kirton, John, 4
Korea: mutual recognition arrangement, 112; trade with, 67, 195–96.

See also Canada-Korea Free Trade Agreement
Korean War, 47, 235
Kukucha, Christopher, 9
Kyoto Protocol, 9, 13, 59, 238; withdrawal from, 17, 59, 121, 124-27, 129, 156

Lagassé, Philippe, 93
Latin America: development assistance, 169, 233; political influence in US, 145; trade with, 196-97
Laurendeau, André, 47
Laurier, Wilfrid, 8, 258
Layton, Jack, 76
League of Nations, 31
Lebanon: evacuation (2006), 13, 107, 215, 250; Israel's attack on (2006), 184, 234
Léger, Jules, 47
Lennon, John, 48
Lewis, David, 44, 49-50
Liberal Party: foreign policy, 235; in opposition, 64-65, 79-80, 83, 95, 99; internationalism, 267; loss of Jewish community support, 51; Quebec, 45; revitalization (2015), 10; uninterrupted rule, 7-8
Libya: Canadian policy on, 12, 67, 96, 99; NATO mission in, 96, 239, 260
Lieberman, Avigdor, 112
Lippmann, Walter, 35, 46
liquid national gas, export proposals, 154-55, 159
Lisitsa, Valentina, 224*n*23
London, Tamar, 73

Macdonald, Donald, 49
Macedonia, 213
MacGuigan, Mark, 246
MacKay, Peter, 100, 107-8, 110, 233
Mad Cow Crisis, 139
Mada al-Carmel, 214-15
majority Parliaments, stability of, 10, 13, 15
Malone, David, 214

Manley Commission. *See* Independent Panel on Canada's Future Role in Afghanistan
Manley, John, 66, 169, 192*n*5, 236, 246, 252, 254
Marchand, Jean, 44, 46-47
Marsden, Lorna, 43
Martin Jr., Paul: appeals to NDP, 17, 169; defence policy, 18, 81-82, 93; development assistance, 77, 168, 170-71, 176, 178*n*1, 233; foreign policy, 5, 7, 12-13, 66-67, 184, 233, 246, 264; leadership style, 76, 156; mission in Afghanistan, 73-74, 77-81; relations with US, 136, 138, 141, 143; resignation, 83; Senate appointments, 250
Martin Sr., Paul, 43-44, 46-47
maternal, newborn, and child health initiative (MNCH), 15, 17, 170, 182-83, 191, 261; exclusion of abortion services, 171, 185, 189, 238, 261; funding for, 173, 175; limitations of, 185, 186; sexual and reproductive health services, 171, 185, 189, 261
McDougall, Barbara, 9
McGovern, George, 52
McKay, John, 170, 250
media relations: 24/7 video stream, 240; CAF in Afghanistan, 231, 236-38, 240; ethnic media, 235; muzzling of public servants, 234, 237, 265; restrictions on access to elected officials, 16, 18, 36, 121, 231-33, 235-36, 239-42, 265; tensions, 16, 231, 233, 235, 239; war against ISIS, 240
Medicare, 41
Merchant, Livingston, 42
MERCOSUR, 197
Mexico: dependence on trade, 142-43, 196, 199; marginalization by Harper, 144-46, 262; US relations, 138
Michaud, Nelson, 9, 11
Middle East: division after First World War, 35; Harper's visit to, 112; human rights issues, 182; peace process, 110; policy on, 12, 107, 182, 214, 246;

source of immigrants, 211; trade with, 196; US oil imports from, 154
middle power, Canada as, 136, 141, 245
Mill, John Stuart, 35, 38
Millennium Development Goals (2000), 185
mining companies: criticism of, 172; influence on development assistance, 174-77
ministerial powers, 57-59
ministerial responsibility, 62, 67
minority Parliaments: effectiveness of, 262-63; influence of politics on, 12, 16-17, 29, 67-68, 85, 122, 259-60, 265; short life expectancy, 9, 85, 242, 258-59
Modi, Narendra, 217, 224n23
Mongolia, 176
Moniz, Ernest, 163
moral relativism, 266
Morocco, 197
Morse, Wayne, 46
Most Favoured Nation status, 198
Mugabe, Robert, 232
Mulroney, Brian, leader of Progressive Conservative Party, 4, 32, 246, 250; foreign policy, 9, 11, 185, 258; relations with US, 199, 258
Mulroney, David, 82
multiculturalism, 213, 219
multilateralism, 198-99; Canadian emphasis on, 123, 144, 195; Canadian shift away from, 141, 145, 186, 200, 234, 264. *See also* United Nations
Museveni, Yoweri, 187
Muskoka Initiative. *See* maternal, newborn, and child health initiative
Myanmar, 176

Natarajan, Jayanthi, 124
National Defence Act, 58
National Energy Board, 159
National Energy Program, 162
National Forum on Canada's International Relations (1994), 32-33
National Research Council, 95

National Roundtable on the Environment and the Economy, 121, 157
national security, 28, 140-41, 247-48
national security advisor, 138
National Shipbuilding Procurement Strategy, 95
Natural Resources Canada, 128, 163
Natynczyk, Walter, 237
neoconservative social policy, 15
Netanyahu, Benjamin, 112
New Brunswick: refineries, 158; trade agreements, 205-6
New Democratic Party: extension of Afghan mission, 3; foreign policy, 235; influence over minority governments, 17, 43-51, 235; neutralism, 44
New West Partnership Trade Agreement (2010), 206-7
New Zealand, 190
Newfoundland and Labrador: international trade negotiations, 205; trade agreement, 206
Nexen, acquisition of, 159
NGO Monitor, 214
Nicaragua, 197
Nicolson, Harold, 35
Nieto, Enrique Peña, 144
Nixon, Richard, 49-50, 52, 198
Nolin, Pierre Claude, 250
non-confidence vote: Harper minority government, 95, 173; Martin minority government, 87n7; tool of opposition parties, 4, 57, 60-61, 67-68, 90, 181
non-governmental organizations: antipathy towards, 9, 14, 18, 151, 161, 172, 177; Canada Revenue Agency audit, 161; funding cuts to, 173, 214, 234, 238; funding for, 174, 176; policy influence, 32-34, 245
North American Aerospace Defense Command (NORAD), 13, 44, 49, 63, 141
North American Energy Ministers' Working Group on Climate Change, 163

Index

North American Free Trade Agreement (NAFTA), 142-44, 196, 199-200, 202, 205, 207
North American Leaders' Summits, 143-44
North American Security and Prosperity Partnership, 143
North Atlantic Treaty Organization (NATO): 2014 Summit, 97; increased Canadian influence, 136, 139, 146; International Security Assistance Force (Afghanistan), 78-79, 81-83, 85-86, 235, 253-54, 264; Libya, 96; NDP opposition to, 44; Pearson support for, 48; training mission in Afghanistan, 12, 77, 80-81, 85; Trudeau position on, 48-49
North-South Institute, 173
Nossal, Kim Richard, 8-9, 11, 100, 218
Nova Scotia, trade agreements, 205-6
nuclear disarmament, 48
nuclear terrorism, 255
nuclear weapons: acquisition of, 7, 40*n*1, 45, 263; Bomarc missiles, 44

O'Connor, Gordon, 93
Obama, Barack, 261; climate change efforts, 17, 129, 156-57; commitment to Afghanistan, 76, 80-81, 85-86; scepticism about pipelines, 139, 151, 157-58, 160, 262
Oda, Bev, 173-74, 176, 215, 238
Office of Religious Freedom, 223*n*5
Office of the Auditor General, 60, 241
Office of the Parliamentary Budget Officer, 60, 84 ,95, 97, 238, 240-42
official development assistance: 3-D approach, 171, 176; Afghanistan, 14, 79-80, 168-69, 171, 175, 177; Africa, 168-70; alignment with foreign policy objectives, 170, 174-75; Americas Strategy, 14, 169-70, 233-34; commercialization of, 14, 167-68, 174-76, 261; cuts to, 172, 175-77, 267; emphasis on measurable outputs, 171, 173; failure of programs, 38, 252;

Kandahar Provincial Reconstruction Team, 80, 169; poverty reduction, 170-71, 176; priority sectors, 168, 170, 176, 233, 252; security considerations, 14, 167, 175; turning point, 167, 177; untying of aid, 171; whole-of-government approach, 171, 176. *See also* mining companies, influence on development assistance
Official Development Assistance Accountability Act (C-293), 14, 170, 177, 250
Offman, Craig, 51
Oliver, Joe, 161
omnibus budget bills, 59, 65
Ono, Yoko, 48
Ontario: alcohol sales, 204; cap-and-trade system, 153, 157, 162; Conservative inroads into, 76, 85; dairy farmers, 205; pipelines through, 158; trade agreements, 205-6. *See also* coal-fired electricity
Operation Medusa. *See* North Atlantic Treaty Organization, International Security Assistance Force
opposition mentality, 8-9, 267
Ottawa Citizen, 232
Ottawa Conference on Combatting Anti-Semitism (2010), 108

Pacific Alliance, 241
Page, Kevin, 238
Pakistan, support for Taliban insurgents, 76, 81
Palestinian State: aid program to, 110; Canadian support for, 185, 214, 261; flag, 109; human rights record, 188; recognition by UN, 188. *See also* refugees, Palestinian
Palmer, Glenn, 73
Panama, trade with, 197
Paquin, Stéphane, 9
Paradis, Christian, 174-76
Paris Peace Conference, 35
Paris, Roland, 6, 266
Parliament: constitutional authority, 11, 25-26, 31, 56, 58, 62, 66-68, 259;

functions of, 11, 30–33, 35, 39–40, 59–61, 259–60; legislative authority, 30, 56–59, 67; limitations on, 26–28, 35–36; policy influence, 34, 60–62, 64, 67–68, 90, 259; public cynicism about, 36–37, 39. *See also* parliamentary committees
parliamentary associations: Canada-China, 249, 256n6; Canada-Japan, 250; Canada-NATO, 248, 250; Commonwealth, 249, 256n6
parliamentary committees: activist role, 10, 238, 265; educational importance, 30, 36–40, 56, 61, 64, 67; expansion in number of, 32; importance in minority governments, 238, 264–65; Liberal pledge to strengthen, 242; required resources for, 38–39; Veterans' Affairs, 239. *See also* participatory democracy
parliamentary diplomacy, 248
parliamentary laundering: definition, 62–63; Harper's use of, 65–68, 90, 96
Parliamentary Press Gallery, 231–32, 235, 239–42, 265
parliamentary vetting: definition, 62–63; Harper's use of, 64–68, 90, 96; King's use of, 63
participatory democracy, 32–33, 48
Partnership Agreement on Regulation and the Economy (2009), 205–6
paternalism, Conservative, 188–89. *See also* child, early, and forced marriage; maternal, newborn and child health initiative
peacekeeping, 48, 141, 245,
Pearson, Lester B., 7, 11, 245; appeals to NDP, 43–47, 51–52, 90; Canadian Club speech, 46; diplomat/foreign minister, 42–43, 51; leadership style, 18, 41–43; legislative record, 41–43; Nobel Prize for Peace, 42; protection of natural resources, 128; Temple University speech, 46–47, 51, 263; relations with US, 42, 44–46, 51;
role of Parliament in foreign policy, 36, 42, 64
Pearsonian internationalism, 48, 258, 266
Pelletier, Gérard, 44–47, 51
Perlin, George, 8–9
Peru: development assistance, 170, 174; free trade with, 15, 64–65, 197, 250; Harper's visit to, 241
Petro-Canada, 50, 263
Petroleum Club (Calgary), 50
Pettigrew, Pierre, 77
Philippines, 216, 219
Phillip, Stewart, 161
Pickersgill, Jack, 43
pipeline development. *See* Enbridge; Energy East; Keystone XL; Kinder Morgan
pipeline safety inspections, 159
pluralism, 9, 136, 141
policy coherence, 10, 176–77
Posner, Eric, 62
Prentice, Jim, 127
Prime Minister's Office, 10, 34, 107–8, 212; centralization of power, 36, 233–34, 239–40; communications strategy, 36, 231–33, 240
Prince Edward Island, trade agreement, 206
privacy rights, 65
private members' bills, 59, 61, 66, 68, 170
procurement: MASH projects, 201, 206, 209n32; military, 12, 89–98, 100; trade negotiations, 197, 200–3, 205–6
Progressive Conservative Party, 4, 8
Progressive Party, 8
prorogation of Parliament, 238
Public Works and Government Services Canada, 97–98
Putin, Vladimir, 216, 234

Qatar, 187
Quebec: cap-and-trade program, 153; Conservative inroads in, 76; dairy farmers, 205; hydroelectric power

emissions, 131; nationalism, 47–48, 263; Pearson's approach to, 43–45, 51; pipelines through, 158; trade agreement with Ontario, 205–6. *See also* conscription crisis; sponsorship scandal; train derailment
Question Period, 239
quiet diplomacy, 5, 36, 42, 51

Rae, Bob, 84
refugees: Palestinian, 106, 109; reduction of benefits to, 212; refugee system, 223n8, 234; Vietnamese, memorial to, 213
Regan, Patrick, 73
regionalism, shift from multilateralism, 234
Reisman, Simon, 50
religious freedom, 187
remediation of land, 152
Rempel, Roy, 5
representative government, 35
Responsibility to Protect, 185. *See also* human security
responsible government, 25–26, 38–39, 57, 67
Responsible Resource Development, 158–59. *See also* energy policy
Richter, Andrew, 89
Rickford, Greg, 163
Rights and Democracy, 173, 185
Ritchie, Charles, 46
Rosen, Stephen, 140
Roussel, Stéphane, 9
Rowlands, Dane, 4
Royal Commission on Bilingualism and Biculturalism, 43
Royal Commission on the Economic Union and Development Prospects for Canada, 199
Royal Commission on the Status of Women, 43
rule of law, 5, 212, 245
Russell, Peter, 9
Russia: conflict with Ukraine, 136, 213, 216; criticism of, 234; diaspora in Canada, 216; possible free trade with, 251
Rwanda, 250

Sarson, Leah, 218
Saskatchewan: carbon capture and sequestration projects, 160. *See also* New West Partnership Trade Agreement, 206
Saudi Arabia, 187
Schmitz, Gerald, 10
science and technology partnerships: Canada-Israel, 112; Canada-US, 163; importance of, 196
Seaborn, Blair, 45
Second World War, 31, 63. *See also* Japan, comfort women
Segal, Hugh, 4, 6
Seizing Global Advantage, 15, 196,
Senate: bipartisan analysis of issues, 16, 36, 244, 247–48, 255; constitutional reform of, 255; impact of Senate reports, 248–49, 251–52; influence on foreign policy, 244, 247–48, 254–56; institutional memory, 249, 255; lack of democratic legitimacy, 244, 255; standing committees, 109, 247–51, 254
Seoul Treaty, 255
shale gas exploitation, 129, 154–56, 159, 162
shale revolution. *See* shale gas exploitation
Sharp, Mitchell, 9
Sierra Club of Canada, 161
Simpson, Jeffrey, 239
Singapore, trade agreement with, 195, 197, 204
Smart Border Accords, 143
Smith, Graeme, 237–38
social democracy, 135
soft diplomacy network, 248
softwood lumber dispute, 4, 139, 141–42, 247, 261
Sokolsky, Joel, 93
South Africa, 124, 232

Soviet Union, 47
sponsorship scandal, 76, 87n7, 156
Sri Lanka: Liberation Tigers of Tamil Ealam, 186, 213, 215, 234; Tamils in Canada, 224n16, 234; war crimes, 186
St. Laurent, Louis, 41
Stairs, Denis, 6, 8, 11
Stand Up for Canada, 4, 156
stimulus spending package, 94
Sudan, 250
Supreme Court of Canada, 58–59, 214, 244, 255
Syria: disenfranchisement of Sunni Muslims, 240; war crimes, 188

Tellier, Paul, 252, 254
temporary foreign workers programs, 220
terrorist attacks in Canada, 99
Thailand, 197
The Third Option, 199, 208n9
Tkachuck, David, 250
Toronto Star, 44, 47, 49, 52
Toronto Symphony Orchestra, 224n23
Trade Commissioner Service, 196–97
Trade and Co-operation Agreement Between Quebec and Ontario (2009), 205–6
train derailment, Lac Mégantic, 29, 159–60
Trans-Pacific Partnership, 139, 197, 204–5
trilateralism, 144
Trudeau, Justin: electoral reform, 7; foreign policy, 68, 267; leader of Liberal Party, 7, 10, 163, 204, 232, 241, 266
Trudeau, Pierre Elliott: anti-nationalist, 49–50, 52, 263; appeals to NDP, 17, 49–52, 90, 263; criticism of Pearson, 266; foreign policy, 7, 11, 18, 47–48, 51–52, 199, 246, 263–64; protection of natural resources, 128; recruitment by Pearson, 44–47, 263; relations with US, 49–50, 263; views on Soviet Union, 47

Turkey, 195–97, 213, 234, 254,
Turner, John, 49–50

Uganda, 187
Ukraine: Canadian observers to parliamentary elections, 216; diaspora in Canada, 211, 216; Holodomor, 234; Russian annexation of Crimean Peninsula, 136, 213, 216; shift in policy towards, 211; trade agreement with, 195, 197
Union of BC Indian Chiefs, 161
United Arab Emirates, 187
United Kingdom: Foreign and Commonwealth Office, 247; friendship with US, 135, 138, 140; House of Lords, 247; parliamentary ratification of treaties, 65; Tamil Tigers as terrorists, 234
United Nations, 41, 108, 139, 183, 184, 187, 260; anti-Israel resolutions, 245; Convention on Enforced Disappearances, 190; Convention on the Rights of Persons with Disabilities, 190; Conservative hostility towards, 186; Convention to Combat Desertification, 121; Economic and Social Council, 109; Educational, Scientific and Cultural Organization, 109; Framework Convention on Climate Change (UNFCCC), 123–24, 127, 130, 153, 156; General Assembly resolutions, 109; Human Rights Council, 109, 190–91; Optional Protocol to the UN Convention against Torture, 190; protocol to children's rights treaty, 190; Relief and Works Agency for Palestinian Refugees in the Near East, 106; scrutiny of Canada, 190–91; Security Council, 109, 188, 239; support for Israel, 108–9
United States: Ballistic Missile Defense Program, 82, 141; Conference of Mayors, 157; decline of hegemonic power, 136–37, 140–41, 198, 262;

Department of Homeland Security, 138, 144–45; Energy Information Administration, 154; environmental protectionism, 157; Gulf coast refineries, 139; imperialism, 44; Internal Revenue Service, 65; oil and gas reserves, 154; protectionism, 208n7; Supreme Court, 139; Tamil Tigers as terrorists, 234; terrorist attacks (9/11), 135, 138, 142–43, 145, 153, 232; trade with Canada, 196; wage and price controls, 198; Watergate crisis, 50, 52; White House Office of Management and Budget, 144
universal child care benefit, 232
Uppal, Tim, 217
Uribe, Alvaro, 232

Van Loan, Peter, 65
Vancouver Winter Olympics, 145
Vermeule, Adrian, 62
Verner, Josée, 233
Veterans Affairs Canada, 239–40
victims' memorials, 214; communism, 215; Holocaust, 215
Vietnam: communist government, 234–35; refugees to Canada, 213
Vietnam War, 44–47, 49, 51, 263; Operation Rolling Thunder, 45; bombing of Hanoi, 52
Von Ranke, Leopold, 52

Wallin, Pamela, 252, 254
war crimes: Canadian participation in, 237. *See also* Sri Lanka; Syria
war on terror, 261
water quality, 152
Weber, Max, 75
Wells, Paul, 89
Welsh, Jennifer, 210
West Coast energy infrastructure, 163
Westminster system, 18, 57
Wilson, Woodrow, 35
Winters, Robert, 43
women's rights, 185–87, 189, 191
World Trade Organization: Agreement of the Application of Sanitary and Phytosanitary Measures, 201–2; Agreement on Technical Barriers to Trade, 201; General Agreement on Trade in Services, 201; means of transferring Western norms, 199; ministerial conference (1999), 36; rejection in favour of bilateral trade, 199; Revised Agreement on Government Procurement (2014), 202. *See also* GATT
Wright, Nigel, 241

Yushchenko, Viktor, 232

Zimbabwe, 232

Printed and bound in Canada by Friesens
Set in Segoe and Warnock by Artegraphica Design Co. Ltd.
Copy editor: Joanne Richardson
Proofreader: Dianne Tiefensee
Index: Megan Sproule-Jones